REGNUM STUDIES IN MISSION

Values and Participation Development in Rural Indonesia

REGNUM STUDIES IN MISSION

Series Preface

Regnum Studies in Mission are born from the lived experience of Christians and Christian communities in mission, especially but not solely in the fast growing churches among the poor of the world. These churches have more to tell than stories of growth. They are making significant impacts on their cultures in the cause of Christ. They are producing 'cultural products' which express the reality of Christian faith, hope and love in their societies.

Regnum Studies in Mission are the fruit often of rigorous research to the highest international standards and always of authentic Christian engagement in the transformation of people and societies. And these are for the world. The formation of Christian theology, missiology and practice in the twenty-first century will depend to a great extent on the active participation of growing churches contributing biblical and culturally appropriate expressions of Christian practice to inform World Christianity.

Series Editors

A full listing of titles in this series
appears at the end of this book

REGNUM STUDIES IN MISSION

Values and Participation Development in Rural Indonesia

Bambang Budijanto

First published 2009 by Regnum Books International

Regnum is an imprint of the Oxford Centre for Mission Studies
P.O. Box 70, Oxford, OX2 6HB, UK
and
Paternoster Press
P.O. Box 300, Carlisle, Cumbria, CA3 0QS, UK

09 08 07 06 05 04 03 8 7 6 5 4 3 2 1

British Library Cataloguing in Publication Data
A catalogue record for this book is available from the British Library

ISBN 978-1-506476-72-8

Typeset by BB Ltd

The financial assistance of the Drummond Trust, Stirling, towards this publication is gratefully acknowledged.

Distributed by 1517 Media in the US and Canada

This book is dedicated to my long-life partners in service and my faithful companions in this journey of life:
Liana, Jemira, Edo and Arvad Jo

This book is devoted to the weak and the marginalized, especially those children who live in extreme poverty and who can not speak for themselves.

Preface

I am indebted for much of my early learning of village life to the late *mbah* Kami of Lopait (a short form of *Kamitowa*, traditional office of vice to the village head) and numerous friends in Lopait village – my neighbors – who helped me gain a deeper understanding and greater appreciation of how their identity, values and religion interacted with the poverty and hard challenges of life.

I am also indebted to numerous individuals who dedicate their lives in service to God among the poor through The Oxford Centre for Mission Studies, Partner in Mission Asia, Pesat Foundation, Compassion International, and Institute for Community and Development Studies who helped me gain a greater insight on how their faith shapes their engagement with the poor.

I thank the late Professor Loekman Soetrisno of the Gajah Mada University and Dr. Nico L. Kana of Percik Foundation for the numerous productive discussions related to this research. I am also grateful for the comments and constructive feedback given by Professor Robert Barnes of Oxford University, Professor Deryke Belshaw of East Anglia University, and Dr. Ian Wallace of the University of Reading. I also gratefully thank Professor Anne Booth, Dr. P. B. R. Carey and Dr. Ines Smyth for their insightful comments on particular chapters.

I must make a very special acknowledgement of the unfailing support and encouragement of Dr. Vinay Samuel, Dr. Chris Sugden and Professor Paul Freston of the INFEMIT. I would also like to convey a special thank to the Drummond Trust for providing the needed funding for this publication. Dr. Wonsuk Ma of the Oxford Centre for Mission Studies worked very hard to convince me to publish this book and Mark Yeadon of Compassion International provides me with needed moral supports and space to finalize this project, for which I am so grateful.

Finally, but by no means least, I want to express my appreciation to my father, and to my children, Jemira Joy, Melzar Edo and Arvad Jo, for willingly sacrificing time and attention which was their due. And I especially thank my wife Liana for her unfailing support, love and patience.

Throughout the entire period of research I have been conscious of divine mercy supplying the inner resources which made this work possible. For this, above all, I am grateful.

Contents

Foreword

Paul Freston

Prof. Paul Freston is Distinguished Senior Fellow and Director of the Program for Studies of Religion in Latin America at Baylor's Institute for Studies of Religion (ISR), and professor of sociology in the Post-Graduate Program in Sociology at the Universidade Federal de São Carlos, Brazil

Bambang Budijanto's work on *Values and Participation: Development in Rural Indonesia* began life as a doctoral thesis at the University of Wales, for which I had the privilege of being on the examining board. Although based on research from the 1990s, it has not lost any of its relevance because it talks of themes which have become even more topical in the last few years: Islam and Christian-Muslim relations; and religious contributions to socio-economic development.

Budijanto writes about his own country, which happens to be the largest predominantly Muslim country in the world. He carries out a careful case-study of how socio-religious values affect development via popular participation, and is scrupulously fair regarding the contribution of diverse religious traditions.

For those who desire a more participatory development strategy, the role of religions and their local leaders is becoming more and more appreciated. Old orthodoxies regarding modernity and secularization are increasingly questioned, and the recognition of multiple ways of being modern opens up new vistas both for religion and for strategists of development. This is not limited to undergirding a work ethic and a rationalization of values; it also includes religion as promoter of notions of justice and solidarity, and as an identity which brings new social actors and movements onto the stage of history. In the developing world today, various forms of Christianity and Islam are the most widespread religious forces at work, and this book constitutes a valuable addition to the literature on exactly how such religions interact with development processes.

Introduction: Religion and Development

1. Socio-Religious Values and Development

Since the publication of Weber's works on *Die Protestantische Ethik und der Geist des Kapitalismus (1904-1905)*,[1] study on the relationship between religion or religious values and economic development has become more significant, both in development studies and in the field of the sociology of religion.[2] The abundant literature which followed this publication has mostly covered the pros and cons of Weber's thesis, which claims that certain religious values seem to support certain economic ethics. Others have developed or added to this argument by applying it in different socio-religious contexts (Geertz, 1956; Bellah, 1957; Eisenstadt, 1968; Alatas, 1973; Stone, 1974; Singer, 1985; Koentjaraningrat, 1993; Abdullah, 1994).

Often, religion is associated with the 'after-life' or with the 'unspeakable', with holiness of life pursued through some kind of self-denial, such as *samadhi* (meditation) in Hinduism, fasting in Islam, or monastic life in Christianity (Ahmad, 1985: ix-xiv). The world is often regarded as a place for the 'fallen' man, of 'indebtedness', or *samsara* (a place of suffering), even though not in an absolute state. 'Salvation' is thus perceived as an escape from such a state. And the way to achieve it is by restraint from seeking material, physical or worldly enjoyment, and distancing oneself from anything which this world regards as valuable, especially things which stimulate desire (Weber, 1948: 323-331).

Development, on the other hand, is usually associated with betterment, prosperity, or material progress. While in religion self-restraint, self-denial and distancing oneself from material enjoyment are among the main paths to 'happiness', development considers that material prosperity and economic progress are among the main indicators of 'success'. Therefore religion and economic development are generally perceived as two separate if not opposed entities (Weber, 1948: 331). The spirit of economic development, which is competition, aggressiveness, and productivity, seems contrary to the spirit of religion, which is self- content, self-restraint, and unconditional love. Even though religion does not ignore the physical aspects of mankind, its main concern is often the spiritual aspect of the 'inner life' of mankind (Weber, 1948: 332). This tension seems to be confirmed by the enormous number of articles on development which consider religion or religious values as inimical

---

[1] The first English edition was published in 1930 entitled, *The Protestant Ethic and the Spirit of Capitalism*, 1930.

[2] Together with Geertz (1973) and Koentjaraningrat (1993), this study employs the term religious values for a certain 'socio-cultural system of beliefs'. For comprehensive discussion on this, see Clifford Geertz, *The Interpretation of Cultures*, 1973; and Emile Durkheim, *Les Formes Elementaires de la Vie Religieuse*, 1912 (E. Ed.-1965).

to the development processes (Mulder, 1986; Koentjaraningrat, 1993; Dove, 1988).

Such a configuration provides at least five alternatives approaches in analysing the relationship between religion and development. First, the modernist approach used by Niels Mulder (1986) and Koentjaraningrat (1993) who set development as the paradigm for their analysis, and consequently proposed a change in people's values. The changes would take place by removing certain socio-religious values considered to be a hindrance to the process of development and by adopting new values which they consider supportive of development.[3]

Secondly, there are those who set socio-religious values as the paradigm for the analysis, and accordingly call for a redefinition of development which could be readily understood by the people (Schumacher, 1985; Dove, 1988). This traditionalist approach, they argue, will generate people's genuine participation in the development process, which in turn will give greater assurance of sustainable development (Selosoemardjan and Breazeale, 1993: 188-189). Those who disagree argue that this approach will not work, because certain socio-religious values breed fatalism, self-contentment, and submissiveness to nature and are completely opposed to the values required for development, and especially economic progress.

Third, there is the typically Weberian position which says that socio-religious values do not necessarily oppose development. They are separate entities but not necessarily opposed to one another. In fact, some socio-religious values and certain development processes are mutually reinforcing. Such is the case with Weber's analysis of capitalism in Western Europe (1904-5) and with Bellah's work on capitalism in Japan (1957). Religion or socio-religious values function to validate certain economic development processes, in return religion gains wider acceptance in a modernised society.

The fourth approach considers that religion and economic development operate in different realms; the 'unseen' realm and the physical realm. Each has merit in its own domain and thus no direct relationship between socio-religious values and development could readily be drawn.[4] The supposed relationship between socio-religious values and development which most people perceive are either insignificant, superficial or exaggerated. They completely dismiss any significant direct implications of socio-religious values for development, and thus any study on the relationship between socio-religious values and development is both inappropriate and unnecessary.

---

[3] Often religion is either regarded as an object of development or is manipulated to justify certain development programmes, see Soedjatmoko, "Iman Amal dan Pembangunan." In LP3ES, *Agama dan Tantangan Zaman*, 1985: 3-7; and especially, Gunnar Myrdal, *Asian Drama: An Inquiry into the Poverty of Nations*, 1968: 57-76.

[4] See for example the revolutionary theories of Antonio Gramsci in Carl Boggs, *Gramsci's Marxism*, 1976.

And fifth, the transformists, as one might call them, are those who believe that even though there is no readily drawn direct relationship between socio-religious values and development, religion or religious values which govern the higher level of human life should have significant implications for the course of development. Such implications are gained by serious meditation on one's own socio-religious values and an attempt to develop an expression that would generate a psychological and moral force to formulate and to undertake a development process which would satisfy both the socio-religious realm and the physical realm (Sider, 1981; Ahmad, 1985).

The problem with most of these approaches is that they often treat religion as a limited normative system of belief and set it apart from the local socio-cultural context of the people (Ahmad, 1985: xlii). These approaches which have made a significant contribution to the theories of social science, are actually difficult to comprehend, especially when the methodology employed is used to explain the relationship between socio-religious values and development in a given local community. In his short analysis of Weber's methodology, Geertz suggested a study of the relationship between religion and development in a smaller unit of analysis with a 'certain socio-religious system' at 'a given time' (because socio-religious values are changing) (1956). This problem has also been indicated by Alatas in his observation:

> The data derived from the South-East Asian setting in particular and the Asian one in general point to the fact that it is impossible to sustain any generalization after concretely analysing cases of each specific religion such as Islam and Buddhism (1973: 157).

Further he also indicated that one of the main problems in analysing the relationship between religion and development is that the observer "is not sufficiently aware of the dynamics of social and cultural interaction when it comes to the interaction between religion and its cultural and social setting" (1973: 157). This leads to the following discussion which will firstly demonstrate that the relation between 'socio-religious values' and 'action' (in this case, participation in development) in a given situation cannot be considered unless the two concepts are defined independently of one another. Secondly, as Geertz (1973) and Alatas (1973) have argued, religion must be understood in a wider sense, which is in its socio-cultural context, and thus the term religion must refer to socio-religious values.

2. Religion and Cultural Values

In the Asian context, religion, whatever its ultimate orientation, is very much bound up with the totality of the social process and concreteness of individual existence. This is especially so in Java, where religion still largely shapes the traditional form of culture.[5] The concept of *aliran* (political streams) as popularised by Geertz (1959) explains that the political organisations in Independent Indonesia were built on pre-existing socio-religious allegiances. According to Geertz, the cultural-religious values that the parties represented provided a basis for a variety of village level organisations and form the primary bond linking the village to the national political and social system.[6] Even though this concept has been criticised for its purported neglect of class (Anderson, 1982: 79) and confusion of ideological constructs with actual social structure (Kodiran, 1971: 342; Kahn, 1982: 92); most scholars do not dispute the strong influence of the traditional cultural religious values in Javanese socio-political structure (Mortimer, 1974: 327; Lyon, 1980: 214; Hart, 1986: 39; Hefner, 1990: 222).

Such phenomena were not, of course, peculiar to the Javanese. The fundamental significance of Durkheim's work on primitive religion was his recognition that "society is a religious phenomenon" (Durkheim, 1965: 419). This means the system of "common ultimate-value attitudes", as Parsons puts it, is indeed inseparable from religious ideas (Parsons, 1951: 427), or to be more precise, religion in most cases shapes the social structure:

> Religion is sociologically interesting not because, as vulgar positivism would have it (Leach, 1954: 10ff.), it describes the social order (which, in so far as it does, it does not only very obliquely but very incompletely), but because, like environment, political power, wealth, jural obligation, personal affection, and a sense of beauty, it shapes it. (Geertz, 1966: 35-6)

Unlike 'action', socio-religious values cannot be directly observed, they must be inferred from some verbal or non-verbal acts (Cancian, 1975:6). Those verbal and non-verbal acts are myths or beliefs or the conceptual aspects of socio-religious life, and rituals, which involve symbolic fusion of ethos and world view (Geertz, 1966: 28; Darmaputera, 1988: 8). And these socio-religious values are mutually dependent upon human behaviours,

> Ultimate-value attitudes, religious ideas and the forms of human action constitute a complex of elements in a state of mutual interdependence . . . (Parsons, 1937: 426).

---

[5] For further analysis, see Neils Mulder's thesis on "Mysticism and Daily life in Contemporary Java", 1975.

[6] Geertz observed that the Nationalist party (*Partai Nasional Indonesia* or PNI) was composed of *priyayi* adherents to the Hindu elements in Javanese syncretism, and the *abangan* followers of the animistic elements of syncretism were associated with the PKI. The orthodox Muslims (*santri*) were aligned to NU, and the modernists with the Masyumi (1965a:127-9)

The best way to explain social actions, or in this case people's participation in development is, therefore, to understand their culture, that is, the "context within which social events and behaviours can be intelligibly described" (Geertz, 1973: 14).

3. Socio-Religious Values and Social Behaviours

Weber defines 'action' as "any human attitude or activity (*Verhalten*) in so far as the actor or actors associate a subjective meaning (*Sinn*) with it" (Weber, 1947:88). And social action is such action which "involves the attitudes and actions of others and is oriented to them in its course" (Weber, 1947:88). Even though it seems that Weber's concept of action deals only with those behaviours which have actors' subjective meaning attached to it, the word he used for 'action' (*Verhalten*) implies very broad aspects of behaviours.[7] Even reactive and conventional (as opposed to consciously deliberate) actions are not, he argued, without meaning, "the conventional behaviour that men in a society take for granted is very often meaningful; it makes sense to them" (Weber, 1978: 4).

Thus, to understand social actions or social behaviours correctly, one must begin any observation from the actors' point of view; and determine what 'meaning' the actors themselves have given to their actions. It has to be done within their cultural context, as Geertz also pointed out:

> Believing, with Max Weber, that man is an animal suspended in webs of significance he himself spun, I take culture to be those webs, and the analysis of it to be therefore not an experimental science in search of laws but an interpretative one in search of meaning (1973: 5).

Therefore, the task of this 'actor-oriented' analysis is to interpret 'subjective meaning' in general terms, that is to describe its 'normalness' despite its 'distinctiveness' (Darmaputera, 1988: 5), in order to be able to grasp the cultural value behind it. Social action (in this case, participation in development) is therefore, best understood from the actors' point of view, i.e. what meaning do the actors give to their actions. Earlier, Parsons (1951) had employed this approach in his influential theory of 'socialized actor', which views 'action' as a process in which an individual chooses between alternatives so as to satisfy their goals and needs.

It needs to be noted, however, that to understand the dynamic of a particular society merely by interpreting 'action' as meaningful for the actors, is simply inadequate. In other words, to explain the dynamic relationship between 'values' and 'action' we cannot confine our inquiry to 'meaning' alone. In a

---

[7] This 'attitude' or 'activity' involving external or internal acts, failure to act or even passive acquiescence (Parsons, 1937: 640; cf. Weber, 1947: 88-89, n. 3).

research study of the Maya community in Latin America, for example, Florence Cancian observed that the Parsonian theory of 'socialized actor' fails to adequately explain the relationship between individual's normative beliefs and his actions (1975: 135). Consequently, she proposed the 'social identity' approach as an alternative theoretical approach. The 'social identity' approach defines values as 'shared-beliefs about what actions and attributes bring respect and approval from oneself and others' (Cancian, 1975:6).[8] Accordingly, action will conform to cultural values so as to validate the actors as good standing members of the community, as well as being an expression of individual beliefs. Thus, individuals conform to values in order to validate an identity (1975: 137). While both the 'social identity' approach and the Parsonian theory of 'socialized actor' have been able to explain the relationship between 'values' and 'action' in a number of different cultural settings, the experiences of the three hamlets of Lopait suggest that no single theory is adequate to explain the relationship between 'values' and 'action.'

Map 1 Indonesia and Central Java

[8] The 'social identity' approach starts with the conception of the collective definition and maintenance of social identities. This approach assumes that values affect behaviour by specifying what action will cause others to validate a particular identity. Therefore beliefs which are perceived to be shared by a group will be related to action, while the personal beliefs of an individual may not be.

Chapter 1

Development and Socio-Religious Context in Indonesia: An Historical Perspective

1. Background

Some forty years ago Indonesia was one of the poorest countries in the world. More than sixty percent of its population were in absolute poverty, the majority being Javanese peasants. In the mid-sixties its GNP per capita was only US$ 50, roughly half that of India and Nigeria (Dirkse *et al.*, 1993; World Bank, 1990). The ruinous hyper-inflation, the sharp falls in rice production and the decline of other domestic production in the mid-1960s brought about the fall of the Soekarno regime and the rise of the New Order government under the then Major General Soeharto.[1]

The 20 years of the Soekarno regime (1945-1965) are usually portrayed as an unending struggle to establish a national unity out of different religious and regional revolts,[2] as well as fractious political parties.[3] The struggle against Dutch rule (1945-1949) was followed by a period of parliamentary government (1950-1957). During these seven years Indonesia was ruled by no less than six different coalition governments, the shortest holding office for six months and the longest for two years (Ricklefs, 1981: 225-244). The intense concern for economic growth which had been a dominant issue in the early post-independence period (1945-1953) was soon overlooked along with growing pressure from the three political fractions, the Communist party (PKI), the modernist Muslim (Masyumi) and the Armed Forces (ABRI) groups for a

---

[1] For extensive reading on the economic turmoil and the political conflicts on Indonesia's mid-sixties, see H. W. Arndt, "Banking in Hyperinflation and Stabilization." In B. Glassburner, ed., *The Economy of Indonesia: Selected Readings*, 1971: 359-395; Rex Mortimer, *Indonesian Communism under Soekarno: Ideology and Politics 1959-1965*, 1974; H. Crouch, *The Army and Politics in Indonesia*, 1978; R. Cribb, ed., *The Indonesian Killings of 1965-1966; Studies from Java and Bali*, 1990.

[2] Among those are the Darul Islam, derived from the Arabic *dar al-Islam* which means territory of Islam (West Java, 1948-1962); the PKI, Communist Party of Indonesia led by Musso (Madiun, 1948); the RMS, South Malucu Republic (Malucu, 1951); Kahar Muzakar (South Sulawesi, 1950-1951); the PUSA, the All-Aceh Union of Ulamas (1953); the Permesta led by H. N. V. Sumual (North Sulawesi, 1957-1961); and the PRRI, Revolutionary Government of the Indonesian Republic (Bukittinggi, 1958-1961).

[3] For detailed accounts of the struggle of the civilian parties to gain greater control over the government, see M. C. Ricklefs, *A History of Modern Indonesia*, 1981: 225-271.

larger share of political (Feith, 1962, Mortimer, 1974) and economic power (Anderson, 1983).

Soekarno had expected that the 1955 parliamentary election would become a 'political panacea' for the government, but it turned out to be disappointing as no single party was able to obtain more than 23 percent of the votes (Kahin, 1995: 50).[4] The election produced no solution and thereby perpetuated the ever increasing factionalism within parliament. Kahin identified this as the key factor behind Soekarno's political shift to 'Guided Democracy' (1995:51). During this period of Guided Democracy (1957-1965) both the army and the Communist party were held in an uneasy relationship by Soekarno who sought to use both for his own ends (Crouch, 1979: 186-188). The growing tension between them culminated in the 'aborted' coup of the 'Thirtieth September Movement', which was followed by probably the worst massacre in the post-war history. Over 500,000 so-called communist activists and supporters were killed between late 1965 and early 1966.[5] While the origins of the coup remain unclear,[6] its consequences for the political system were apparent. The 'aborted' coup gave the Armed Forces a spurious legitimacy to become the unchallenged power in post-1965 Indonesia. The socio-political system would soon be transformed.

The political climate of the 'Guided Democracy' period had a ruinous impact on plans for economic development. National resources and energies were diverted to the campaigns to recover West Irian (1961-1963) and the confrontation against Malaysia (1963-1966). Toward the end of 1965 the social, political and economic structures of the nation were near to collapse. During the first ten weeks of 1966 massive student demonstrations broke out in Jakarta leading to a state of near anarchy (Crouch, 1979: 192), hyper-inflation peaked, with the price of rice rising at an annual rate of 900 percent (Ricklefs,

---

[4] There were twenty-eight parties gaining seats in the parliament, but only four had more than eight seats: PNI (Nationalist party), Masyumi, NU (traditionalist Muslim), and PKI. The large number of smaller parties had caused difficulties of forming a governing coalition, G. McT. Kahin, "Soekarno tak Ingin ada Pertumpahan Darah." *Tiras*, 5 October 1995: 50; M. C. Ricklefs, 1981: 238.

[5] The exact number of deaths was unknown but most scholars accept a figure of about 500,000 deaths, see H. Crouch, "The Trend to Authoritarianism: The Post-1945 Period." In H. Aveling, ed., *The Development of Indonesian Society*, 1979: 192; and M. C. Ricklefs, 1981: 274.

[6] There have been several attempts to analyse the origin of the Thirtieth September Movement; among those is a view propounded by Benedict Anderson and Ruth McVey, in a preliminary analysis widely known as the 'Cornell Paper' (1971), which interprets the event as a movement of dissident junior officers from Central Java in co-operation with Air Force officers against the army leaders in Jakarta. Harold Crouch gives a brief overview of some of these views (1979: 188-192).

1981: 268),[7] while the value of the 'rupiah' fell drastically. Between 1962 and 1965 the black market exchange value of the 'rupiah' compared to the United States dollar changed from Rp. 470 to Rp. 50,000 (Ricklefs, 1981: 192; Anderson, 1990: 108).

The stagnation of economic development was not solely the responsibility of the political climate of Soekarno's Guided Democracy. The country was saddled with a war shattered economy as well as burdened with a heavy inherited debt from the Netherlands Indies colonial government (Kahin, 1952: 433-452). Moreover, until 1957 Dutch businesses continued to dominate much of the advanced revenue-producing sectors, as well as international shipping (Anderson, 1990:102). It is in the whole context of a general reaction against Western imperialism in the fifties, an inherited shattered economy with a limited access to revenue-producing sectors, the feebleness of the central government during the parliamentary period (1950-57) and the rise of the Communist Party (PKI) with its successful mobilisation of the Javanese peasantry (1953-1965), which together culminated in the killing of top army generals. This sets the scene in which the post 1965 Indonesian political-economic system must be viewed.

2. Rural Development Policy of the New Order

The New Order government under General Soeharto immediately set a different course. The self-reliant economy of Soekarno was replaced by an open market economy with a massive influx of Western economic aid (Anderson, 1990: 112-113; Crouch, 1979: 196; Dirkse *et al.*, 1993: 5). Hyper-inflation was perceived as one of the key factors which had destroyed Guided Democracy (Anderson, 1990); therefore the New Order government set a priority to bring inflation under control, which they managed to achieve within three years (Mortimer, 1973: 54). Price stabilisation which demands an adequate supply of goods became the next priority. The state was then still too chaotic to raise the necessary resources domestically, therefore massive external aid and investments were essential. The government well understood that to gain this support, policies designed to win the sympathy of the Western world would be required.[8] Soon the results were evident, from 1968 a huge quantity of foreign aid and investments began to flow into Indonesia,[9] which enabled the government to reconstruct the national economy.[10]

---

[7] Arndt illustrates the deteriorating macro-economic situation, from a base of 100 in 1954, the consumer price index rose to over 600 in 1961 and reached 61,000 by 1965 (1971: 373).

[8] Some of those were to put an end to confrontation with Malaysia in 1966, the return of many nationalized enterprises and the Foreign Investment Law of 1967, see B. Anderson, *Language and Power: Exploring Political Cultures in Indonesia*, 1990: 112.

[9] At the beginning of the first five-year development plan (*Pelita*), more than a quarter of total budgetary revenues were derived from foreign aid and borrowing. As the

In 1969 the government launched the first *Pelita* (*Pembangunan Lima Tahun*, Five Year Development Plan). The aim was for economic and political stabilisation, the strategy was the 'floating mass' and the modernisation of the agricultural sector, and the main target was the attainment of rice self-sufficiency. The policy was essentially political in nature, as Husken and White identify that 'self-sufficiency' was interpreted in terms of urban middle class society, which in turn would ensure political stability (1989: 235-236).[11] By 1972, the impact of the programme was being felt: GNP was registering an annual growth rate estimated to be above six percent, inflation rates were down and exports were showing spectacular rates of increase (Mortimer, 1974: 54).

It was Sajogyo in his authoritative study, ***Modernisation without Development in Rural Java*** (1972) who began to pinpoint the social effects of the Indonesian growth model. It was followed by a growing number of concerns with regards to the uneven distribution of the benefits of the development programme, as illustrated in Table 3.1 (Mortimer, 1974; Collier *et al.*, 1973; Collier, 1978; Booth and Sundrum, 1976; 1980). A number of studies indicate that the majority poor of rural Java had been excluded from the benefits of increased production. It has been suggested that the benefits of the agricultural modernisation programme had mainly, if not exclusively, gone to the urban middle class and to the richer farmers (Hinkson, 1975; Palmer, 1977; Manning, 1988).

Table 1.1. Rural-Urban Income Disparities in Indonesia and Selected Developing Countries

Country	Year	Ratio of Urban to Rural Income	Relative Urban-rural incomes disparities
Malaysia	1970	214	86.2
Philippines	1970	208	81.6
Colombia	1970	232	73.0
Sri Lanka	1969-70	172	65.5

'balanced-budget' policy of the New Order administration involved a rapid growth in government external borrowing, by 1993/1994, the total foreign debt service ratio still stood at over 30 percent, see A. Booth, "Indonesian Economic Development in the Soeharto Era." Paper prepared for the SBU-CAFOD-CIIR seminar on UK/Indonesia Economic Relations, South Bank University, 17 July 1996, pp. 1-2.

[10] For a negative assessment of this approach, see C. Payer, *The Debt Trap*, 1974. Earlier Benjamin Higgins had identified the neocolonial aspects of Indonesia's economic strategy, see B. Higgins, "Survey of Recent Development." *Bulletin of Indonesian Economic Studies* 8.1 (1972): 7.

[11] Peter C. Timmer in his article "The Political Economy of Rice in Asia" (1975) demonstrated the strong correlation between rice self-sufficiency and political stability in the Soekarno era. See also Sjahrir, *Basic Needs in Indonesia; Economics, Politics and Public policy*, 1986.

South Korea	1971	187	56.4
Taiwan	1972	122	19.4
Indonesia	1969-70	142	39.8
Indonesia	1976	184	73.2
Java	1976	209	91.6

Source: Anne Booth and R. M. Sundrum, "Income Distribution in Indonesia: Trends and Determinants." In R. G. Garnaut and P. T. McCawley, eds., ***Indonesia: Dualism, Growth and Poverty***, 1980: 461.

From Table 3.1 it appears that in Indonesia as a whole, the urban-rural economic gap grew wider between 1970-1976, and, in the case of Java, the rural-urban economic disparity was significantly higher (91.6 percent). Sritua Arief (1980) reported the rise of income inequality as measured by the concentration ratio of consumption expenditure per capita, that is, from 0.33 in 1970 to 0.41 in 1976.[12] Using three poverty thresholds for urban and rural areas, Sajogyo (1977) defined urban poor with a consumption of less than 480 kg. of rice equivalent per capita per annum; urban very poor: less than 360 kg; urban destitute: less than 270 kg; rural poor: less than 320 kg; rural very poor: less than 240 kg; and rural destitute: less than 180 kg. In applying his categories to the 1970 and 1976 *SUSENAS* (*Survey Sosial Ekonomi Nasional,* National Socio-economic Survey) Sajogyo calculated that while the proportion of the poor had slightly decreased, the proportion of the very poor in rural areas had slightly increased, and the proportion of the destitute in rural areas increased quite significantly (Table 1.2).[13]

While Booth and Sundrum (1976: 94) in their analysis of the agricultural censuses in 1973 concluded that the size distribution of farms between 1963 and 1973 had only changed slightly,[14] others, on the basis of village level

[12] Sritua Arief based his calculation on the method developed by Kakwani and Podder. For further reading, see Sritua Arief, "Who Benefits from Economic Growth: The Indonesian Experience." *The South East Asian Economic Review* 1.1 (1980): 1-12.

[13] There have been a number of objections to Sajogyo's approach to measuring poverty in rural Java (White, 1979; Oey Meesook, 1978; Booth and Sundrum, 1980). The key issue was that Sajogyo divided the total households expenditure by the average household size for the entire population. This criticism was based on the assumption that poorer households tend to be smaller than the average (Bose, 1982, n.15; Booth and Sundrum, 1980: 464). The analysis of the Central Bureau of Statistics on the 'Poverty and Income Equality in Indonesia 1976-1990', however, revealed that the average size of poor rural households was 6.1, which was considerably bigger than the 4.1 of the average size of the non-poor rural households (1992: 35). But both Sajogyo (1977) and his critics basically agreed on the significant number of rural households which remained untouched by the increase in agricultural production up to 1976 (Mubyarto and Soetrisno, 1985).

[14] According to their analysis of the macro data, between 1963 and 1973 the size of the average Javanese farm fell from 0.70 to 0.66 hectare. Although this figure indicates that landholding inequality remained moderate by third World standards, they had excluded the many rural people who owned no land at all, which comprised more than 40 percent

studies, maintain that fairly rapid concentration of land holding had been occurring (White, 1979; Collier, 1978; Sajogyo, 1978).

Table 1.2. Estimates of the Extent of Poverty Using Sajogyo's Measure

Categories	Poverty line in rice equivalents (kg./Capita/Year)	Percentage of total in 1970	Percentage of total in 1976
Rural poor	320	55	52
Rural very poor	240	35	35
Rural destitute	180	19	21
Urban poor	480	58	43
Urban very poor	360	42	28
Urban destitute	270	24	17
Total poor		59	51
Total very poor		36	33
Total Destitute		20	20

Note: Population of Indonesia 1970: 117.4 million (83% in rural areas); 1976: 135.2 million (81% in rural areas). Source: Sajogyo's calculations in, "Garis Kemiskinan dan Kebutuhan Minimum Pangan" (Poverty Line and Minimum Consumption Needs), ***Kompas***, 17 November 1977.

The *Inpres* programmes (*Instruksi Presiden*, Presidential Instruction for Special Grant Programmes) which were intensified at the beginning of this period were among several programmes designed as a response to the growing concern at both the rural-urban economic gap and regional disparities.[15] It was meant to carry out medium and small projects, while at the same time improving rural employment. The programme was funded by the central government on a per capita basis. Since its inception in 1970, the *Inpres* programme has been successful in building large numbers of schools, markets and health centres as well as constructing and repairing many kilometres of urban and rural roads. But it failed to make a significant impact on rural employment. Birowo and Hansen (1981) argued that the principal failure lay in the way private urban contractors were recruiting the urban work force to carry out projects in the rural areas. Beyond this direct deficiency of the *Inpres* programme, Mubyarto and Loekman Soetrisno in their regional study of the district of Sleman considered the self-reliant development style which the government aims to

of the population in wet-rice areas, see R. Hefner, *The Political Economy of Mountain Java*, 1990: 13.

[15] Two other programmes closely related to the *Inpres* programme are the *Bandes* (*Bantuan Desa,* Village Grants) and *proyek padat karya* (Labour Intensive Construction Project).

promote, has been stifled by the *Inpres Kabupaten* programme.[16] The central government subsidy, they argued, required a great deal of paper work and meetings, which eventually prevented the local people from field level involvement in identifying and initiating local projects (1985: 57).

The *padat karya* (labour intensive) programme initiated earlier in 1969, was directed at the improvement and expansion of the infrastructure in rural areas by means of mobilising work forces, especially in the slack season. The projects undertaken were small scale and private contractors were not involved. The sub-district government carried out the organisation. As the funds allocated for this project were increased in 1976, as a result of increased national revenues from the 1973 oil price boom, hundreds of projects comprising road construction, irrigation canals, fish ponds, *et cetera* were embarked on annually (Simanjuntak, 1987). While the number of projects completed annually was enormous, the long-term benefits on productivity and employment were marginal. Birowo and Hansen (1981) identified severe shortcomings in the processes of project identification, preparation and supervision of project implementation, resulting in poor project outcome. In addition Hardjono (1983) reported the way in which *padat karya* has allowed the richer farmers to continue benefiting from development projects at the expense of the poor.

> Since these hastily arranged 'jobs' usually involve the digging of canals and drains or road improvements undertaken in a haphazard way when funds are available, the work is not integrated into long-term regional development plans. Local land-owners benefit from improvements made to the infrastructure by the poor, who under this labour-intensive system work for a wage that is about half of the wage of an agricultural labourer (Hardjono, 1983: 54).

The *Bandes* programme was an annual cash grant subsidy allocated to every village in Indonesia. The funds were mostly used to carry out small-scale improvements in local infrastructure such as roads, bridges, public buildings and to repair small-scale irrigation networks. In 1981 the grants were approximately US$ 635 per village, by 1990 US$ 800, and US$ 2600 in 1993. As the funds were limited and the projects chosen were often biased towards the rural elite, the direct contribution to village welfare was usually insignificant. However, the government considered this programme an important way of encouraging popular participation in the development process (Hardjono, 1983; Huisman, 1994).

The economic growth at the national level was impressive. It grew by 8.8 percent annually during the first *Pelita* (1969-1974) and 7.2 percent on the second *Pelita* (1974-1979). Although the improvement among the very poor

---

[16] The *Inpres kabupaten* programme is a central government's direct aid to the district level (*kabupaten*) administration, thus bypassing a number of structural bureaucratic levels.

and destitute in the rural areas was disappointing, urban areas benefited more from the economic growth as indicated by a sharp decline in urban poverty.[17] Between 1976 and 1978 the inequality worsened as indicated by the rise of the Gini coefficient from 0.34 to 0.38 (Cheetham and Peters, 1993). In spite of the implementation of numerous rural development programmes in response to the question of unequal distribution of development benefits the field evidence remained unchanged. In fact, in some cases, opportunity for the rural poor to reap benefit from agricultural development actually declined (Mubyarto and Soetrisno, 1985: 38).

Beginning with the third *Pelita* (1979-1984), the increase in national revenue from the oil boom (1973-4), and perhaps the *Malari* affair (1974),[18] drove the government to give more emphasis to alleviating poverty in rural areas in its development policy. The *Inpres* programme was intensified, and by 1981 there were eight *Inpres* programmes in operation. These comprised grants to provinces, districts, villages, for construction of primary school buildings, health infrastructure, road improvements and reforestation (Daroesman, 1981). The Provincial Development Programmes were launched in 1979. These programmes were funded mainly by American and West German sources, designed to reach the rural poor through credit, employment, industrial and other programmes (Daroesman, 1981: 16). Furthermore, the government promulgated what was known as 'the eight tracks to equity'. The priority of the development process which was expressed in the sequence of the *Trilogi Pembangunan* (three development principles), which until 1979 was 'national stability', has now been replaced by 'equitability of development benefits'.

> Indonesia's economic growth during *Pelita*-II became a guarantee for an equitable distribution of development efforts, so as to enable all layers of the society and especially those with low income to equally enjoy the gains of development. During *Pelita*-III, the emphasis of the trilogy of development is laid on the principle of an equitable distribution of development and its gains in the achievement of social justice for the whole of the Indonesian nation. This

[17] Nearly all urban poverty measurements for the period of 1970-1976, including Sajogyo's and his critics', indicate sharp declines in urban poverty (among the very poor) from approximately 42 percent in 1970 to 28 percent in 1976.

[18] In January 15, 1974 when the Japanese Prime Minister, Kakuei Tanaka, arrived on a state visit, thousands of students demonstrated in the streets of Jakarta calling for a reduction of prices, an end to corruption and the disbanding of Soeharto's private assistants (*Aspri*). This incident became known as the *Peristiwa Malari* (*Malapetaka Januari* or January Disaster) or *Malari* Affairs. While the analysis of the political nature behind the incident is still unclear, the socio-economic message for the New Order administration was plain. The economic growth and the improvement of living standards were not always mutually compatible objectives. For further discussion on the *Malari* Affair, its origin and implications in Indonesia socio-political life, see H. Crouch, 1978; and Adam Schwarz, *A Nation in Waiting: Indonesia in the 1990s*, 1994.

> principle is being applied through the various steps and activities, among other things through the so-called eight channels of equitable distribution (*delapan jalur pemerataan*)[19] . . . (Republic of Indonesia, 1987: 35-36, emphasis added).

It was followed by a series of presidential decrees (*Keppres*) designed to allow greater local participation in government contracts (Republic of Indonesia, 1987: 37). *Keppres* 14 of 1979, and 14A of 1980 further define conditions under which budget funds may be used. The main objective was for preference to be given to 'weak economic groups' in the allocation of government contracts. A 'weak economic group' was identified as an enterprise where at least 50 percent of the capital was *pribumi* (indigenous)[20]owned, the net assets of the enterprise were not to exceed Rp. 25 million (US$ 12,000) in the case of trade and other services, or Rp. 100 million (US$ 48,000) in the case of industry and construction. Local co-operatives, which in rural areas meant *KUD* (*Koperasi Unit Desa* or Village unit Co-operatives), were also considered as 'weak economic groups' for the purpose of this legislation (Daroesman, 1981: 12-15).

Both macro data analysis and a large number of micro village studies indicate impressive growth in agricultural production between 1978 and 1983, growth which contributed to the reduction of rural poverty by real significant increases in rural wages.[21] It has been suggested that the increase in rice production during this period was due to the introduction of rice varieties (IR-32 and IR-36) resistant to the brown planthoppers.[22] Furthermore, the

---

[19] They were the equitable fulfilment of the basic needs (food, clothing, housing); the equitable provision of an opportunity to obtain education and health care; the equitable division of incomes; the equitable provision of work opportunities; the equitable provision of entrepreneurial opportunities; the equitable provision of opportunities to participate in development (especially for the younger generation and women); the equitable distribution of development throughout the entire territory of the country; and the equitable provision of opportunities to obtain justice (Republic of Indonesia, 1987: 36).

[20] Refering to 'ethnic Indonesians' as distinct from the Arab and Chinese Indonesian citizens.

[21] See W. L. Collier *et al.*, "Acceleration of Rural Development in Java." *Bulletin of Indonesian Economic Studies* 18 (1982): 84-101; G. Wiradi and C. Manning, *Landownership, Tenancy and Sources of Household Income; Community Pattern from a Partial Recensus of Eight Villages in Rural Java*, 1984; World Bank, *Indonesia: Policies for Growth and Employment*, 1985; G. Hart, *Power, Labor and Livelihood: Processes of Change in Rural Java*, 1986; and R. J. Cheetham and R. K Peters Jr., "Poverty Reduction during the New Order Government." In Jan-Paul Dirkse *et al.*, eds., *Development and Social Welfare; Indonesia's Experiences under the New Order*, 1993: 17-36.

[22] The brown planthoppers attacked 352,000 hectares of lowland rice areas in 1975, 317,000 hectares in 1976, and 562,900 hectares in 1977 causing estimated losses of 747,000 tons in 1975, 713,000 tons in 1976 and 1,144,000 tons in 1977. For further

substantial public infrastructure constructed during the first and second *Pelita* began to yield benefits for rural Java.

Table 1.3. The Increase in Rice Production, 1960-1981

Year	production ('000 metric tons milled rice)	Per capita availability (kg/person/year)
1960	9,401	98.4
1970	12,681	108.0
1975	15,141	114.6
1976	15,799	116.9
1977	15,829	114.4
1978	17,547	124.4
1979	17,918	124.5
1980	19,908	136.4
1981	22,000	149.3

Source: R. H. Bernsten, B. H. Siwi, and H. M. Beachell, "The Development and Diffusion of Rice Varieties in Indonesia." Paper presented to the International Rice Research Conference, 29 April , 1981: 59.

More recent studies have largely claimed that government development policies of the eighties have benefited the rural poor in general. While the rapid growth in rice output in the late 1970s and 1980s has generated increased employment in agriculture, Jones (1984) and Manning (1988) observed that increased public spending in rural areas has been more important for the employment situation in rural areas than agricultural growth. Findings elsewhere on Java by Rietveld (1986), Kasryno (1986) and Manning (1987) indicated the increasing importance of the non-farm sector for the income of rural households.[23] This could mean that the dynamic growth of the agricultural production has less significance in improving rural income than previously suspected. By the late eighties the prevalent view of the socio-economic impact of the broad-based economic growth policy of Indonesia remained unchanged, that is the

---

reading, see O. Mochida, "Brown Planthoppers Reduce Rice Production." *Indonesian Agricultural Research and Development Journal* 1.1 (1979): 2-8.

[23] On the basis of a micro-study on various parts of rural Java, Kasryno (1986) found that, while the relative share of income from all farm-related activities remained largely unchanged, the component of farm labour income declined from 42 percent to 28 percent of the total income during this period. This was accompanied by an increase in income generated by off-farm employment from 12 percent to 23 percent of the total income, see F. Kasryno, "Structural Changes in Rural Employment and Agricultural Wage in Indonesia." In Yang Boo Choe and Fu Chen Lo, eds., *Rural Industrialization and Non-Farm Activities of Asian Farmers*, 1986: 183-208.

discrepancy between the rich and the poor had increased over the years (Tjondronegoro, 1993: 159; Dirkse *et al.*, 1993: 10).

At the beginning of the fifth *Pelita* (1989-1994) another policy toward equality of income was introduced. This policy emphasised the development of the *KTI* (*Kawasan Timur Indonesia,* Eastern Indonesia), which consists of nine poor provinces.[24] It was followed by the *IDT* (*Inpres Desa Tertinggal, Inpres* for the poor villages) programme. In 1993 President Soeharto created a new post, Assistant to the Chairman of *Bappenas (Badan Perencanaan Pembangunan Nasional,* National Development Planning Board), who was charged with setting up an *Inpres* programme targeted at alleviating poverty in some 20,633 villages considered to be in a state of absolute poverty (BPS, 1993c). The *IDT* programme distributed Rp. 20 million (US$ 9,500) per annum to each of these villages for up to three successive years. Within the programme poor households were encouraged to form groups among themselves to facilitate the development of small-scale business enterprises. The *IDT* programme would then facilitate the group with capital, as well as technical and managerial advice.

It is probably far too early to evaluate the impact of the *IDT* programme as far as rural poverty is concerned. However, numerous reports on the ignorance of rural people on how to spend the money, as well as the misuse of *IDT* funds by some local bureaucrats, have overshadowed the whole issue of rural poverty (Mubyarto, 1995). The latest official evaluation on the impact of *IDT* programme in alleviating poverty reports an 'indication' that the programme has in some degree been able to empower individuals in poor villages (***Republika***, 20 October 1995). Such conclusions have not been supported by any detailed research. Indeed, the statement itself seems to have been biased toward the political interest of the ruling party, as was then expressed by the Secretary General of the Interior Department, Mr. Surjatna: "*Karena jika program IDT gagal, ini akan berdampak politis dan akan mempengaruhi*

[24] The negligence of the development process in the Outer Islands, especially in Eastern Indonesia since the beginning of the New Order has deepened inter-regional disparities. In his study on these regional imbalances, Cornelis Lay of Gajah Mada University concluded that any solutions would have to go beyond a greater share of economic investment in Eastern Indonesia. As political authority in Indonesia is concentrated in Java, and Javanese culture tends to dominate (see, MacAndrews *et al.*, 1982), Cornelis Lay called for a new expression of Javanese political culture (cf., Anderson, 1972). The present Javanese political culture, he argued, had contributed to the formation of the 'centre-periphery' relationship between Java (Jakarta) and the outer islands, and had generated dependency and underdevelopment of the Eastern regions of Indonesia. The new expression of the Javanese political culture would have to empower local and regional leaders to have a greater influence and participation in developing their own regions and districts as well as at the national level. See, C. Lay, *Ketimpangan dan Keterbelakangan di Indonesia* (Imbalances and Under Development in Indonesia), 1993.

kredibilitas pemerintah" (If the *IDT* programme fails, it will have a political impact and affect the government's credibility) .

Writing in 1993, Cornelis Lay perceived that despite the policy of giving priority investment to the Eastern Regions of Indonesia, inter-regional disparities persisted. Unless effective remedies can be found for this imbalance of development, he argued that Indonesian national unity will be affected (1993: 73-75). While the majority of the rural population is believed in one way or the other to have benefited from the development programmes under the New Order administration, the issue of rural-urban and regional disparities are still considered the major threat to government credibility approaching the 1997 general election.[25]

In defending national development policy against the criticism of a widening of the rural-urban disparity, Prof. Ali Wardhana (1995) argued that the World Bank report reveals that in the past ten years the Indonesian Gini coefficient remained fairly static.[26] It was 0.33 in 1983 and was 0.34 in 1994 (World Bank 1995).[27] His view is however, debatable, since the World Bank report relies solely on the *SUSENAS* (National Socio-Economic Survey) data published by the Central Bureau of Statistics (BPS), which was based on household expenditure. This household expenditure approach is perceived to be inadequate to illustrate the real income distribution in specific social groups, as BPS have also acknowledged.

> The public welfare status can be partly indicated by its level of income. However, it cannot be denied that data collection of income is often difficult to do, primarily because of the technical problem in the field during interview. Due to this problem, household income was deduced from household expenditure data. It should be remembered that expenditure distribution is not always consistent with the Gini ratio for income or welfare distribution (BPS, 1993b: 89-90).

Few governments in recent history have undertaken significant poverty alleviation measures and reduction of socio-economic as well as regional disparities. In this respect the New Order government is phenomenal. As early as the mid seventies Indonesia committed itself to the principle of 'growth in equity'.

---

[25] Harmoko, the Chairman of Golkar, the ruling party (*Republika*, 18 October 1995), as well as Ginanjar, the Chairman of *Bappenas* (*Republika*, 13 October 1995) and May-Gen. Syarwan Hamid (*Republika*, 19 October 1995) were among the officials who perceived the implication of such an issue for the 1997 general election.

[26] Gini ratio is a measure of income distribution based on income class. It is between nil (zero), which expresses perfect distribution, and 1 (one), perfect unequal distribution (BPS, 1993b: xxv).

[27] A. Wardhana "Indonesia, Asia-Pacific, and the Global Economy: New Dimension and the Challenge of Regional Building", Paper prepared for the CSIS (the Centre for Strategic and International Studies) seminar, Jakarta, 17 October 1995.

> Implementation of development should, besides increasing the national income, also secure an equal distribution of income for the whole of the people in accordance with the sense of justice so that, on one hand, development is not only aimed at the increase of production, but it should at the same time **prevent a widening of the gap between the rich and the poor** . . . (Republic of Indonesia, 1983: 16-17, emphasis added).

While the World Bank reports (1995) on poverty reduction and income distribution equality seem to commend Indonesia's achievements, a large number of micro studies referred to in the present study are almost unanimously less optimistic. Many are sceptical or even suggest that the impact of the New Order's development policy has had a completely different impact, that is an increase in the discrepancy between the rich and the poor (Dirkse *et al.*, 1993: 10). Significant concerns were expressed about the rhetorical nature of those policies (Hart, 1986: 56). Tjondronegoro observed that, while the government committed itself to equity since the third *Pelita* (1979-1984), "the organisational infrastructure that would carry out this commitment, however, has remained largely unchanged" (1993: 159).[28]

There have been several independent studies and seminars dedicated to evaluating the first 25 years of New Order policy on poverty alleviation (1965-1990). Prominent here was a colloquium on 'Poverty and Development in Indonesia', held in the Hague in April 1991. This was considered particularly significant, given the prestige of the participants and the objectivity of the presentations. While some of the contributors maintained that current government policy on development is on the right track and will be able to proceed in the same general direction, with some adjustments in policy design and implementation,[29] others, including Sjahrir, Sajogyo, Benjamin White, Ines Smyth, Tjondronegoro, Hafidz, Van Tuyl and Witjes have called for more drastic policy changes. Most have in one or other way indicated the need for a real 'bottom-up development policy' which gets beyond mere rhetoric (see, Dirkse *et al.*, 1993).

At the heart of the New Order economic development programme was the Green Revolution. While the top-down macro policy has been criticised for discouraging the participation of the rural poor in development, and thus creating a larger discrepancy between the rich and the poor, the Green Revolution, has largely been praised for significantly raising rice production, and thus increasing the income of the rural population in general. The following section will examine the impact of the Green Revolution on the alleviation of rural poverty.

---

[28] For further readings on the administrative and organisational problems of rural development in Indonesia, see S. Tjondronegoro, *Social Organization and Planned Development in Rural Java*, 1984; and N. G. Schulte Nordholt, 1987a.

[29] Among others were, Cheetham and Peters, Thorbecke and Budhy Tjahjati, and Soetjipto, see Dirkse *et al.*, 1993.

3. Indonesia and the Green Revolution

The rural development policy adopted in Indonesia since 1950 has been focused around the need for rice self-sufficiency. Soekarno (1950-1965) considered that the unequal distribution of land in rural areas was a major obstacle in increasing agricultural production, therefore improving agricultural structure by, for example, land reform was given top priority.[30] The New Order administration (post-1965) relied more on the use of modern agricultural inputs to increase production. It is of course inappropriate to compare the Soekarno Old Order administration and the New Order's performance in terms of the quantity of rice production, instead the socio-economic performance of independent Indonesia is to be viewed from the perspective of historical continuity. As Peter Timmer has observed, any economic achievements of the New Order administration would not have been possible without the development of socio-political concepts during the previous two decades (foreword in Sjahrir, 1986).

Development policies immediately after 1965 denote the government's renewed attempts to achieve self-sufficiency in rice production through intensified cultivation. With the improvements of irrigation networks as a first step, the government initiated the Green Revolution through a *Bimas* (*Bimbingan Massal,* Mass Guidance) programme in 1969. Under this programme farmers were provided with a package of services that included short-term credit and subsidised inputs such as high-yielding variety (HYV) seeds, fertilisers and pesticides. Due to the widespread occurrence of the brown rice planthoppers and the accumulated debt problem of the participating farmers, the growth in production output was rather slow. The *Inmas* (*Intensifikasi massal*, Mass Intensification) programme was then introduced in 1973, mainly to provide services to those farmers who could not be given new loans because of their rising accumulated debt, and to tenants who did not qualify for *Bimas* (Hardjono, 1983). Since the incentive to join *Inmas* programme was limited, as it offered no cash assistance, the number of *Bimas* and *Inmas* participants decreased from 3.6 million in 1974 to 2.1 million in 1978 and declined further to about 1 million in 1980 (Huisman, 1994). The third major programme called *Insus* (*Intensifikasi khusus*, Special Intensification) was introduced in 1979 to overcome the stagnation in the intensification campaign and to increase the cropping intensity in irrigated areas. Unlike the two previous programmes, *Insus* provided bank credits on the basis of group farming rather than individual farmers, and as an incentive the

---

[30] While several intensification programmes, such as the establishment of 'Rice Centres' (*Padi Sentra*) programme by the Department of Agriculture in 1959, and the introduction of *Denmas* (*Demontrasi Massal*, Mass Demonstration) in 1963, of special significance during Soekarno's administration was the land reform programme which was initiated in 1960. For a comprehensive analysis of this land reform programme and its political implications, see Rex Mortimer, 1974.

government bought all *Insus* rice at a price 2.5 percent higher than the current floor price. Together with the introduction of the IR-32 and IR-36 rice varieties, which were resistant to the brown plant hopper, the *Insus* programme was able to substantially increase rice production. Hardjono reported on these encouraging results showing that in 1980-81 *Insus* groups obtained average yields of 4.7 tonnes of milled rice per hectare as against 2.5 tonnes on *Bimas* land (1983: 51).

Indonesia was transformed from being one of the world's major rice importers in the seventies, to being self-sufficient in 1983-1984 (Sudaryanto and Kasryno, 1994: 107). Despite the significant increase in rice production since 1978 (see, Table 1.3), the Green Revolution in Indonesia, as initiated by the *Bimas* programme, has been criticised. It was criticised first, because the concentration of effort on rice production reportedly had a negative impact on non-rice crops, both as the secondary crops grown in irrigated areas and as the main crops in the upland and drier areas. Commodities such as cassava, soya beans, maize and peanuts were all affected (Falcon *et al.*, 1984; Booth, 1979; Timmer, 1981; Huisman, 1994).[31] Second, it has been argued that the various Green Revolution programmes increased the income of only the small upper class of farmers who own over 0.5 hectares of land (Mubyarto and Soetrisno, 1985: 29) and did not change the position of the very small and landless farm labourers (Soewardi, 1976: 100-107; Penny and Singarimbun, 1973: 29-34; Prabowo and Sajogyo, 1981). In summing up the findings of his field research in several villages in Java between 1973-1974, Maurer observed that:

> ...everywhere the rich and the better-off landowners were participating massively in the official *Bimas* credit program and had access to relatively cheap subsidised agricultural inputs, whereas the small and poorest ones remained virtually excluded from it (1984: 113).

In fact, as has been indicated by Hardjono (1983), the significant growth of national rice production has mostly been attained through government patronage of large landowners (see also, Husken, 1984).

Third, the Green Revolution has been criticised for major displacement of rural employment as the result of the technological innovations in the agricultural sector (Mortimer, 1973; Sinaga, 1978; Collier, 1981a). Many farmers replaced the hand-held harvest knife (*ani-ani*) with the sickle, thus reducing demand for harvest labour (Stoler, 1977a; Collier *et al.*, 1973; Collier,

---

[31] Peter C. Timmer reported that while the rice production increased some 41 percent from 1967-1971, production of the major dry-field food staples such as maize, cassava and sweet potatoes fell at an annual rate of 10, 7 and 5 percent respectively (1981: 43). In the Tengger Highlands, East Java, per hectare yields for maize had fallen to 0.80 metric tons by the late 1960s, see R. Hefner, 1990: 17; and Anne Booth, "The Agricultural Survey, 1970-75." *Bulletin of Indonesian Economic Studies* 15 (1979) : 49.

1978; Palmer, 1977).[32] One study showed that rice-harvesting using the *ani-ani* required about 200 man-days per hectare of agricultural unit compared with 75 man-days when sickles were used (Collier *et al.*, 1973: 41). Another study in West Java showed that the use of only 9 small tractors in soil preparation covering as large an area as 20 hectares of land would result in the decline of farm wage labour from as much as 5400 man-days to 2600 man-days (Sinaga, 1976: 5). Furthermore, the introduction of the mechanical rice huller has displaced some 7.7 million part-time (hand) pounders (Timmer, 1973; Collier *et al.*, 1974). In order to determine the potential impact of mechanisation on agricultural employment in Java, Collier developed a comparison of labour use between an average traditional rice farm in Java in 1968-1969 with a hypothetical totally mechanised rice farm along the IRRI model. He found that the mechanised small rice farm uses only 111.1 man hours per hectare, as compared to the 1275 man hours in traditional farm rice. If the comparison were to be applied to all the irrigated land area in Java, i.e. approximately 2,628,000 hectares (1981), mechanisation would displace some 3,058,729,200 man hours of labour per season (1981a: 39-44). Although this finding is unrealistic due to the impossibility of mechanising all the irrigated land in Java, this illustration and other village studies (Utami and Ihalauw, 1973; Sinaga, 1978) have revealed that increasing and significant numbers of rural poor are being excluded from traditional farm employment. The Green Revolution, they argue, has mostly benefited land owners, large farmers and skilled labourers. It eventually leads to a concentration of land control, labour surplus and declining welfare of the poorer rural households (Sinaga, 1976; Tjondronegoro, 1978). As has also been indicated by Sritua Arief, from 1971 to 1974 the level of real wages in rural Central Java has declined by 12 percent, in Yogyakarta by 17 percent, and in West Java by 28 percent (1978: 74-75).

Such phenomena are not of course peculiar to Indonesia. Elsewhere in developing countries sharp changes in tenancy arrangements, displacement of employment and the increasing number of landless peasants have been frequently reported. This occurred under the impact of the Green Revolution in the Philippines (rice) and the Punjab (wheat).[33] Ishak Shari and Jomo Kwame Sundaram similarly identified the changes of tenancy arrangement in rural Malaysia as the result of the growing mechanisation of the production process, which has driven the tenants away from the land, and thus increasing the number of rural unemployed (1982: 233-236).[34]

[32] The *ani-ani* is used to harvest only the panicles, whereas the sickle is used to harvest the entire rice stalk. Because modern varieties have shorter stalks and are more susceptible to shattering than traditional varieties, threshing results are best when a crop is harvested by sickle.

[33] See Eric H. Jacoby, "Effects of the 'Green Revolution' in South and Southeast Asia." *Modern Asian Studies* 6.1, January 1971.

[34] For further reading on the negative impact of Green Revolution on employment in Southeast Asia, see S. K. Jayasuria and R. T. Shand, "Technical Change and Labor

While acknowledging the potential of the Green Revolution in overcoming food shortages and poverty, most of the literature cited above has basically pointed to a similar prospect of increasing inequalities in the rural population by the process of introducing modern seed varieties. As with Java in the seventies, the field evidence was alarming. Writing in the late seventies, White summarised what were considered to be the major findings of micro-studies on socio-economic development during this period:

> A perusal of available case studies of agrarian and other socio-economic developments in rural Java would point out the following changes in recent years: unequal distribution of the direct and indirect benefits of new biological and chemical technologies in rice production, new technologies in cultivation, weeding, harvesting and processing which cut the costs for the larger farms but reduce the employment and income opportunities of labourers;...declining real agricultural wages; unequal access to agricultural and other form of subsidised government credit,...increasing landlessness and an acceleration in the purchase of agricultural land by wealthy villagers and urban elite; . . . (1979: 8).

This labour displacement and the unequal distribution of development benefits have led some observers to conclude that increasing rural class polarisation was inevitable (Penny and Singarimbun, 1973; Collier *et al.*, 1974; Soewardi, 1976; Collier, 1978, 1979, White, 1976).[35]

The problem with most of these analyses is that they view rural change exclusively in terms of technology, credit allocation or land distribution. From the various analyses of the impact of Green Revolution on the Javanese rural population, it is evident that most development related policies have been accompanied by complex changes in rural income and employment. Furthermore, it becomes clear that the impact of the Green Revolution differs greatly inter-regionally, intra-regionally, between households and in time (Huisman, 1994). While such evidence would obviously repudiate any generalisation, it is interesting to note that the earlier studies of the seventies were often rather negative on the employment and the income distribution

---

Absorption in Asian Agriculture: Some Emerging Trends." *World Development* 14.3 (1985): 415-428. Particularly important has been series of studies sponsored by the United Nations Research Institute of Social Development (UNRISD), which includes Southeast Asia, summarised in A. Pearse, *Seeds of Plenty, Seeds of Want*, 1980.

[35] These findings have undermined Geertz's well-known thesis of 'agricultural involution' and 'shared poverty' in rural Java (1963). Unlike the process of agrarian change in other developing countries, Geertz observed that the concept of 'involution' and 'shared poverty' had enabled the Javanese in 'Mojokuto' to accommodate the growing population on an increasingly over-crowded island with a minimum socio-economic differentiation. In his view, they were able to maintain their social homogeneity in an egalitarian and symmetrical structure (1963).

effects of the Green Revolution.[36] On the other hand the publications of the eighties and early nineties tend to express general opinions on the overall impact on employment, income and other socio-economic changes in rural Java.[37]

More recent studies on economic change in the wet rice growing community in rural Java suggested that the Green Revolution of the seventies and early eighties has indirectly contributed to the increase in real rural wages. The poorer rural households seem to have benefited from finding employment in urban locations, and as a consequence, this led to widespread rural agricultural labour shortage (Manning, 1988; Collier *et al.*, 1988). These findings suggest a remarkable change in the welfare of the poorer rural households, as compared to Geertz's apprehension on the outcome of the 'involution' process of the Javanese rural community (1963). It also suggests a marked departure from the classic analysis of the Green Revolution, which identifies the labour displacement and unequal distribution of income that would eventually lead to a rural class polarisation (Collier *et al.*, 1973; Sinaga, 1976; Mortimer, 1973; Palmer, 1977; Stoller, 1977a).

It was Hayami and Kakuchi (1982) who pointed out that although labour use per hectare for modern rice varieties is still lower than for traditional varieties, due to the increasing cropping intensity of modern rice technology, the Green Revolution has heightened labour demand, especially in irrigated areas of Java.[38] The cropping intensity itself was the result of growth in the proportion of irrigated land and the spread of the short-growth-duration modern varieties.[39]

---

[36] It appears that these earlier studies seemed to overstate the polarising tendencies generated by the Green Revolution as a reaction to Geertz's involution thesis. It is also suspectible that it springs from a tendency to generalise from the Green Revolution experience of other Asian countries, see C. Manning, *The Green Revolution, Employment and Economic Change in Rural Java: A Reassessment of Trends under the New Order*, 1988: 1-2.

[37] See Y. Hayami and M. Kikuchi, *Asian Village Economy at the Cross-Roads: An Economic to Institutional Change*, 1982; G. Wiradi and C. Manning, 1984; F. Kasryno, 1986; G. Hart, 1986; C. Manning, 1988; R. Hefner, 1990; T. Sudaryanto and F. Kasryno, "Modern Rice Variety Adoption and Factor-Market Adjustments in Indonesia." In C. C. David and K. Otsuka, eds., *Modern Rice Technology and Income Distribution in Asia*, 1994: 107-127.

[38] Modern varieties were mainly adopted in irrigated and in some favourable rain-fed areas, mostly in Java and parts of Sumatra. On the other hand, the upland and tidal swamp villages, mainly located on the outer islands, where waterlogging, acidity, salinity, and other soil fertility problems are prevalent, only traditional varieties are grown. Jatileksono's (1994) village study in Lampung revealed that while the adoption of modern rice varieties in favourable irrigated areas has increased labour demands, however, in the upland less favourable areas, where traditional varieties continue to be grown, the yields continue to stagnate.

[39] Sudaryanto and Kasryno observed that in the irrigated villages, the ratio of irrigated land had increased significantly, from 76 percent in 1970 to 93 percent in 1987 (1994: 110).

It has also been suggested that higher farm income due to the increasing labour demands has generated an added value in the non-farm sector (Manning, 1988; Collier *et al.*, 1988; Naylor, 1991). Such effects have also been reported in India (Hazell and Ramasamy, 1991), Malaysia, Nigeria (Hazell and Roell, 1983), and the Philippines (Gibbs, 1974). Given recent evidence that modern variety adaptation has tripled Indonesian rice-farm income (Heytens, 1991), it was suspected that significant employment effects on the non-agricultural sector have also occurred (Rietveld, 1986; Manning, 1987; 1988).

As a marked departure from the earlier analyses on rural employment, Kasryno (1986) identified a shift of employment away from agriculture among the young rural population (age 10-29, across 'class stratification'). While it is true that agriculture is unlikely to be able to provide sufficient employment opportunities for the increasing rural work force, this exodus to out-of-farm employment seems to have been motivated by the higher returns of the non-farm activities, especially in urban areas (Manning, 1988).[40] This present research, as will be described in Chapter Three, confirms this trend of labour mobility of the younger generation, as it occurred in the three hamlets under investigation. It further identifies these young commuting urban employees as a new rural middle class. The exodus has eventually generated an increase in agricultural labour intensity. The higher earnings from commuting employment in urban areas (Hugo, 1978) and the increase of demand and intensity of the agricultural employment in rural areas (Collier *et al.*, 1988; Manning, 1988) could have resulted in a higher income for those remaining in agriculture as well.

To sum up, the discussion in this section has highlighted the overall trends of the impact of the Green Revolution on employment and income distribution in rural Java. While considering the 'success' of the Green Revolution in raising agricultural output, village studies in the seventies generally agreed that the Green Revolution inputs had generally benefited larger farmers. These studies identified the increasing gap in income distribution which unavoidably led to rural polarisation (Collier *et al.*, 1974; Sinaga, 1976; White, 1976; Stoler, 1977a). This finding is quite different from the prevalent socio-economic analysis of the sixties and early seventies, which believed that rural Java had undergone a unique process of agricultural involution, and had been able to maintain the egalitarian and symmetrical structures of rural community (Geertz, 1963).

---

[40] Earlier studies have mainly emphasised the lack of employment opportunity in the agricultural sector in Java as the major factor contributing to the search for urban jobs, see G. Temple, "Migration to Jakarta." *Bulletin of Indonesian Economic Studies* 11.1 (1975): 76-81; G. Hugo, *Population Mobility in West Java*, 1978; and H. Kano, "The Economic History of Javanese Rural Society: A Reinterpretation." *The Developing Economies* 17 (1980): 3-22.

Differing from these two analyses, more recent studies have tended to look at the overall employment (both farm and non-farm activities), income and other socio-economic impacts of the Green Revolution. Evidence from these later studies indicate the increasing importance of the non-farm sectors for the income of rural households, especially for the temporary migration and commuting urban employment (Kasryno, 1986; Manning, 1988). It is argued that the higher earnings of urban jobs has indirectly increased the earnings of the farm employment in rural areas (Huisman, 1994). Related to these data, the identification of segmented labour markets and of unequal income distribution, which led to the process of polarisation in rural Java seems to be far from conclusive.

The role of the Green Revolution itself in the process of social change of the rural Javanese might have been much less than scholars have suspected. Hayami and Kakuchi (1982), Sairin (1975) and Ihalauw (1974) argued that long before the Green Revolution, new agricultural technologies had been introduced into different parts of rural Java. For example, the replacement of the hand-held harvest knife (*ani-ani*) with the sickle, and the shift from the *bawon* (share-harvest) harvesting system to the *tebasan* (broker) system, had very little, if any, impact on the polarisation of the rural Javanese society. Meanwhile, Temple (1976) suggested a gradual and rather slow evolution of rural Javanese society from a communal type of society into a more commercial one. This gradual process had probably begun during or even before the colonial period. Therefore, to suggest that the Green Revolution of the seventies was the central factor contributing to rural inequality and polarisation is speculative and to some extent misplaced.

While both the New Order's policies on rural (economic) development and the implementation of the Green Revolution have to various degrees been benefiting the majority of the population, poverty is still prevalent within some thirty-five percent of Indonesian villages (BPS, 1993c). At the conclusion of his analysis of the New Order development policy, Hardjono (1983) pointed out that the government's current policies have resulted in an all pervading top-down approach to rural development, which for most development theories, are considered to have failed to touch the lives of the needy and poorer households (Castillo, 1983; Pearse, 1980).[41] The national-level policy makers complain of the 'static' attitudes of the rural people, yet overlook the highly centralised socio-political sphere which has eroded traditional village institutions and

[41] Recent theories on rural development have generally identified empowerment and popular participation as central aspects for sustainable development, see for example, R. Chambers, 1983; P. Oakley *et al.*, 1991; S. Burkey, *People First: A Guide to Self-Reliant, Participatory Development*, 1993; M. Cernea, *Putting People First: Sociological Variables in Rural Development*, 1985; M. Bamberger, ed., 1986; C. T. Castillo, *How Participatory is Participatory Development: A Review of the Philippine Experience*, 1983; D. Ghai, *Participation in Development: Some Perspectives from Grass-Roots Experience*, 1988.

prohibited village-level political activities, that should otherwise promote people participation in development (Tjondronegoro, 1984; Mubyarto and Soetrisno, 1989). It is therefore appropriate to dedicate the following sections to a discussion on the New Order's policies related to socio-political aspects of rural life.

4. Socio-Political Policy of the New Order

It has been a major concern that Indonesia's impressive economic growth has not been accompanied by political developments at a comparable rate. In fact, as a number of observers have repeatedly expressed, the significant increase of overall food production was achieved at the expense of rural 'depoliticization' (Mubyarto and Soetrisno, 1985; 1989; Hardjono, 1983; Hart, 1986; Sjahrir, 1986). The government seems to consider that the involvement of the rural poor in politics as an impediment to rural development (Mubyarto, 1988:47). The intense competition of the political parties prior to 1965 was perceived as the source of conflicts within the rural population. Therefore, to protect the peasants from the 'bad influence' of political parties and concentrate on economic development, the government introduced the 'floating mass' policy, which prohibited political parties from operating and carrying on any activities in villages except for the few weeks of campaign prior to general elections (Mubyarto and Soetrisno, 1985: 37).

The idea of 'floating mass' was suggested by Nurcholis Madjid of HMI (*Himpunan Mahasiswa Islam*, a modernist Moslem youth organisation) in June 1971, with the intention of allowing political parties to concentrate themselves on "interest aggregation, interest articulation and political communication" (Ward, 1974: 190).[42] However, the government's main motive behind the adoption of this floating mass concept was neither to allow the political parties to draw up workable programmes, as had probably been in Madjid's mind, nor to increase rural income, as the government itself has repeatedly argued.[43] While the rice policy was primarily aimed at winning over the urban middle class (Husken and White, 1989: 235-236), the floating mass policy was a means of isolating the political parties from their grass-roots support in villages

[42] Quoted from the "Pandangan HMI terhadap Masalah-Masalah Dewasa Ini" (HMI's Views on Contemporary issues), 23 June 1971:10 as cited by Ken Ward, *The 1971 Election in Indonesia, An East Java Case Study*. Monash Papers on Southeast Asia, 1974: 189.

[43] It would be wrong however, to suggest that the government's concern was entirely political consolidation. Since economic growth validates politics, it is similarly true that a stable political climate would encourage foreign investment, and facilitate economic growth. In the long run, this economic growth was expected to improve the living standards of the mass of the people (Crouch, 1978: 273-275).

(Ali Moertopo, 1973: 85-86; Crouch, 1978; Liddle, 1973; Utrecht, 1974).[44] Although Madjid's speech took place in mid-1971 and the floating mass policy was not enforced until late 1971, the intention to diminish the influence of political parties in the villages appears to have been dominant in the New Order regime from its inception in 1966 (Crouch, 1978; Mubyarto, 1988).[45]

Between September 1971 and April 1972 the concept of floating mass received broad attention from the media and its implementation was widely discussed among the New Order supporters.[46] Since the *aliran*[47] was perceived as the strongest force in the villages' resistance to the spread of communism with its class struggle, a principal objection was raised against the disruption of *aliran* that might be caused by the floating mass concept (Ward, 1974). Mortimer, a prominent analyst of the PKI (The Communist party of Indonesia) observed that the PKI's strategy of mobilising the rural poor was fatally undermined by the strength of the *aliran* attachments:

> The Communists had tried to fight on class lines for once, and to an extent they had succeeded; but in the end, *aliran* loyalties tended to swamp them. The traditional socio-cultural cleavages among the population, which had been an important factor in dictating the PKI's strategic avoidance of class agitation in past years, could not be overcome in the short period in which they cultivated a class approach in the villages (1974: 327).

For Geertz, an *aliran* was more than a mere political party and it was more than a mere ideology. It was a "transformation of the *santri*, *abangan* and *priyayi* traditions into modern universalistic ideologies." (1965: 127-128). Accordingly, the PNI (*Partai Nasional Indonesia*, The Nationalist Party) and

---

[44] Ken Ward considered it as an attempt to transplant a feature of 'stable' Western political system, "wherein most of the population are not members of political parties and only interest themselves in politics on the occasion of elections" (1974: 78).

[45] Within the Army itself, there were different views over the question of what role the political parties would be permitted under the New Order. The militant anti-Soekarnoist officers represented by Sarwo Edhi, H. R. Dharsono and Kemal Idris had called for a major overhaul of the political system, which would drastically reduce the role of the political parties, see H. Crouch, 1978: 234-252; and E. Utrecht, "The Military and the Elections." In Oey Hong Lee, ed., *Indonesia after the 1971 Election*, 1974: 84.

[46] *Harian Kami*, 3 August 1971; *Kompas*, 25 September 1971; *Abadi*, 22 October 1971; *Sinar Harapan*, 5 April 1972; *Suara Karya*, 6 April 1972, *Mahasiswa Indonesia*, 10 October 1971., see K. Ward, 1974: 189.

[47] By *aliran* (stream) is usually meant the political alignments of a variety of village level organisations, e.g. Women Clubs, Youth Groups, boy scouts, private schools, peasants unions, art groups, trade organisations -which form the primary bond linking the village to the national political system. According to this *aliran* system, people were politically divided not by class or ideology, but according to religious beliefs and socio-cultural values that found expression in the post-independence Indonesia political party system. See Geertz, "The Javanese Village", in G. William Skinner, ed., *Local, Ethnic, and National Loyalties in Village Indonesia*, 1959.

the PKI were composed of both the *priyayi* adherents to the Hindu elements in Javanese syncretism with a tendency to be white-collar employees and the *abangan* followers of the animistic elements of syncretism which were mostly poorer peasants. Opposing these nominal Muslims were the devout *santri* who showed a marked tendency to be businessmen or richer peasants. The more orthodox of whom were associated with the NU (*Nahdlatul Ulama*) and the modernists with the Masyumi Party (1965: 127-129). The cleavage between, on the one hand, Muslim parties, who based their appeal on *santri* dominated areas, and, on the other, the PNI and PKI, with their support in the Javanist regions seemed to confirm Geertz's *aliran* thesis.

While the Communist party had failed to fight the *aliran*-party *nexus* through an agrarian mobilisation, Golkar (*Golongan Karya*, government political party) appears to confront the *aliran* pattern of the Indonesian political system through political tinkering. Neither political observers nor Golkar's leaders were quite optimistic that 'Sekber-Golkar'[48] would be able to develop popular grass-roots support in the short period before the 1971 election (Ruth McVey, 1970; Crouch, 1978). Mackie in an analysis of the 1971 election wrote:

> If any transformation of the *aliran* pattern is to be expected. . . it will require a broad cluster of economic and social changes reaching throughout Indonesia, particularly rural Java, probably over several generations (1974: 62).

It was clear from Golkar's electoral strategy then, that instead of fighting against the deeply rooted *aliran* pattern of the Indonesian political system as others have observed (Mortimer, 1973; Schulte Nordholt, 1987a; Hefner, 1990), their strategy tended to enforce the vertical alignment of *aliran* and political party. Significantly, Golkar did not present a coherent political ideology of its own which could unite former supporters of PNI, the Muslim parties and even the PKI, and thus erode the *aliran* cleavage. Instead, Golkar in realising the potential power of the *aliran* alignments of rural Java, created a patronage machine that would win over supporters from other parties. Utrecht observes:

---

[48] Sekber-Golkar (*Sekretariat Bersama Golongan Karya*, the Joint Secretariat of Functional Groups) was established by army officers in October 1964, to coordinate anti-PKI organisations within the National Front. In the first year it was a federation of 146 organisations, it swelled to 210 in 1967 and further to 249 in 1968. It was later used by Soeharto as the government party, through which his supporters would compete in the elections. Although most of these affiliated bodies were civilian, the most influential were led by army officers. In fact, six out of seven *Kino* (*Kesatuan Induk Organisasi*, Basic Organisation Units) were led by army officers, including Brigadier-General Suhardiman and Major General Sughandi, see K. Ward, 1974: 25-26; and H. Crouch, 1978: 266.

> After Golkar functionaries had succeeded in winning over the village authorities and landowners to side with Golkar it was not difficult to obtain the support of the rest of the inhabitants of the village. . . . It was the economic dependence on landowners and village authorities, who themselves were dependent on facilities granted to them by Golkar functionaries, that made the small farmers-for the greater part poor sharecroppers-voted for Golkar (1974: 85).

Sustained by Golkar's overwhelming victory in the 1971 election (62.8 percent), the government launched another political manoeuvre, namely the reform of the political structure. Apart from Golkar, the parties were to realign themselves into two new parties. The first, PPP (*Partai Persatuan Pembangunan,* United Development Party) consisted of the Muslim parties: NU, Parmusi, PSII *(Partai Serikat Islam Indonesia,* Indonesian Islamic League Party) and Perti *(Pergerakan Tarbijah Islamijah* or Islamic Educational Movement). The Second, PDI *(Partai Demokrasi Indonesia,* Indonesian Democratic Party) consisted of PNI, Parkindo (Christian Party), Catholic Party, Murba (left-nationalist party) and IPKI *(Ikatan Pendukung Kemerdekaan Indonesia,* The League of the Upholders of Indonesia's Independence). The grouping of these parties seems to further confirm government's intention to maintain the *aliran* pattern between the Islamic *santri* and the Javanist *abangan.*

It is interesting to note that prior to and during the massacre of the alleged PKI supporters in 1965-1966 the army worked very closely with the *santri*, and especially the Ansor (NU's youth organisation) against the peasants *abangan* supporters of the PKI.[49] Mackie's analysis on the 1971 election concluded that Golkar was just another party of the *abangan* (1974: 75). Crouch also writes,

> Drawn from much the same Javanese a*bangan* background, the army and PNI leaders "understood" each other in a way that excluded the Muslim leaders and the "modernists" of the Action fronts. Obliged to hold elections but fearing that they lack of effective vote-getting organisation of their own, the army leaders seemed to be relying on the PNI to block whatever challenge might be offered from the Muslim quarter (1978: 265).

Mackie's analysis seemed to have been confirmed by the fact that the great expectation of the Masyumi's supporters that the New Order would rehabilitate Masyumi never came to pass. Instead, to co-ordinate the activities of the ex-Masyumi supporters the government established a new Muslim party, Parmusi (*Partai Muslimin Indonesia,* Muslim Party of Indonesia) with none of the

[49] In East Java, where the major killing took place, the clash was initiated by the Ansor's leaders. Moreover, the major youth rallies in Bandung and Jakarta which intensified the anti-Soekarno feeling and proclaimed the birth of the New Order was strongly supported by the Masyumi's leaders (the Modernist Muslim party banned by Soekarno in 1960 on alleged involvement in PRRI revolt). For extensive reading, see H. Crouch, 1978: 147-157, 197; and B. May, *The Indonesian Tragedy*, 1978: 120-123.

former charismatic Masyumi's leaders being allowed to sit on the party's leadership (Crouch, 1978: 259-263; Solichin Salam, 1970: 269-270). The votes gathered by Parmusi in the 1971 election reveal that the majority of the former Masyumi's supporters did not see Parmusi as the new Masyumi. While Masyumi was one of the major parties winning 20.9 percent of the votes in 1955 election, the government created Parmusi only gathered 5.36 percent in 1971 election. But, with only a small number of the ex-Masyumi's supporters who voted for the other Muslim parties, the majority must have supported Golkar. The significant number of modernist Muslims (*santri*) within Golkar was well recognised by the army officers. In response to the British journalist, Brian May's, question on why the army had not fully trusted Golkar, a general once said: "There are too many Moslems (ex-Masyumi/modernist *santri*) among them."[50] Moslems continued to be considered a potential danger, even after the parties had been demolished. Up until the late eighties these *santri* elements of Golkar seemed to have gone unnoticed. Accordingly, most political observers including Mackie (1974) and Crouch (1978), tended to regard Golkar as a party of the *abangan*. Such a view was undoubtedly false. The ability of these *santri* (modernist Muslim) elements in Golkar to take control of the party's leadership in the early nineties proves that while the army officers were determined to maintain the *aliran* pattern, they did not establish Golkar simply to strengthen the Javanist *abangan*. Instead, they have been taking advantage of the *aliran* cleavages, as well as Golkar, to retain the power.[51] In a recent interview, the retired lieutenant-general Sayidiman, who was the deputy of the army in 1973-1974 said,

> The armed forces regarded Golkar as a co-ordinating institution through which the armed forces would be able to perform 'development' according to their own wishes. . .Every armed forces leader has his own tactical adjustment. If he feels that he would still need to make use of Golkar, it is all right (Forum, 6 November, 1995: 82). .

In the early nineties as the political climate briefly appeared to allow greater *keterbukaan* (openness), two significant phenomena had been taking place in the national political arena. First, the modernist Muslim elements in Golkar

[50] The interview took place in 1972, see B. May, 1978: 300.

[51] Even with 261 out of 460 seats in the *DPR* (Parliament, 1971), Golkar itself was not the key player in Indonesia's political arena, as its supporters might had expected. In his book, Brian May reported, "In January 1973 I invited Liem Bian Kie, who was one of the coterie, to produce evidence of any initiative that Golkar had taken in parliament. . . after a long discussion it appeared that all they had been able to achieve was to present a report on the 1972 rice crisis. Measures such as making Pertamina accountable to parliament, bringing all the army revenues under strict parliamentary control and the setting up of a commission to examine the Soeharto's circle's financial empire had not been considered" (1978: 301).

had taken over the party leadership in 1993 with Soeharto's blessing. It appears that by the late eighties as Soeharto felt that he could no longer obtain full support from the army, he turned his attention to the modernist Muslim, *santri*, who had been marginalised by the New Order from the late sixties (Adam Schwarz, 1994: 37, 274-289).[52]

The 'Islamisation' of Indonesia's politics goes beyond Golkar leadership. The formation of the parliament (1992) as well as the appointment of the cabinet members (1993) and the armed forces leadership (1994) have clearly been affected by this trend of *ijo royo-royo* (very green/very Islamic in nature). Second, the growing prominence of ICMI (*Ikatan Cendekiawan Muslim Indonesia*, Indonesia Association of Muslim Intellectuals) in Indonesia's politics since 1990, has encouraged the nationalists who were mainly from the *abangan* Javanist background to consolidate their supporters. By mid-1995 the births of PCPP (*Persatuan Cendekiawan Pembangunan Pancasila*, Association of *Pancasila* Development Intellectuals), YKPK (*Yayasan Kerukunan Persaudaraan Kebangsaan,* The Harmonious Brotherhood Nationhood Foundation) and the 'New PNI' (*Persatuan Nasional Indonesia,* Indonesia National Unity) were announced. Most observers are in agreement that these new nationalist organisations have been founded to counterbalance the influence of the *santri* ICMI in the political arena.[53] It has therefore been identified as the reawakening of the *aliran* pattern in Indonesia's political system. These two new significant phenomena in Indonesia's politics confirm the argument of this thesis, which believes that in spite of burying the *aliran* pattern, the New Order has distilled its essence, within the Golkar framework. The fact that the manifestation of the *aliran* cleavage had been less clear in the seventies and the eighties could only be attributed to the unfavourable political climate, where a 'security approach' was strictly enforced.

In line with the general socio-political policy of maintaining the patron-client relationship of the *aliran* pattern and the introduction of the floating mass concept, the New Order administration has also dismantled all institutions within the village that were introduced by the Soekarno government to erode the feudalistic nature of village bureaucracy and to accelerate the process of democratisation of village government (Mubyarto and Soetrisno, 1985; Schulte Nordholt, 1987a). In 1980, the *LSD* (*Lembaga Sosial Desa,* the Village Social Institute) for example, was replaced by a body known as the *LKMD* (*Lembaga Ketahanan Masyarakat Desa*, Institute for the Resilience of Village

---

[52] Recent articles by Muslim's leaders on the New Order of the seventies and the eighties have openly blamed Ali Moertopo for creating an antagonistic relationship between the army and the *santri* community, see especially, *Gatra*, 21 October 1995: 39-40; Abdul Haris Nasution, "Catatan 50 Tahun Indonesia" (a Remark on Indonesia 50th Year), *Gatra*, 19 August 1995: 40-41; Interview with A.M. Fatwa in *Tiras*, 9 November 1995: 52; and with Sayidiman Suryohadiprojo in *Forum*, 6 November 1995: 80-84.

[53] See Harold Crouch's comment on this issue as cited in *Gatra*, 11 November 1995:24; and Liddle's comments on *Forum*, 20 November 1995:13.

Community). The significant difference between the two is found in leadership; in the past *LSD*'s leadership was a non-governmental position, whereas now the village head is the leader of *LKMD*. Moreover, the way the government has made the village head the sole ruler of the village and has uniquely attached the *pamong desa* (village administrators) into the civil servant organisation (*Korpri*), has significantly transformed the village head and his leadership team (*pamong*) into agents of the central government. The absence of political parties and peasants' organisations in the village have consequently deprived the peasants of an effective channel through which to express their aspirations in the development sphere (Schulte Nordholt, 1987a; Mubyarto and Soetrisno, 1989).

These policies which were meant to maintain political stability have eventually undermined peasant participation in the process of rural development.[54] Participation in development was thus defined only in terms of involvement in project implementation and sometimes of increased shares in project benefits.

> The **active participation in development** of all layers of the community should continue to increase and to expand, both with regard to **shouldering the burden of development** and **bearing the responsibilities in implementing** development, but also in **receiving the fruits of development** (Republic of Indonesia, 1983: 17, emphasis added).

As it will be demonstrated in Chapter Four, the experience of the three Lopait hamlets as well as other field studies on rural Java suggest that the lack of peasant participation in the identification and planning stage of rural development has often led to failures (Mubyarto and Soetrisno, 1985: 38; Prijono and Prijono, 1983: 78; cf., Development Alternatives Inc., 1975).

5. Conclusion

While no one can deny the achievement of the New Order administration in maintaining the overall economic growth in the last 25 years, there is mounting evidence of an unequal distribution of development benefits. The widening of the economic gap between the rich and the poor which was perceived in many field studies from the mid-1970s has been increasingly recognised by the New Order administration. In response to this growing concern of inequitable distribution of development benefits, beginning in *Pelita*-III (1979-1984), the government made a deeper commitment to an equal distribution of development benefits. This commitment, which began to take effect in the mid-1980s, has in varying degrees benefited the rural population. A number of

---

[54] It has been a general concern that over time the importance of political stability with its 'security approach' in development has been overstated. The result, as Mubyarto put it, is a passive and indifferent society (1988: 47).

field studies on rural Java in the 1980s and early 1990s, as well as this present study (see Chapters Three and Four) indicate that out of the different rural development programmes implemented by the state, the infra-structural developments and the establishment of new industrial towns have benefited the rural people most, in terms of employment opportunity and increase in overall household income.

However, while the rural development programmes adopted by the New Order administration have no doubt been aimed at helping the rural poor, they have fallen short of what can be done in many ways. As has been identified earlier in this chapter and will be described further in Chapters Three and Four, the floating mass policy, the collaboration between the (traditional) village elite and the supra-village structures, the uprooting of village level grass-roots organisations and the lack of people's participation in the decision-making process have, together with other factors, prevented the government from delivering on its commitment to equitable distribution of development benefits. As a result, although the number of rural people who benefited from government development programmes has increased, in many parts of Java development benefits are yet to be equally distributed, and, poverty is still prevalent within some thirty-five percent of Indonesian villages (BPS, 1990).

The socio-political policies of the New Order since 1966 have largely discouraged peasant participation in both political and economic development. Instead of eroding the *aliran* cleavages of the Indonesian political system, as most observers have assumed, the government has deliberately enforced the vertical alignments of the *aliran* pattern to retain the political balance of power. As a result, rural people have not only been excluded from the political sphere but more tragically they have gradually been made more 'dependent' on the supra-village powers.

Moreover, as has been argued above, and will be demonstrated later, in Chapter Three, the rapid process of commercialisation in rural economy does not necessarily lead into rural class polarisation. Furthermore, in spite of the rural 'depolitization' policy of the New Order, the *aliran* cultural-religious allegiance of *santri* and *abangan* remained strong both at national and local levels. As the specific effects of these policies have varied across villages throughout Indonesia, the following chapter will examine the extent to which these development policies and programmes have been affecting the rural population in the Tuntang sub-district.

Map 2 Administrative Boundaries and Sub-Districts of Semarang District 1995

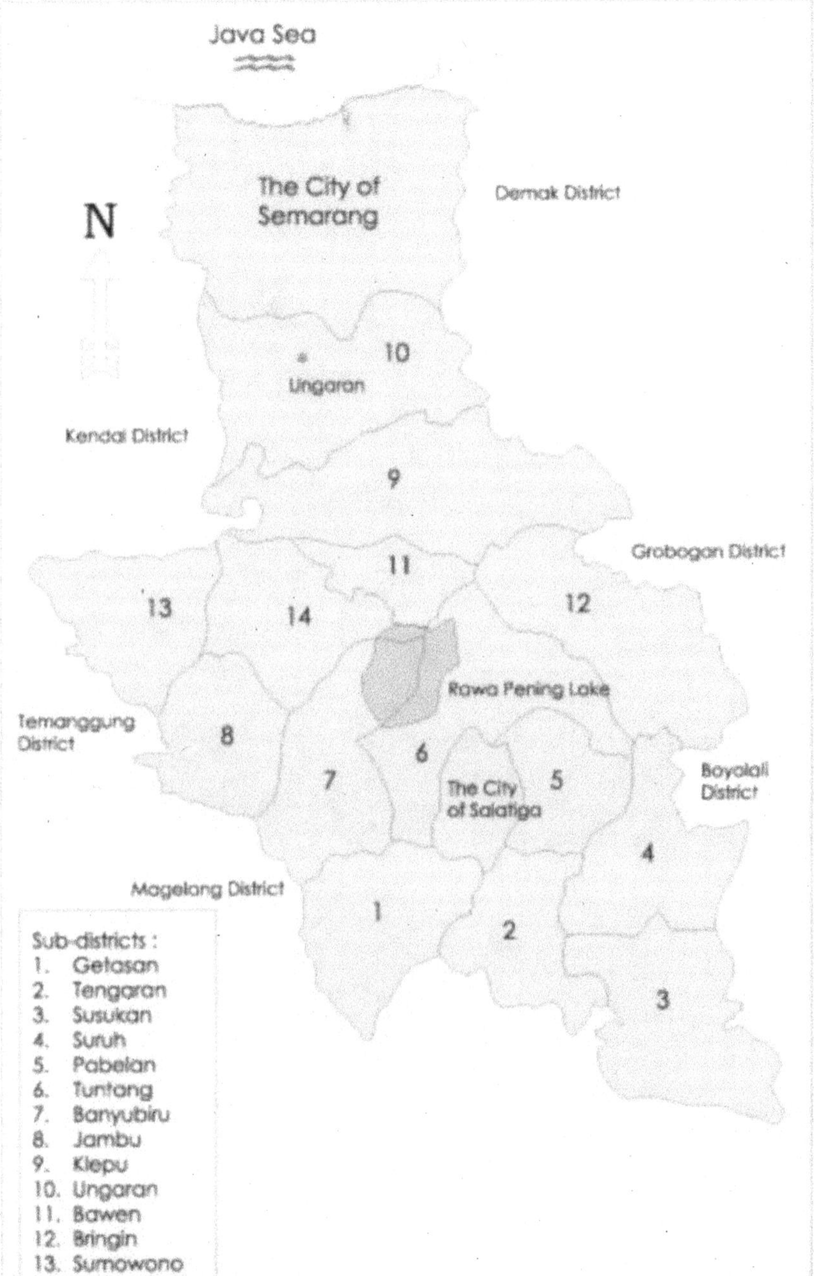

Chapter 2

The Sub-District Level Analysis: Tuntang Sub-District

1. Local Administrations: An Historical Perspective

Prior to the rise of Mataram as the main power in Java in the seventeenth century, the *mancanagara*[1] and the *pasisir* consisted of a number of smaller independent states or kingdoms governed by their own kings (Burger, 1957: 51-52).[2] Later, when Mataram subjugated them, these smaller states remained administratively independent.[3] The rulers were then called *bupati,* which originally (Old Javanese) means leader (Kartodirdjo, *et al.*, 1987: 4).[4] Between 1743-1746 VOC (*Vereenigde Oost-Indische Compagnie*) administration was

---

[1] G. P. Rouffaer (1931) described four regional divisions in Mataram kingdom. First, the *nagara,* the centre or capital where the king had absolute control. Second, the *nagaragung,* regions surrounding the *nagara,* were *pelungguh* (appanages) of the high officials living in the court. Third, the *mancanagara,* outside the *nagaragung,* were smaller states subjugated by Mataram and were governed by *bupati* (regents). Fourth, the *pasisir* were north coast regions of the *mancanagara* stretching from Cirebon to Surabaya, see G. P. Rouffaer , "Vorstenlanden." In *Adatrechtbundel* Vol. 34, 1931: 236-259. See also Moertono Soemarsaid, *State and Statecraft in Old Java: A Study of the Later Mataram Period, 16th to 19th Century*, 1968. These regional divisions have been perceived as a reflection of Javanese cosmology, see Selosoemardjan, *Social Changes in Jogjakarta*, 1962: 24; and W. H. Van Ossenbruggen, "Mancapat, Mancalima." In P. E. de Josselin de Jong, ed., *Structural Anthropology in the Netherlands, A Reader,* 1977: 30-60.

[2] In the fourteenth and fifteenth centuries, prior to the rise of Demak as an independent Islamic state, these coastal kingdoms were subjugated to the Majapahit kingdom. Reportedly their rulers had to pay annual homage to the king of Majapahit. See H. J. de Graaf and Th. G. Th. Pigeaud, "De Eerste Moslimse Vorstendommen op Java, Studien Over de Staat-kundige Geschiedenis van de 15e en 16e Eeuw." *VKI* 69 (1974): 75; and Th. Pigeaud, *Javaansche Volksvertoningen; Bijdrage tot de Beschrijving van Land and Volk*, 1938: 347, 398, 478, 515.

[3] See Ann Kumar, "Development in Four Societies over the Sixteenth to the Eighteenth Century." In Harry Aveling, ed., *The Development of Indonesian Society*, 1979: 33-34; and M. Soemarsaid, 1968: 120-123.

[4] Raffles referred to regents or head of indigenous regencies as *bupati*; previously, under Daendels *patih* (chief official of Javanese Kingdom) were also referred to as *bupati,* see R. H. Kleyn, *Het Gewestelijk Bestuur op Java*, 1889: 206; and H. J. de Graaf and Th. G. Th. Pigeaud, 1974: 99, 133. For an in-depth discussion on different titles given to *bupati,* see Sartono Kartodirdjo, *et al.*, *Perkembangan Peradaban Priyayi*, 1987: 46-52.

set up in the coastal ports of Surabaya, Rembang, Jepara and Semarang (Ricklefs, 1981: 91).[5] Under VOC's jurisdiction, *bupati* (district heads) of Java's *Noord-en Oostkust* were required to enforce the coffee cultivation and levy taxes for the East India Company. Following the take over of the East Indies Company in 1795 by the *Bataafsche Republiek* (Dutch colonial government between 1795-1806),[6] these practices were maintained. On this M. C. Ricklefs wrote:

> There was little immediate change in Indonesia, however, for the same personnel remained in their jobs and pursued their old ways. . . On the north coast, the Dutch ruled directly in theory, but in practice local lords (*bupati*) acted as their agents (1981: 106).

And later, in an endeavour to 'protect' the people from the abuse of power by *bupati,*[7] Governor-General Daendels (1808-1811) gave these *bupati* new status as '*ambtenaar van Zijne Majesteit den Koning van Holland'*. They were thus attached to the administrative hierarchy of the Dutch colonial government

---

[5] In 1677 the court of Plered fell to the rebel leader Trunadjaja, who drew much of his support from the *pasisir* (Ricklefs, 1981: 72). Prior to his death (in 1677), the ousted king, Amangkurat I (reign: 1648-1677) turned to the Dutch East Indies Company for assistance. Soon the Company's forces intervened and succeeded in enabling Amangkurat II (reign: 1677-1703) to succeed to his father's kingdom. To repay the costs of the war, Amangkurat II ceded to the Company the ports of *pasisir*. The Dutch's effective control over the whole *pasisir*, however came late in the mid-1740s (Rickefs, 1981: 73, 89). In 1743 the Dutch restored Susuhunan Pakubuwana II (reign: 1726-1749) to his throne after the Chinese insurrection joined by several princes of the House of Mataram. To repay the Dutch, Susuhunan signed over the entire *pasisir* (north coast). See contract of 19 Oct. 1677, in J. K. J. De Jonge and M. L. van Deventer, eds., *De Opkomst van het Nederlandsch Gezag in Oost-Indie Verzameling van onuitgegeven Stukken uit het Oud-Koloniaal Archief* Vol. 7, 1862-1909: 163-166; and P.B. II - VOC Treaty, 11 Nov. 1743, in De Jonge and Van Deventer, eds., *De Opkomst*, Vol. 9, 1862-1909: 434-447. See also F.W. Stapel, *Geschiedenis van Nederlandsch-Indie*, 1930: 116; and M.C. Ricklefs, *Jokjakarta Under Sultan Mangkubumi 1749-1792, A History of the Division of Java*, 1974: 19-20, 38-39.

[6] The investigation on the affairs of the VOC by the Dutch government (in the 1790s) revealed bankruptcy, scandal and mismanagement in all quarters, see J. S. Furnivall, *Netherlands India, A Study of Plural Economy*, 1939: 37-38; and Clive Day, *The Policy and Administration of the Dutch in Java*, 1966: 130-131. The VOC was formally dissolved in January 1800, see Ricklefs, *A History of Modern Indonesia, c. 1300 to the Present*, 1981: 105-106.

[7] Reports of power abuse by *bupati* and other local chiefs were numerous, see Djoko Suryo, "Social and Economic Life in Rural Semarang in the Later 19th. Century." Ph.D. Thesis, Monash University, 1982: 66-71. Djoko Suryo also identified maladministration as the main cause of the decline of economic life and population movement of the 1850s in rural Semarang (1982: 303).

(Kartodirdjo, *et al.*, 1987: 12-15).[8] Ricklefs noted that following his anti-feudal instinct, Daendels "treated them (*bupati*) not as lords over their society but as officials of the European Administration, and reduced their power and income" (1981: 107). While for the *bupati*, this change meant loss of autonomy, for the rural population, they were seen to be further distanced from the policy maker ('central government').

In the mid-nineteenth century when a more intensive form of direct rule on the villages was required, the Dutch colonial rule created a post of Assistant *Wedana*, referred to as *Onderdistrict Hoofd* (Kleyn, 1889: 208-211). Under the Indonesian administration this position which involved co-ordinating a number of villages is referred to as *camat* (sub-district head).[9] In the mid-fifties Soetardjo Kartohadikoesoemo asserted that the function of *camat* was similar or related to that of the Sundanese *cutak,* a leader of a federation of villages who was elected locally. Based on this argument he urged the government to make the *kecamatan* a third level of local government (1965:67). The historical data does not support his claim. There are no records whatsoever which indicate that the sub-district head was elected by the people, nor that it reflected the needs of the villagers, as did the *cutak.*[10]

The Dutch colonial state chose the 'village' as the main instrument of its welfare effort (Ricklefs, 1981: 148).[11] However, since the Dutch considered the traditional Javanese village to be an inefficient administrative unit, a policy of amalgamating villages was introduced to produce a more rational administrative structure.[12] This effort however, failed. Ricklefs also observed,

---

[8] The central issue behind this administrative reform was initially based on the colonial concept of 'how to manage Java in a way that would be profitable for the Netherlands' (Djoko Suryo, 1982: 61-63). See also J. S. Furnivall, 1939: 58; Clive Day, 1966: 131-132; and S. van Deventer Jsz., *Bijdragen tot de kennis van het Landelijk Stelsel op Java*, Vol. 1, 1865: 282-283.

[9] A *kecamatan* (sub-district) consists of approximately 20 villages. There are 62,061 villages in Indonesia which are co-ordinated under 3,639 sub-districts (Central Bureau of Statistics, 1993).

[10] According to a Dutch source, before 1854, village headmen were directly co-ordinated under the *bupati* (district head). This source also indicates that sub-district heads were appointed by the colonial government, see S. Tjondronegoro, *Social Organization and Planned Development in Rural Java*, 1984: 83; Soetardjo Kartohadikoesoemo, *Desa*, 1965: 67; Marsono, *Peranan Pamong Praja dalam Administrasi Pemerintahan Daerah di Indonesia*, 1968: 51; and Selosoemardjan, 1962: 31-32.

[11] In an attempt to avoid dealing directly with the rural population of Java, the Dutch colonial government found the autonomous nature of Javanese villages was the perfect solution. See S. van Deventer Jsz., Vol. 1, 1865: 330; C. van Vollenhoven, *De ontdekking van het Adatrecht*, 1928: 2; R.H. Kleyn, 1889: 228; and N. G. Schulte Nordholt, 1987b: 205.

[12] See "Gouvernement Besluit omtrent de Vereniging en Splitsing van Desa's op Java, en Madoera met uitzondering van de Vorstenlanden", 28 October, 1919, no. 13. In 1897 there were 30,500 villages recorded in Java with an average population of 800 each. In

> These new administrative units often had no indigenous basis and fail to grow into the autonomous welfare organisations the colonial government sought. Village banks, rice-stores and other projects were encouraged, with mixed results. There was considerable corruption and maladministration. Population pressure led to ever-decreasing field sizes, and poverty and unemployment encouraged violence and criminality (1981: 184).

In his report on the implementation of the government's (Dutch East Indies) *besluit* on the unification and the bifurcation of villages in Java and Madura (1920), Resident Laceuille of Semarang (1929) concluded that it was a rather fruitless effort to combine villages.[13] Toward the end of Dutch rule in Java, spontaneous movements to de-unify villages became rather popular. In any case, the heavy hand of Dutch paternalism encouraged by this and other colonial policies on village administrative structure have gradually undermined the traditional Javanese village autonomy (Ricklefs, 1981: 148).

2. Power Flow in the Post War Indonesia

At present, the dilemma of choosing the autonomous third level local government (below the provincial and district levels) is far from being resolved. In contrast with the *UU* (legislation) No. 1/1957 which referred to *desa-praja* (village) as the third level of local government, the *UU* (legislation) No. 5/1974 seems to regard the *kecamatan* as the third level local administration (Schulte Nordholt, 1987b: 69-70; Tjondronegoro, 1984: 84). In reality, however, recent macro-development policy suggests that it is the villages which have been considered as the third level territorial units.[14] The government's inconsistency in selecting the autonomous third level unit for decentralisation of development programmes has to some degree reduced the effectiveness of both the *camat* (sub-district head) and *lurah* (village head) in accomplishing their tasks. At best this uncertainty would only extend the bureaucratic-chain between the central government and the rural population, with the village being a 'fourth' level of local government.

1927 there were only 18,584 amalgamated villages with an average population of 1,800 each (Ricklefs, 1981: 148).

[13] See F. A. E. Laceulle, *Eindverslag over het Desa Autonomie Onderzoek op Java en Madoera,* 1929.

[14] The *IDT* programme (special fund for poor families living in poor villages; which number more than 20,000 villages all over Indonesia), the *Lomba Desa Teladan* (annual contest to be awarded as the 'model' village) and the *Tabungan Keluarga Sejahtera* (a kind of matching-fund saving for poor families living in non poor villages) are among recent major national development programmes which operate on village level administration, although supervision is still required from the sub-district head. See also N. G. Schulte Nordholt, *Ojo Dumeh, Kepemimpinan Lokal dalam Pembangunan*, 1987b: 205.

Questions and concerns have been raised in response to the increasing attention given to the village level administration as the third level local unit for the implementation of rural development programmes. First, questions have been raised on the capability of the village administrators to govern their own village affairs. That is, to what extent they would be able to carry this responsibility of becoming an autonomous third level administration unit (Dohrenwend, 1957: 3). The common perception on the setting of Javanese rural life up until the late nineteenth-century was often related to the 'autonomous' nature of Javanese villages. The increasing supra-village socio-economic interference has gradually undermined this autonomy (Ricklefs 1981: 184). The exposure of the villages to world market forces as the result of improved infra-structure and transportation in rural Java has eventually made villages more dependent on the supra-village structures.[15] Deeper integration of Javanese villages into the larger world forces and the further impositions of the New Order government's centralised policy on rural development have not been adequately balanced by sufficient improvement in the quality of village administrators.[16]

Second, according to the ***Statistical Pocketbook of Indonesia 1992*** there are 62,061 villages and 242 districts in Indonesia. If the village is to be considered the autonomous third level of administration after the provincial and district levels, there would be, on average, some 257 village heads directly responsible to each *bupati* (district head). In the case of Central Java the ratio is even higher with 293 village-heads per *bupati*. In his concern at the weakness of the village level administrations in Central Java, Schulte Nordholt argued that a good supervision mechanism, rather than government training courses, is the key aspect in developing the village level administration.

> These village administrators are not stupid or 'lacking in education', but in fact, in terms of politics they have learned well how to survive. The technical administrative programmes, such as government training courses, brought very little impact. It is through a good supervision mechanism at village level administration, that an effective improvement could be expected (Schulte Nordholt, 1987b: 205).

---

[15] Although such supra-village economic interference had frequently occurred during the time of Mataram kingdom, prior to Dutch colonialism, of most importance in terms of their impact on village autonomy were the imposition of Raffles's landrent system and the *Cultuur Stelsel* introduced by Van den Bosch (in office 1830-1834), see D.H. Burger, *De Ontsluiting van Java's Binnenland voor het Wereldverkeer*, 1939: 39; S. Tjondronegoro, 1984: 69; and Djoko Suryo, 1982: 231-232.

[16] Since the beginning of the Five-Year Development Plan in 1969, *lurah* has been increasingly burdened by additional workloads relating to various credits and Green Revolution programmes, see N. G. Schulte Nordholt, 1987b: 199-207; and Mubyarto and Loekman Soetrisno, "Rural Development in Indonesia; Past Experience and Future Policies." In R. P. Misra, ed., *Rural Development; Capitalist and Socialist Paths*, 1985: 56-60.

With a ratio of one *bupati* to supervise 292 *lurah* in Central Java, one could hardly expect any effective development in village level administration. Moreover, the gaps in the socio-cultural, economic and educational backgrounds between the district level and the village level administrators are extremely difficult to reconcile. The former are urban, middle class, and college educated, while the latter are rural, poor or lower middle class and secondary educated.[17]

Third, with regard to the importance of people's participation in development, questions have been raised concerning the extent to which rural people identify themselves with the village (*desa*) community. In their recent evaluation of the impact of development on socio-cultural change in Indonesian villages, Selosoemardjan and Kennon Breazeale (1993) identified the gap between the government's objectives and the people's value system as the main obstacle for participation in rural development.

> Through this mechanism, a link should be established between the objectives of the modern development program and the value system of the *adat*-oriented villagers. If that link can be created, there is a chance that a given program will work well. Otherwise, it is very likely that the villagers will not be induced to participate, at least not actively (1993: 198).

And rightly so, they directly related people's participation with the success of development programmes. Further they observed that despite various efforts to bridge the gap between government objectives and local value systems, which were mostly undertaken at village (*desa*) level, the problem persists.[18]

In regard to the present research, the question has been raised; in which territorial unit (village level or hamlet level) has successful socialisation mostly occurred?[19] With which social institutional unit do people mostly align themselves, or which social institution has the largest contribution to people's identity? In an extensive research in Kendal and Cibadag sub-districts, Tjondronegoro (1984) suggested implicitly that a hamlet (*dukuh*), rather than a

---

[17] See government acts on village administration, especially in Section 3-5-14 of the *UU* (legislation) No. 5, 1974 and in Section 2-3-14 of the *UU* (legislation) No. 5, 1979.

[18] To bridge this gap the government created a village level institution known as the LKMD (*Lembaga Ketahanan Masyarakat Desa,* The Village Council for Development Planning and Guidance), see Selosoemardjan and Kennon Breazeale, *Cultural Change in Rural Indonesia, Impact of Village Development*, 1993: 198-199.

[19] Social order or social institution is an ongoing human product of the materialisation of collective and co-operative felt-needs of a group of people. On the other hand, 'successful socialisation', produces identities which are socially predefined and profiled to a high degree. Identity is highly profiled in the sense that it represents "fully the objective reality within which it is located" (Berger and Luckmann, 1966: 184). A 'successful socialisation', as Berger and Luckmann put it, is "the establishment of a high degree of symmetry between objective and subjective reality (as well as identity)" (1966: 183).

village (*desa*) is the basic territorial unit for rural development programmes in Java. He found that at hamlet level, community ties are stronger and "grassroots participation finds its greatest manifestation" (1984: 19).

> Observations in the villages encompassed in this insight stimulating case study seem to support the proposition that organizational ties and communal unity, in so far as loyalty toward voluntary associations and their elected leaders is displayed, can be found at sub-village rather than village level (1984: 260).

It is probably the belief that the founder of the hamlet is their common ancestor which leads to a strong cohesion and social identity within hamlet community (Selosoemardjan, 1962: 94-98).[20] Furthermore, a comparative study between village level organisation and hamlet institutions in two different sub-districts under his investigation reveals that the latter appears to be more oriented to the needs of the rural people.

> A classification of rural organisations and institutions as they appeared in the two separate research areas seems to have in common the distinction between village- and hamlet-oriented groupings. The former is at least more apt to give support to supra-village interest, whereas the latter is more clearly oriented toward the needs of the hamlet community (Tjondronegoro, 1984: 20).

Although economic pressure might occasionally hold back rural people from committing themselves to a more active role in development (White, 1976), individual interests and group interests often play a greater role in either strengthening or weakening people's initiative (Selosoemardjan and Breazeale, 1993: 198; Tjondronegoro, 1984: 37). To some extent, these needs were reflections of the value system of the hamlet community.

The preceding discussion suggests that the village level administration has neither satisfied the needs of the rural population, nor has it satisfactorily served the government's objectives. Ironically, villages (*desa*) have increasingly been referred to (implicitly) as the third level local administration.[21] Based on this discussion and on the numerous micro studies of people's participation on the (village level) development programmes,[22] this present study focuses on the hamlet territorial units. Since no hamlet in Java is

---

[20] Ina Slamet in her book, *Pokok-Pokok Pembangunan Masyarakat Desa*, 1965: 78-80, also argued that 'primitive democracy' is firmly rooted and is still functioning in the hamlets.

[21] *UU* (legislation) No. 5, 1974, chapter 3, point 1, just mentions the first and second autonomous levels of local government. Point 2 of the same chapter opens the possibility of creating the third autonomous local government as the political, economic, socio-cultural and national security required.

[22] S. Tjondronegoro reported that village initiative (participation) has on the whole been weak in rural development activities (1984: 37). Similar trend was also reported by Ina E. Slamet (1965) and Selosoemardjan and K. Breazeale (1993).

politically or economically isolated, to gain a complete picture of the external forces which contribute to formation of the present value systems as well as to the socio-economic developments, we will look first at larger territorial units, namely the *kecamatan* (sub-district) and the village levels.

3. Geographical Setting of Tuntang

Tuntang is located within the district of Semarang, Central Java, 42 kilometres south of Semarang and 58 Kilometres north of Surakarta (see Map 1 and 2).[23] It lies on the north-east foot of mount Merbabu at approximately 500 metres above sea level. The fertile soil and the mild weather of Tuntang and its surroundings attracted among others, the 'NV Cultuur Maatschappij Tlogo' in Amsterdam to develop a coffee plantation in 1809 in the village of Delik, which was then under the administration of the district of Salatiga. But this plantation estate was small compared to those in the neighbouring sub-districts of Ambarawa and Bawen.[24]

4. Historical Background of Tuntang

In pre-colonial times, Tuntang was located on an important road connecting the *nagaragung* (the centre of the old Javanese kingdom) and the coastal town of Semarang. The existence of this road is reported by Rijklof van Goens on his journey from Batavia to Mataram in 1648 (Van Goens, 1856).[25] During his journey from Semarang he passed through a series of mountains (hills) near the

---

[23] In the mid-nineteenth-century (1858) Tuntang village and the surrounding areas were under the administration of Salatiga regency. Between 1843-1857 Salatiga was a sub-regency headed by a *rangga*. In 1857 it was promoted to become a regency. Several other administrative changes, which concerned the boundary of Semarang residency, took place in 1901, 1929 and in 1930s, see E. Waal, *Aanteekeningen over Koloniale Onderwerpen*, Vol. 10, 1867: 217; and Djoko Suryo, 1982: xvii-xviii.

[24] See "Perusda Perkebunan Tlogo Tuntang Salatiga", 1992: 36. This plantation estate had been operated long before the *Cultuur Stelsel* began in 1830 (see, Djoko Suryo, 1982: 24). In 1870 reportedly the contractor (long lease-holder) was 'H.G. Larch *et al.*', covering the land area of 425 *bau* or approximately 301 hectares, see *Handboek voor Cultuur en Handelsonderneming in Nederlandsch-Indie*, 1888: 43-90. The present plantation estate covers some 400 hectares and is operated under the management of the Central Java "Perusda (regional/provincial company) Aneka Industri" (Governor's decree no. 07.63/1980).

[25] This report was first published in, Van Goens, Ryckloff Volckertsz., "Reijsbeschrijving van den weg uijt Samarangh nae de Konincklijke hoofdplaets Mataram, mitsgaders de zeeden, gewoonten ende regeringe van den Sousouhounan, groot machtigste koningk van 't eijlant Java." (Itinerary of the Way from Semarang to the Royal Capital Mataram, as well as the Morals, Customs, and Government of the Susuhunan, Mighty King of the Island of Java) *BKI* 4 (1856): 307-350. (Reprinted in H. J. de Graaf, ed., *De Vijf Gezantschapsreizen van Rijklof van Goens, naar het Hof van Mataram, 1648-1654*. 's-Gravenhage: Martinus Nijhoff, 1956).

village of 'Tjandhi', which is probably the present-day Candirejo village in Tuntang sub-district. Among other important places, he also mentioned passing through the villages of Tuntang and Kesongo, which are the northern and the southern borders of Lopait village. Rijklof van Goens described the three main roads connecting Mataram and the *pasisir* (north coast) as follows:

> First the road most used, leading from Mataram to the north towards Semarang, which road going past the toll gate at Taji, is used most as being the easiest and shortest. The second road, leading out to the west, in the neighbourhood of Tegal. This road is very difficult to travel. The main toll gate along the road lies close to Trayem. The third road leads to the east and ends somewhere around Blambangan, while a branch runs to Gresik and Jaratan (1856: 348).

The decline of Demak and Jepara as trading ports of Java in the late sixteenth or early seventeenth century increased the importance of the road which connected Mataram to Semarang (Schrieke, 1957: 105). The importance of this road was first observed from the expedition of Pieter Franssen in 1630 (Fruin-Mees, 1926). Later, in 1656 van Goens described the road, which joined Semarang to the plains of Kedhu, passed through Ungaran, Tuntang and Salatiga as the "*meest bewandelt ende ordinair bereijst werd*" (the road which is the most travelled and commonly used).[26] As early as 1678 there is already mentioned "the great through road" between Semarang and Mataram.[27] In 1746 Governor General Willem van Imhoff (in office: 1743-1750) was the first to travel from Semarang to Surakarta by six-horse coach. Apparently, it was not possible at that time to go beyond Surakarta using the same coach (van Milaan, 1942: 221-224).

Mataram considered the northern regions toward the northern coastal towns as a significant political and economic gate to the outside world. Different from the other regions in the Mataram kingdom, there was a great deal of involvement of the central government in these regions.[28] Located within such an historically important region, Tuntang was obviously far from being isolated from the outside world. Surprisingly, this advantage of being located on an important route did not seem to breed either any remarkable historical

---

[26] See Van Goens, 1865: 348; and P. W. Van Milaan, "Beschouwingen over het 17e Eeuwse Mataramse Wegennet." *Sociaal Geographische Mededeelingen* 4 (1942): 224.

[27] See De Jonge and Van Deventer, *De Opkomst*, Vol. 7:155; Vol. 9: 377, 385; Vol. 10, n. 44. See also B. Schrieke, *Ruler and Realm in Early Java.* Part 2 of *Indonesian Sociological Studies: Selected Writings of B. Schrieke*, 1957: 105-107; and P.W. Van Milaan, 1942: 205-239.

[28] Most of the other regions outside the *nagaragung* were governed by local nobles or by the king's relatives with much less involvement from and loosely controlled by the *Kraton* (court), but, for important coastal towns such as Semarang, Jepara, Lasem and Juwana a new post was created, namely the *syahbandar*, see M. Soemarsaid, 1968: 120-121, 141; and B. Schrieke, 1957: 169, 192.

background nor significant economic progress for Tuntang.[29] Until late in the second half of the nineteenth-century little was mentioned in the history of Java, concerning Tuntang.

The southern border of Tuntang Sub-district is the historically significant town of Salatiga.[30] De Graaf mentioned the *Masjid Watu* (Stone Mosque) in Salatiga, dated around the second half of the fourteenth century (1958: 19).[31] In March 1757 a peace conference was held by Governor Hartingh in Salatiga,[32] where Mas Said swore allegiance to the Mangkunagaran, the Dutch East Indies Company and the Sultan. The Dutch Company (and later the Dutch Colonial state), considered Salatiga and its surroundings politically significant.[33] First, because it lies on the border of the *vorstenlanden* (*nagaragung*), where most resistance was based.[34] Second, Salatiga and its surroundings were also the border between two main socio-religious traditions, the *pasisir* (coastal) Demak tradition and the inland Mataram tradition. The former represents a trade-oriented, Malay-Islamic tradition and the latter represents an agriculture-oriented, Javanese tradition (Koentjaraningrat, 1984: 313-318; Carey, 1979: 49, 91).[35]

---

[29] Even after the Tuntang railway station was opened in 1873, the population of Tuntang remained comparatively poor. Some of the older respondents in the area recall their impoverished childhood. It was then common for people to speak of "*kere Tuntang*" (poor people of Tuntang), who begged along the Tuntang bridges and the railway station. Djoko Suryo noted that the significant growth of *kecu* (robbery) in Tuntang and Salatiga in the late nineteenth-century was primarily caused by economic pressures (1982: 275, 278). See also Liem Thian Joe, *Riwajat Semarang; Dari Djamannja Sam Poo Sampe Terhapoesnja Kongkoan*, 1931-1933: 131-133.

[30] For the developments of the administrative status and boundary of Salatiga in the nineteenth and early twentieth centuries, see E. de Waal, Vol. 10 , 1867: 217; and Djoko Suryo, 1982: xvii-xviii.

[31] See H. J. de Graaf, "De Verdwenen Tjandi te Salatiga." *BKI* 114 (1958): 117-120.

[32] Nicolaas Hartingh served as Governor of Java's Northeast Coast, based in Semarang (1754-1761). Technically, until Daendels's treaties with the courts in 1811 this Government of Java's Northeast Coast (stretching from eastern border of Cirebon to the strait of Bali) belonged to Mataram, and was leased to the East Indies Company. In reality, the area was effectively under Dutch control, see P. B. R. Carey, Aspects of Javanese History in the Nineteenth Century." In Harry Aveling, ed., *The Development of Indonesian Society*, 1979: 49.

[33] Salatiga seems to be had been among the common conference or meeting places between the Dutch and Javanese rulers, see M. C. Ricklefs, 1974: 318.

[34] Ricklefs mentioned a Dutch commandant at Salatiga (fort 'de Hersteller') in 1789, when rumours spread out that the Susuhunan and his religious advisors were plotting to slaughter all Europeans in Java. It seems that the Dutch regiment (*cavalerie*) had been firmly established in Salatiga for some time prior to the peace conference in 1757 (1974: 316, 318, 357).

[35] Apart from the socio-religious reasons, H. J. de Graaf and Th. G. Th. Pigeaud also identified economic causes of the continuous conflicts between '*wong Mataram*' (the inland Mataram people) and the coastal people in the sixteenth and seventeenth centuries (1974: 301-303).

Following the introduction of the Cultivation System in 1830, the need for efficient transportation was apparent. In 1870 the first railway in Java was opened, connecting the coastal town of Semarang to the *vorstenlanden.*[36] Unlike other railway routes in Java which were operated principally for economic reasons, the route which connects Semarang to Magelang, through Tuntang and Ambarawa (1873-1905) was built for security or military reasons.[37] This route was not economically feasible because the railway had to pass through extremely steep mountainous areas, especially between Gemawang and Jambu. The government's main intention was to connect the Dutch military strongholds in Magelang, Ambarawa and Semarang (Perumka, n.d., p. 6). In accord with these developments, Tuntang Railway Station was built in 1873.

Adding to the significance of this area is the Rawa Pening lake. This semi-natural lake covers the area of 2500 hectares at about 463 metres above sea level during rainy season and 650 hectares at about 460 metres above sea level during the dry season (Jratuseluna and NEDECO, 1974). Although the first dam at the Tuntang river was not built until 1916 (Polak, 1951), Rawa Pening lake has existed as the source of living for the fishermen in surrounding villages for quite a long time.[38] A novel written in the 1920s spoke of a long tradition of fishery as livelihood of the villagers surrounding Rawa Pening.[39]

> Kaoe sebenarnja ada anak dari Siswo Soepeno, satoe orang jang pernah mengoembara ke mana2, tetapi achirnja soeda tinggal di sini . . . Siswo hidup sebagai toekang panjing (You are actually the daughter of Siswo Soepeno, one who had travelled to many places, but finally lived here . . . He made his living as a fisherman) (Lovely, 1929: 75).

---

[36] The work was started in 17 June 1864. The route Semarang-Tanggung was opened for the public in 1867, Semarang-Surakarta in 1870, and Semarang-Yogyakarta in 1872. This railway was operated by the Nv. Nederlands Indische Spoorweg Maatschapij (NIS). See N.H. Henket, *De aanleg van Spoorwegen op Midden-Java*, 1886: 17-19.

[37] The first section, from Kedungjati to Ambarawa was finished in 1875. Apart from military considerations this route was intended to transport agricultural products and other goods from the surrounding areas of Salatiga, Bayalali, Tengaran and other districts (Henket, 1886: 81-82). The second section between Ambarawa and Magelang was primarily built for military considerations. Magelang and Ambarawa (also Salatiga), had been important military towns for the Dutch Colonial state. While in Salatiga the Dutch built 'de Hersteller' fort for its regiment, in Ambarawa the Dutch built the famous 'Willem I' fort.

[38] Apart from the Legend of 'Baru Klinting' concerning the origin of Rawa Pening, no one seems to know when the lake took its form and began to function as the main source of living for the surrounding inhabitants.

[39] See Madame d'Eden Lovely, *Itoe Bidadari dari Rawa Pening*, 1929: 56-57. So it was unlikely that prior to 1916 Rawa Pening was merely a "marshy area of a peat soil" as Polak (1951) has assumed. Equally wrong-headed was Rukmadi Warsito's (1979) assertion that prior to 1930 there was no one in surrounding villages whose principal livelihood was fishery.

Fish was only one among many resources Rawa Pening had to offer for the surrounding inhabitants. Local tourism also developed in the 1920s, when people from Salatiga and other neighbouring towns used to rent a fishing boat in *dhusun* Calombo to enjoy the beauty of Rawa Pening (Lovely, 1929: 2-5).

In 1938 the construction of the second dam was completed. Accordingly, Rawa Pening has been able to irrigate some 24,000-40,000 hectares of rice fields, particularly in the coastal plains of Semarang and Demak. It has also generated some 20 MW hydro-electricity per year (Goeltenboth, 1978: 7).[40] There have been numerous studies undertaken to measure the socio-economic impact of the construction of the second dam for the population of the surrounding villages.[41] Reportedly, twenty-eight hamlets in four sub-districts were submerged, their inhabitants being moved to neighbouring villages. In order to increase the capacity of the hydro-electric power, in 1967 the government decided to increase the water level by 40 centimetres, since when, more than 600 hectares of rice fields have been covered with water for at least six months per year (Warsito, 1979: 249). As a whole these developments of Rawa Pening lake, which were meant to increase the irrigation and the hydro-electric capacity for the coastal plains of Semarang, have been accomplished at the cost of the surrounding inhabitants.[42] Fortunately, as some researchers have revealed, the decline of agricultural income affected by the increase of water level at Rawa Pening lake has to some degree been compensated by the increase of income from non-farm employment. Although the contribution of non-farm employment seems to have been greater in villages with easy access

---

[40] For further reading on Rawa Pening and its habitat, see Jratunseluna and NEDECO, "Report of Prefeasibility of Rawa Pening." Internal Report, 1972; B. Polak, "Construction and Origin of the Floating Island in the Rawa Pening", 1951; F. Goeltenboth, ed., *Proceedings of the First Seminar in Aquatic Biology and Aquatic Management of the Rawa Pening Lake*, 1978.

[41] See K. Suwondo, "Changes in the Means of Obtaining Income of the Inhabitants Around the Rawa Pening." In F. Goeltenboth, ed., *Proceedings of the First Seminar in Aquatic Biology and Aquatic Management of the Rawa Pening Lake*, 1978: 167-195; P. Pramonosidhi, "The Rate of Intensification of Farm Management in the Area Around Rawa Pening." In F. Goeltenboth, 1978: 196-237; R. Warsito, "Pergulatan Hidup Kaum Nelayan di Tengah-Tengah Pemanfaatan Rawa Pening." In F. Goeltenboth, ed., *Proceeding of the Second Seminar in Aquatic Biology and Aquatic Management of the Rawa Pening Lake*, 1979: 234-283; R. Nuningsih and B. Sukardjo, "Kehidupan Sosial-Ekonomis Masyarakat Desa-Desa di Sekitar Rawa Pening." (Socio-economic setting of the villages around Rawa Pening lake), 1979: 366-405; and Pradjarta Dirdjosanjoto, *et al.*, "Socio-economical Aspects of the Population Around the Rawa Pening Lake: Pilot Study in the Village of Candirejo", 1978: 102-250.

[42] Between 1875-1891 the first major irrigation project on the *Kali Toentang* (Tuntang river) was undertaken, especially to irrigate the districts of Manggar, Sambung, Wedung, Demak (regency of Demak) and Singen Kidul and Grogol (Regency of Semarang), see L.H. Slimkers and J.E. de Meijer, "De Waterwerken in de Afdeeling Demak", in *TKII* (1891-1892): i-xxi.

to public transport, the increase of non-farm activity has affected almost all the villages in the region.[43]

In present-day Indonesia, Tuntang still remains located on the strategic road linking the two most important cities of Central Java, namely Semarang and Surakarta. But, as in pre-colonial and colonial times, this strategic location has not led to significant economic and political advancement for the population. Different aspects including the macro (national and regional) development policy on Tuntang and Rawa Pening, the ecology the geographical location, employment and the character of the local administration, have to some degree contributed to this rather slow economic development.

5. The Territorial Context

Tuntang is one of the fourteen sub-districts (*kecamatan*) in the district (*kabupaten*) of Semarang.[44] The seat of the district administration is located in the town of Ungaran. Situated 18 kilometres north of Tuntang, Ungaran has developed to become one of the most important industrial towns in Central Java. The availability of cheap land and low cost labour could have encouraged business people to open factories in this region.[45] As land for industrial development became more scarce and expensive in Ungaran during the past five years, people have begun to build factories along the provincial road southward in the neighbouring districts of Klepu and Bawen (the northern border of Tuntang). Unlike the development of the textile industry in Majalaya in West Java (Antlov and Svensson, 1991), and of the *kretek* cigarette industry in East Java (Saptari, 1991), which had developed largely from traditional domestic industries, the large industries in Ungaran were mostly developed by large urban-based companies and foreign capital. This ongoing industrial

---

[43] In a socio-economic study of Candirejo village in Tuntang sub-district, P. Dirdjosanjoto, *et al.* (1978) further argued that the poorer households and the landless farm labourers have benefited more from non-farm employment (1978: 246).

[44] The formation of the Tuntang sub-district was partly a result of nineteenth-century infrastructural development, especially the construction of railroad from Kedungjati to Ambarawa in 1875. In 1877 the sub-district of Tuntang was created, with its seat at Tuntang village, both located on the railroad line. This sub-district, however, remained under the administration of Salatiga district, see "Grondgebied", in "Algemeen Verslag der Residentie Semarang over het Jaar 1877".

[45] Compared to other provinces in Java the regional minimum wage of Central Java is the lowest. In January 1996 the regional minimum wage of Central Java is 3,200 rupiah (US$ 1.42)/daily. The average regional minimum wage for West Java is 4,125 rupiah (US$ 1.83), and for East Java is 3475 rupiah (US$ 1.54) (*Kebijaksanaan*, 1996: 128-130). Other advantages of this region are the easy access to the seaport of Semarang, the excellent roads connecting major cities in Java, and the proximity of the provincial administration offices in Semarang.

development has, to various degrees, influenced the employment of the rural population in the surrounding villages.[46]

6. A Glimpse of the Sub-District Town of Tuntang

Tuntang covers a land area of 5,623 hectares, with a population of 47,159 (1993).[47] It is divided into 16 villages and 98 hamlets (see Map 3). The population density is 839 persons per square kilometre, slightly below the average density of Central Java (863), and far lower when compared to Java's major rice producing regions, such as Sleman (1,160 in 1980) and Klaten districts (1,771 in 1993) on the southern borders of Central Java abutting on the *Daerah Istimewa* (Special Region) of Yogyakarta.[48] The seat of the sub-district administration is in the village of Tuntang. As in most sub-district towns of Java, rows of houses, schools and government offices are situated along both sides of the main provincial road.

Travelling from the north, after passing through the vast Asinan tea plantation of the Bawen area, the road leads to the Tuntang bridges which stand as the "north gateway" of Tuntang sub-district.[49] From these bridges, the beauty and majesty of Rawa Pening lake seems to show its full expression, especially in the evening as the sun goes down. Immediately beyond the bridges, on the right-hand side of the road is a huge sign-post, saying "*Selamat Datang di Restoran dan Taman Rekreasi Tuntang Asri*" (Welcome to the Restaurant and Recreation Garden of Tuntang Asri). On the left, is the old police office. The

---

[46] According to the official report (Semarang district office), there were 15 large industries in Ungaran, 29 in Klepu and 7 in Bawen sub-districts in 1995. 50 percent of the large industries in Ungaran and 80 percent in Klepu were founded in the last ten years. 86 percent of the industries in Bawen were founded in the last five years. These large industries alone have absorbed more than 35,000 labourers from the surrounding villages.

[47] Prior to 1991 there were 19 villages under the administration of Tuntang sub-district, with 6,500 hectares of land and a population of 57,000 (1989). In 1991, as the town of Salatiga expanded its territory, 3 villages were included as part of Salatiga, namely Blotongan, Kecandran and Pulutan.

[48] Significantly both Sleman and Klaten have been among the main rice producing areas since colonial times. Today, Sleman is the 'rice granary' of Yogyakarta, while Klaten is the major food supplier for Central Java. Although it may appear to support Geertz's analysis which relates *sawah* ecosystem to population density, where he argued that while "swidden overpopulation results in a deterioration of the habitat, in a wet rice regime it results in the support of ever increasing numbers of people within an undamaged habitat" (1963: 33), there is no evidence that agrarian involution has ever occurred within these two districts, see Thomas Schweizer, *A Century of Change in the Javanese Rural Economy*, 1988; Mubyarto and Loekman Soetrisno, 1985; Irwan Abdullah, *The Muslim Businessmen of Jatinom*, 1994.

[49] In his journey to Mataram (1746), Van Imhoff mentioned the existence of the, already well-known, two wooden bridges over the *Kali Toentang* (Tuntang river), see Van Milaan, 1942: 221.

sub-district police headquarters were moved to the new site in 1993, some 300 metres southward on the right-hand side of the road. Behind this old police office is the Tuntang railway station, which was closed in 1977. In the same year the Railway Museum in Ambarawa opened to the public and the Ambarawa-Tuntang railway is one of the tourist attractions in the area. Tourists, mostly from the Netherlands, are offered a short nostalgic rail journey from Ambarawa (Willem I) railway station to Tuntang along the shores of Rawa Pening lake.

Only a few hamlets in Tuntang sub-district have easy access to public transport, most have to rely on 'Ojek' (motorcycles used as taxis) for transportation between their hamlets and the main roads. The main 'Ojek' station ('Ojek' stop) for Tuntang area is located on the road side next to the old police station. On a normal day between ten and fifteen motor cycles are lined up on the road side, while the drivers sit nearby chatting and waiting for passengers. At night the number of 'Ojek' are less, usually between four to eight.[50] In 1988, the total number of 'Ojek' was only 15, but it had grown to 51 in 1993, and 139 in 1995.[51] Approximately, half of these are on a part-time basis, which means the drivers have other main jobs. The main beneficiaries of this transport are the local traders and the *warung* (prepared food stall) owners at the hamlets located far from the main roads. Although there has not been any research on the contributions of 'Ojek' transportation to rural trading, certainly this twenty-four hour transportation service has, to some degree, stimulated trading, especially in the more isolated local hamlets.

200 metres further on, on the left, is the *puskesmas* (local health centre) and, on the other side of the road, the sub-district office. With the exception of the police head-quarters, all major sub-district level government offices are located within this single compound. The sub-district office is located in the centre rear of the compound. Near the front gate on the left is the *Koramil* (sub-district level army head-quarters) and in-between are the offices of the education, religion, Statistics and other departments. Unlike most sub-district towns in Java, the economic and educational activities of Tuntang are not centralised in the sub-district town.[52] Although many economic transactions

---

[50] There are three other 'Ojek' stations in Tuntang at a smaller scale.

[51] This phenomenal growth is due to the considerable local road construction undertaken by the village and sub-district administrations, as well as by the hamlet leadership, beginning in the late 1980s.

[52] The four major local markets are located in the villages of Kesongo, Candirejo, Tuntang and Gedangan. The only senior high school in the sub-district is located in Kesongo. The KUD (Village Unit Co-operation) is also located In Kesongo. Prior to 1991, when the village of Blotongan was under the administration of Tuntang sub-district, it had been the leading trading activities. In most cases, along with the government offices, the major market place, the busiest economic activities, the terminal for public transport and the highest level of schools are located in the sub-district town, see Jennifer Alexander, *Trade, Traders, and Trading in Rural Java*, 1987: 39.

take place in the four local (daily) markets and the four *selapan* (periodic) markets in Tuntang sub-district, larger transactions usually take place at the market towns of Ambarawa and Salatiga, which are eight and seven kilometres respectively from Tuntang.

Transportation from the sub-district town to Semarang and Surakarta is abundant. The inter-city bus runs every ten minutes during day time and at an hourly basis during the night. The competition among the bus drivers for passengers is very intense, and often pursued at the cost of passengers' safety. Traffic accidents of different degrees of severity happen several times a month.[53] Other forms of public transport includes the 'Izuzu', (mini-bus of 20 passengers) and the unique old slow bus, the 'Esto'. The 'Izuzu' runs from Ungaran or Bawen to Salatiga and back. It is slightly more expensive but more convenient for passengers travelling a short distance. The old slow 'Esto' connects the market towns of Ambarawa and Salatiga. The sub-district town of Tuntang has no terminal for any public transport. These public transport services were not meant primarily to serve the needs of the people in Tuntang, therefore to judge the development progress of Tuntang in terms of this abundant public transport would mostly be misleading. This is not to say however, that this public transport service has made no significant contribution to the development processes in this area. Public transport has indeed made a significant socio-economic contribution to this area. These contributions have, however, generally benefited those hamlets located on either side of the provincial road, and have much less impact on the isolated hamlets.

7. The *Camat* and his Administration

The present *camat* (sub-district head) began his term in late 1992. His predecessor was replaced after Golkar lost some 20 percent of its votes in 1992 general election. Previously he was the *camat* of Sumowono, a more remote sub-district in Semarang district. His promotion to the less remote sub-district of Tuntang is considered as the government's acknowledgement of his success. Apart from his simple life-style, he precisely fits Schulte Nordholt's description of typical "*pejabat Orde Baru yang maju*" (progressive New Order official) (1987b: 80-81). Unlike the village head and the hamlet head, who are elected by adult members of their respective villages or hamlets, the *camat* is appointed by the government. The introduction of *UDKP* (*Unit Daerah Kerja Pembangunan,* Development Unit Area) by the Ministry of Interior in 1974 established the *camat* as the central government agent to co-ordinate all the

[53] One of the respondents in the present research is a retired bus driver, who lost his job after three major accidents with the bus he drove. During the field research in second half of the 1993, from Lopait village alone three people were killed and another lost his memory due to traffic accidents.

development programmes and different departmental or sectional activities within his *wilayah* (administrative region).[54]

Nico Schulte Nordholt in his dissertation: *Opbouw in Opdracht of Ontwikkeling in Overleg*? (1981)[55] illustrated the struggle of the *camat* to function as both the extension of central government and as a channel for people's aspirations and needs to be conveyed to government.[56] As was already apparent in the 1980s (Schulte Nordholt, 1987b; Tjondronegoro, 1984), the institution of *camat* in the 1990s is being perceived in its former function, as an extension of the central government. In an attempt to make a success of his second appointment, the present *camat* of Tuntang seems to be setting his priority as one of building trust with the ordinary people. Almost every night he is out, either attending meetings and celebrations, or simply visiting people in one of the villages under his administration. Even in the afternoon one often finds him talking with people on the road side. This approach is somewhat unusual, generally a *camat* would restrict himself to establishing co-operation with village heads and other local leaders. In his research in Gunung Sari Sub-district, in Central Java, Schulte Nordholt observed,

> A *camat's* visitations to villages usually do not get beyond the village office. If he has to walk to a village, he may occasionally converse with people he meets on the way, but usually this conversation is just for the sake of courtesy (1987b: 179).

As the *lurah* (village heads) have been increasingly transformed into central government agents, co-operation between *camat* and *lurah* has often led to the hindrance of two-way communication between the rural people and the central government. This has had the effect of isolating the rural people from participating in development (Schulte Nordholt, 1987b: 498-499).

It will probably take a much longer time for the *camat* of Tuntang to change people's perception on the role of *camat*. First, he has to win people's confidence by altering the traditional understanding of the *camat* as being a central government agent, whose main jobs include policing and tax collection.[57] It seems that the *camat*'s hard work to transform this traditional perception has yet to attain significant achievement. Rural people who went to

---

[54] See, sections 80-81 of *UU* (legislation) No. 5, 1974, concerning the territorial government structure. See also N. G. Schulte Nordholt, 1987b: 69-70; and S. M. P. Tjondronegoro, 1984: 92-93.

[55] See, the Indonesian edition, *Ojo Dumeh: Kepemimpian Lokal dalam Pembangunan* (Local Leadership in Development), 1987b.

[56] See also D.D Fagg, "Authority and Social Structure; a Study in Javanese bureaucracy", 1958; S. M. P. Tjondronegoro, 1984; Soetardjo Kartohadikoesoemo, 1965; M. Surianingrat, *Wewenang, Tugas dan Kewajiban Camat* (The Authority, Function and Responsibility of Sub-District Head), 1976.

[57] See Surianingrat, 1976: 7; S. Kartohadikoesoemo, 1965: 67; H. A. Sutherland, *Pangreh Praja; Java's Indigenous Administrative Corps and Its Role in the Last Decades of Dutch Colonial Rule*, 1973: 59-60; and Marsono, 1968: 51.

the sub-district office (and met the *camat*) of Tuntang between January and July 1994, for example, mostly either attended to request letters of recommendation[58] or to undertake land transactions.[59] Land transactions in rural Indonesia are administered and legalised by a *camat*, and he levies a 0.5-1 percent commission. At the same time, he has to collect administrative and other charges assigned for village and sub-district administrations. However, to avoid these charges and tax, a large number of land transactions in rural Java are done unofficially (*di bawah tangan*).

Second, this unusual approach has, to some degree, threatened the interests of some village headmen.[60] It is unlikely that the *camat* can afford to lose the support of the village headmen. As a result, he has been trying to balance his intention to be well rooted in the rural community with the need to retain support from the village headmen. The outcome of this dual approach is often a lack of decisiveness.

8. Population and Employment

Population change and its relation to socio economic development in Java, especially following the introduction of the *Kultuurstelsel* (1830-1860)[61] has been among the most popular subjects of socio-economic research on rural Java.[62] The impact of the Cultivation System on Java's rural population has

[58] Almost 50 percent of 4247 people who visited the sub-district office during this period came to obtain the *SKKB/SKTT (Surat Keterangan kelakuan baik/Surat keterangan tidak terlibat* or recommendation letter of good conduct / had not been involved with the Communist Party or other forbidden ideologies). The data on the number of people visiting the sub-district office is obtained from the *kecamatan* guest-book.

[59] Excluding the unofficial ones, there were 108 land transactions between January-July 1994. Only in the case of land transactions, would the *camat* himself present to witness. Most people who came to the sub-district office to obtain letters of recommendations would normally be dealt with by the members of *camat*'s staff.

[60] Power abuse by village headmen in Java is not a recent phenomena, it has a long history, going back even before the colonial times. See D.H. Burger, 1939: 42; It was supposed to have been one of the cause of famine in rural Java between 1849-1850 (Djoko Suryo, 1982: 94-97); see also S. van Deventer Jsz., Vol. 2, 1865-1866: 460.

[61] Johannes van den Bosch's ideas for the Cultivation System were principally for Javanese villages to set aside one-fifth of their land for planting cash-crops designated by the government. The government would then buy the produce at fixed prices. This money, which the people earned, in Van den Bosch's calculation, would have been sufficient to pay the landrent of the whole village. Those who did not own land were to contribute obligatory labour (66 man-days). For extensive reading on the Cultivation System, see Clive Day, *The Policy and Administration of the Dutch in Java*, 1966; and C. Fasseur, *Kultuurstelsel en koloniale Baten, De Nederlandse Exploitatie van Java 1840-1860*, 1974.

[62] See C. Geertz, *Agricultural Involution*, 1963a; R. E. Elson, *Sugar and Peasants: The Social impact of the Western Sugar Industry on the Peasantry of the Pasuruan, East Java, from the Cultivation System to the Great Depression*, 1980; M. R. Fernando,

been the subject of very different historiographical interpretations. Cornelius van Vollenhoven (1919) argued that the Cultivation System had encouraged the villages to communalize landholding rights, thus destroying the older individual's right to land. In similar vein, Geertz (1963a) argued that Javanese rural community had moved toward a symmetrical, egalitarian and homogeneous system as the result of the Cultivation System. Geertz's thesis has provoked responses from many scholars. Elson (1978), in an attempt to test Geertz's thesis in Pasuruan district, concluded that far from resulting in egalitarian and homogeneity, the Cultivation System had strengthened the position of the village elite, thus creating a class of wealthy landholders. Among Geertz's other dominant critics in the 1970s and '80s was William L. Collier (1981a, b) who, in a similar way argued that the 'involution' thesis is an inadequate explanation for socio-economic, as well as population change, in nineteenth-century rural Java.[63]

While the vast body of literature on the Cultivation System has shed light on the socio-economic change of rural Java in the nineteenth-century, there is a marked tendency to generalise the *modus operandi* and impact of the Cultivation System and thus overlook significant local variations. As Van Niel also indicated,

> There is a marked tendency in the historical literature on the Cultivation (Culture) System in Java to attribute a greater conceptual and operational unity to the System than it deserves (1992: 30).[64]

Further, in an analysis of the relationship between economic change and population movement in nineteenth-century rural Semarang, Djoko Suryo confirmed that "generalizations based upon general concepts or theories have failed to explain the contemporary realities of rural life." He called for further analyses to be carried out at levels lower than district (1982: 56).

As has been stated already, the sub-district of Tuntang was formed in 1877 under the administration of Salatiga district. Formerly, this area consisted of villages governed directly by the *rangga* in Salatiga. Since statistical data on the Cultivation System at below the district level is not available, the closest account of Tuntang under the Cultivation System would be to look at the data

---

Peasants and Plantation Economy; The Social impact of the European plantation economy in Cirebon residency from the Cultivation System to the end of the first decade of the twentieth century, 1982; R. van Niel, *Java Under the Cultivation System*, 1992.

[63] For a summary of the historical debate on the subject, see Robert van Niel, 1992.

[64] Van Niel pointed out that the land used for government cultivation was, at most, only five percent of all cultivated land. Moreover, he also identified diverse patterns of relationship between landrent assessment and payments made by the government for the crops due to regional varieties (1992: 69-72). Unfortunately, Van Niel himself did not avoid the trap of generalising the socio-economic impact of the Cultivation System in rural Java (1992: 226-227).

on Salatiga district. Djoko Suryo categorised Salatiga and other major coffee producing districts in Semarang Residency as 'profitable coffee districts,'[65] which means, the coffee payment was higher than the landrent assessment of the entire district.[66] On the other hand, all other sugar producing districts in lowland Semarang residency were unprofitable except the Perbuan district (1982: 43). As a whole, between 1837-1851, the Cultivation System in Semarang residency had been seen as unprofitable.[67] With regard to this district categorisation, Djoko Suryo's calculations of district 'profitability-unprofitability' are misleading. Djoko derived the figures of district 'profitability-unprofitability' from the per capita amount of coffee payment. The figure for this coffee payment is obtained by dividing the district's total income from coffee (the coffee payment minus the landrent assessment) by the total population (1982: 35-38; 50-53). This method of calculation assumed that there was no per capita income apart from coffee, which was, of course, untrue. In Salatiga district, for example, in 1837 there were 2747 non-coffee planter households out of the 8255 'all crops' planter households, or 33 percent of the total planter households (Suryo, 1982: Appendix VII).

Table 2.1 shows that between 1837 to 1845 the total income from coffee payment in the Salatiga district increased by an average of 2.1 percent annually. At the same time, the population of the district grew by an average of 3.2 percent annually. However, as Djoko Suryo has already argued at residency level, economic change alone is an inadequate explanation for the population movement. His study reveals that, while there are cases where a profitable year was followed by a significant increase in population growth, there are also cases where an unprofitable year was followed by population decline. In contrast, there are also cases where the population growth occurred in sequence with an unprofitable year. In fact, the highest population growth occurred in 'unprofitable coffee districts' (1982: 42-43).

---

[65] Together with Ambarawa, Limbangan, Cangkiran, Selakaton, and Tengaran districts. The only major coffee producing district in Semarang residency where the landrent assessment exceeded the coffee payment was in Ungaran district. In 1845, the total coffee trees in each of the above districts were between 804,666 (Limbangan) and 6,107,337 (Ambarawa), Ungaran district was next, with some 792,321 trees, see Djoko Suryo, 1982: 43, 316.

[66] There were only two major commercial crops planted in Semarang Residency, namely coffee and sugar. The other crops such as tobacco, tea and cotton were grown in relatively small amounts. Salatiga's involvement in Cultivation System was limited to coffee plantation, see Djoko Suryo, 1982: 24.

[67] In 1843 and 1851 the government payments were slightly above the land-rent assessments, only in the year of 1850 Semarang residency obtained substantial profit from the Cultivation System, see R. van Niel, 1992: 70.

Table 2.1. Population Change and the Cultivation System at Salatiga District, 1837-1845

	1837	1845	Annual Growth in %
Total population	36,845	47,412	3.2
Total coffee Trees	722,976	2,021,022	13.7
Total coffee planter households	5,508	4,771	-1.8
Total planter households (all crops)	8,255	5,267	-5.5
Average trees/Households	131.3	423.6	15.8
Coffee payment	f. 77,979.60	f. 92,347.40	2.1
Average coffee payment/household	f. 14.16	f. 19.36	4.0[68]
Land-rent assessment	f. 37,545	f. 43,270	1.8
Average incomes/planter household	f. 7.34	f. 10.29	4.3
Total land planted (all crops)	5,145 *Bau*[69]	5,756 *Bau*	1.4

Sources: "Verslag der Kultures", in "Algemeen Jaarlijk Verslag der Residentie Samarang over 1837-1840"; Th. S. Raffles, ***The History of Java***, Vol. 2, 1817: 264-269; and P. Bleeker, "Fragmenten eener Reis over Java", in ***TNI*** 1 (1850): 4-8.

Concerning the Salatiga district, Table 2.1 points out the fact that while the population, the coffee payment, and the average income of the planter households increased, the number of coffee planter households declined by 1.8 percent. At least four possible explanations can be suggested for this trend. First, that there was other produce grown in the Salatiga district, which was more profitable than coffee. Such a suggestion presumes a significant increase in the number of the 'non-coffee' planter households in the district. The historical data, however, does not support this. Between 1837-1845 the 'non-coffee' planter households in Salatiga district declined by 19.3 percent every year.[70]

The second suggestion is that the phenomenal population growth was mostly a result of biological reproduction by the local community. Although biological reproduction might have contributed to this substantial population increase, it alone fails to give adequate explanation. Apart from the period of the early implementation of the Cultivation System (1837-1845), the annual growth had always remained below 2.0 percent. The population growth was

[68] Fifty percent of this average coffee payment growth was contributed by the decreasing number of coffee planter households.

[69] 1 *bau* is a traditional measurement which equal to 0. 70965 hectare.

[70] In 1837 the total number of planter households (all crops) was 8,255. There were only 5,267 households by 1845, see "Verslag der Kultures", in "Algemeen Jaarlijk Verslag van der Residentie Samarang over 1837-1840"; and P. Bleeker, 1850: 8.

1.5 percent between 1815-1839, was 1.9 percent between 1845-1879, and was 1.6 percent between 1879-1995[71]

Third, as elsewhere in nineteenth-century Java, population movements from sugar districts to coffee districts were not uncommon. The burden of compulsory labour in sugar districts was reportedly more severe compared to other districts (de Vries, 1931: 99). Shocked by this burden, the population of sugar districts declined in the early years of Cultivation System (Elson, 1978: 26). Ong Hok Ham also identified population movement from sugar districts to coffee districts caused by the inequities in the practice of compulsory labour in Madiun residency (1975: 215). An analysis at the residency level of Semarang, however reveals a contrary picture. The population of the sugar districts in Semarang residency had increased by 2.9 percent between 1837-1845.[72] There was, of course, a possibility of population movement from sugar districts outside Semarang residency to the coffee districts in Semarang residency. The data to support this assumption is, however, unavailable. The limitation of data on population movements in nineteenth-century Java has prevented the tracing of the origin of new settlers beyond the residency of Semarang.

The fourth explanation suggests that the total income of an average coffee planter household was much less than the average income of the coffee planter households as shown above. Table 2.1 clearly indicates that between 1837-1845 Salatiga district had undergone a rapid process of concentration of landholdings. In 1837, the average coffee trees per planter household was 131.3. By 1845 each planter household owned an average of 423.6 coffee trees, representing an annual increase of 15.8 percent. As noted, this fifty percent average annual increase in coffee payments per household was made possible partly by the decline of coffee planter households. The earlier picture of Salatiga district, drawn by Djoko Suryo as being reasonably 'prosperous', gained from the good profit of coffee plantation (1982: 43), is thus ambiguous. This picture is even further shattered by the existence of the private plantation company, the N.V. Cultuur Maatschappij Tlogo. This private plantation company had been developing since 1809 and covered a plantation area of 301 hectares.[73] This vast plantation area which had been developed long before the beginning of the Cultivation System (see Hefner, 1990: 40-42; Suryo, 1982: 24), certainly made a significant contribution to the overall 'profitability' of

---

[71] The total population of Salatiga district in 1815 was 25,902. It was 35,487 in 1839, 78,528 in 1879, and 98,027 in 1895, see Djoko Suryo, 1982: 308-313 (Appendix I); and Benjamin White, "Population, Involution and Employment in Rural Java." *Development and Change* 7 (1976): 1.

[72] There were two sugar districts in Semarang Residency, namely Kendal and Perbuan. The total population of Kendal and Perbuan districts in 1837 was 35,830, it grew to 44,143 in 1845, see Djoko Suryo, 1982: 36.

[73] *Sertifikat Hak Atas Tanah* (land certificate) no 424-428, 31 October 1809, and *Surat Ukur* (land measurement certificate) no. 8615, 1 January 1856, see "Perusda Perkebunan Tlogo", 1992: 36.

this area. This further proof of the large landholding concentration of coffee plantations in Salatiga district suggests that the income of the average planter household was probably much less than suspected (Table 2.1). It, therefore, explains the decline of the planter households.

Interestingly, the significant increase of coffee trees in the district between 1837-1845 (see Table 2.1) was not accompanied by any corresponding increase in the amount of cultivated land. While the number of coffee trees increased by 15.8 percent annually, the planted area rose only 1.4 percent. The substantial population growth was presumably correlated with the huge increase in the number of coffee trees. While the increased concentration of landholdings, especially by the private plantation companies, explains the decline of the planter households,[74] it appears that "employment", rather than district "profitability" or even 'land availability' played the more significant role in population movement in Salatiga district. As Robert W. Hefner also indicated,

> At the height of the Cultivation System, the number of peasants mobilized for coffee cultivation exceeded the number involved in the cane cultivation, at times by a ratio of three to one. The amount of labor required was massive (1990: 41-42).[75]

Just like Ungaran, Bawen, and Klepu sub-districts today, where the big industries and factories have contributed massively to population movement in the area, Salatiga district in the mid-nineteenth-century witnessed a similar movement with its private plantation companies. It needs to be stressed here, however, that the complexity of this issue of population movements in nineteenth-century Java, prevents both any exclusive explanation, as well as any generalisation, of a theoretical concept.

Rural Javanese population density has often been looked at as an important component of past and present poverty (de Vries, 1972; Koentjaraningrat, 1971). However, the nineteenth-century Salatiga district has a different story to tell. As the preceding discussion and other studies have revealed, man-land ratio was not necessarily the major determinant of the socio-economic state of rural Java.[76] The response of the rural Javanese to population pressures in the 1930s, which de Vries described as "*dapat berpikir sehat*" (wise), particularly by choosing not to overcrowd the cities, but to move to the more remote areas of Java, has long been abandoned (1972: 18). In post Independence Indonesia, and especially as a result of the rapid industrialisation in the 1970s and '80s, the

---

[74] See Clifford Geertz, 1963a: 56; for the role of private land-holders in coffee plantations, see J. Metcalf, *The Agricultural Economy of Indonesia*. Monograph 15, US Department Of Agriculture, 1952: 70.

[75] See also Benjamin White, "Agricultural Involution and Its Critics: Twenty Years after Clifford Geertz", 1983: 28.

[76] See Jean-Luc Maurer, "Some Consequences of Land Shortage in Four Kelurahan of the Kabupaten Bantul." Mimeograph, 1973: 8; and Djoko Suryo, 1982: 43.

role of farm employment in the rural economy has declined considerably, on the other hand, non-farm activities have gained an increasing role in rural socio-economic lives.

In post-Independence Indonesia, the population growth of Tuntang sub-district has been relatively low. Between 1973 and 1993 the average annual growth rate was 0.6 percent. This is mainly due to the successful family planning programme implemented in this area. The birth rate declined by 8.7 percent annually between 1981-1988, and by 24.9 percent between 1988-1995.[77] Table 2.2 shows that the number of children, especially the 'under fives' dropping sharply between 1982-1988, and a further decline can be noted of 0.2 percent between 1988-1995 (see, Tables 2.2, 2.3).

In the seventies there were significant numbers of people moving out, mostly to join the transmigration programme. There are at least, two main reasons which encouraged people to leave their villages either for transmigration or urbanisation. The first was the impact of the government's decision to raise the water level of Rawa Pening lake in 1967. Between 1959-1967, Rawa Pening lake became badly silted, probably caused by a lack of maintenance. To maintain the capacity of the hydro-electric power, which serves the needs of Semarang and its surrounding areas, the government decided to increase the water level of the lake. As a result, 600 hectares of *sawah* were submerged during the rainy season (Warsito, 1979: 249). In June 1977, the village head of Rawasari wrote that, in his village, more than 95 hectares of *sawah* (wet-rice field), mostly under the *Bimas* intensification programme and 17 houses were destroyed by the Rawa Pening annual flood.[78] The population of the villages affected by this misfortune responded in many different ways, with the transmigration programme as one of the major options. Between 1976-1979 for example, 188 people from Rawaboni and 263 from Rawasari alone transmigrated to other islands.[79]

Second, as stated above, coffee plantations, especially the Tlogo Plantation Estate, had made an important contribution to the population movement in

[77] Between 1980-1982, the average number of live births per year in Tuntang sub-district was 1055; between 1986-1988 it was 609 and between 1993-1995 only 82, see *Statistik Kecamatan Tuntang* (Annual Statistics of Tuntang Sub-district), 1982, 1988; and *Formulir Isian Monografi* of Tuntang sub-district (statistics of Tuntang sub-district, updated every six month), 1993-1995.

[78] A report from the sub-district head of Tuntang to the district head of Semarang reveal that 38 hectares of *sawah* in the village of Tuntang, 90 hectares in the village of Candirejo, 33 hectares in the village of Sraten and more than 92 hectares in Rawasari have been severely damaged by this annual flood. Statistics for the other three villages (Jombor, Kesongo and Lopait) suffering from this flood are not available, see LPU UKSW, "Rawa Pening Project II", 1977: 109.

[79] In 18 July 1977, the *bupati* of Semarang gave an instruction that the lands which had been deserted by the people who had joined transmigration programme should not be used as settlement, see LPU UKSW, 1977: 111; and Rukmadi Warsito, 1979: 245.

nineteenth-century Tuntang. Significant numbers of people moved into the sub-district seeking employment at this coffee plantation estate. During the course of the 'great depression' in 1930, as the price of coffee in the international markets fell drastically, the management decided to diversify the plantation.[80] Accordingly, cocoa became one of the major crops, with other crops such as pepper, rubber and cloves being planted in smaller amounts. In the period of the Japanese occupation (1942-1945) the plantation estate was neglected. Following the Indonesian Revolution, between 1952-1980, the plantation estate underwent several managerial changes.[81] In practice, however, from the late forties until 1967, most of the land was occupied and utilised as a resource by the people living in the surrounding villages. Reportedly people made quite good fortunes out of it. A change in management practice took place in 1967. In accordance with the priority the New Order administration gave to restoring the economic state of the country, land was taken back by the management. Between 1967-1973 people were still allowed to utilise the land for their second crops, using the spaces between the government's rubber trees. Finally, in 1973, the management of the plantation estate completely refused to give permission for the people to plant any crops on estate land. People responded to this economic pressure in several different ways, the transmigration programmes and urbanisation in Jakarta were among the major alternatives.[82]

---

[80] See J. S. Furnivall, 1939: 442; Jan G. L. Palte, *The Development of Java's Rural Uplands in Response to Population Growth: An Introductory Essay in Historical Perspective*, 1984: 37.

[81] *SK Gubernur* (Governor's decree), No. 19 /52-6/7/10, 12 March 1952, the plantation was registered under the administration of *Yayasan* (Foundation) *Senapati*. *SK Gubernur* No. 6.41/1953-6/59/6, 12 November 1954: under the administration of the District office of Semarang. *SK Gubernur* No. 2/14/ka/64, 19 March 1964: under the administration of the "Perusda (*Perusahaan Daerah,*Government regional company) Aneka II". *SK Gubernur*, No. 6/62/1971-7/54.9, 16 July 1971: under the administration of the economic administration of Central Java province. *SK Gubernur*, No. G.7160/1973-60/3/6, 15 May 1973: under the administration of the "Pinda Minyak dan Es", Central Java. *SK Gubernur*, No. O.P.173/1978, 16 May 1978: under the administration of the Board of Directors of the Central Java *Perusda*. *SK Gubernur*, No. 07.63/1980, 17 September 1980: the estate was under the administration of the "Perusda Aneka Industri", Central Java.

[82] According to church elders in Celengan hamlet, during these years of increasing economic pressure, the *Yayasan* (Foundation) 'Salib Putih' of Salatiga, along with the provincial government, have funded quite a large number of people to go for transmigration to Central Lampung district in South Sumatra. In early 1982, reportedly some 275 people of Watuagung village alone were transmigrated. Both Celengan and Watuagung are located at the border of the Tlogo plantation estate, see "Annual Statistics of Tuntang Sub-District", 1982: 26. Unfortunately, there were no official records as to the exact number of people migrated to Jakarta during this period. However, the information gathered from the local informants suggest that most of the

The causes of population movements around Tuntang in the seventies have thus been characterised by economic pressures produced by government (supra-village) policies. The socio-political situation in the late sixties and early seventies prevented people from pleading their cases. Prior to 1966, the PKI (*Partai komunis Indonesia*, Communist Party of Indonesia) was the largest political party in the town of Salatiga and in the district of Semarang, including Tuntang sub-district.[83] The majority of farmers in this area were members of BTI (*Barisan Tani Indonesia,* Indonesian Farmers' Front). In 1966, as the PKI was banned and hundreds of thousands of its supporters were either killed, imprisoned or exiled to Buru Island, it was not uncommon to accuse a rival of being a PKI supporter, in order to remove him from his post as village head, as an owner of land, or as a supplier of certain products. It was in this context of fear and intimidation following the 30 September 1965 (GESTAPU) coup, that the policies of increasing the water level of Rawa Pening and of prohibiting the people to utilise estate land were introduced. Although there is no official evidence suggesting that the execution of these policies was politically motivated (i.e. to put pressure on the former members of BTI), the people were left with very little choice.[84]

In contrast to the late 1960 and '70s, population movement of the 1980s and early 1990s was relatively low. This was mainly due to improved transportation and the development of the neighbouring sub-districts into new industrial areas. The significant improvement of the infrastructure has tended to socio-economically merge Tuntang into the urban sprawl of Semarang and Salatiga. Moreover, the remarkable progress of the Ungaran, Klepu and Bawen sub-districts as new industrial areas has contributed to the formation of a new cluster of 'commuting urban employees'.

In 1995, 52.5 percent of the work-force of Tuntang was involved in farm related employment. The proportion of people employed in farm related work has continued to decline. It was 53.7 percent in 1984 and 62.3 percent in 1976.[85] While the total number of people working in farm-related employment

---

more well-to-do population of Celengan hamlet (i.e. Those who own a permanent [brick] house) were amongst those who migrated to Jakarta in the seventies.

[83] In the 1955 general election, the PKI gained 60 percent of votes in Salatiga and 53 percent in Semarang district, see "Kota Madya Salatiga, Suatu Laporan Survey Tentang Keadaan Sosial-Ekonomi dan Pembangunan Daerah", 1976: 68.

[84] A number of respondents in Celengan hamlet interpreted the government policy which prohibited them from utilising the lands of the plantation estate as a political strategy to put pressure on them. The population of Kumpulrejo and Kalipinggang hamlets also gave a similar political interpretation to the economic pressure caused by the government's policy on Rawa Pening, see Pradjarta Dirdjosanjoto *et al.*, 1978: 235, 242-244.

[85] See Direktorat Pembangunan Desa Propinsi Jawa Tengah, "Laporan Hasil Survey Mikro Kecamatan Tuntang, Kabupaten Dati II Semarang, Propinsi Jawa Tengah" (Report on the micro level survey of Tuntang sub-district, in the Semarang district, Central Java), 1984-1985: 3.

has declined, the number of owner farmers has slightly increased by 0.3 percent (see Table 2.4). This increase is however, insignificant compared to the spectacular increase in employment outside farming.

Table 2.2. Demographic Profile of Tuntang Sub-District, 1982-1988

YEAR	1982			1988			Annual Growth in %		
AGE	*M*	*F*	*T*	*M*	*F*	*T*	*M*	*F*	*T*
0-4	4006	4016	8022	3121	3106	6227	-4.1	-4.2	-4.1
5-9	3137	3580	6717	3124	3317	6441	-0.1	-1.3	-0.7
10-14	3201	3167	6368	3061	3236	6297	-0.7	0.4	-0.2
15-24	5156	5445	10601	5672	6002	11674	1.6	1.6	1.6
25-49	7419	7977	15396	8709	9262	17971	2.7	2.5	2.6
>50	3360	3374	6707	3915	4025	7940	2.6	3.0	2.9
Total	**26287**	**27532**	**53819**	**27602**	**28979**	**56581**	**0.8**	**0.9**	**0.8**

Source: Annual Statistics of Tuntang Sub-District, 1982; 1988.

Table 2.3. Demographic Profile of Tuntang Sub-District, 1988-1995

AGE/ YEAR	1988[86]	1995	Annual Growth in %
0-4	5034	4959	-0.2
5-9	5173	5697	1.4
10-14	5153	5616	1.2
15-24	9594	10081	0.7
25-39	9875	10102	0.3
>40	11226	10704	-0.7
Total	**46055**	**47159**	**0.3**

Source: Annual Statistics of Tuntang Sub-District, 1988; 1995.

Table 2.4 shows that non-farm employment (excluding the civil service and Armed forces) personnel increased by 9.5 percent annually. Interestingly, this increase was not obtained at the cost of other 'stable income' employment. The two employment categories mostly affected were the landless farm labourer and the 'under employed'. With the total number in the work-force remaining the same, this indicates that employment mobility or changes in people's employment in Tuntang sub-district between 1976-1995 was relatively small. The process of change in employment structure shown in Table 2.4 must then

[86] In 1991 there was an administrative reorganisation of Salatiga, in which three villages of Tuntang were administratively taken over by the town of Salatiga, namely Blotongan, Pulutan and Kecandran villages. To be able to assess the population growth of Tuntang in 1988-1994, these three villages are, therefore, excluded from Tables 2.3, 2.4, 2.5, 2.8.

be interpreted in terms of the ability of non-farm sector in 1995 and preceding years to absorb the huge percentage of the under-employed population of Tuntang as well as to give additional jobs for the rest of the population.[87] It should not be assumed, however, that significant change, namely the increase in non-farm employment and decline in the 'under employed' category, was simply a direct employment shift.[88]

Table 2.4. Employment Mobility of Tuntang Sub-District, 1976-1995

Employment	1976		1995		Annual Change
	Number	%	Number	%	%
Owner Farmer/Share-Cropper	6715	24.7	7089	25.8	0.3
Landless Farm Labourer	9524	35	6833	24.8	-1.7
Fisherman	703	2.6	546	2	-1.3
Enterprise/Industry/ Business	107	0.4	3822	13.9	20.7
Trading	630	2.3	2303	8.4	7.1
Industrial Salaried Employee	177	0.7	2377	8.6	14.6
Unskilled Casual Non-Farm Labourer	913	3.4	1570	5.7	2.9
Transportation	140	0.5	945	3.4	10.6
Civil Servant/Armed Forces Personal	2645	9.7	1514	5.5	-2.9
Retired	280	1	534	1.9	3.5
Others (Under Employed)	5352	19.7	Nil	-	-
TOTAL	27186	100	27533	100	0.1

Sources: LPU-UKSW, 1977; The Annual Statistics of Tuntang, 1995.

The two most remarkable growth areas in employment were related to industry. The spectacular growth of private enterprises and industries (including home industry) by 20.7 percent annually was made possible by the socio-economic integration of Tuntang into the market economy of Semarang, Ambarawa and Salatiga. As has been discussed above, the rapid development of road networks and of the means of transportation in the eighties has merged Tuntang into the larger socio-economic sphere of Semarang city, Semarang district and Salatiga. The improved access to a larger market and market expansion have, therefore,

[87] The improvement of road and transportation networks in the village of Candirejo in the late seventies has enabled its population to take on additional employment. Reportedly, in 1977, more than 65 percent of the work force had two or more means of employment, see K. Suwondo, 1978: 180-184.

[88] The slight increase (2.9 percent) of the waged labourers was an evidence of a modest employment mobility within the unskilled lower level of the population.

provided major stimuli for the population of Tuntang to engage in medium and small-scale industries. Furthermore, the road improvements in a number of villages have reduced real transport costs of goods being traded to nearby market towns, and thus increased the competing power of the products (Booth, 1979: 51). Hefner also related the opening of a road in 1980 to the 37 percent decline of the real transport costs in four communities in the mid-slope Tengger highlands (Hefner, 1990: 85). Since only few hamlets in Tuntang sub-district have immediate access to public transport, while others remain accessible only by footpaths and 'Ojek routes', the increase of the number of people engaged in industry and trade is unequally distributed among the villages.

Table 2.5. Improvement of Road Facilities, 1984-1995

Types of Road	1984		1995		Annual Change
	Length in km.	*%*	*Length in km*	*%*	*%*
Asphalt Road	33.25	20.1	52.66	28.4	4.3
Stone surface Road	68	41.1	72.26	39	0.6
Soil-Road	64.15	38.8	60.5	32.6	-0.5
TOTAL	165.4	100	185.42	100	1.0

Source: Micro Survey of Tuntang Sub-District, 1984-1985; and Statistics of Tuntang Sub-District, 1995.

The other two employment sectors which have undergone significant increases are industry and transport. The rapid development of the Ungaran, Klepu and Bawen sub-districts into new industrial areas has largely contributed to the increasing number of commuters from Tuntang.

In comparison, road improvements in Tuntang have been modest. In the Tengger highlands, for example, the length of asphalt road in the seventies increased from 47 to 92 kilometres and the villages with vehicular road access (i.e. stone-surfaced and asphalt) had increased from 20 to 80 percent (Hefner, 1990: 85).[89] In Tuntang sub-district, the roads increased from 101.25 kilometres in 1984 to 124.92 kilometres in 1995 (see Table 2.5). Out of these 23.67 kilometres of improvements, 19.41 kilometres (or 82 percent) were asphalt, providing the main access roads in the area. As in most rural areas of Java, the construction of access roads was subsidised by the *Inpres* (Presidential Instruction) programme, while the feeder roads which link individual hamlets to the main access roads were the responsibility of the local communities (Booth and McCawley, 1981: 8).

---

[89] The road improvements of Tuntang was certainly much less drastic compared to the rice producing areas such as Jatinom in Klaten district, see Irwan Abdullah, 1994: 60.

The fact that the stone-surfaced vehicle roads increased by only 0.6 percent annually and soil roads declined by only 0.5 percent, indicates that people's contributions to the recent employment changes was small, especially when contrasted with the massive impact of the road networks on employment change of the population of Tuntang sub-district (see Table 2.4).[90] On the other hand, the expansion of the asphalt roads and the existence of vast lengths of stone-surfaced and soil roads have generated remarkable employment opportunity for 'Ojek' drivers, which serve to link them.[91]

9. Agricultural Development

The wide range of sectoral rural development activities administered at sub-district level includes a number of agricultural development programmes such as *BIMAS* (*Bimbingan Massa*, Mass Guidance), *INMAS* (*Intensifikasi Massa*, Mass Intensification) and *INSUS* (*Intensifikasi Khusus*, Special Intensification)[92]; health programmes such as the *Puskesmas* (*Pusat Kesehatan Masyarakat*, Rural Health Centre); the *Posyandu* (*Pos Pelayanan Terpadu*, Rural Health Cadre); and the *PKK* (*Pendidikan Kesejahteraan Keluarga*, Family Welfare Movement). It also includes education programmes such as *Kejar Paket-A* (*Kelompok Belajar Paket-A*, a government literacy programme), and *SD Inpres* (*Sekolah Dasar Inpres*, Presidential Grant for Elementary Education). As well as road construction, infra-structural developments include the *Listrik Masuk Desa* (Rural Electricity), and the *Koran Masuk Desa* (Rural Newspaper). To facilitate the economic development the government offers some formal small-scale credit, such as *Kupedes* (*Kredit Umum Pedesaan*, General Rural Credit programme), *KMKP* (*Kredit Modal Kerja Permanen*, Permanent Working Capital Credit Programme), and *KIK* (*Kredit Investasi Kecil*, Small Scale Investment Credit Programme).[93]

In Tuntang sub-district, the rural health programmes of *Puskesmas* and *Posyandu* have been quite successful, both in promoting family planning programmes and in raising the life expectancy of the villagers, as discussed earlier in this chapter. The three programmes most directly related to employment change and improvement of household income in Tuntang have

---

[90] Since the development of the feeder roads were the responsibility of individual hamlets, an explanation of this phenomenon needs to be sought at the hamlet level.

[91] As has been stated above the number of 'Ojek' in Tuntang have increased from 51 in 1993 to 139 in 1994.

[92] For a general discussion on these agricultural development programmes, see Chapter Three. For a detailed description of these programmes, see H. Huisman, *Planning for Rural Development: Experiences and Alternatives*, 1994: 39-42.

[93] For a brief discussion of the operation of some of these programmes at village and hamlet levels, see Chapters Five and Six. For a detailed description of these programmes, see S. Maskun, *Pembangunan Masyarakat Desa*, 1993: 249-300; and H. Huisman, 1994: 43-52.

been the infra-structure (road and transport) development, the establishment of new industrial sub-districts of Ungaran, Klepu and Bawen, and to some extent the improvement in the standard of education. While the other rural development programmes have in varying degree benefited the population of Tuntang, they are generally less significant in contributing to household income than those mentioned above.

At the heart of Indonesian rural development programmes is agricultural development. This is probably based on the fact that although non-farm activities have gained increasing significance in improving rural income as a whole, in many parts of rural Java farm-related employment remained very dominant in absorbing the work force (Mubyarto, 1988; Huisman, 1994). This was also the case in Tuntang sub-district (Table 2.4). Moreover, a significant proportion of the non-farm activities in rural Java are still closely related to farm-related activities (Mubyarto, 1988).

The master development plan of Semarang district categorises Tuntang sub-district as a "W*ilayah Pengembangan* III" (The Third Development Sector), which means the emphasis or the main objective of the development in Tuntang sub-district was to facilitate the development process of the larger regions.[94] Rawa Pening lake is expected to produce the vast hydro-electric power required for Semarang and to irrigate between 24,000 to 40,000 hectares of wet-rice fields in the plains of Semarang and Demak districts. With such a status, one could hardly expect spectacular agricultural development in Tuntang sub-district. It has, however, led to a significant increase in non-farm activities such as industry, trading and transportation. In fact, significant increases of these non-farm activities in the recent years have been largely responsible for the stagnation of the farming sector. Moreover, the increases were made possible by the fact that these income-earning activities did not depend on the natural and public resources, which were to a large measure designed to facilitate the development progress of the larger regions.

In Tuntang sub-district itself, well-irrigated wet-rice fields constituted only 142.5 hectares in 1982, or 7.9 percent of the total *sawah* (wet-rice) fields. Seventy percent of the total *sawah* in Tuntang was either poorly irrigated or rain-fed. Most of these well-irrigated fields were formed in the late seventies and early eighties. In 1995 the figure was slightly reduced, the well-irrigated area falling to 141 hectares. Both the expansion of the well irrigated areas in the late seventies and its decline in the late eighties and early nineties were not at all unique. Earlier Sudaryanto and Kasryno have identified significant increases of irrigated fields between 1970-1987 in the areas they were

[94] See Direktorat Pembangunan Desa Propinsi Jawa Tengah, "Laporan Hasil Survey Mikro Kecamatan Tuntang" (Micro Study on Tuntang Sub-District), 1984-1985: 14.

researching.[95] The decline of well irrigated fields was also a national phenomena. In a workshop organised by CIDES (Center for Information and Development Studies) and Bappenas (National Development Planning Board), Soni Harsono, the Minister for Agrarian Affairs, stated that 50,000 hectares of well-irrigated wet-rice fields are being converted into industrial and housing estate annually (*Republika*, 11 October 1995).

During the heyday of the Green Revolution in Indonesia (1978-1983), the rice output of Tuntang was also raised. In a similar amount of harvested lands, rice output increased from 5,990.12 tons in 1979 to 8,167.39 tons in 1981. This means that the intensification programme of the Green Revolution was able to increase per hectare output from 3.33 tons to 4.59 tons (see Table 2.6). In the 1990s, consistent with the decline of well-irrigated fields, rice fields in Tuntang also suffered a decline. Despite this decline from 1508 hectares in 1993 to 1290 hectares in 1995, Tuntang has been able to maintain both the intensity (per hectare output) and the quantity (total output) of its rice output.

Table 2.6. Rice Output in Tuntang Sub-District, 1979-1981, 1993-1995

Year	The Harvested Rice fields (in Hectares)	Tons/hectare	Total Output (in Tons)
1979	1801	3.33	5990.12
1980	1867	3.96	7396.77
1981	1779	4.59	8167.39
1993	1508[96]	3.58	5394.64
1994	1364	4.53	6178.92
1995	1290	4.92	7089.72

Sources: The Statistics of Tuntang Sub-District, 1982; 1993-1995.

Table 2.6 shows that the average productivity of rice farmers recovered in the first half of the 1990s. Apart from the increase of the per hectare yields from 4.59 tons in 1981 to 4.92 tons in 1995, during this time the number of farmers declined by two percent annually.

---

[95] See T. Sudaryanto and F. Kasryno, "Modern Rice Variety Adoption and Factor-Market Adjustments in Indonesia." In Cristina C. David and Keijiro Otsuka, eds., *Modern Rice Technology and Income Distribution in Asia*, 1994: 110.

[96] The sharp decline of the harvested rice fields between 1981-1993 was partly due to the change of administrative border of Salatiga to include Blotongan, Kecandran and Pulutan villages, which were formerly under Tuntang administration.

Table 2.7. Growth of (Wet-Rice) Farmer's Productivity 1981-1995

	1981	1995
Total Yields in Tons	8167.39	7089.72
Yields (Ton) per Hectare	4.59	4.92
Lands Harvested (in Hectare)	1779	1290
Number of Farmers	18,503	13,922
Average Harvested Lands Cultivated per Farmer (in Hectare)	0.1	0.1
Average Rice Output per Farmer (in Ton)	0.44	0.51

Source: Calculated from The Annual Statistics of Tuntang Sub-District, 1982: 28, 40; and *Daftar Isian Monografi Kecamatan Tuntang*, 1995: 26, 29.

Table 2.7 demonstrates 16 percent growth of average productivity (rice outputs) per farmer between 1981-1995. The real amounts of outputs and of the average lands cultivated per farmer in both years (1981 and 1995) are actually higher than the numbers appearing on the Table. This is especially because Table 2.7 includes the *tegalan* (dry land) farmers in its calculation, which numbers around 25-30 percent of the total farmers, without calculating the output from the non-rice fields.

The number of owner farmers increased from 6715 in 1976 to 8621 in 1982. This 4.3 percent increase has largely been caused by the success of the Green Revolution during those years. At least for a few years the Green Revolution was able to convince the rural population of Tuntang that rice farming under the *Insus* (*Intensifikasi khusus,* Special Intensification) programme could increase their income. In the following years, agricultural development became rather stagnant. The attractions of urban employment made available through the improved road networks and development of new industrial areas had encouraged some farmers to leave their farm activities. In the early nineties, the improved road networks and the integration of Tuntang into the market towns of Semarang, Salatiga and Ambarawa have largely contributed to the increase of rice outputs (Table 2.7). The increase of rice output was naturally followed by increase in the number of owner farmers (Table 2.8).

Table 2.8. Change in Farm Employment

Employment	1982	1992	1995
Owner Farmer/Share-Cropper	7606	6182	7089
Landless Farm Labourer	7812	7304	6833

Source: Annual Statistics of Tuntang, 1982; 1993; 1995

The decline in the number of landless farm labourers has been very dramatic. Even during the heyday of the Green Revolution in Tuntang (1978-1984), the number of landless farm labourers declined by more than 3.6 percent annually. There were 12,643 landless farm labourers in 1976 and only 9,882 in 1982. The field data points to the fact that the landless farm labourers had neither benefited from the increased output of the Green Revolution, nor been driven out of farm employment, as the result of the mechanisation of the Green Revolution. It needs to be noted, that during this period, improvements in road networks and means of transportation were beginning to take place in a number of villages, such as Candirejo, Jombor, Sraten (see Dirdjosanjoto, *et al.*, 1978). It was this infrastructural improvement, rather than the mechanisation of the Green Revolution, which has mostly encouraged the landless farm labourers of Tuntang to leave farm employment for urban jobs.

Between the mid-eighties and mid-nineties, the number of landless farm labourers was somewhat stable (Table 2.8). During this time, the road networks improved, people had easier access to market towns, and more urban commuting employment was available, as a large number of new industries were established in Ungaran, Klepu and Bawen sub-districts. Moreover, the way in which the landless farm labourers tended to remain in their farm employment, despite other attractions and opportunities, indicates that the landless farm labourers of the early nineties had a better share of the agricultural output. The sharp decline in the number of landless farm labourers in the late seventies and early eighties had heightened labour demand in farm activities by the early nineties (see Manning, 1988). The heightened labour demand has, in turn, increased farm incomes.

It is inadequate to speak of the Green Revolution in terms of new agricultural inputs alone (seeds, fertilisers and mechanisation). Among other things, it involves markets, transport, and regional policies (Hefner, 1990: 85). In fact, as far as Tuntang sub-district is concerned, these three factors have more dominant roles in the overall employment and income change of the population than the new agricultural inputs *per se*.

10. Land Distribution

As has already been shown, concentration of landholdings and unequal distribution of lands in Tuntang sub-district occurred during the Cultivation System in the nineteenth-century. A number of village studies in Tuntang sub-district in the seventies confirmed the ongoing process of concentration of landholding and the unequal distribution of lands in these villages (Suwondo, 1978; Nuningsih and Sukardjo, 1979).[97] A village study in Lopait village (see

---

[97]These pilot studies reveal that 70 percent of the farmers in Candirejo village and 56 percent in Rawasari village owned less than 0.2 hectares of farm land, see K. Suwondo,

Chapter Three) suggests that, while unequal distribution of land existed between 1982-1989, there was no evidence of continuing process of concentration of landholding. During this period the number of farmers owning their own fields increased by 7.1 percent, while the amount of farm land declined by 1.7 percent and the owners of large (more than one hectare) farm lands declined by 12 percent.[98] The most likely explanation for such data is the process of fragmentation of landholdings. The Statistics at sub-district level, point in a similar direction. Between 1972-1995 the wet-rice fields as a whole (including the rain-fed) declined by 9.2 percent. The total farm lands, including the *tegalan* (swidden) fields, declined by 4.6 percent. At the same time, the farmers owning their own fields increased by 6.0 percent.[99] This Statistic suggests that the process of the concentration of landholding in Tuntang, which has occurred since colonial times, has halted over the last two decades. This process of fragmentation of landholding does not necessarily lead toward 'shared poverty' nor was it produced by it (Geertz, 1963a). On the contrary, a number of factors, such as improved road network, increased urban migration, the growth of new industrial areas, and heightened demand for farm labour, have been making a considerable contribution to this process. One should, however, be aware, that this process of fragmentation of landholding has yet to make a significant contribution to the equality of landholding in Tuntang sub-district. The distribution of landholding is still very unequal.

In the mid-seventies, the government began to show greater interest in non-rice farming, when maize, soybeans, peanuts and cassava were included in the *BIMAS* extension programme (Hefner, 1990: 83). In the second half of the seventies, the programme was expanded to cover two million hectares (Mears and Moeljono, 1981: 35). Dry land farmers were given greater access to credits in order to purchase fertilisers at very low prices.[100] This policy, however, had very little impact on the productivity of cassava in Tuntang sub-district. The average per hectare yield of cassava in Tuntang was 9.9 tons in 1994 and 9.25 tons in 1995 (Tuntang sub-district, 1994-1995: 26),[101] not much different from

---

1978: 177; R. Nuningsih and B. Sukardjo, 1979: 388; and Gillian Hart, *Power, Labor and Livelihood*, 1986: 100.

[98] See, Monthly statistic of Lopait (*Daftar Monografi Desa*), December 1989; Annual Statistics of Tuntang Sub-District, 1982.

[99] The average amount of farm land owned by a farmer declined from 0.48 hectares in 1972 to 0.35 hectares in 1995.

[100] Due to large government subsidies, the fertiliser were sold at amongst the lowest prices in Asia, see Randolph Barker, Robert W. Herdt and Beth Rose, *The Rice Economy of Asia*, 1985: 88; F. Husken and Benjamin White, "Java: Social Differentiation, Food Production and Agrarian Control." In G. Hart, A. Turton, and B. White, eds., *Agrarian Transformation: Local Processes and the State in Southeast Asia*, 1989: 252.

[101] Between 1981-1983 the average per hectare yields of cassava was 10.4 tons, see The Annual Statistics of Tuntang, 1982: 41; and The Annual Statistics of Semarang District, 1983: 163.

that of the early 1950s.[102] Concerning maize, this intensification programme had a stable impact on Tuntang only after the mid-eighties. In the early adoption of this intensification programme, per hectare yields were very unstable. From 1.6 tons in 1979, it grew to 2.0 tons in 1980, and then declined sharply to 1.1 tons in 1981. Both cassava and the maize production were particularly unstable. Table 2.9 shows that the instability of the annual outputs were very much determined by the amount of land cultivated for the crops.[103]

Table 2.9. Cassava and Maize Production in Tuntang Sub-District, 1981-95

Year	Cassava			Maize		
	Lands cultivated (hectares)	*Per hectare yields (tons)*	*Per ton price (US $)*	*Lands cultivated (hectares)*	*Per hectare yields (in tons)*	*Per ton price (US $)*
1981	422	9.4	21.13	445	1.1	107.98
1982	463	11.6	46.95	1114	2.1	169.01
1983	850	11.7	53.33	825	2.4	119.11
1994	364	9.9	28.70	420	3.1	139.53
1995	409	9.25	76.75	675[104]	1.96	203.16

Source: The data were calculated from The Annual Statistics of Tuntang, 1982: 41; *Daftar Isian Monografi of Tuntang*, 1994-1995: 29; The Annual Statistics of Semarang District, 1982: 203; 1983:209; 1994: 236-7.
Note: The price of 1981-1983 were taken from the market price in Bringin sub-district. The price of 1994-1995 were the average market price in Semarang district. The exchange rate for US$ were 1065 rupiah in 1981-1982, 1125 rupiah in 1983, 2150 rupiah in 1994 and 2215 rupiah in 1995.

Table 2.9 also indicates that it was the market prices, rather than the 'intensification programme' (mainly of fertilisers) which was the dominating factor for determining the amount of land to be cultivated for the crops. In accordance with the rise in the price of cassava in 1982 and a further increase in 1983, the land cultivated for cassava was also increased from 422 hectares in 1981 to 850 hectares in 1983. Between 1984-1993 the price of cassava declined, which accords with the decline of the lands cultivated for cassava during the period. In 1993 the land cultivated for cassava was 298 hectares. In 1994 and 1995 the price of cassava rose again which was followed by the

---

[102] Frederick C. Roche, "Critical Lands in East Java: Development Problems and Potentials." *Economic Problems* 26 (1984): 9.

[103] In 1975 the average per hectare maize yields in Indonesia remained very low. It was only 1.09 metric tons or 77 percent of the all-Asia average, see R. Hefner, 1990: 83; L. A. Mears and Sidik Moeljono, "Food Policy", 1981: 53. For the stagnation of cassava production in this period, see Frederick C. Roche, 1984, 26: 1-6.

[104] Some 600 hectares of these were ravaged by pests, leaving only 70 hectares to be harvested.

increase in land cultivated for this crop. The fluctuations of the annual maize production of Tuntang seem to have followed a similar pattern.

Coffee production in Tuntang today does not reflect its historical role in the region. During the Cultivation System, Tuntang was considered as a 'profitable coffee district' (Suryo, 1982: 43). During the second half of the sixties there were 5.1 hectares of land cultivated for coffee. The productivity was low, the annual per hectare yield was between 246-259 kilograms of dried beans. The coffee was traditionally cultivated, usually requiring no pruning and less fertilisers, thus little capital or labour was necessary (Hefner, 1990: 93).[105] In spite of the fluctuation of coffee price in the seventies and eighties (Godoy and Bennett, 1987: 22), coffee production in Tuntang rose steadily. Encouraged by the easy access to fertilisers in the mid-eighties the average per hectare yields grew to 480.6 kilograms. Coincidentally, between 1982-1984, the land cultivated for coffee increased to 15.8 hectares. The recovery of the coffee prices by the middle nineties has further encouraged the increase in land cultivated for coffee.[106] By 1993 there were 26.0 hectares, and 40.45 hectares by 1995.

11. Market and Trading

One of the main factors which impeded economic development of Tuntang was the absence of a central market town in the sub-district. There are four rather small village markets, located in Candirejo, Kesongo, Tuntang and Gedangan villages which mainly served their local surroundings. As in much of Java, economic transactions are not limited to official markets. Smaller scale transactions are found in the 65 *toko* (shops), 119 kiosks and 213 *warung* (prepared-food shops) scattered in 16 villages. Fish-trading takes place on several traditional wharves along the eastern coast of Rawa Pening. However, the most important trading places for the population of Tuntang are the *pasar kabupaten* (district market places) of Ambarawa and Salatiga, which are eight and seven kilometres away.

As in other traditional small village markets of rural Java , the traders of Kesongo market simply set their commodities out along both sides of the village road. In a larger village market of Candirejo there were also a few "loses" (sheds without interior walls) and a number of kiosks. Of the four village markets in Tuntang sub-district, the one in Candirejo is the busiest. Presumably, this is primarily due to the good transport links connecting the village market with Salatiga. The *honda mini* (smaller pick-up) runs from Salatiga to Candirejo (and return) almost every ten minutes. The road

[105] See also Hans Ruthenberg, *Farming System in the Tropics*, 1980: 298.

[106] The price per kilograms coffee was US$ 0.81 in 1992. It grew to US$ 1.15 in 1993 and US$ 2.93 in December 1994, see The Annual Statistics of Semarang District, 1994: 218.

improvements in the late seventies and the addition of market facilities in the mid-eighties have been major contributors to the development of the transport networks in this village.

The importance of markets and market places for rural economy in Java has been extensively discussed by Jennifer Alexander in her book, ***Trade, Traders and Trading in Rural Java*** (1987). She observed that, for the Javanese, trading is a legitimate means of livelihood, and by no means a despised activity (Dewey, 1962: 75; Alexander, 1987: 31).[107] This is especially true for rural women in village markets (Stoler, 1977b). The village markets in Tuntang sub-district open a few hours in the mornings. There are no fixed times either to open or to close transactions. The peak periods are normally between 6.30 am to 9.00 am. While the size of each village market varies, the number of traders would be around 70 to 200 in a normal day.[108] Apart from a couple of small-scale wholesalers from Tuntang, Salatiga and Ambarawa, there were also some middlemen within the village.[109] The majority of traders, however, were rural women from within the village and its neighbouring hamlets.[110] Most of these rural women are not full-time specialist traders (Dewey, 1962: 77). They carry small amounts of cash-crops such as a few kilograms of maize or cassava, vegetables (cucumber, chilli) and fruits (banana, jackfruit) grown in their own or their neighbour's yards (*pekarangan* and *kebon*), and even a dozen of eggs. Since most of these women carry their commodities in a *bakul* (bamboo basket carried on a woman's back),[111] the total quantity would not normally exceed 25 kilograms.[112] A large number of these tradeswomen are also customers, they sell and buy among themselves. And for them village markets, especially the

[107] Earlier literature portrayed trading as a despised income activity, especially by the *priyayi*, see, for example, J. H. Boeke, *Economic and Economic Policy of Dual Societies as Exemplified by Indonesia*, 1953: 24-25; and G. N. Chandler, *Periodicity, Mobility and the Distribution of Consumer Durables: A Study of Village Market Trade in D. I. Yogyakarta, Indonesia*, 1982.

[108] The figure is considered lower than the estimated traders in the village market of Krakal in Kebumen District (200-400 traders), see J. Alexander, 1987: 39; other regions of Java, however, gave rather similar estimations, see Alice G. Dewey, *Peasant Marketing in Java*, 1962: 75; and A. G. Anderson, "The Rural Market in West Java." *Economic Development and Cultural Change* 28 (1980): 767.

[109] For the description of different types of traders in rural Java, see A. G. Dewey, 1962: 76-77; and J. Alexander, 1987: 55-60.

[110] J. Alexander found that 40 percent of the women in her sample were traders (1987: 30).

[111] In the early usage of the term, the tradeswomen were often referred to as *bakul*. Later, a middleman (Dewey, 1962: 76); and a wholesaler (Alexander, 1987: 59) were also referred as *bakul*.

[112] In most cases larger quantities will be sold in the market town of Ambarawa or Salatiga. In such cases, most often the crops have been sold to a *penebas* (wholesaler) before even ripe. The *penebas* was the one who harvests the crops and brought them to the market town or to a larger (town) wholesalers.

traditional ones, mean more than just economic transactions, in a way they provide social interactions among rural women across neighbouring hamlets.

12. Participation in Development

One way in which participation in development has been measured in Indonesia was by the amount of money the local people are willing to sacrifice for the advancement of development projects in their areas. These *swadaya* resources ('voluntary' contributions from the people in terms of man power, food, money and other items)[113]were calculated into monetary value, and then were compared to the amount of the central government's subsidies. So, when it appears in the sub-district annual statistics that, in 1995 Tuntang sub-district received 68 million rupiah (US$ 30,225) of central government subsidies, while the *swadaya* resources calculated were equal to 96 millions rupiah (US$ 42,670), the implication was clear; the population of Tuntang was considered, as actively participating in the development process in their areas.[114]

Although such a procedure could be a useful indicator for measuring the *camat*'s (sub-district head's) success in mobilising people to become involved in development projects, it has very little significance in measuring people's participation in development. First of all, the way in which these *swadaya* resources was calculated is ambiguous. Second, the way in which participation was defined is obscure and partial. The third and the most important factor for measuring participation, namely the motives and processes of participation were left undescribed.

Mubyarto and Loekman Soetrisno suggested that the central government's funding and subsidies to the lower level autonomous administrations have been counter-productive (1985: 57). They attributed the failure of the government in promoting self-reliant development to the top-down development policy,

> The impact of the development from above can be felt in the villages, at the regency as well as provincial levels. One result is that the region expects a continually growing allocation from the central government every year. A self-reliant development style which the government aims to promote is not only watered down but also stifled (1985: 57).

While the development process in Tuntang seems to display a similar tendency, it is difficult to adequately measure people's participation at sub-district level. The difficulties of using village or sub-district levels as a basic unit for implementing the development programmes and measuring development success have been thoroughly discussed in the beginning of this chapter. This

---

[113] The term was used to describe the "*pemasukan/sumbangan dari penduduk yang berbentuk barang dan tenaga, dinilai dengan uang*" (local resources in the forms of items or man power, calculated in monetary value).

[114]See *Daftar Isian Monografy* of Tuntang Sub-district, 1995: 21.

study is therefore suggesting that the hamlet be used as the basic unit for measuring people's participation. Although no thorough analysis of people's participation at sub-district level was undertaken, the field observation in Tuntang sub-district suggests a rather low people's participation in development.

13. Summary

Based on historical evidence and present observations, this chapter began by suggesting the hamlet be the basic unit for the implementation of development programmes. The unresolved problem of the government in choosing the third level local administrative unit has produced inefficient, unnecessary bureaucracy and eventually impedes two-way communication between the rural people and the central government. The following chapters will focus on the three hamlets of Lopait as the basic unit for the implementation of development programmes, as well as for the measurement of development success.

There is evidence of considerable economic growth in Tuntang sub-district. The regional per capita GNP grew from US$ 81 in 1984 to US$ 228 in 1990 and further increased to US$ 297 in 1993.[115] The improvement of road networks and the government policy on Rawa Pening and on the plantation estate in the seventies and eighties have significantly contributed to the major employment change. Reportedly a large number of people moved into non-farm employment either as their main occupation or as additional income activities. Temporary urban migration and commuting for urban employment have been among the most significant activities for economic development of poor rural households. At the same time the development process in Tuntang has pointed toward a better distribution of landholdings.

The dominating factors for economic development of Tuntang in the past two decades have been either policies from above (both development and pressures) or resources from outside (Ambarawa and Salatiga market places). While it is true that a large number of the population have benefited economically from these policies, there is little evidence that rural people have been empowered to engage in self-reliant development of their areas. In fact, as we shall see in the next chapter, top-down government policy and subsidies have stifled the initiative of the rural people.

---

[115] The Annual Statistics of Semarang District, 1994: 257.

Map 3 Tuntang Sub-District

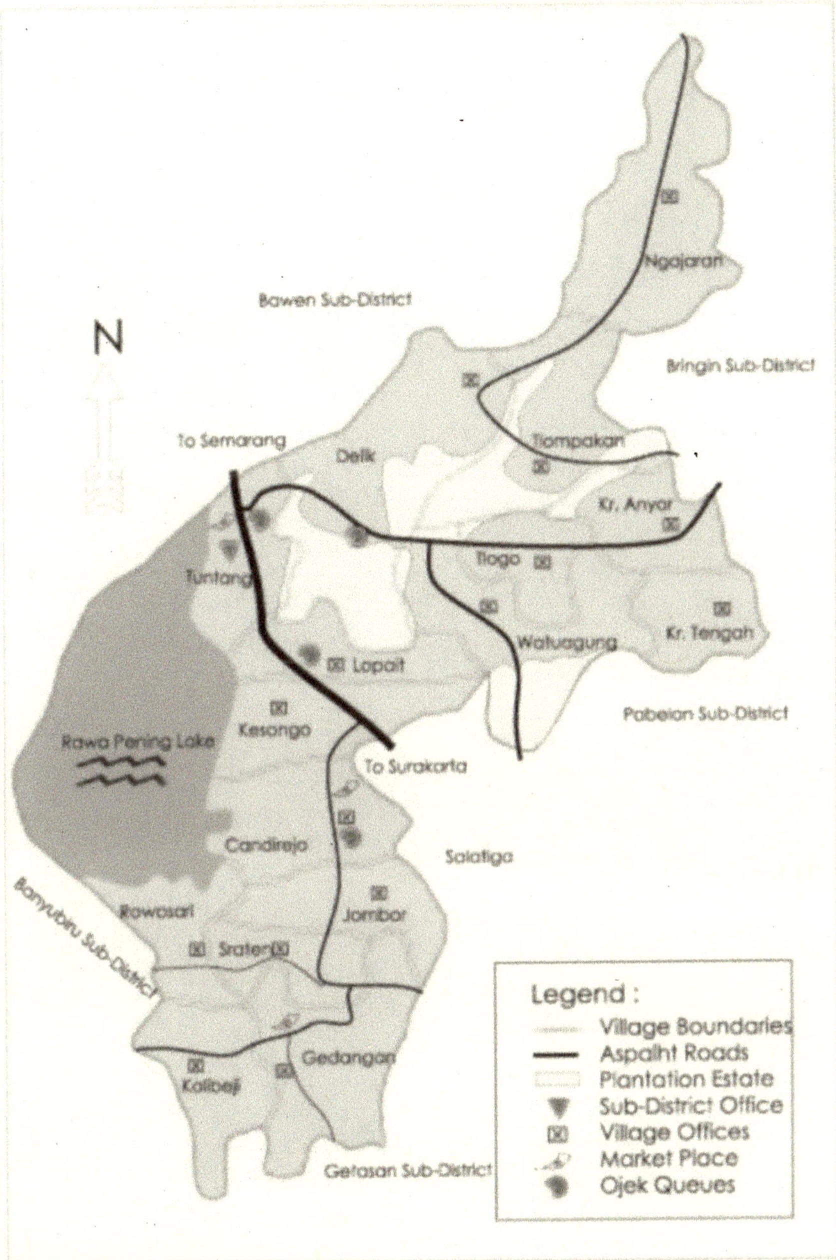

Chapter 3

The Socio-Economic Setting of the Three Hamlets of Lopait

1. The Village of Lopait

Lopait village is located two kilometres south from the sub-district town of Tuntang. It covers an area of 373.9 hectares, of which 70.9 hectares are wet-rice fields, 224 hectares are dry farm fields, 100 hectares are *rawa* (lake), and the rest are settlements, fish ponds, and public infrastructures. These lands are distributed into four 'traditional' grouping of hamlets, namely Gudang, Celengan, Calombo, and Lopait.[1] These groupings represent different ecological settings, and to some extent, diverse historical backgrounds (see Map 4).

2. Historical Backgrounds

2.1. Lopait in the Nineteenth Century

Among the sixteen villages in Tuntang sub-district, only three are located along the Semarang-Surakarta provincial road, Lopait is one of them. The other two are the village of Tuntang, where the sub-district administration is located, and the village of Kesongo, where one of the major village market places is located. They are on the southern and northern borders of Lopait respectively. At a local level, therefore, the population of Lopait would go to their northern village neighbour of Tuntang for governmental-administrative needs, and to their southern neighbour Kesongo for purposes of trade. Among these three villages Lopait seems to be the most recently established.

Unlike Tuntang and Kesongo villages which had originally developed along the 'great-through road' which connected Mataram to the coastal town of

---

[1] As has been stated in the Introduction, Lopait hamlet is excluded from the present research, primarily because Gudang hamlet and Lopait hamlet have very similar social settings (belief system, livelihood, local political structure, and sub-cultural orientations), making it possible to eliminate one of the two. Moreover, Prior to the Dutch Colonial policy on the unification and bifurcation of villages in Java and Madura in the 1920s, the traditional village (*dhusun*) of Lopait covered the area of the present Gudang and Lopait hamlets, thus, they are also having similar historical background. See also, Bijblad No. 9308. "Regelen Omtrent de Vereniging en Splitsing van Desa's op Java en Madura met unitzondering van de Vorstenlanden." Gouvernementsbesluit No. 13, 28 October 1919; and S. Kartohadikoesoemo, *Desa*, 1965: 68.

Semarang (Van Goens, 1856),[2] Lopait seems to have been largely developed around the N. V. Cultuur Maatschappij Tlogo (Tlogo Plantation Estate).[3] In the 1890s the majority of the population of Lopait resided on the border of this 'coffee' plantation estate. The settlement along the 'Mataram (Surakarta)-Semarang' road was comparatively small. The population of Lopait who lived along this road was probably much less before the nineteenth century. This probably explains why Van Goens (1856), while mentioning Tuntang and Kesongo villages, says nothing of Lopait in his report. However, the existence of the well laid-out wet-rice fields along the 'Mataram-Semarang' road in the nineteenth century suggests that the first inhabitants of Lopait also resided along this 'great-through road'.

A missive of the Resident of Semarang to the Governor-General of the Netherlands-Indies in 1878 mentioned a rich farmer in the village of Lopait by the name of Katam. It was reported that on 15 October 1877 his house was attacked by a *kecu* (robber) band numbering some twelve armed men. The investigation shows that the robbers were from the surrounding villages of Rawadanis, Karang Kulon, and Rawa Kancing.[4] The large agricultural lands owned by his descendants as well as the leadership roles they have played for the past century[5] suggests that Katam belonged to the *golongan cikal-bakal* (founding fathers and their descendants) of Lopait village,[6] and, most probably

---

[2] As has been mentioned in Chapter Four, in his journey from Batavia to Mataram in 1648, Van Goens described this road as the "*meest bewandelt ende ordinair bereijst werd*" (the most travelled and commonly used) (1856: 348). For the increased significance of this road in the 18th. and 19th centuries, see M. Soemarsaid, *State and State-Craft in Old Java: A Study of the Later Mataram Period, 16th. to 19th. Century*, 1968: 120-121; and M. C. Ricklefs, *Jogjakarta Under Sultan Mangkubumi 1749-1792: A History of the Division of Java*, 1974: 357. In modern Indonesia this road has become one of the busiest provincial roads in Java.

[3] As has been mentioned in Chapter Four, this coffee plantation estate was laid out in 1809, see "Perusda Perkebunan Tlogo Tuntang Salatiga", 1992; and *Handboek voor Cultuur en Handelsonderneming in Nederlandsch-Indie*, 1888: 43-90.

[4] See the missive of the Resident of Semarang to the Governor-General of the Netherlands-Indie, 2 March 1878, in "Algemeen Verslag der Residentie Semarang over het Jaar 1878" (Arsip Nasional Republik Indonesia).

[5] His son, Atmoredjo was *lurah* (village head) of Lopait until 1925. His office was continued by his son (i.e. Katam's grandson), Sastroprayitno or Kuslan (1925-1941). After a short interval, one of his great-grandsons, Samsukin, became *lurah* between 1947-1965. His other great-grandson is the present *lurah*, Rosjidi (1989-1997). At least two of his descendants also held the office of *kamituwa* (vice-*lurah*). Most of these people and a number of their relatives have been large farmers. For some of the roles and privileges of the *golongan cikal-bakal* (the descendants of founding fathers), see Ina Slamet, *Pokok-Pokok Pembangunan Masyarakat Desa*, 1965: 71; N. G. Schulte Nordholt, *Ojo Dumeh, Kepemimpinan Lokal dalam Pembangunan*, 1987b: 212; and Robert R. Jay, *Javanese Villagers*, 1969: 291.

[6] According to the older respondents the first settler, or founding father, of Lopait was *mbah* Mertotolo. He was, according to tradition, a fugitive from the Dutch colonial

as village sources have suggested, was himself a descendant of a member of the Yogyakarta ruling house who married a resident of Lopait, and consequently moved to Lopait in the early formation of the village administration.[7]

It appears that clusters of settlements in Lopait had existed before the nineteenth century. However, the establishment of the village administration seems to have taken place either at the end of the Java War (1825-1830) or shortly after, when the *mancanagara* was annexed by the Dutch (cf., Schulte Nordholt, 1987b: 253). As has been discussed in Chapter One, during the heyday of the Cultivation System (1837-1845), the population of Salatiga district grew by more than three percent annually (see Table 2.1). Not surprisingly these newcomers, who had come for employment at the Tlogo coffee plantation chose to reside around the estate. As employment at the estate provided the main resource for the surrounding population, the surrounding settlements gained increasing socio-economic importance. Thus, even though the first settlers of Lopait have resided along the 'Mataram-Semarang' road, at the present Gudang hamlet, in the 1830s the socio-political (village administration) centre of Lopait shifted toward the 'interior' settlements around the plantation estate. Later, Dutch Colonial policy on the unification and bifurcation of villages in Java and Madura in the 1920s established this 'interior' settlements into a separate hamlet, which has since become the present Lopait hamlet.[8] The village administration remained here until 1941, when Kasbin, a resident of Gudang was elected to become *lurah*.

---

state. He and his brother, Sukmotolo resided in Kresekan, Gudang. A large number of his descendants had married into the family of *mbah* Katam, who moved to Lopait slightly later. Unlike *mbah* Katam, Mertotolo's descendants have mostly resided outside Lopait. The present *carik* (village secretary) and *kaurbang* (*Kepala urusan pembangunan*, village staff in charge of development) of Lopait are descendants of *mbah* Mertotolo. The tomb of *mbah* Mertotolo is situated between the Lopait and Gudang hamlets. As in much of rural Java, the tomb of the founding father is considered to be a sacred place, and is located near the principal spring water. In order to win the people's heart, following his election as *lurah*, Harjadi (Lopait's village-head, 1981-1989) constructed a neat cement tomb on what was previously a simple rural soil (earth) grave.

[7] According to some respondents he was the son of Dipoyono (Bendara Pangeran Harya Dipowiyono), who was the grandson of Sultan Hamengku Buwana I of the Sultanate of Yogyakarta (reign: 1755-1792), see K. P. H. Mandoyokusumo, *Serat Raja Putra Ngayogyakarta Hadiningrat*, 1988: 16. According to tradition, during the Java War (1825-1830), Dipojono or Honggogali and his brother Honggodrono fled from the court of Yogyakarta and resided in the village of Ndoplang, Ambarawa. Honggodrono had no children. In the mid-nineteenth century, one of Dipojono's son, Dipodrono (*mbah* Katam) married a resident of Lopait.

[8] See Bijblad No. 9308. "Regelen Omtrent de Vereniging en Splitsing van Desa's op Java en Madura met unitzondering van de Vorstenlanden." Gouvernementsbesluit No. 13, 28 October 1919.

2.2. Calombo Hamlet

Calombo and Celengan hamlets have come from different traditions. Calombo (Tjilamba or Tjlombo) hamlet did not develop along the 'Mataram-Semarang great-through road'. Instead, tradition has it that it grew out of local fishing communities. In the nineteenth century, when the settlements in Lopait developed mainly at the western border of the Tlogo coffee plantation estate, Calombo had merged into the socio-economic amalgamation of the villages around Rawa Pening.[9] The existence of Rawa Pening lake as a common resource had driven the population of villages around the lake into a rather exclusive rural social setting, and this strong social tie seems to have existed for a long time.[10]

In general, these small villages were not made up of exclusive bodies of close kin, but individual immigrants from different localities (Lovely, 1929: 11, 75). It seems that seeking a livelihood in the lake and intermarriage with earlier settlers have been the major reasons for Calombo and its sister villages' population growth. As a result, unlike Lopait, there is no group of *cikal-bakal* (descendants of the founding fathers) in Calombo.

2.3. Celengan Hamlet

Celengan hamlet, on the other hand, mostly developed during the heyday of the Cultivation System (1830-1870). Unlike Lopait hamlet which was part of the expansion of the early settlements of Gudang (along the Mataram-Semarang road) toward the western border of Tlogo coffee plantation, the population of Celengan was developed from the population over-spill of Watuagung village on the south-eastern border of the estate (see Map 4).

Watuagung and other 'interior' villages of Tuntang were considered as more '*asli*' (original),[11] which probably means that these villages, because of their location far from the main roads, have had fewer immigrants moving in (see Map 3). Most of these villages were formed because of the fertility of the surrounding fields (cf., Schulte Nordholt, 1987b: 253).[12] 80 percent of all the well irrigated *sawah* (wet-rice fields), or 65 percent of the total of the irrigated *sawah* and 100 percent of the plantation estate of Tuntang sub-district, were located in these villages. In the mid-nineteenth century, as large numbers of workers were required in the coffee plantation, populations of these villages,

[9] See D'Eden Lovely, *Itoe Bidadari dari Rawa Pening*, 1929: 17, 56-57.

[10] D'Eden Lovely related a conversation which implicitly indicates that those who did not earn their living in Rawa Pening lake were considered foreigners (1929: 11-13).

[11] These villages are located at least one kilometre east of the provincial road, which includes Ngajaran, Tomplakan, Karanganyar, Karang-Tengah, Delik, Tlogo and Watuagung.

[12] In his research Schulte Nordholt found that within this kind of village the number of landless farm labourers were comparatively small (1987b: 253).

were attracted to villages closer to the estate. As most of the early population of Celengan hamlet were employed by the Tlogo plantation estate, private land ownership was limited. This scarcity of land has been felt more acutely since 1967, when the government took over the lands belonging to the plantation estate which had previously been cultivated by the people.

The implementation of the *gouvernementsbesluit* (government's decree) No. 13, 28 October 1919[13] concerning the unification and the division of village administration in Java and Madura has brought Celengan, Calombo and Lopait (including Gudang) traditional villages (*dhusun*) into one village administrative unit.[14] As Laceulle (1929) rightly observed, this village unification policy largely failed to create a new identity for the population. While, some traditional villages eventually detached themselves and returned to their former village units, many others, which remained in the new administrative units, succeeded in maintaining their former identity.[15] The improved road network between Celengan and Gudang hamlets in recent years has brought the former into a closer socio-economic link with Gudang and Lopait hamlets. However, it has not succeeded in creating a new identity for the people. Social identification remains with the populations' respective hamlets. Thus, people are identified by '*wong* (people of) *Celengan*', '*wong Calombo*', and '*wong Gudang*'.[16]

3. Village Administration and Local Politics

According to the *Regeeringslement* (legislation) of 1855 concerning village administration, village heads were to be directly elected by the adult male population of the respective villages (Kartohadikoesoemo, 1965: 243).[17] Traditionally the village head was appointed (through a consensus) by the *golongan cikal-bakal* based on a hereditary system (Schulte Nordholt, 1987b:

---

[13] See Bijblad No. 9308, "Regelen Omtrent de Vereniging en Splitsing van Desa's op Java en Madura met Unitzondering van de Vorstenlanden".

[14] Under this policy, between 1918-1927 there were 4515 cases of 'unification' of traditional (smaller) villages into a single administrative unit. Resident Laceulle reported, however, that after the pressure from the government had eased a number of these traditional villages separated themselves from the new village administration and returned to their former village units; see S. Kartohadikoesoemo, 1965: 96, 102; and M. C. Ricklefs, *A History of Modern Indonesia*, 1981: 148.

[15] See S. Kartohadikoesoemo, 1965: 95-102; and especially J. J. Schrieke's comments on this policy in, *De Lagere Inlandsche Rechtsgemeenschappen in Indonesie*, 1921.

[16] In a recent village study in Central Java, Schulte Nordholt (1987b) discovered that 90 percent of the male population claim to have a close family relationship with the hamlet leaders as compared to only 57 percent who claim to have close contact with the *pamong desa* (village administrators); see also Robert R. Jay, 1969: 290.

[17] For an extensive discussion on the development of colonial policies on village administration, especially on the election of village head in rural Java, see S. Kartohadikoesoemo, 1965: 236-254.

211; Kartohadikoesoemo, 1965: 195).[18] In a number of villages the policy was only partially adopted. The people would elect through a referendum, a candidate who had been prepared by the former village head (Schulte Nordholt, 1987b: 239). In most of these cases the candidate was either the son or close relative of the former village head who had been *magang* (to work voluntarily for the purpose of learning) in a village administration.[19] However, in general, the implementation of this system of free election of the village head did not take place until the mid-twentieth century (Slamet, 1965: 71; Schulte Nordholt, 1987b: 213, 239). Even when free elections did take place later, a hereditary system of election of *lurah* remained a dominant aspect in many parts of Java.[20]

3.1. Village Administration

Since the establishment of the village administration in Lopait, the post of *lurah* (village head) has always been held by residents of either Lopait or Gudang hamlets (the original Lopait village). More specifically, six out of seven *lurah* of Lopait in the last hundreds year have come from only one *cikal-bakal* family, namely the root family of Atmorejo (the son of *mbah* Katam) who was *lurah* of Lopait until 1925.[21] The free election system was introduced in 1941, following the death of *lurah* Sastroprayitno. As a result, Karsopuspito, a resident of Gudang and a close relative of the former *lurah* was elected.[22] In those days, as in many parts of Java, the village office was located at the *lurah*'s house (Schulte Nordholt, 1987b: 259), so the appointment of Karsopuspito as *lurah* implied a shift in the location of the village administrative centre from Lopait to Gudang. There were probably other reasons which encouraged this shift, such as the decline of the economic role of the Tlogo coffee plantation (as a result of the great depression of the 1930), and

---

[18] In pre-colonial times, the descendants of the founding fathers which formed the core-group of a village were known under many different names, such as *wong baku, kuli kenceng, wong ajek, gogol-kenceng.* There are two other groups of inhabitants, namely the *kuli setengah kenceng*, were immigrants who did not own cultivated land; and the *pemondok*, who neither owned cultivated land nor a separate house of their own, see S. Kartohadikoesoemo, 1965: 195-196; and I. Slamet, 1965: 46.

[19] Other village studies have however, suggested that the implementation of the policy across Java was varied, see S. Kartohadikoesoemo, 1965; R. R. Jay, 1969; I. Slamet, 1965; N. G. Schulte Nordholdt, 1987b.

[20] The eight new *lurah* of what Schulte Nordholt called 'Gunungsari' sub-district elected in 1975 and twelve out of the twenty *lurah* of what he calls 'Pasisir' sub-district were descendants of the earlier *lurah* (1987b: 219, 257).

[21] This is by no means exceptional, such phenomena occurred elsewhere in Java, see for example, P. Dirdjosanjoto, *Memelihara Umat*, 1994: 182; and S. Tjondronegoro, *Social Organization and Planned Development in Rural Java*, 1984: 167.

[22] Karsopuspito's daughter married Samsukin, who was the nephew of the deceased *lurah*, and thus, the grandson of Atmoredjo. Later, Samsukin replaced his father-in-law (1948-1965).

the development of Gudang hamlet as a pooling station for agricultural products of the surrounding villages before they were sent to Magelang and Ambarawa.[23]

Karsopuspito's term did not last very long. He was considered an ally of the Dutch, and as a result, was assassinated in 1948 by Indonesian freedom fighters.[24] His son-in-law, Samsukin was then elected as *lurah* until his death in 1965.[25] Samsukin was succeeded by his brother-in-law (the son of Karsopuspito), Ismin. A major change in village administration all over central Java took place in 1975, when the *Perda* (*Peraturan Daerah*, Provincial Decree), No. 1, 1973 was implemented. Accordingly a candidate for *lurah* should be under 45 years of age[26] and has completed junior high school education. The term was limited to eight years, with a possibility of serving a maximum of two terms. As in many other villages, the *lurah* of Lopait was affected by the *Perda.*

In 1975, when *lurah* Ismin was dismissed on charges of tax fraud, it seemed that no representative of the *cikal-bakal* family was prepared to meet the new requirements to run for *lurah* in Lopait. Nor was any other resident prepared to challenge the *cikal-bakal* family. As a result, between 1975-1980 there was no *lurah* in Lopait. Timin, the (hamlet head) of Celengan, was given the responsibility to run the village administration as an 'acting' *lurah.*

Although, throughout the history of the Lopait village administration, *golongan cikal-bakal* played a dominant role, this does not mean that other groups in the village were passive subjects and had no power to influence the election of *lurah.* As in many parts of Java, the success of a *kyai* (Muslim religious teacher) in bringing large numbers of nominal Muslims to become true adherents earns him significant socio-political influence,[27] as was true for

[23] The name of 'Gudang' (warehouse), presumably emerged in the early twentieth century as the Dutch built several warehouses to pool the agricultural products of the surrounding villages. According to elderly respondents the warehouses were located at the present primary school and were administered by two Dutchmen, known to local people as Prom and Hegh. Reportedly there were two other Dutch families in Gudang, namely De Bus and Premis who owned a dairy farm.

[24] Apparently this incident of a *lurah* being kidnapped and murdered was quite common in those days, see N. G. Schulte Nordholt, 1987b: 239, 255.

[25] In 1819 the colonial government tried to limit the term for *lurah,* but it was totally ignored (Kartohadikoesoemo, 1965: 241). In practice *lurah* remained a life-time job until the implementation of *Perda* (*Peraturan daerah,* Regional Decrees), No. 1, 1973 and the *UU* (legislation) No. 5, 1979, concerning village administration.

[26] *UU*, No. 5, 1979 revised the age limitation to 60.

[27] *Kyai* is a respected title normally given to a teacher of Islamic faith, in most cases they run a *pesantren* (traditional Islamic school). In his recently published Ph.D. Thesis entitled *Memelihara Umat* (1994), P. Dirjosanjoto distinguished *kyai pesantren* and *kyai langgar* (a less respected status). For the role of *kyai* in the colonial times, see Harry J. Benda, *The Crescent and the Rising Sun,* 1958: 54-55; and S. Kartodirdjo, *Protest Movements in Rural Java,* 1973: 7. For the roles of *kyai* in post-independence

kyai Fatekurohman of Calombo hamlet.[28] Reportedly since the early eighties, candidates for *lurah* always came to him for a blessing. According to the respondents in Calombo hamlet, in the last two elections, the candidates which had had the blessing from the *kyai* were finally elected as *lurah*. The socio-political influence of the *kyai* on his adherents, both in Calombo and Gudang hamlets has increased significantly during the seventies and eighties. Since all the candidates of the village head in 1979 and 1988 elections came to him for a blessing, the *kyai* did not need to campaign for his candidate (even if he had favoured any). It sufficed for him to signify to his adherents the candidate of his choice. In doing so, the *kyai* would not openly mention any name but for a few weeks prior to the elections his adherents would normally be able to read the signs expressed by the *kyai* through his sermons delivered at the Friday prayers.

In the 1988 village head election, for example, there were two candidates, Rosjidi and the wife of Harjadi (the former village head). The *kyai* did not campaign for Rosjidi nor attack the other candidate, he simply reminded his adherents that Islam only recognises a male *imam*/leader. The *kyai* did not even directly relate this religious conviction concerning leadership with the coming election, thus avoiding any public attack on the female candidate. It sufficed for him to repeatedly remind his adherents of Islam's teaching on *imam*/leadership in his sermons. This sign was well understood by his adherents. At the same time, he did not set himself in opposition to the supporters of Mrs. Harjadi. As had been predicted, Rojsidi won the election by a large margin. This result further established the role of *kyai* in the socio-political life of Lopait.

The third and the most powerful influence on Lopait's socio-political life are supra-village interests. After some four years with no village head (1975-1979), an election was finally set for 1979. Among the five candidates Harjadi was the youngest (in his late twenties). Without firm support from the supra-village (sub-district) authorities, he probably would not have entered into this competition in the first place. Harjadi had a long list of disadvantages apart from his age and experience. He had just moved to Lopait in 1974 (five years

---

Indonesia, see C. Geertz, "The Javanese Kijaji: The Changing Role of a Cultural Broker." *Comparative Studies in Society and History* 2 (1960): 200-249. For the roles of *kyai* in social change, see Hiroko Horikoshi, *Kyai dan Perubahan Sosial*, 1987: 211-236, and for their roles on preserving the *pesantren* tradition, see Z. Dhofier, *Tradisi Pesantren*, 1982.

[28] *Kyai* Fatekurohman is a native of Gading hamlet in the village of Tuntang. Intensive religious teaching in Calombo in the late 1940s and '50s was started by his father (the *kyai* of Gading) when the future *kyai* Fatekurohman was still very young. In later years Fatekurohman married a resident of Calombo, accordingly he moved to Calombo hamlet. He was very successful not only in erecting the mosque and the *pondok pesantren*, but also in attracting people from surrounding villages to attend his lectures, his preaching and the *pengajian* (recitation of the Qur'an and study sessions).

prior to the election),[29] which implied he was less knowledgeable of the local situations and less rooted socio-culturally. Moreover, Harjadi was Roman Catholic and did not belong to the *cikal-bakal* families of Lopait. In a normal situation it would be anomalous for a predominantly Muslim village to be headed by a non-Muslim *lurah*.

The government's support for Harjadi was very much in line with the concern of the New Order administration in general, which was to create stable village administrations supportive of the government's development policy.[30] As in many other parts of rural Java, political life in Lopait prior to 1965 was subject to division. Calombo hamlet contained predominantly NU (*Nahdlatul Ulama*, the East Java-based conservative Muslim party) supporters.[31] The PKI (Communist Party of Indonesia) gained much support from the population of Celengan hamlet, and a significant number of PNI (nationalist party) supporters were in Gudang hamlet. Within such a context, Harjadi was regarded as a better choice by the government. He had not been allied to any of the earlier conflicting groups, nor was he traditionally rooted in the community. He was expected to draw his support from and thus be dependant on the supra-village structures.

Although the *golongan cikal-bakal*, the *kyai* and the *camat* (sub-district head) were major players in *lurah* elections, it cannot be suggested that the rest of population of Lopait were just passive actors. There were other social or socio-religious groups in the village which had not been accommodated by the *kyai* and by the *golongan cikal-bakal*, forming the majority of the population in Celengan hamlet. It should be noted that the total number of households in Celengan hamlet were equal to the total number of households in Gudang plus Calombo hamlets, every candidate for village head realised, therefore, the importance of support from the population of Celengan.

As stated already, the socio-cultural and socio-religious orientation of the population of Celengan was more toward the village of Watuagung. Unlike the villages of Tuntang, which are located around Rawa Pening lake, where the Muslim orthodoxy is very dominant, Watuagung and its neighbouring villages in the eastern half of Tuntang sub-district were not dominated by the orthodox

---

[29] His mother resided in Lopait since 1950. Harjadi was born in 1951 and was brought up by a relative in Jambu, Ambarawa. Since 1965 he studied in Salatiga and resided there until 1974, when he moved to Lopait.

[30] The 'floating-mass' policy (see the discussion in Chapter Three), the *Perda* (*Peraturan daerah*, Provincial Decree) , No. 1, 1973, and the *UU* (legislation) , No. 5, 1979 are to be seen in this respect, see L. Soetrisno, "Kelembagaan Desa dan Kelembagaan Masyarakat Desa: Prospek pada Program Umum HKTI dan Pencapaian Tujuan-Tujuan HKTI" (Village Organisation and Village Institution: Prospects of the "Indonesian Farmers Association" in Achieving its Goals), a paper prepared for the "Workshop on the Formulation of HKTI's General Programme," 4-6 April, 1989: 3-4.

[31] In the 1955 general election, NU obtained close to a hundred percent of the vote in Calombo hamlet.

Muslims. Instead, the notion of tolerance and harmony of *Kejawen* (Javanese mysticism) was valued. Eleven church buildings, and 3 *vihara* (Buddhist temples) in Tuntang sub-district are all located within these villages, together with 20 mosques. However, religious tension was less apparent in these villages compared to the orthodox Muslim villages around Rawa Pening lake.[32]

For the *Kejawen* people of Celengan, *restu* (blessing) from the ancestors, and from the guardian spirits of the hamlet, is fundamental for their activities. The ceremony of '*bersih makam*' (graveyard cleansing) is conducted twice a year, in the second and eight month of *Sapar* and *Ruwah* of the Javanese calendar. According to respondents in Celengan, most of the past candidates for village head, and especially the present and the previous Lopait *lurah*, had come to the sacred grave (*makam keramat*) in Celengan for a blessing prior to their election. The candidates' motives for these rituals (overnight prayer on the grave) varied. Some really came for a blessing from the guardian spirits, while others simply came in order to identify themselves with the people of Celengan, and obtain their support in the election. Whatever the motives, such a political ritual is, in fact, a common practice in much of rural Java (Schulte Nordholt, 1987b: 216).

Overall, despite the increasing influence of the *kyai* of Calombo, the major key players of Lopait socio-political life remained in the alliance between the traditional elite and the supra-village structures. The experience of Lopait in the New Order administration has thus, confirmed findings elsewhere in rural Java which suggest that *lurah* have been mostly functioning as agents of the supra-village government (Mubyarto and Soetrisno, 1989; Schulte Nordholt, 1987a; Tjondronegoro, 1984).[33]

3.2. Local Politics

The political orientation of Calombo, Gudang and Celengan hamlets was individually distinct. In the 1955 and 1971 general elections, approximately 98 percent of the population in Calombo hamlet voted for the NU.[34] The effective

---

[32] Two Protestant churches were located in Lopait and Tuntang villages which are considered 'middle villages', consisting of mixed hamlets. Some hamlets were oriented toward the villages around the lake and others were oriented toward the *Kejawen* villages in the western half of the sub-district. There was no single church or *vihara* in the seven villages around the Rawa Pening lake.

[33] As has been indicated earlier by Soetrardjo Kartohadikoesoemo, this is not a new phenomenon. The role of *lurah* as an agent of the central government has developed during the colonial period. It was probably initiated by the introduction of 'Revenue Instruction' by Sir Thomas Stamford Raffles in 1814 (1965: 236-254).

[34] Since the official data on the result of 1955 and 1971 general elections in Lopait village has been lost, this research relies on the information given by the older village administrators (*pamong*) and informal leaders such as the *kyai* of Calombo and the retired *kamituwa* of Lopait (in office: 1942-1993).

leadership of the *kyai* has, to a large degree, contributed to the consistent homogeneity of their political orientation. Throughout general elections of the New Order period the population of Calombo has almost unanimously voted for the PPP (*Partai Persatuan Pembangunan*, United Development Party), the only officially sanctioned Muslim Party since the fusion of political parties in 1971. In the 1992 general election, apart from a few village administrators who voted for the Golkar (the government party), the rest of the population voted for PPP.

In the 1955 general election more than 65 percent of the population in Celengan hamlet voted for the PKI (*Partai Komunis Indonesia*, Communist Party of Indonesia). Most of its farmers were members of the BTI (*Barisan Tani Indonesia*, Indonesian Farmers Front, associated to the PKI). Following the aborted 'coup' of the 'Thirtieth September Movement', two of the hamlet leaders were arrested. Then in 1967 the government reclaimed the lands which originally belonged to the plantation estate which had been cultivated by the local people since independence. This has been interpreted by the population of Celengan as a form of punishment by the government for past political orientations. In the general elections which took place in 1971 and 1987, the population of Celengan, mostly voted for Golkar, both out of fear and as a means of survival. In the 1992 general election,[35] however, when a brief period of political 'openness' (*keterbukaan*) allowed the population of Celengan to express their political orientations more freely, the PDI (*Partai Demokrasi Indonesia*, Democratic Party of Indonesia) gained an overwhelming victory. PDI gained 159 votes in 1987 and doubled to 322 in the 1992 general election. On the other hand, Golkar's vote dropped from 305 to 153.

Table 3.1. General Elections in the Three Hamlets of Lopait, 1987-1992

Hamlets	Number of votes cast, 1987			Number of votes cast, 1992		
	PPP	Golkar	PDI	PPP	Golkar	PDI
Calombo	168	47	5	215	35	8
Celengan	31	305	159	57	153	322
Gudang	68	185	36	108	175	59

Source: *Mantri Statistik* (Statistic Officer) at Tuntang sub-district office.

Although most of the population in Celengan hamlet had been members of the BTI, very few understood the communist ideology. As Tjondronegoro has rightly observed, "apart from several strongholds established around towns, political ideologies never became deeply rooted in rural Java" (1984: 32).

[35] Most political observers have so far considered the 1992 general election as the best general election of the New Order era, in terms of the neutrality of the Armed Forces and the 'openness' of the political climate.

Likewise, the exodus of Golkar's voters to PDI in the 1992 general election was not primarily based on ideological considerations. It appears that the people had not fully identified themselves with the ideology and the vision of the PDI. The exodus was primarily meant to express their frustration, caused by the blockage of their socio-political aspirations.

The decline of Golkar's vote in Celengan hamlet offers at least three explanations. First, for years since 1965, the people have been constantly the target of government suspicion on account of their pre-1965 pro-PKI sympathies. Their support for the government party (Golkar) in the general elections throughout the New Order era did not change the government's attitude. Secondly, it was probably caused by the government's policies on the plantation estate which had damaged their livelihood. Thirdly, it was a socio-political reaction against the domination of the Gudang-based *golongan cikal-bakal* over the village administration. Since they constantly held the office of village administrator, these *golongan cikal-bakal* were naturally strong supporters of Golkar.

At the 1955 general election in Gudang hamlet, the PNI (the nationalist party) and the Communist party (PKI) shared some forty percent of the votes. The population of Gudang have been able to identify themselves with the government party (Golkar) far more successfully than those in Celengan. Throughout the general elections of the New Order era Golkar always gained a substantial victory in Gudang hamlet. In the 1992 general election, even when Golkar's village level votes dropped drastically from 59.1 percent in 1987 to 33.4 percent in 1992, support for Golkar in Gudang remained strong. The votes Golkar lost mostly went to the PPP (the Muslim Party), which significantly increased its share from 23 percent in 1987 to 34 percent in 1992. This success of PPP in Gudang has been attributed to the success of the *kyai* and his family in bringing large numbers of nominal Muslims to become 'true' adherents of Islam. Even though no research has been undertaken on this process of '*santrinisasi*' (bringing nominal Muslims to become true adherents of Islam) in post-1965 Java, a number of micro studies indicated that elsewhere in Java, the process of '*santrinisasi*' has accelerated (see, e.g. Dirdjosanjoto, *et al.*, 1978: 175; and Hefner, 1990: 216).

From its inception, Golkar put forward no new party ideology apart from the strong emphasis on 'economic growth' and 'national stability'. As Ken Ward observed, Golkar's strategy to maintain its rural support was mainly, "to restore the villagers to the traditionalist influence of rural and higher officialdom" (1974: 176). This coalition between the central government and the traditional village elite was not only meant to ensure the success of government development programmes (Schulte Nordholt, 1978b:16; Hart, 1986: 41-42), but primarily to protect the New Order regime from the challenge of the ideologies of the right and left.

In the case of Lopait in the seventies and eighties, the supra-village administrations suspected Celengan as a potential breeding ground for left-wing ideology (i.e. communism). Calombo hamlet, in contrast, was considered a potential support base for the extreme right. Golkar had strategically restored the traditional influence of the *golongan cikal-bakal* in Gudang (and Lopait), while ensuring their dependence on the central government. The more intensive contact and exposure of Gudang to the New Order development programmes, such as the *SD Inpres* (Presidential Instruction for the establishment of rural public schools), and the *PKK* (*Pendidikan Kesejahteraan Keluarga*, Family welfare programme), have contributed to the identification of the population of Gudang with the government party.

The two elementary schools in Lopait village are both located in Gudang hamlet. The better access of the population of Gudang to education, as compared to the other hamlets in Lopait, has contributed to the increasing number of Gudang-born people who became candidates for the civil service. The existence of a substantial number of civil servant families in Gudang hamlet, was also an important support for Golkar and the New Order government, especially in regards to the implementation of its development policies. The creation of a new class of '*pegawai*' (civil servant) in Gudang has thus, been an effective way in which Golkar and the New Order government have established a support system in the local population.

The 1992 general election in Lopait revealed that the New Order policies on the '*monoloyalitas*' (single loyalty)[36] and the 'floating mass'[37] have not eroded the cultural-religious cleavage (*aliran*) of the rural Javanese described by Geertz and his MIT team in the 1950s (Geertz, 1959; Jay, 1963). The majority of Calombo hamlet remained supporters of the Muslim Party (PPP) as was the case in 1955. The majority of Celengan supported the PDI (Democratic Party), primarily because they could neither identify themselves with the ruling party nor with the Muslim Party. Moreover PDI described itself as the party of '*wong cilik*' (small people; commoners as opposed to the elite), a notion which the people of Celengan could easily identify with. In Gudang hamlet, the '*monoloyalitas*', and 'floating mass' policies, together with the implementation of development programs such as school buildings and family welfare programmes, made Golkar the best alternative for the former adherents of the PNI (Nationalist party) and for the new class of '*pegawai*' (civil servants).

These socio-political groupings were by no means static. While cultural-religious cleavages had shaped the socio-political groupings in the pre-1965 Lopait (cf., Geertz, 1959), it was the New Order's suspicion toward Celengan and Calombo hamlets as ex-PKI and NU strongholds respectively, which encouraged the realignment of these older socio-political groupings in Lopait. Furthermore, the significant progress of the '*santrinisasi*' (leading a nominal

---

[36] The policy was originally introduced by Interior Minister Amir Mahmud in 1969, according to which all civil servants have to vote for the government party, Golkar.

[37] No party political activity below the *kabupaten* (district) level is permitted except at general elections.

Muslim to become a devout one) in Gudang hamlet, which had widened the influence of the local *kyai* in Calombo, started to form strong local socio-political affiliations which stretched far beyond the hamlet's boundaries.[38]

Regardless of the different factors which have shaped and encouraged it, the socio-political groupings of all three hamlets in Lopait remain very strong. Socio-politically each of the three has maintained its separate identity. This situation was clearly evidenced by the result of the 1992 general election, and suggests that the government imposed village boundaries have failed to integrate or reshape the cultural-religious values of the traditional villages (hamlets) in rural Java.[39]

4. Population and Employment

4.1. Population Change in Lopait Village

According to the analysis of demographic changes, the family planning programme in Lopait village has been exceptionally successful since the early eighties. Between 1982-1988 the total population of Lopait grew by only 0.7 percent annually. This low population growth largely resulted from an intensification of the family planning programme. During the same period the population of the 'under fives' had declined by 5.5 percent annually.[40]

---

[38] At the national level, a devout Muslim (*golongan santri*) does not necessarily vote for PPP (the Muslim party). In orthodox Muslim communities such as Calombo and other *Nadhlatul Ulama* areas in rural Java, the role of the *kyai* in local political issues, such as village head elections or general elections is very recognisable. Throughout the history of New Order general elections, *kyai* have been effective vote-gatherers for all three political parties, especially for Golkar, see "Peran Dai dalam Pemilu." *TIRAS*, 18 April 1996: Appendix A-H.

[39] This local political setting is by no means unique to Lopait, in many parts of rural Java, political affiliations of a hamlet based on cultural-religious cleavages are common. In a micro study of the village of Candirejo, P. Dirdjosanjoto *et al.*, identified a '*santri* hamlet' where the majority of the inhabitants voted for the NU (the orthodox Muslim party) in the 1971 general election, and an '*abangan* hamlet', where most of the inhabitants voted either for the PKI (the Communist Party) or the PNI (the Nationalist Party) in the 1955 general election. This socio-political grouping by hamlet remained a determinant of local political events in the New Order period, such as elections of village head. Unfortunately, these socio-political groupings have formed a basis for differently privileged socio-economic groupings and an uneven distribution of employment opportunities within the village (1978: 138, 173); see also K. Suwondo, "Changes in the Means of Obtaining Income of the Inhabitants Around the Rawa Pening." In F. Goeltenboth, ed., *Proceedings of the First Seminar in Aquatic Biology and Aquatic Management of the Rawa Pening Lake*, 1978: 185.

[40] Between 1982-1988, at the sub-district level, the population growth was higher than Lopait by 0.2 percent annually. The decline of the 'under five' at the sub-district level was 3.7 percent, which was 1.8 percent lower to that of Lopait. The figures show that

Table 3.2. Demographic Structure of Lopait Village, 1982-1988

Year/ Age	1982	1988	Change	Annual Change in %
0-4	508	361	-147	-5.5
5-9	334	346	12	0.6
10-14	324	364	40	2.0
15-24	520	695	175	5.0
25-49	946	882	-64	-1.2
50-59	232	241	9	0.6
> 60	30	130	100	27.7
TOTAL	2894	3019	126	0.7

Sources: Annual Statistics of Tuntang sub-district, 1982 and 1988.

Significantly, for the same period, the population aged between 25 and 49 years also declined by 1.2 percent annually. The sharp decline in this working age group was mostly due to the twin vectors of the transmigration programme and urbanisation. In Celengan hamlet, the substantial exodus was largely attributed to the local economic pressures, caused by the reclaiming of the lands originally belonged to the Tlogo plantation estate, in the early seventies.[41] Moreover, during this period Lopait had much better access to road and transportation networks which linked the rural population to big cities such as Jakarta and Semarang.

Between 1988 and 1994 Lopait underwent rapid infrastructural development. Until the late eighties, cars could only pass through the main roads to Celengan and Calombo hamlets during the dry season. However, by 1991 most of the main village roads had been macadamised (stone-surfaced). The better access to national road and information networks, together with improved educational standard amongst the younger generation, all contributed to the demographic, employment as well as economic changes in Lopait in the nineties.

---

the family planning programme in Lopait was exceptionally successful, compare Tables 1.2 and 2.2.

[41] See the discussion on Chapter Four. The substantial exodus from Lopait for transmigration and urban jobs during this period was not shared by its neighbouring villages. At the sub-district level this working age group of 25-49 grew by 1.7 percent between 1982-1988.

Table 3.3. Demographic Structure of Lopait village, 1988-1993

Year/ Age	1988	1993	Change	Annual Change in %
0-4	361	406	45	2.4
5-9	346	497	151	7.5
10-14	364	452	88	4.4
15-24	695	580	-115	-3.6
25-49	882	992	110	2.4
50-59	241	280	39	3.0
> 60	130	274	144	16.1
TOTAL	3019	3481	462	2.9

Sources: Annual Statistics of Tuntang Sub-district, 1988; *Laporan Monografi Desa Lopait* (village monthly statistics), December 1993

The significant growth of the 'under ten' population indicates that, during the second half of the eighties and early nineties, the family planning programme was not so intensive. However, the bulk of the population growth during this period was principally due to a substantial increase in the numbers of elderly people. The improvement of road networks, better access to health centres, together with the increase of average family incomes, all seemed to have increased life expectancy of the population of Lopait.

It needs to be noted, however, that while all the other age groups have registered significant increases during this period, the younger working group of 15 to 24 year old has declined by 3.6 percent annually. These Statistics support the finding of Kasryno,[42] and indicates significant labour mobility of the younger generation from farm-related employment to urban non-farm employment. The improved access to education seems to have been the major contributor for this younger population of Lopait to seek urban employment.

4.2. Employment in Calombo Hamlet

4.2.1. Fresh-Water Fishing

Calombo is a fishing hamlet, 65 percent of the households earn some of their income from fresh-water fishing.[43] The percentage would be higher if some local women, who engage in local fish-trading, are included. These women act as local brokers. They buy fish direct from the fishermen and sell them to the wholesalers, who then sell them on to consumers in Magelang, Surakarta and Semarang. Unlike most rural Javanese markets, the daily fish transactions in Calombo are carried out at a fixed prices.

---

[42] See Faizal Kasryno, "Structural Changes in Rural Employment and Agricultural Wage in Indonesia." In Yang Boo Choe and Fu Chen Lo, eds., *Rural Industrialization and Non-Farm Activities of Asian Farmers*, 1986.

[43] The total number of fishermen in Calombo was 85 in 1994, or 26 percent of the total work force in the hamlet.

Table 3.4. Changes in Pattern of Employment in Calombo Hamlet, 1980-1994[44]

Employment	1980	1994	Annual Change in %
Owner Farmers/Share-Croppers	11	57	12.5
Landless Farm Labourers	23	11	-5.1
Fishermen	52	85	3.6
Self-Employed/Home Industry	5	62	19.7
Businessmen/women	2	4	5.1
Rural Salaried Employees	3	10	9.0
Urban Employees	1	55	33.1
Traders	15	20	2.1
Unskilled Casual Non-Farm Labourers	2	0	-5.1
Civil Servants/Armed Forces/Retired	3	6	5.1
TOTAL WORK FORCE	117	310	7.2

Source: primary data.[45]

In 1994, there were ten local fish brokers, and six wholesalers from outside the hamlet. Interestingly, there was no competition among the local brokers. Each fisherman has a fixed buyer from among the ten local brokers. A fisherman would neither sell his fish to any other than his own regular buyer nor sell directly to any of the outside wholesalers. Each of these local brokers also has her own buyer among the six outside wholesalers. Only in the rare case of disagreement over price, when for certain reasons the local price went up and the outside buyers dared not take the risk of buying the fish, would the local brokers then sell the fish directly to market places in Kesongo or Salatiga.

Most of these households who were recorded as earning some of their income from fishing in 1994, belong to the rural middle income group.[46] The

---

[44] Women and unmarried children are included only when they earned their own separate income, for further reading on the contribution of children employment for family income in rural Java, see B. White, "The Economic Importance of Children in a Javanese Village." In Moni Nag, ed., *Population and Social Organization*, 1973: 127-146.

[45] Since official statistics at the hamlet level were not available, all the hamlet-level data presented in this thesis are primary data, produced during the field research.

[46] As has been stated already, this present research divides the rural households of Lopait into three socio-economic income groups. The rich (*tiyang gadhah*), the middle (*cekapan*) and the poor (*tiyang mboten gadhah*). This class categorisation of the

income from fishing alone was relatively small;[47] however, as in many other parts of rural Java, a large number of households in Calombo have more than one source of income.[48] The fourteen households categorised as poor in Calombo hamlet were mostly landless farm labourers and fishermen who engaged in single employment. Although the number of fishermen in Calombo increased from 52 in 1980 to 85 in 1994, the overall contribution this made to individual household income has significantly declined. Other sources of employment, especially off-farm activities, have made increasingly important contributions to family income.

4.2.2. Agriculture

Most of the wet rice fields in Calombo were *bengkok* (village lands temporarily given to village administrators as part of their salary) and *bondo desa* (village lands as a source for village incomes). Although no modern technologies, apart from the Green Revolution inputs (seeds and fertilisers) were applied in these fields, agriculture in Calombo seemed to offer a good return. This was apparent in the significant increase of the numbers of owner farmers in Calombo hamlet between 1980 and 1994 (see Table 3.4 above).[49] This increase of owner farmers, which was accompanied by a substantial decline in the number of landless farm labourers (farm wage labourers), is an indication of significant economic growth in Calombo. Obviously during this period, a large number of landless farm labourers and poor fishermen in Calombo have been able to accumulate capital obtained mostly through non-farm jobs. As rice farming was considerably profitable, and ownership of farm lands was still

---

households in each hamlet was primarily developed by the local people and the hamlet leadership themselves. In the latter process of this categorisation, statistical data on the households incomes were taken into account so as to adjust and monetarily quantify this local categorisation. For this socio-anthropological approach to social analysis, see Mubyarto and L. Soetrisno, "Rural Development in Indonesia, Past Experience and Future Policies." In R. P. Misra, ed., *Rural Development, Capitalist and Socialist Paths*, 1985: 5.

[47] In 1994, the average price of fish bought by the local brokers per kilogram was Rp. 1.700 or US$ 0.81. In a normal day a fisherman caught between two and three kilograms of fish; with an average of 22 working days a month the annual income from fishing was US$ 534.60 per household. With an average of five people in a household, the per capita income from fishing alone was US$ 107 annually, far below the poverty line set by the World Bank (1990) of US$ 275.

[48] See A. Stoler, "Some Socio-Economic Aspects of Rice Harvesting in a Javanese Village." *Masyarakat Indonesia* 2 (1975): 55-56; and J. Alexander, *Trade, Traders and Trading in Rural Java*, 1987: 28-29.

[49] The term 'owner farmers' (*tani*) as opposed to landless farm labourers (*buruh tani*), is used to describe farmers who either own their own farm-land or who have control over farm-lands through some tenurial arrangements, or both. Following G. Hart, this definition of land ownership includes *tanah bengkok* (a rice land allocated to village administrators in lieu of payment). See G. Hart, *Power, Labor, and Livelihood: Processes of Change in Rural Java*, 1986: 95-96.

considered a key investment to be passed on to descendants, accumulated capital was usually invested in farms.

Significantly, 32 out of these 57 owner farmers, have control over farm lands through sharecropping. Thus farmland ownership in Calombo remains relatively unequally distributed, with only 25 out of 110 households (22.7 percent) owning land. Compared to other parts of rural Java, where the Green Revolution has seemingly encouraged the concentration of landholdings (White, 1979; Soentoro, 1981; Amaluddin, 1987), one could even speak about a 'sub-division' of landholdings in Calombo in the past decade and a half. Whilst farmers who owned farm lands grew from 11 in 1980 to 25 in 1994, the rich farmers who owned more than a hectare of farm land declined from 5 in 1980 to 2 in 1994. This process was not necessarily a direct result of the Green Revolution inputs (HYV seeds, fertilisers, and pesticides) and technologies, rather it was an outcome of the overall impact of rural development programmes as a whole, which included infra-structure such as roads, transportation networks, and markets (Hefner, 1990: 85).

4.2.3. Non-Farm Employment

The growth of the self- employment (including home industries), and urban employment in Calombo has been very fast over the past 15 years since 1980. Between 1980 and 1994 the number of people involved in self-employed economic activities has grown from five to sixty-two. Most of the self-employed were women, who used their spare time to make *icir* (fish nets). Since the industry was not organised on a professional basis and markets were limited to those fishermen actually resident within Calombo hamlet itself and the villages nearby, the impact of the growth of this rural activity on household incomes was modest.

Similar to the trend of the self-employed activities, the number of people in Calombo hamlet who were involved in off-farm urban employment also grew substantially from one in 1980 to fifty-five in 1994. Significantly, fifty-four percent of them were women, and fifty-seven percent of these were under 25 years old. The educational background of these urban employees was also distinctive. In 1994, a hundred percent of the population of Calombo who completed senior high school education (*SMTA*) and fifty-one percent of those who completed junior high school education (*SMTP*) worked in urban areas (cf., Hugo, 1978: 181). Unlike the self-employed activities, urban employment has made a significant contribution to the overall income of the population in Calombo hamlet.

There is no indication that those who went for urban employment represented a certain class in local society. The improved transport, information and education networks in the past decade have encouraged the younger generation of Calombo of all socio-economic groups and classes, to seek urban employment. Earlier studies have mainly emphasised the lack of employment opportunities in the agriculture and farm-related sectors in rural

Java as the major factors contributing to the search for urban jobs.[50] Although it was true that both agriculture and fresh-water fishing in Calombo could not adequately absorb the additional work force created by the population expansion, most of the urban employees seem to have commute from Calombo hamlet with a motivation either to obtain a better income (cf., Manning, 1988), or to make contribution to the overall household incomes.[51] Moreover, as in many other parts of rural Java, the average income from non-farm rural employment in Calombo is below that of the agricultural labourer.[52] It was higher earnings from urban employment which has eventually enabled the urban employees to make significant contributions to the household's incomes.[53] In 1994, eighty-two percent of the urban employees in Calombo belonged to either the richer or the middle income households.

It appears that real employment mobility in Calombo has mostly occurred among the poorer households, where a population largely regarded as of 'unstable income' such as landless farm labourers and other unskilled casual non-farm labourers, has now found new forms of employment. The additional household income provided by other family members, especially those who worked in urban areas, have enabled the heads of poorer households to engage in more 'stable income employment' (see Table 3.4). The number of people belonging to these two groups, namely the landless farm labourers and the unskilled casual non-farm labourers, have substantially declined from 25 in 1980 to 11 in 1994. Apart from these farm and non-farm wage labourers, most heads of household have tended to remain in their occupations. Among the other poorer and middle income households of Calombo, employment mobility has mostly occurred in terms of additional jobs taken by other family members. The lower earnings from both the farm and off-farm rural employment have

---

[50] See G. Hugo, "Circular Migration." *Bulletin of Indonesian Economic Studies* 13 (1977): 57-66; H. Kano, "The Economic History of Javanese Rural Society: A Reinterpretation." *The Developing Economies* 17 (1980): 3-22; and Gordon P. Temple, "Migration to Jakarta." *Bulletin of Indonesian Economic Studies* 11 (1975): 76-81.

[51] As has been stated above, a large number of the urban employees from Calombo are younger women with either senior or junior high school education. In 1991, an average first year salary, for working as an employee at an industrial company in the district town of Ungaran, was US$ 28 per month. Even though this amount was relatively small by urban standards, these younger women could not have otherwise earned as much, from both farm and non farm employment within Calombo hamlet.

[52] In many parts of Java, the incomes from the rural non-farm employment were much lower than those of the agricultural sectors, see D. Penny and M. Singarimbun, *Population and Poverty in Rural Java: Some Economic Arithmetic from Srihardjo*, 1973; B. White, "Population, Employment and Involution in a Javanese Village." *Development and Change* 7 (1976): 267-290; and Mubyarto, "Strategi Pembangunan Pedesaan." In Mubyarto and S. Kartodirdjo, *Pembangunan Pedesaan di Indonesia*, 1988: 28-29.

[53] See G. Hugo, *Population Mobility in West Java*, 1978; and C. Manning, *The Green Revolution, Employment and Economic Change in Rural Java*, 1988.

been largely compensated by the involvement of additional members of the family in off-farm employment. On the other hand, among the richer households there are indications that fewer family members are now involved in off-farm employment and the generation of additional incomes.

To sum up, the improvements of road, transport and educational networks, have contributed to the integration of Calombo into the developing national economy. This integration has encouraged the younger generation of Calombo travel out of the hamlet to seek urban jobs and to obtain better incomes. Eventually, the higher earnings from urban employment have made a substantial contribution to the household income, across the economic strata. Between 1980 to 1994 the number of poorer households in Calombo hamlet declined from 43.4 percent to 12.7 percent (see Table 3.5).

Table 3.5. Poverty Reduction in Calombo Hamlet, 1980-1994

Economic Status	**1980**		**1994**	
	No of Households	%	No of Households	%
Richer Households	7	8.4	14	12.7
Middle Income Households	40	48.2	82	74.6
Poorer Households	36	43.4	14	12.7
TOTAL	83	100	110	100

Source: primary data.

4.3. Employment in Celengan Hamlet

4.3.1. Agriculture

Celengan hamlet is a typical upland rural Javanese village, where the farmlands are mostly rain-fed fields (Hefner, 1990: 8). Most of the farmers plant cassava in the dry season and maize in the wet season. In terms of the agriculture intensification programme, there was very little Green Revolution input applied in Celengan. With some exceptions, the cassava and maize were mostly local varieties and most farmers used manure only perfunctorily. With the average per hectare yields of 9.9 tons for cassava and 3.1 for maize in Tuntang sub-district in 1994 (see Table 2.9), being calculated at the 1994 price of US$ 28.70/ton for cassava and US$ 139.53/ton for maize, at least 1.9 hectares of rain-fed farm lands would be needed to meet the basic needs for a family of five.[54]

[54] Using the standard of US$ 275 per capita developed by the World Bank in 1990.

As has been stated earlier, since the government reclaimed the lands originally belonged to the Tlogo plantation estate between 1967 and 1973,[55] only a few households in Celengan hamlet owned farm lands. In 1980 only 15.1 percent of the households were owner farmers. Interestingly, despite the relatively small returns from the agricultural sector, the number of the owner farmers grew to 32.6 percent, or 79 farmers, in 1994. Out of these, only six were relatively large farmers owning 1.9 hectares of farm land or more, whereas thirteen farmers owned between 1 to 1.5 hectares and the rest owned less than 0.2 hectares.

Table 3.6. Employment Change in Celengan Hamlet, 1980-1994

Employment	1980	1994	Annual Change in %
Owner Farmers/Share-Croppers	36	79	5.8
Landless Farm Labourers	319	251	-1.7
Self-Employed/Home Industry	16	86	12.8
Businessmen/women	3	12	10.4
Rural Salaried Employees	20	51	6.9
Urban Employees	16	110	14.8
Traders	24	156	14.3
Unskilled Casual Non-Farm Labourers	11	26	6.3
Civil Servants/Armed Forces/Retired	8	36	11.3
TOTAL WORK FORCE	453	807	4.2

Source: primary data.

Between 1980 and 1994 most of the ownership of the large farms remained largely unchanged. The fragmentation of landholding only occurred among farmers owning less than one hectare of land. It appears that agricultural return had very little influence on the increase of the owner farmers in Celengan hamlet. Although the number of owner farmers registered a significant 5.8 percent annual increase, farm land transactions in Celengan seem to have been made more for socio-cultural than economic motives. Security and the maintenance of personal and family social status, both, seem to have been the dominant factors in the increase of land ownership in Celengan hamlet. Apart from large landowners, agriculture has made little contribution to household income.

---

[55] See the discussion on the impact of government policies on Tlogo plantation estate in Tuntang Sub-district (1967-1973), in Chapter One section 1.8.

4.3.2. Rural Non-Farm Employment

The scarcity of good farm land in Celengan hamlet has led to members of the poorer households engaging in more than one occupation. Unlike Calombo, Celengan has no other natural resources within the hamlet, such as the Rawa Pening lake which borders Calombo. Those who prefer to seek additional income from within the hamlet have mostly engaged in either self-employed jobs or work at the chicken breeding business owned by a Chinese businessman from Semarang.

The self-employed jobs were mostly home industries which produced plaited bamboo, used for ceilings and partitions in village houses. Therefore, the market for these products is limited to the needs of the rural population. Similarly, those who work as employees at the chicken breeding business, may enjoy stable income, but have little opportunity for full-time employment. In order to be able to absorb as many unemployed as possible, the company has developed a shift policy. Under this policy, most of the employees only work a half-day. Thus income from rural non-farm employment in Celengan contributes relatively little to household income.

4.3.3. Trading and Urban Non-Farm Employment

Table 3.6 shows that between 1980 and 1994 trading and other urban employment underwent extremely high growth of some forty percent annually. Unlike the traders of Gudang and Calombo hamlets who have mostly traded within their respective hamlets, more than eighty percent of the Celengan traders traded outside the village. A large number of them were 'urban commuters'. They traded as far as Semarang, Solo, Magelang, Salatiga and Ambarawa. Apart from these commuting traders, there was also a significant number of Celengan residents who were temporary migrant traders in Jakarta.[56] It appears that for the past two decades, trading and urban employment have played an increasingly important role in the socio-economic life of the population of Celengan.

It should be noted, however, that the majority of the Celengan traders are women, a similar situation to traders and non-farm employees in Calombo.[57] This means most of these households have other sources of family income from their men and children. There were only six traders from Celengan hamlet who owned large farmlands (above a hectare). Four out of these six were men. This further confirms the trend among the richer households where there were fewer

---

[56] In Table 5.6, these temporary migrant traders were recorded under urban employment. Apart from the urban commuting traders and the temporary migrant traders, there were traders from Celengan hamlet who have moved permanently to Jakarta and other cities in the seventies. They were excluded from the figures in Table 5.6. They are no longer recorded as residents of Lopait village, even though most of them keep on returning to Lopait once a year during the *Riyaya* (Muslim holiday).

[57] As we shall see latter, the traders of Gudang hamlet were mostly men.

family members involved in earning additional incomes. The heads of the households tended to have multiple jobs.

Compared to the urban employees of Calombo hamlet, the urban employees of Celengan have a relatively better educational background. Fifty percent of the urban employees have at least completed junior high school education, and the other forty-three percent have completed elementary education.[58] However, similar to Calombo hamlet, most of the educated youth (i.e. those in the 15-24 age bracket) in Celengan have commuted (or temporarily migrated) from the hamlet for urban jobs, either in Jakarta or in the nearby district town of Ungaran.[59] Their educational background determined the type of urban jobs available to them. While the largest group of urban employees in Calombo worked as house-maids, a large number of the urban employees from Celengan hamlet worked in private companies and industries.

Trading and urban employment have obviously made a significant contribution to household income in Celengan. In 1994, seventy percent of those who obtained some of their household incomes from either trading or urban employment, belong to the middle income group of Celengan hamlet.

4.4. Employment in Gudang Hamlet

4.4.1. Agriculture

Gudang hamlet is a typical lowland agricultural village. The housing settlements are surrounded by vast wet-rice fields to the north, south and west. In the east, on the border with Celengan are dry fields (*tegalan*). Most of the wet-rice fields are well irrigated and are cultivated under the *Inmas* (Indonesian Green Revolution) programme. The Green Revolution inputs, such as the HYV seeds, the fertilisers and the pesticides are distributed locally by the *KUD* (*Koperasi Unit Desa*, Village Unit Co-operative) 'Bina Dharma' in the village of Kesongo, some 2.5 kilometres south of Lopait (see Map 3).

Table 3.7. Employment Change in Gudang Hamlet, 1980-1994

Employment	1980	1994	Annual Change in %
Owner Farmers/Share-Croppers	69	81	1.2
Landless Farm Labourers	77	48	-3.3

[58] Among the urban employees of Calombo hamlet, only thirty-five percent have completed junior high school education and forty-one percent have completed elementary education.

[59] A hundred percent of those who completed university and senior high school education, and eighty-seven percent of those who completed junior high school education were urban employees.

Self-Employed/Home Industry	25	62	6.7
Businessmen/women	2	11	12.9
Rural Salaried Employees	9	22	6.6
Urban Employees	10	59	13.5
Traders	26	68	7.1
Unskilled Casual Non-Farm Labourers	14	19	2.2
Civil Servants/Armed Forces/Teachers/Retired	10	51	12.3
TOTAL WORK FORCE	242	421	4.0

Source: primary data.

As in much of rural Java, the farmlands of Gudang hamlet are unevenly distributed. In 1994, some seventy-four percent of the owner farmers possess or have access to farmlands of less than 0.2 hectare. Twenty percent owned between 0.2 to one hectare, and only six percent owned more than one hectare. There is no indication that between 1980 and 1994 Gudang hamlet saw any concentration of landholdings. Indeed, the number of the large landowners has declined from eight in 1980 to five in 1994. The farm lands controlled by these richer farmers have also declined from the total of 14.7 hectares in 1980 to 7.5 hectares in 1994.

Although there were instances where these richer farmers sold some of their farm lands to fund wedding feasts, usually farmlands were sold for more profitable incomes. During field research in 1993-1994, farmlands were sold to purchase a kiosk in Salatiga (urban) market place, to purchase a more profitable piece of land (closer to the main road), and most often, to pay unofficial costs (e.g. Bureaucratic bribes) to be appointed as a civil servant or to be accepted in military academies (i.e. as a candidate for Armed Forces personnel). Earlier, in the late eighties, farmlands were also sold to fund a campaign for *lurah* (village head) election.

As elsewhere in Java (Penny and Singarimbun, 1973; Maurer, 1984), and other developing countries (Jayasuria and Shand, 1984; Jacoby, 1971), the owner farmers of Gudang hamlet have enjoyed a better share of the benefits from the agricultural sector. Both the extensive use of the Green Revolution inputs and the application of new agricultural technologies have, to some extent, contributed to the decline in the number of landless farm labourers. The displacement of landless farm labourers in Gudang hamlet from agricultural employment has not, however, been exclusively caused by the technological innovations of the Green Revolution.[60] The improved transportation and

[60] Village studies in the seventies and early eighties identified a major displacement of rural employment as a result of the technological innovations of the Green Revolution. Reportedly, a large number of landless farm labourers were driven out of farm employment, see, A. Stoler, "Rice Harvesting in Kali Loro." *American Ethnologist* 4 (1977a): 678-698; R. Sinaga, "Implications of Agricultural Mechanisation for

information networks seem to have also been largely responsible for the employment changes of these landless farm labourers.

Those landless farm labourers who were forced out of farm employment and had to take up rural non-farm income-earning activities have remained on the whole poor. Rural non-farm activities, such as plaiting bamboo offered less income to that of the agricultural sector. On the other hand, those who went for urban jobs, such as labourers on construction sites in Jakarta or small-scale trading activities in Salatiga market place seem to have become better placed economically.

4.4.2. Civil Service

Between 1980 and 1994, farmland ownership in Gudang increased only by 1.2 percent. Apparently, despite the success of the *Inmas* (Indonesian Green Revolution) programme, agriculture remained less attractive as compared to civil service (*pegawai negeri*) jobs or other salaried employment in private companies (*pegawai swasta*). Even the large owner farmers have preferred not to invest the surplus in the agricultural sector, either through capital improvement or the purchase of larger farm lands. Most have saved these surpluses to help their children be appointed as civil servants, and a few have invested their profits in non-farm businesses, such as auto repair shops, tailoring enterprises, and rice hulling mills.

Significantly, between 1980 and 1994, civil servants (including teachers) and armed forces personnel in Gudang increased by 12.3 percent annually. More than seventy percent of the respondents in Gudang hamlet wanted their children to find work as a civil servant. Three main motives which emerged from the questionnaire were first, the assurance of a monthly income, second, a pension, which would give assurance for their old age, and third, social respect.[61]

Employment and Income Distribution." *Bulletin of Indonesian Economic Studies* 14.2 (1978): 102-111; and W. L. Collier, "Improved Cropping Patterns, Labor Absorption, and Small Rice Farm Mechanization in Java." Paper prepared for the joint A/D/C-IRRI Workshop on Consequences of Small Rice Farm Mechanization. Los Banos, Philippines, 14-18 September 1981(a).

[61] As in many other parts of Central and East Java, those who work in an office, behind the table, are considered by their fellow villagers as *priyantun* (educated Javanese, elite). The term is used by the villagers in Lopait to address this group of *pegawai kantor* (office clerk). It refers to the 'clean' and 'refined' jobs they undertake (as compared to farmers in the fields and traders in the market places), which require no excessive physical strength. Hart (1986) designated this group of people as '*new priyayi*', Koentjaraningrat referred to them as '*kaum intelegensia*' (intellectual group), while Nagazumi (1972), classified them as "*priyayi rendahan*' (low-class *priyayi*). For the development and classification of *priyayi*, see S. Kartodirdjo, *et al.*, *Perkembangan Peradaban Priyayi*, 1987; Koentjaraningrat, *Kebudayaan Jawa*, 1984: 235-285; and A. Nagazumi, *The Dawn of Indonesian Nationalism; The Early Years of the Budi Utomo, 1908-1918*, 1972: 36.

4.4.3. Women and Trading

As Gudang hamlet is the centre of administration for Lopait village, a large number of economic transactions occur within the hamlet itself. Many of these traders are *warung* (ready-made food shop) and kiosk owners within the hamlet. Significantly, apart from a number of women who traded in the nearby village market of Kesongo (see Map 3), a large number of Gudang's traders, even those who traded in the market places of Ambarawa and Salatiga, were men. Compared to Calombo and Celengan hamlets, there were fewer women and other family members in Gudang hamlet who were involved in making contributions to household incomes by engaging in trade. Eighty-two percent of the traders in Calombo and sixty-five percent in Celengan hamlets were women as compared to only seventeen percent in Gudang hamlet. Similar trends also occurred in rural self-employment and urban employment of Gudang hamlet.

However, it is not true to say that the women of Gudang do not make a contribution to household incomes. Even though the heads of the households were usually registered as the owners of a kiosk, on most occasions when the husband had another job (in Gudang this was mostly farming), the wife would look after the kiosk. Similar trends occurred in both farm and non-farm employment. In the agricultural sector, for example, while the owner farmers were mostly men, quite often when the husband had another job, it was the wife who did the hard work in the field. In one Gudang household, the husband went to Salatiga every afternoon to sell *mie-bakso* (meat-ball and noodle). In the morning, while the husband worked his wet-rice farm, his wife went to Salatiga market to buy meats and made the meat-ball at home. The pattern of the involvement of many Gudang women in making a contribution to household income was similar to the finding of Jennifer Alexander in her study among the elite women in the village of Babadsari (1987: 26).[62]

5. Poverty Alleviation

For the purpose of the present study, the households of the three hamlets in Lopait have been divided into three local income grouping, the *tiyang gadah* (rich household), the *tiyang cekapan* (middle income group) and the *tiyang mboten gadah* (poor peasants).[63]

[62] The role of women in Gudang was, to some extent, shaped by their '*priyayi*' tradition, where men do not normally encourage his wife to engage in a separate income earning activity, see S. Kartodirdjo *et al.*, 1987: 130.

[63] See the method of data collection for employment and income of the three hamlets as well as the classification of income group estimation in Instrument D, Appendix 1.

Table 3.8. Poverty Reduction in Three Lopait Hamlets, 1980-1994

Hamlets	Income Groups	1980[64]		1994	
		Number of Households	%	Number of Households	%
Calombo	Richer Households	7	8.4	14	12.7
	Middle Income Households	40	48.2	82	74.6
	Poorer Households	36	43.4	14	12.7
	TOTAL	83	100	110	100
Celengan	Richer Households	19	9.5	32	13.9
	Middle Income Households	94	47.2	112	48.5
	Poorer Households	86	43.2	87	37.6
	TOTAL	199	100	231	100
Gudang	Richer Households	16	16.3	19	13.3
	Middle Income Households	60	61.4	83	58.5
	Poorer Households	22	22.4	40	28.3
	TOTAL	98	100	142	100

Source: primary data.

The richer groups in Calombo and Gudang hamlets are comprised of civil servants, retired government servants on pensions, large-farm land owners, businessmen/women and some traders. In Celengan hamlet the richer group comprises traders, urban employees, civil servants and large farm-land owners. Apart from the civil servants, most of them have other sources of income. Urban employment has made a substantial contribution to the richer groups in the three hamlets. Twelve out of fourteen richer households in Calombo earned some of their income from urban employment. Twenty-four out of thirty-two richer households in Celengan and fifteen out of nineteen richer households in Gudang hamlet also earned some of their income from urban employment.

However, urban employment has not exclusively benefited the richer group. 40.2 percent of middle income households in Calombo, 51.8 percent of middle income households in Gudang and 69.1 percent of middle income households in Celengan have also benefited from urban employment. Ten out of fourteen poorer households in Calombo earned some or all of their income from urban employment. The percentage of the poorer households in Celengan and Gudang hamlets who earned some or all their income from urban employment is very small. They are only 11.2 percent and 10 percent respectively.

[64] The 1980 household classification data were not based on household incomes, Instead they are estimations given by the village officials and counter checked by other key informants, See Instrument D-3, Appendix 1.

The incomes from urban employment are also very varied, ranging from Rp. 40,000 (US$ 18) a month for a house-maid, to Rp. 250,000 (US$ 115) a month for a middle ranking civil servant. The salaries of civil servants and the payments received by pensioners are substantial by village standards. In Gudang, therefore, where the richer households are mostly civil servants working in urban areas, the contributions of the additional incomes from other family members (wife and children) are much less significant. In Calombo and Celengan hamlet the picture is quite different. The contributions of additional incomes from other family members here are very significant.

To sum up, in the past decade Calombo hamlet has undergone a significant reduction in poverty. The poor households in Calombo declined from 43.4 percent in 1980 to 12.7 percent in 1994. The percentage of poor households also declined slightly in Celengan hamlet, but grew significantly in Gudang. It appears that to some extent, the access of poor households in each hamlet to urban employment coincides with the percentage of poverty reduction in each hamlet.

6. Education

The population of Gudang hamlet has been and still is better educated than those of Celengan and Calombo hamlets. This reflects the existence of two elementary schools in Gudang, and the closer distance of Gudang hamlet to the provincial road, which gives better access to the junior and senior high schools in Salatiga. Table 3.9 shows significant increases in the number of those completed junior and senior high schools. Overall there were only 9.9 percent of Gudang population in 1980 who had completed junior high school. By 1994 the percentage of those completing junior high school had grown to 27.1 percent. It needs to be noted, however, that a large number of these people (45.5 percent), did not continue to study in the senior high school. While there could be a number of explanations, it appears that this phenomenon has been mostly motivated by the educational qualifications set for a civil servant, i.e. junior high school. Table 3.9 also indicates that the percentage of the population of Gudang hamlet who had completed elementary school grew from 39.2 percent in 1980 to 54.3 percent in 1994. Moreover, the percentage of school enrolment also increased from 75.8 percent in 1980 to 89.7 percent in 1994.

Educational improvements in Celengan in the past decade and a half, have occurred in almost every level. Significant improvement is registered at the percentage of those who completed elementary education. It rose significantly from 22.7 percent in 1980 to 45.9 percent in 1994. As has been stated above, the economic pressures in Celengan hamlet, especially in the 1980s, caused by the scarcity of land and the lack of employment opportunities within the hamlet itself have driven the youth into the labour market after elementary schools. In many households of Celengan, it required two or more members of the same household to be able to provide a livelihood for the family. As most unskilled urban employment (including small scale trading) in the 1980s required no higher qualifications than elementary education, many parents in Celengan saw an elementary school certificate as their target in educating their children. Table 3.10 also indicates that those who completed junior high school grew from 6.0 percent in 1980 to 14.5 percent in 1994. This growth was a recent phenomenon, as a response to the rising of educational qualifications required for most of urban jobs in Jakarta. Overall the school enrolment in Celengan increased from 74 percent in 1980 to 86 percent in 1994.

Table 3.9. Educational Profile of Gudang Hamlet, 1980-1994

Level of Education	1980		1994	
	No. of people	% of total pop	No of people	% of total pop.
University Graduates	1	0.2	7	1.1
Completed Senior High School	10	1.9	54	8.7
Studying at the Senior High School	29	5.5	31	5.0
Completed Junior High School	26	4.9	77	12.4
Studying at Junior High School	30	5.6	40	6.4
Completed Elementary School	113	21.2	129	20.7
Studying at the Elementary School	52	9.8	67	10.7
Drop-out from Elementary School	101	19.0	98	15.7
Below school age	41	7.7	56	9.0
Never gone to formal education	129	24.2	64	10.3
Total	533	100	623	100

Source: primary data.

Table 3.10. Educational Profile of Celengan Hamlet, 1980-1994

Level of Education	1980		1994	
	No. of people	% of total pop.	No of people	% of total pop.
University Graduates	2	0.2	4	0.3
Completed Senior High School	5	0.5	36	2.7
Studying at the Senior	24	2.2	36	2.7

High School				
Completed Junior High School	35	3.2	115	8.8
Studying at Junior High School	47	4.3	92	7.0
Completed Elementary School	136	12.4	320	24.3
Studying at the Elementary School	301	27.4	238	18.1
Drop-out from Elementary School	164	14.9	189	14.4
Below school age	98	8.9	101	7.7
Never gone to formal education	285	26.0	184	14.0
Total	1097	100	1315	100

Source: primary data.

Table 3.11. Educational Profile of Calombo, 1980-1994

Level of Education	**1980**		**1994**	
	No. of people	**% of total pop.**	**No of people**	**% of total pop.**
University Graduates	-	0.0	-	0.0
Completed Senior High School	2	0.4	4	0.7
Studying at the Senior High School	9	2.1	19	3.5
Completed Junior High School	8	1.7	30	5.5
Studying at Junior High School	21	4.5	36	6.6
Completed Elementary School	49	10.4	84	15.3
Studying at the Elementary School	144	30.7	116	21.2
Drop-out from Elementary School	54	11.5	97	17.7
Below school age	36	7.6	49	8.9
Never gone to formal education	146	31.1	113	20.6
Total	469	100	548	100

Source: primary data.

Changes in educational standards in Calombo during the past 15 years have been quite modest. Those who completed junior high school have increased from 4.1 percent of the total population in 1980 to 9.7 percent in 1994. Most of these people have worked either as civil servants in Salatiga or as employees at private companies in Bawen and surrounding sub-districts. Those who completed elementary education had also increased slightly from 19.0 percent in 1980 to 31.6 percent in 1994. The geographical location of Calombo is one of the principal obstacles preventing its children from obtaining higher education; to get to the elementary schools in Gudang, these small children have to cross one of the busiest provincial roads in Central Java with no pedestrian crossing. As a whole, school enrolment percentage in Calombo increased from 68.9 percent of the total population in 1980 to 79.4 percent in 1994.

7. Summary

Historically, ecologically and socio-economically the three hamlets of Lopait were distinct from one another. Calombo is a fishing hamlet, developed around the Rawa Pening lake. The socio-economic as well as religio-political orientations of Calombo are towards the villages around Rawa Pening lake. Celengan is an upland rural Javanese hamlet. The population here was originally formed from the overspill of Watuagung and its surrounding villages toward the Tlogo plantation estate. Gudang is a typical lowland agricultural Javanese hamlet, which developed along the provincial road. The family of the founding fathers of Gudang trace its origin back to nobility from the court of Yogyakarta in the early nineteenth century.

In the 1920s the Dutch colonial administration unified these hamlets under one village administrative unit of Lopait. As in much of rural Java, this administrative unification proved to be ineffective. In 1994 the population of the three hamlets largely identified themselves with their respective hamlet, rather than with the village of Lopait. To some extent, the local policies and interests of the New Order administration in Lopait village have contributed to the polarisation of the three hamlets of Lopait, both socio-economically and socio-politically. In the past two decades, political affiliations at both local and national levels, the choice of livelihood and how the population in each hamlet regarded education have largely determined their responses to the government's interests and policies in Lopait.

As a whole, the three hamlets have benefited from the government's development programmes, and especially the substantial improvement of road, transport and information networks. This infrastructural development has contributed to the overall increase in 'school enrolment' percentage in all three hamlets, and the increasing number of population, especially from Gudang and Celengan, who have completed junior and senior high school (see Tables 3.9; 3.10; 3.11). Our earlier discussions have also identified the contribution of this infrastructural development to family income, especially by providing better access to urban jobs in all three hamlets. However, since each hamlet reacted differently to government policies and programmes, the extent to which each hamlet benefited from the development programmes differs considerably. The following chapter will look more closely at these development programmes, and analyse the way they have been implemented in the three hamlets of Lopait. With regard to programme sustainability, it is similarly important to examine the extent to which these development schemes have been able to generate people's participation in the three hamlets under investigation.

Map 4 Lopait Village

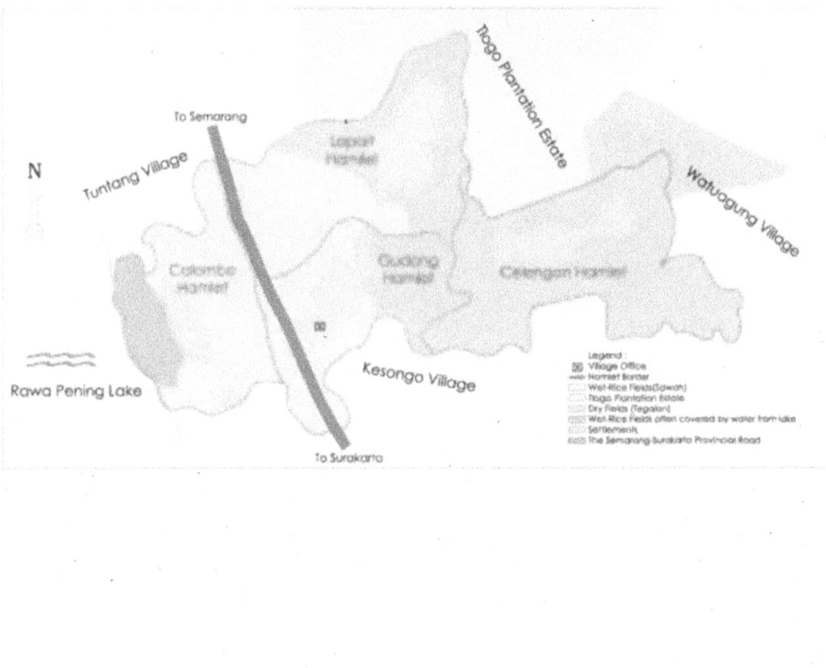

Chapter 4

Participation in the Three Hamlets of Lopait

The aim of this chapter is to assess people's participation in the development projects implemented in the three hamlets of Lopait between 1989 and 1994.[1]

1. The Forms of Participations

In the Indonesian context, participation in rural development projects was often perceived in terms of the extent of the rural people's support for or involvement in the government's development programmes. In smaller (local) projects this support was measured by the amount of contributions by the people. As these contributions were expected to ease the burden of the central government in financing these projects, participation was often perceived in terms of either the amount of government money being saved or the percentage of the budget being paid by the local people (Republic of Indonesia, 1983: 17).[2] In larger projects, such as provincial roads, school buildings, hospitals or clinics where the funding came from the central government and the implementation was carried out by professional developers from the cities, people's participation was less expected. The people were already considered to be participating in these development projects if they did not do anything to obstruct the execution of the projects. Thus often 'being quiet means to participate' (Mubyarto, 1988: 36-37).

Participation in rural Java has also been associated with *gotong-royong* (co-operative labour). In *gotong-royong*, members of the community regardless of their economic status are socially obliged to participate. The tools which are employed by the government to measure the degree of participation have implied that 'incentives' and 'instructions' are inferior to voluntary

---

[1] As has been stated already, the fifth *PELITA* (*Pembangunan Lima Tahun*, Five Year Development plan), which ran from the fiscal year of 1988/1989 until the fiscal year of 1993/1994 was selected for this study mainly because it stood as the last *PELITA* in the Indonesian *PJP I* (*Pembangunan Jangka Panjang I*, the First 25 Year Long Term Development Phase).

[2] The forms of the *Daftar Monografi Desa* and *Daftar Monografi Kecamatan* (the village and sub-district periodic reports), to be filled by the village and sub-district administrators, compared the amount of money contributed by the local people and the amount of government subsidies, see Mubyarto, "Strategy Pembangunan Pedesaan", 1988: 36.

involvement in the development projects.[3] The rapid change in rural employment towards more heterogeneous, urban-oriented income generating activities in many villages, as well as major changes in land tenure arrangements as a result of Green Revolution technologies, have to some extent changed the practice of *gotong-royong*. The rural poor, especially landless farm labourers and urban employees could hardly be expected to take part in *gotong-royong* for more than one day a week. For these people, no work means no income. Therefore, it is unacceptable to regard the poor wage labourers who worked in the development projects for payment as participating less than the rich farmers who contributed some money (Mubyarto, 1988: 37).[4]

Paul (1987) defined participation as an active process by which beneficiaries 'influence' the direction and execution of a development project with a view to enhancing well-being in terms of income, personal growth, self-reliance or other values which are cherished. This definition seemed to balance the short-range (income growth) and long-range (self-reliance) expectations of the rural people as the beneficiaries; the decision-making stage (direction) with the implementation stage (execution) of the projects; and between the inputs of the development projects (direction and execution) with the outputs of the projects (well-being). While the definition was comprehensive and all-encompassing, in practice it is hard to develop a measuring tool to assess 'personal growth' and 'other values which are cherished', especially when it is applied to evaluate participation in a short term development project such as village road construction.

In a more practical and measurable way Cohen and Uphoff (1976) defined participation as people's 'involvement' in decision-making processes, in implementing programmes, in sharing the benefits, and in efforts to evaluate the programmes. In accordance with the definition above, this present study employed the indicators for participation which were set out by Finsterbusch and van Wicklin (1987) and Oakley *et al.*(1991). Under the heading of a 'decision-making' stage, this study examines three sub-stages, namely, the stage of project identification, the stage of project selection,[5] and the stage of project planning, which includes taking responsibility as a committee member. The 'implementation' stage classifies people's contributions in terms of money and labour. This study also divides the examination of the output of development projects into two stages, namely the sharing of benefits and people's involvement in the maintenance stage. Since performance or

---

[3] See, Direktorat Pembangunan Desa Propinsi Jawa Tengah, "Laporan Hasil Survey Mikro Kecamatan Tuntang, Kabupaten Dati II Semarang, Propinsi Dati I Jawa Tengah Tahun 1984/1985" (Micro Studies on Tuntang Sub-District 1984/1985), 1985: 12.

[4] For an extensive reading on the development of *gotong-royong* practice, see Koentjaraningrat, *Some Social-Anthropological Observations on Gotong-Rojong Practices in Two Villages of Central Java,* 1961.

[5] To be applied only to cases where there were more than one project being identified at the previous stage.

involvement in each stage of development projects was determined by different factors, such as gender, types of employment, educational background, social status, macro development policies and the local culture, it is inappropriate to accumulate the points (levels of performance) obtained in all the stages.[6]

This study interprets participation within the socio-cultural, political, and economic context of each hamlet.[7] Such analysis would not only describe the levels of people's participation in each hamlet, but more importantly, it explains different factors which determined participation. Further, it examines whether their involvement in the projects was socio-culturally, politically, economically, or religiously motivated. In most rural development projects these reasons for participation were not mutually exclusive.[8] Even though experience reveals that very often the basis for participation is likely to be stronger where there are mutually reinforcing impetuses (Cohen and Uphoff, 1976: 86), a greater proportion should be expected to come from the people's 'initiative', as compared to 'enforcement' from outside (political or social pressures). 'Initiative' from within, regardless of the motives behind it, generally offers a greater guarantee for more sustainable development (Cernea, 1987; Stinson, 1987).

2. The Process of Participation

The 'why' and 'what' of participation have been endlessly discussed and indicated, the 'how' question has, however, been much less frequently raised. Rural development studies have often taken "participation" for granted as if it is a desirable good for both the development agency and the rural poor. In

---

[6] Culturally, a rural Javanese woman, for example, would not be expected to earn points in the decision-making stage. Moreover, the measurements used to assess participation in the 'sharing of benefits' stage differed from those applied in the "decision-making" and the 'implementation' stages. In this stage, any one making use of the facilities provided by the projects were considered as participating in the projects. For the sake of the accuracy of the assessment, it is therefore important for each individual to have a set of three different points (scores), namely the participation points (scores) for the 'decision-making' stage, the participation points (scores) for the 'implementation' stage and the participation points (scores) for the 'sharing of benefits' stage, see Y. Slamet, *Pembangunan Masyarakat Berwawasan Partisipasi*, 1993: 96-99; and Mubyarto, 1988: 38-39.

[7] The scoring system was only added at the latter part of the analysis both to cross-check the findings of the qualitative analysis at the implementation stage, and to enable the local people do parts of the evaluation themselves (see Table 3.1). As will be illustrated in the following sections, each hamlet under investigation has a distinct factor which determined people's participation in the development projects. To undertake a comparative study among such diverse contexts, employing a mere quantitative measurement would certainly be inadequate and the findings could be deceptive.

[8] See, Development Alternatives Inc., *Strategies for Small Farmer Development: An Empirical Study of Rural Development Projects*, 1975: 95-101.

reality, people's participation involves some form of cost for both parties, and often requires more than just economic incentives. Targeting the participation of the rural poor involves greater risks, time, energy and commitment.[9] Since it involves some form of cost, apart from its usefulness and its desirability, 'feasibility' is to be among the main considerations (Uphoff, Cohen, and Goldsmith, 1979: 28). As a result of failure to recognise these costs, a number of projects have failed both to increase the problem-solving capacity of the poor in the longer term and to channel benefits to the poorest members of society (Johnston and Clark, 1982: 163-164).[10]

The rural poor are only likely to actively participate when the projects or the local organisations that undertake them are responsive to their strongest needs (Hunter, 1971; Buijs, 1979).[11] Although it is true that the poor do not always make wise investments in development projects, the choices as to which projects they would put their participation into are made on the available perceptions (Johnston and Clark, 1982: 172). These perceptions are developed within the framework of their context and perceived needs. Johnston and Clark were right in saying that, "the investment of effective participation cannot be commanded by policymakers" (1982: 173). They further asserted:

> The requirement of effective policymaking for local organizations is therefore not omniscience but entrepreneurship: the ability to recognize and design programmes capable of mobilizing participation (1982: 173).

In a pioneering work on the concept of measuring participation, Cohen and Uphoff (1976) listed a set of factors which influence participation in rural development projects. There are at least three factors which were very relevant to this present research, namely the socio-economic, the political and the socio-cultural factors. In regard to socio-economic composition, Mulder (1973) maintained that in participation processes socio-economic homogeneity is preferable. Cohen and Uphoff (1976) also mentioned 'disproportional participation' which often occurred in a socio-economically heterogeneous composition.[12]

---

[9] See Bruce F. Johnston and William C. Clark, *Redesigning Rural Development: A Strategic Perspective*, 1982: 171-173; and H. Y. Buijs, *Access and Participation*, 1979: 25.

[10] See, UNRISD, *Rural Cooperatives as Agents of Change: A Research Report and a Debate*, 1975; D. C. Korten, "Community Organization and Rural Development: A Learning Process Approach." *Public Administration Review* 40.5 (1980): 480-511.

[11] See for example, the rejection of modern co-operatives by the farmers in Mali, in N. S. Hopkins, "Participatory Decision Making and Modern Cooperatives in Mali." In J. Nash, J. Dandler, and N. S. Hopkins, eds., *Popular Participation in Social Change*, 1976; see also some other cases reported in D. C. Korten, 1980.

[12] See also Inayatullah, *Cooperatives and Planned Change in Asia*, 1970; and Y. H. Landau, M. Konopnicki, H. Desroche, P. Rambaud, eds., *Rural Communities, Intercooperation and Development*, 1976.

Politically, while a positive supporting attitude of the government towards participation is desirable, from several cases it emerged that external (supra-village) threats have in fact encouraged solidarity among the rural community. This solidarity often functions as a mechanism that promotes participation of the members of the community. To outwit the hostile supra-village policies and thus to secure its existence the group has to creatively consider every option in order to find structures which will be most effective (Buijs, 1979: 29).[13]

The socio-cultural context of the community often holds the key for success or failure of participation in development projects. The traditional village structure, with a strong pattern of differentiation and often dominated by a small powerful local elite, has generally been considered the major obstacle for people's participation.[14] These elites are usually linked to the poor in some form of patronage relationship. A vast body of literature and reports on rural development demonstrates how the development agencies have continuously overlooked this patronage relationship in rural communities. As a result, most attempts to organise the rural poor have been thwarted by the local elite (Johnston and Clark, 1982: 167).[15]

3. Development Projects in Lopait 1989-1994

The research identified 19 development projects in Gudang hamlet, 17 in Celengan hamlet and 16 in Calombo hamlet which were carried out between the 1988/1989 and 1993/1994 fiscal years. Due to the limitation of time and resources, the author selected seven projects from each hamlet. A number of considerations were taken in selecting the projects. First, the projects selected were to cover different aspects of local community life, such as education, infrastructure, health or hygiene, and religion. Second, the research considered the different sources of the funding for the projects, whether they were subsidised by the central government or were locally funded. Third, they should represent two types of development projects, namely 'intensive' one-off projects such as road construction and mosque refurbishment, and the

[13] See also B. F. Galjart, *Peasant Mobilization and Solidarity*, 1976; and G. Huizer, *Boerenverzet in Latijns-Amerika*, 1976.

[14] Robert Chambers described these elite as "nets" which filter out benefits before they reach the rural poor, see R. Chambers, *Rural Development: Putting the Last First*, 1983; and G. Hunter, *Modernizing Peasant Society: A Comparative Study in Asia and Africa*, 1969.

[15] See also R. Chambers, *Managing Rural Development: Ideas and Experience from East Africa*, 1974; and G. Hunter, "Research on Cooperatives in East Africa: Review/Note," Mimeographed, 1971.

'extensive' programmes such as literacy (*Kejar Paket A*)[16] and the *Posyandu* (*Pos Pelayanan Terpadu*, local health cadres).

3.1. Participation in Calombo Hamlet

Among the three hamlets under investigation, the local community in Calombo was the most homogenous in terms of socio-economic stratification, political affiliation and religious orientation. As has been stated above, this social context has created wider opportunities for the rural population of Calombo to participate in the development processes.

The seven development projects in Calombo hamlet which had been selected for this research were: the Construction of the main road in Calombo hamlet (1989/1990); the construction of the bridge in *RT* I (1990/1991); the construction of the bridge in *RT* IV (1990/1991); the construction of the road in *RT* IV (1991/1992); the construction of the building for the Islamic kindergarten (1992/1993); the refurbishment of the Mosque (1991/1992) and the refurbishment of the public water supply (*MCK*)[17] (1989/1990).

It needs to be noted that two infrastructure projects in Calombo were decided in some kind of *rembug dhusun* (traditional village meeting) forum, where all the heads of the households in the hamlet get together.[18] At this forum every participant has a vote in the decision-making process. Although at village level, this 'traditional' or 'primitive' democratic forum has mostly been abandoned, at hamlet level and mostly at *RT* (*Rukun Tetangga*, Neighbourhood association)[19] levels the *rembug desa* or *selapanan* forum remained functional

---

[16] *Kejar Paket A,* the abbreviation of *Kelompok Belajar Paket A* (Group Learning of Packet A), is the government's literacy program.

[17] *MCK* is abbreviation of *mandi, cuci, kakus* (taking a bath, washing and latrine or toilet). In rural Java, an *MCK* is two cemented partitions (for males and females), with neither doors nor roofs. It is either constructed on a water spring, a river or a well. The public water supply (*MCK*) in Calombo is constructed in the Mosque area, therefore the functions are limited primarily for *wudhu* (washing before prayer), washing and cooking.

[18] In the past, most rural Javanese villages practised *rembug dhusun (desa)* or *selapanan*, which was a regular meeting of the *pamong desa* (village officials) with the heads of households, conducted every 35 days (*selapan*). For further reading on traditional village meetings, see E. de Vries, *Landbouw en Welvaart in het Regentschap Pasoeroean: Bijdrage tot de Kennis van de Sociale Economie van Java*, 1931.

[19] The *RT* (*Rukun Tetangga*, Neighbourhood Association) consists of approximately 20 households. The *RW* (*Rukun Warga*, Association of the members of the local community) consists of several *RT*. In the case of Lopait village, the *RW* in Calombo consists of four *RT*. The *RW* in Gudang consists of five *RT*, and the *RW* in Celengan consists of nine *RT*. In rural Java there are two local leaders at the hamlet level, the *bekel* (*Kadus*, hamlet headman) and the chairman of the *RW*. The first are the traditional and formal leaders of the hamlet, and the latter are perceived as the informal leaders of the local community. The *kadus* has recently been considered by the central government as the extension of the village administration, and the chairman of the *RW*

in many parts of rural Java (Slamet, 1965: 78-80; Koentjaraningrat, 1984: 205-206).

Three other projects in Calombo hamlet were identified and selected at the *rapat dusun* (hamlet leaders meeting). In these *rapat dusun* the people were mainly represented by the chairmen of the *RT*. Other attendants in the meeting were the *tokoh masyarakat* (informal leaders), the chairman of the *RW* and the hamlet head (*kadus*). The three projects were the construction of the village road in *RT* IV (1990/1991), the construction of the village bridge in *RT* IV (1991/1992) and the construction of the building for the Islamic kindergarten in *RT* IV (1992/1993).[20] Apart from the discussion on the construction of the building for the Islamic kindergarten, which was the continuation of an earlier discussion at the mass prayers in the Mosque, the other projects were selected through voting.

The other two projects were mainly motivated by religious concerns, namely the refurbishment of the public water supply (1989/1990) and the refurbishment of the Mosque (1991/1992). Although the public water supply might be used for other purposes, such as cooking and washing, the main function of the site was for *wudlu* (washing/cleansing oneself before prayer). There were no decision-making processes for these two projects. The projects were selected, planned, and funded by the *kyai* (Islamic religious teacher) and his family. Only later in the implementation stage did the neighbourhood voluntarily take part, organised by the eldest son of the *kyai*. It appears that apart from the two religious projects above, the population of Calombo hamlet had been very much involved in the decision-making processes of the development projects implemented in their hamlet. In a number of cases the selection of the projects was made through voting either by all the household heads or by their representatives.

It needs to be noted that at the planning stage, local participation was significantly high. Apart from the construction project of the bridge in *RT* I, which was initiated and planned by the university students on *KKN*,[21] the rest of the projects were planned by the informal leaders of Calombo hamlet. With the exception of the religious projects of the refurbishment of the Mosque and of the public water supply attached to the Mosque,[22] in most cases the planning for the implementation of the projects was discussed in the sub-committees. Each

---

as the representative of the local community with no administrative responsibility. The *RT* and *RW* groupings were introduced during the Japanese occupation. For further reading, see W. M. F. Hofsteede, *Decision-Making Process in Four West Javanese Villages*, 1971; Taliziduhu Ndraha, *Beberapa Catatan tentang Kemungkinan Pembinaan Struktur Organisasi Pemerintahan Desa*, 1973.

[20] The main village road in *RT* IV is the gateway to Calombo hamlet.

[21] *KKN* or *Kuliah Kerja Nyata* is a mandatory programme for all university students which involves their carrying out two months of social outreach in a rural setting.

[22] There was no committee for these two religious projects. The projects were initiated, planned and funded by the *kyai* and his two sons.

segment in the committee proposed plans to implement the projects within their respective responsibilities. Even though at its final stage the plans for implementation had to be presented and approved at the whole committee meeting, this process allowed the plans for the projects to be largely drafted at the lowest possible level in the community.

At the implementation stage, participation in Calombo was very much apparent. The spirit of *gotong-royong* (co-operative labour) was still considerably strong. None of the seven projects under investigation was implemented by hiring professional labourers. Members of the community took their turn to voluntarily work for the projects. In terms of money, apart from the religious projects of refurbishing the Mosque and the public water supply, where the *kyai* as (considered to be) the owner had provided all the funding, in all the other projects each household in the hamlet contributed either voluntarily or the amount set by the hamlet leaders.

While the degree to which each development project has benefited each household was varied, as a whole, the seven projects under investigation have benefited the majority of Calombo people, regardless of income group or type of employment.[23] Quite interestingly, participation in the maintenance of the projects was less apparent. Apart from the Mosque and the public water supply, there was no arrangement for the maintenance of the other projects. Only when parts needed some repairs would the chairman of the respective *RT* call upon the household-heads to participate in a *kerja bhakti* (mutual/voluntary work). This phenomenon was not at all unique; elsewhere in developing countries the problem of maintenance has repeatedly been raised.[24]

Among the seven projects under investigation, the highest participation occurred in two projects, namely the construction of the bridge in *RT* IV and the construction of the building for the Islamic kindergarten. Both proposals were first rejected by the village and supra-village administrations. The completion of the projects was mostly due to the persistence of the local leaders in carrying them out, including the fund-raising from within the hamlet and seeking donations from outside the village. At the project identification stage the economic motive (the importance of the bridge for income earning activity) was only secondary. The initial motivation for the construction of the bridge in *RT* IV was its function as the gateway to Calombo. Similarly, the initial motive for the construction of the building for the Islamic kindergarten was not primarily for the improvement of educational standards, but for the expansion of the *pesantren* (Islamic traditional school). Before this Islamic kindergarten existed, the only kindergarten officially acknowledged by the sub-district administration was the Christian kindergarten in Celengan hamlet. The academically superior students at the local elementary schools in Gudang were

---

[23] See, Table 5.8 on the poverty reduction in the three hamlets of Lopait.

[24] Similar phenomena also occurred in Celengan and Gudang hamlets.

mostly graduates from this Christian kindergarten. This to some extent contributed to the identification of an Islamic kindergarten as a need.[25]

The lowest level of participation occurred in the construction of the bridge in *RT* I. This project was identified in conjunction with the *KKN* programme (university students on social outreach). Even though the project itself was apparently useful for the people, it did not meet their perceived needs. It was selected primarily because the route across the bridge was considered much safer for students of Calombo who go to school in the village of Tuntang.

The excessive involvement of the 'outsiders' right from the beginning until the end of the implementation stage mostly discouraged the local people from actively participating in the project. Both the identification and the planning were mainly undertaken by university students from the Diponegoro University in Semarang. At the implementation stage the university students carried out the main jobs. Even when the funds for the project were insufficient, it was the students who took full responsibility for paying the balance.

Although *KKN* programme was meant to mutually benefit both the university students and the village population (Kusnaedi, 1995: 109), in reality the academic aspects were over-emphasised so as to become the core motive. Accordingly the university students and not the local population had come into the centre of the programme and become the main actors or subjects of the development projects. The people were well aware of the nature of *KKN* programme, as primarily meeting the requirements for university graduation. The resources and especially the time limitations[26] for the implementation of programme have often caused problems in project selection. The alternative projects to be selected were very limited, and accordingly the selected projects often did not meet the real needs of the people. The whole approach of the *KKN* programme was to look at the university students as a 'source of knowledge and technology', and the rural population as the ones expected to respond by adopting the knowledge and technologies (Kusnaedi, 1995: 109-110). As a result, 'projects', have become the centre of the *KKN* programme rather than 'people'.

3.2. Participation in Celengan Hamlet

The seven development projects in Celengan hamlet selected for this research were: the construction of the village road in *RT* IV (1989/1990); the

---

[25] There were Islamic kindergartens in Celengan and Gudang hamlets, but they were officially unrecognised by the Sub-District administration. The kindergartens were not professionally managed and therefore had low education standards. Moreover, the locations of these kindergartens were not at all convenient for the children of Calombo. To get to these kindergartens these 4-5 years children had to cross the provincial road which separates Calombo hamlet from Gudang and Celengan hamlets.

[26] Usually the *KKN* programme was limited to two to three months only. Moreover the students have to raise the funding for the projects themselves.

construction of the Church building (1989/1993); the health cadre programme (1989/1990); the construction of the Mosque (1990/1991); the construction of the guard posts (*pos kamling*) (1991/1992); the Islamic kindergarten (1991/1992); and the *padat karya* (mobilisation of work force) construction project of the main road (1993/1994).

Compared to the Calombo hamlet, participation at the decision-making process in Celengan hamlet was much less apparent. The development projects implemented in Celengan hamlet were mostly identified by 'outsiders'. The construction of the main road was identified by the district (*kabupaten*) administration; the guard post project was identified and initiated by the village head; the health cadre programme was an extension of the Sub-District programme; and the Islamic kindergarten was identified by a *KUA* (*Kantor Urusan Agama*, religious department at sub-district level) officer from Tuntang sub-district.

There are, however, three development projects which were identified and selected by the local leaders of Celengan hamlet. Two of these were religious projects, namely the construction of the Mosque and the construction of the Church building. The third was the construction of the village road in *RT* IV. The selection of the construction projects of the Mosque and of the village road in *RT* IV took place at the *rapat dusun* (hamlet leaders meeting) attended by the hamlet head, the chairman of the *RW*, the chairmen of the nine *RT* and some of the informal leaders. The construction of the Church building was identified and selected at the Church elders meeting. In all these project-selection meetings, decisions were made through traditional Javanese system of *musyawarah* (deliberation) and *mufakat* (consensus). In no instance was decision made by voting, as occurred in Calombo.

The largest development project in Celengan hamlet during this period was the construction of the main village road. The whole decision-making process of this project, from identification, selection and right up to the planning stage had mainly been facilitated by the district administration. Prior to implementation, meetings were held with the representative of the district administration, the sub-district head, the *Koramil* (sub-district level Army commanding officer), and the village administrators of Lopait, including the village head. Although the meetings were open to suggestions from the village leaders, in most cases the content was mainly a briefing regarding the implementation of the project given by the representative of the district administration.

As the road construction was a *padat karya* (labour intensive) project, all the funding came from central government under the supervision of the district administration. The people of Celengan who worked in the implementation of this project were paid at Rp. 1,000 (US$ 0.46) per day, which was less than a half of the regional minimum wage of US$ 1.05.[27] Therefore, the involvement of a large number of people in this project could either be seen as an expression of people's active participation or more likely the scarcity of rural employment. The *padat karya* programme itself was introduced both to encourage active people participation as well as to provide the peasants with short-term employment during the slack seasons.

The funds allocated by the central government for this project were US$ 11,193. At the end of the third month, there were only US$ 930 left, while the project was far from complete. Accordingly the committee decided to assign the completion of the project to the people of Kesongo village. With such limited funds and limited time little could actually be expected from the people of Kesongo. As a result the quality of the road was relatively poor.[28]

At first, the people of Celengen did not consider this project as one of their needs. One of the main purposes of this particular *padat karya* road project was to integrate the Celengan hamlet with Gudang and the other hamlets in the village of Lopait. As has been stated already, socio-culturally and economically Celengan has its orientation mostly toward the Watuagung and Kesongo villages, at the south and east borders of the hamlet respectively. This project has therefore had only slight significance for the population of Celengan.[29] A significant number of respondents who had worked for this project were motivated by the opportunity for employment. However, a gradual change of attitude took place after the project was completed. Although the socio-economic orientation of Celengan remained toward the Watuagung and Kesongo villages, the main road which connects Celengan with the Gudang hamlet officially stands as the gateway of Celengan hamlet (see Map 6). Encouraged by the realisation that this road was theirs, and even more, was their official gateway, the people of Celengan organised themselves to refurbish this poor quality road two months after the completion of the *padat karya* project.

At this second stage of the construction of the main road in Celengan, people participation was significantly higher. Both the planning and implementation

---

[27] To some extent the *padat karya* projects are benefiting the richer households at the expense of their poorer neighbours. In most cases the richer households, who owned motor vehicles, used the road more often, while the poorer households who worked for the projects were paid much less, see J. Hardjono, "Rural Development In Indonesia: The 'Top-Down' Approach." In Lea and Chaudhri, eds., *Rural Development and The State*, 1983: 38-66.

[28] Birowo and Hansen also identified severe shortcomings in the planning and supervision of the *padat karya* projects which resulted in poor project outcome. See Achmad T. Birowo and Gary E. Hansen, "Agricultural and Rural Development: An Overview." In Gary E. Hansen, ed., *Agricultural and Rural Development in Indonesia*, 1981: 1-27.

[29] In general the rural poor will invest active participation only in an organisation that is responsive to their 'most intensely felt needs', see G. Hunter, 1971.

of this refurbishment was undertaken by the local people through *gotong-royong*. It appears that the 'sense of ownership' of the project has to some extent encouraged participation in Celengan hamlet. This was not of course peculiar to Celengan; elsewhere in developing countries a sense of ownership has significantly encouraged rural people participating in development.[30]

The socio-political and the economic pressures from the supra-village structure have to some extent discouraged participation in Celengan.[31] As discussed in Chapters One and Two, following the government's policy on reclaiming the lands which originally belonged to the Tlogo plantation estate, the population of Celengan was socio-economically devastated. As a result, some were compelled to join the government's transmigration programme, while a significant number of others chose to pursue urban employment in Jakarta. This 'exodus' has contributed to the lack of strong local leadership in Celengan hamlet.[32]

As a whole, apart from the two religious projects, the construction of the Mosque and the Church building, participation in the decision-making processes was relatively low. In all the other programmes, none of the 60 respondents in Celengan was involved in the project committees. To make a comparison, more than thirty percent of the respondents in Calombo and Gudang hamlets were involved in the project committees.

The implementation of the development projects in Celengan took a different shape. Even though social binding within the population of Celengan was significantly strong, *gotong-royong*, which expressed the harmony and to some extent, the egalitarian nature of Javanese villages (Koentjaraningrat, 1993: 56) has played an insignificant role in the implementation of the major development projects in Celengan. Six out of the seven development projects selected in Celengan were carried out by professional labour.

It would be misleading, however, to measure people's participation in Celengan hamlet only through their involvement in voluntary work (*kerja bhakti*). The arrangement of the project implementation stage was significantly influenced by the pattern of livelihoods of the Celengan hamlet, which was made up mostly of commuting traders and urban employees. With the addition

---

[30] See a number of cases from Brazil, South India and Morocco which were reported in Daniel W. Bromley, ed., *Making the Commons Work*, 1992: 183-266.

[31] Prior to the rise of the New Order government, almost all of the population of Celengan hamlet were supporters of the Communist Party (PKI). In 1966 when the PKI was banned, some of the local leaders of Celengan were sent to jail and others were intimidated. Until recently, a large numbers of households in Celengan remained on the government's list of those who were ideologically suspect.

[32] Since the mid-sixties the heads of Celengan hamlet have not been natives of Celengan. Until 1993 the hamlet-head of Celengan was Timin of Gudang hamlet and in 1994 he was replaced by Bisri, a native of Kesongo. Both Timin and Bisri married residents of Celengan. Moreover, most of the educated and well-to-do of Celengan are among those who seek urban jobs.

of the economic pressures caused by the scarcity of lands, a *kerja bhakti* requirement of one full day or more could certainly harm their livelihood. For these commuting traders and the wage-labourers, a day off meant no income (Mubyarto, 1988: 37). In most cases, therefore, the people of Celengan participated in development through their donations.

As in many other developing countries, participation in some projects was low when the projects did not meet the perceived needs of the local people (Hunter, 1971). One factor which might have influenced the seeming lack of participation in Celengan was the fact that most of the projects were identified by the village and supra-village structures, and did not meet the perceived needs of the people. The *padat karya* construction project of the main road which connects Celengan to Gudang hamlet was one example of this inaccurate identification of projects. The construction of the guard posts, which was initiated by the village head, in order to meet village administrative requirements from central government, was another example.

People's participation in activities which are seen to serve in strengthening the social bond of the hamlet community was significantly high. Such activities might well include *kerja bhakti* for maintenance of the road networks within the hamlet and the *sambatan* (helping a neighbourhood to build a house or preparing a feast).[33] These activities have not only improved public facilities within a neighbourhood, they have also strengthened the social bond of the hamlet community.[34] The socio-political as well as the economic pressures from the village and supra-village structures (see Chapter Two) have added to the importance of this social bond. As the pressure from outside has increased so the need for identity within the hamlet community has also increased. This explains, for example, why at one stage the construction of the main road to Gudang was not considered important, while a few months later the people of Celengan considered the same road as very important, because it was now looked upon as the official gateway of their hamlet.

In terms of benefits, only 35.6 percent have actually had their needs met by the projects. In comparison, out of 93.6 percent of the respondents in Calombo who claimed to have benefited from the projects, more than eighty percent made use of the facilities to meet their needs. In Gudang hamlet, 60 percent of the respondents claimed that the projects implemented in their hamlet have met their needs. The question in regard to the sharing of development benefits in Celengan was not so much as to who or which group in the community has

---

[33] The words *kerja bhakti* and *sambatan* could have different meanings in other parts of Java, see Koentjaraningrat, *Kebudayaan Mentalitas dan Pembangunan*, 1993: 58-61.

[34] This weekly *kerja bhakti* for village public facilities was practised mainly for social purposes. Accordingly, people worked for only one or two hours on Sunday to do some maintenance work such as mending the road within the neighbourhood or other minor construction jobs. In terms of work, little was achieved. However, in terms of socialisation *kerja bhakti* has successfully strengthened the identity and harmony of the hamlet community.

benefited the most, but to what extent these development projects have really met the perceived needs of the people.[35]

It appeared that throughout the decision-making process, the implementation stage and the sharing of benefits, the 'quality involvement' of the people of Celengan was low. This seeming lack of participation did not necessarily imply stagnation of the socio-economic development. In fact, in the field of education, Celengan has grown faster than the other hamlets in Lopait village (see Table 2.10). In terms of poverty reduction Celengan has also made marked progress (see Table 2.8). The low percentage of the needs which were met through these projects indicates that most of the development projects implemented in Celengan hamlet between the fiscal year of 1988/1989 and 1993/1994 had very little relevance to the socio-economic needs of the hamlet.

3.3. Participation in Gudang Hamlet

The seven development projects in Gudang hamlet selected for this research were: the refurbishment of the rural water supply and sanitation (*MCK*) of 'Kaligedog' in *RT* IV (1990/1991); the refurbishment of the village road in *RT* III (1992/1993); the refurbishment of the village road in *RT* V (1992/1993); the refurbishment of the *mushola* (Muslim prayer house) 'Al Hidayah' in *RT* III (1992/1993); the refurbishment of the rural water supply and sanitation (*MCK*) 'Kaliwates' (1993/1994); the *Posyandu* (village health cadre) and the *Kejar Paket A* (government literacy programme).

The refurbishment of the village road in *RT* V was identified and selected at the annual *LKMD* (*Lembaga Ketahanan Masyarakat Desa*, the village resilience institution) meeting.[36] The project identified was the main road which connects Gudang to Lopait hamlet. This road used to be the main route for vehicles to Lopait hamlet, especially in the rainy season. Before the road which connects Lopait hamlet directly to the provincial road was constructed in 1989, all the vehicles to Lopait hamlet had to pass along this road (see Map 6). It appeared that the construction of the road in Lopait hamlet in 1989 has to some extent threatened the income of some industries and traders in Gudang hamlet. The refurbishment of this road in *RT* V could therefore be seen as economically

---

[35] There was no indication of any social or income groups within Celengan which exploited other groups in the hamlet.

[36] The agenda for the annual meeting of the *LKMD* was, amongst other things, to allocate the *Bandes* fund (*Bantuan Desa*, village grants from the central government) for the next fiscal year. For discussion on the replacement of the grass-roots institution of *LSD* (*Lembaga Sosial Desa*, the Village Social Institution) with the *LKMD*, and how this change has undermined participation in rural development, see N. G. Schulte Nordholt, "From *LSD* to *LKMD*: Village Level Participation." In Philip Quarles van Ufford, ed., *Local Leadership and Programme Implementation*, 1987a: 31-53; also Mubyarto and Loekman Soetrisno, *Integrated Rural Development: Indonesia*, 1989.

significant for Gudang.[37] The project was meant to maintain the function of the main road of Gudang hamlet as a gateway for vehicles to go to other hamlets within the village, which would of course have some political and especially economic implications.

This project was identified by the chairman of the development board of *LKMD*, a large farmer, wealthy trader and close friend of the village head. He mainly traded unhulled paddy (*gabah*), and since much of the wet-rice fields were in Lopait hamlet, most likely his business was badly affected by the construction of the alternative road which connected Lopait hamlet directly (bypassing Gudang hamlet) to the main (provincial) road. It was probably expected that once this road in *RT* V had been refurbished, some of the old customers from Lopait hamlet would return.

The funding for the project came mostly from the *Bandes* fund for the fiscal year of 1992/1993 and donations from local businessmen. Like no other project implementation in Gudang, this project was carried out through purely *kerja bhakti.* With some twenty people working voluntarily every day (in turn, under social obligation), the project was completed within a month.[38] As in many other parts of rural Java, the identification and the selection processes of this road improvement project were biased toward the richer households of Gudang (Hardjono, 1983: 54).

The role of the rural elite (the traditional elite which are also belonged to the richer income group)[39] in the decision-making process of most of the development projects implemented in Gudang has been very substantial. Their influence on the project selection and on the project planning of the refurbishment of the *MCK* 'Kaligedog' in *RT* IV (1990/1991), the *MCK* 'Kaliwates' in *RT* II (1993/1994) and of the refurbishment of the village road in *RT* III (1992/1993) was very strong, which left the beneficiaries without a say. Throughout the decision-making processes there were no major disagreements, and therefore, no voting for the selection of the projects. Any projects identified by the hamlet leaders (the elite) were generally accepted without argument.

The decision to undertake the refurbishment of the *mushola* (Muslim prayer house) 'Al Hidayah' was made without the involvement of the ordinary congregations. The project was identified, selected and planned by a small group of wealthy farmers, who were then the caretakers of the *mushola.* The literacy and the rural health cadre projects were extensions of the central

---

[37] The poor condition of this road in *RT* V, especially during rainy seasons had encouraged the construction of the road in Lopait hamlet in 1989.

[38] In most cases, those who have contributed donations for the project may be exempted from the 'obligation' of *kerja bhakti.*

[39] The most influential person among the rural (traditional) elite was the chairman of the *RW*, who was a police officer. The other members were mostly either civil servants or wealthy farmers.

government programmes and therefore, no decision-making processes occurred at village level.

Evidently, people's participation in the decision-making process had been seriously undermined by the excessive involvement and strong influence of the rural elite in the project identification, selection and planning. The implications were clear, as has been shown in the case of the refurbishment of the village road in *RT* V discussed above, the rural elite benefited most from the development project.

Apart from the refurbishment project of the village road in *RT* V, the implementation stages of other projects were carried out through a combination of employing professional labourers and *kerja bhakti* by the local and mostly the poorer households, who were unable to contribute much in terms of money. In most cases the professional labourer(s) would lead a team of local voluntary workers who would assist them in activities which required no complex skills. The organisation of the *kerja bhakti* was arranged by the hamlet leaders, who assigned the household-heads to participate (in turn) in the *kerja bhakti.*

As a whole, the excessive influence of the rural elite of Gudang has to some extent impeded people's participation at the decision-making stage. The research has also revealed that vested interests of the rural elite have been evident in the processes of project identification, selection and planning. The considerable degree of participation in the actual implementation stage through *kerja bhakti*, as demonstrated in the cases under investigation, has to some extent implied an exploitation of the poorer households by the rural elite. As for the sharing of benefits, although 60 percent of the respondents in Gudang hamlet claimed to have benefited from the projects, it was the elite who have benefited the most.

4. Discussion and Summary

Among the development projects implemented in the three hamlets of Lopait between the fiscal years of 1988/1989 and 1993/1994, the highest participation occurred in the hamlet of Calombo.[40] In most of these projects, the people of Calombo had been very much involved in the decision-making processes, both directly (through the forum of *rembug dhusun*) or indirectly, through the chairmen of *RT* as their representatives in hamlet leaders meetings (*rapat dusun*). On the contrary, most of the projects in Celengan were identified and planned by the village and supra-village structures (outside the hamlet), leaving

[40] The findings of this analysis on people's participation in these three hamlets did not ascertain whether the people of Celengan and Gudang hamlets were less eager to be developed than the people of Calombo or whether the people of Calombo were more modern than their counterparts in Celengan and Gudang hamlets. The findings were conditional on the socio-cultural, political as well as the economic settings of these three hamlets, and on the particular projects being implemented in these three hamlets.

the local people with very little involvement in the decision-making processes. In regards to the development projects in Gudang hamlet, with only few exceptions, they had been identified and planned by the rural elite within the hamlet. In most cases the local people simply accepted the projects proposed by the rural elite.

Most of the official assessments on participation in Indonesia have focused on the actual involvement of the rural people in the implementation stage. In fact, in a large number of village level development studies, the implementation stage in development projects was the most difficult stage to assess. This is especially true with a comparative village study such as this present research, when different socio-economic settings as well as different means of employment were important determinants of the forms of participation in the implementation of the development projects. It was difficult to quantify whether the implementation of the development projects in Calombo, which was mostly through *kerja bhakti* was more participative than that of Celengan hamlet, which took the form of donations. Similarly, it was difficult to compare the *kerja bhakti* in Calombo with the use of paid (skilled) labourers in Celengan and Gudang hamlets; let alone to quantitatively distinguish the use of the skilled labourers in Celengan and Gudang hamlets. It was apparent that the use of the skilled labourers in Celengan hamlet was related to the types of the income earning activities engaged in by the people, who were mostly traders and urban employees. This was very different from the motives of Gudang in hiring professional labourers. In Gudang, effectiveness in project implementation was one of the main considerations in hiring skilled labourers. Furthermore, to comparatively assess people's participation by comparing the amount of donations collected for the projects in each hamlet would certainly be ambiguous.

In order to do justice to the different aspects which underlie the data on participation at the implementation stage, two phases of assessment have been undertaken in this present analysis: first, the qualitative analysis based on the in-depth observation, as extensively discussed earlier in this chapter; second, to separately analyse the reasons for participation[41] (or not participation) in each hamlet. These reasons were then classified into four groups.[42] First, those who were, for whatever reasons, self-motivated to participate in the projects. Second, those who were 'forced' to participate or in a situation where they could not avoid but to participate in the projects. Third, those who were unable to participate in the projects, such as elderly and sick people, commuting

[41] In terms of both donations and the peoples' involvement in the actual work, either without payment (*kerja bhakti*) or with some form of payments, as in the case of *padat karya* projects.

[42] In order to minimise bias in the interpretations of the answers from the respondents and for the sake of the applicability of the scoring system in rural Java, where education level is relatively low, this analysis only divided the answers into four groups.

traders and urban employees. And fourth, those who, for whatever reasons, did not wish to participate. A simple scoring system was then attached to each group (see Table 3.1).[43]

There were at least two dangers in employing a scoring system in a comparative study. First, the question on the reasons for not participating in development projects might be understood differently in each hamlet. Second, the scoring was often biased toward the subjective feeling of the researchers. However, since the questions were asked only after in-depth observation of the local socio-cultural values in the three hamlets had been undertaken, both pitfalls were sufficiently addressed.

Table 4.1. Scoring System to Assess Participation at the 'Implementation Stage' in the Three Hamlets of Lopait

Classification of reasons for participation and their scores	Calombo		Celengan		Gudang	
	Percent of respondents	Scores	Percent of respondents	Scores	Percent of respondents	Scores
Self-motivated to participate (Score: 2)	48.4	96.8	27.9	55.8	30.6	61.2
'Forced' to participate (Score: 1)	16.5	16.5	23.8	23.8	41.9	41.9
Unable to participate (Score: -1)	34.4	-34.4	45.9	-45.9	18.1	-36.2
Did not wish to participate (Score: -2)	0.7	-1.4	2.4	-4.8	9.4	-18.8
Total Scores	**100**	**77.5**	**100**	**28.9**	**100**	**48.1**

Source: calculated from primary data.

[43] It needs to be noted that the scoring system developed in this analysis was neither meant as a universally applicable tool nor as a comprehensive measurement for assessing the whole process of participation in development projects. There are several limitations on the use of this scoring system. Firstly, it served only to counter-check the data or the findings which had already been established through in-depth qualitative observations. Secondly, as the scoring system was expected to be used by the rural population of Java, 'simplicity' had been among the main considerations in developing the scoring systems. It would be inappropriate to expect rural Javanese, given their low level education, to apply sophisticated tools in assessing their participation in development (PRA). Thirdly, the scoring system was developed out of the socio-cultural as well as political context of rural Java and was meant specifically to quantitatively measure the 'implementation stage' of a development project.

The result of the comparative analysis of the scoring system was largely consistent with the data which had already been established by the in-depth qualitative observations (as extensively discussed earlier in this chapter). Both by qualitative observation and by the quantitative scoring system, the highest level of participation at the implementation stage was recorded in Calombo hamlet.

It appeared that the sharing of benefits stage was very much related to the decision-making process. As most of the development projects in Calombo hamlet were identified by the local people, the projects have mostly met the needs of the people. Accordingly, 93.6 percent of the respondents in Calombo claimed to have benefited from the development projects and more than eighty percent made use of the facilities on a daily basis. In Celengan, only 35.6 percent of the respondents claimed to have benefited from the development projects. This figure indicates that most of the projects in Celengan had not met the needs of the people. As has been discussed already, this was mainly caused by inaccurate project identification, since most of these projects had been identified by the village and supra-village structures. We have also shown in this study that once a project met the needs of the people of Celengan, participation was significantly higher. In Gudang, the benefits of the development projects have not been equally distributed. The rural elite have benefited most from them. In a number of cases these benefits had been obtained at the expense of the poorer households.

Throughout the discussion it has become apparent that the socio-cultural, political as well as religious homogeneity of Calombo hamlet has to some extent contributed to substantial people participation in development processes. It is also apparent that, as development programmes implemented in Gudang failed to recognise the socio-economic differentiation, kinship loyalty and patronage relationships both between the supra-village structures and the rural elite, and between the elite and the poor, the projects have delivered fewer benefits to the poorer households. As the poorer households made little contribution to the decision-making processes, they also have shared less in the benefits, compared with the elite.

The socio-political pressures on Celengan, which produced the excessive involvement of the supra-village structures in the development processes there (especially in the decision-making stage), have not actually suppressed people's participation in socio-economically developing their hamlet. While it is true that the above analysis indicates minimal participation in a number of projects (especially those identified by the supra-village structures), the external pressures have strengthened the bond of the hamlet community. Hamlet identity has not only become one of the perceived needs of the people of Celengan, it has also produced the motivation to socio-economically develop their hamlet through different means and opportunities available to them. The success in creating urban employment opportunities (mostly in Jakarta) for their fellow peasants from Celengan, for example, has significantly contributed to the overall increase in average income of the hamlet.[44] The seemingly lower participation in the government's development projects, and evidently higher participation in the projects which either meet their needs of hamlet identity or were motivated by it, was their very strategy, not only to survive (Slamet, 1982), but to effectively respond to the external pressures (Scott, 1976).

In order to fully understand the process of people's participation, one needs to consider both the external and internal factors which influence people participation in development. While it is important to acknowledge the contributions of the external factors, such as politics, means of employment, and economic structures, it is similarly important to analyse the contributions of the socio-religious values (the internal factor) of the people in these three hamlets to development processes. Therefore it is appropriate to dedicate the next chapter to the analysis of the contributions of the socio-religious values of these three hamlets to people's participation in development.

Map 7 Celengan Hamlet

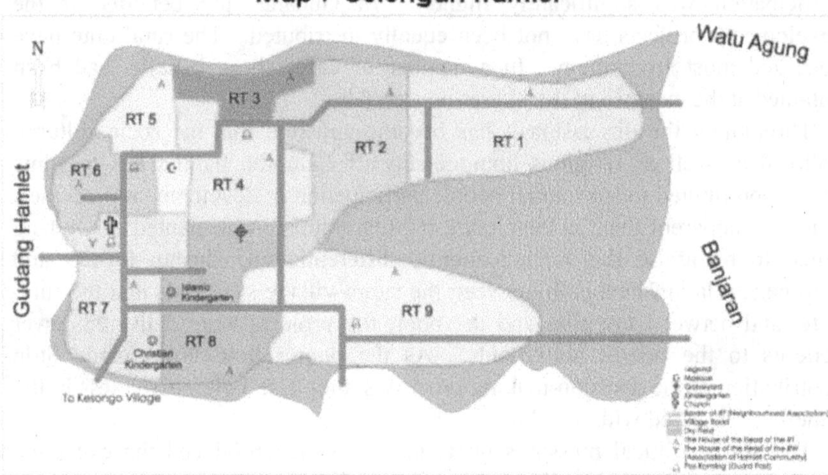

---

[44] The temporary migrant (urban) employees and traders of Celengan in Jakarta would normally return to their hamlet once in a year, during the Muslim holiday (*Riyaya*). It is not uncommon then for them to bring some of their fellow peasants back to Jakarta after the *Riyaya*.

Map 5 Calombo Hamlet

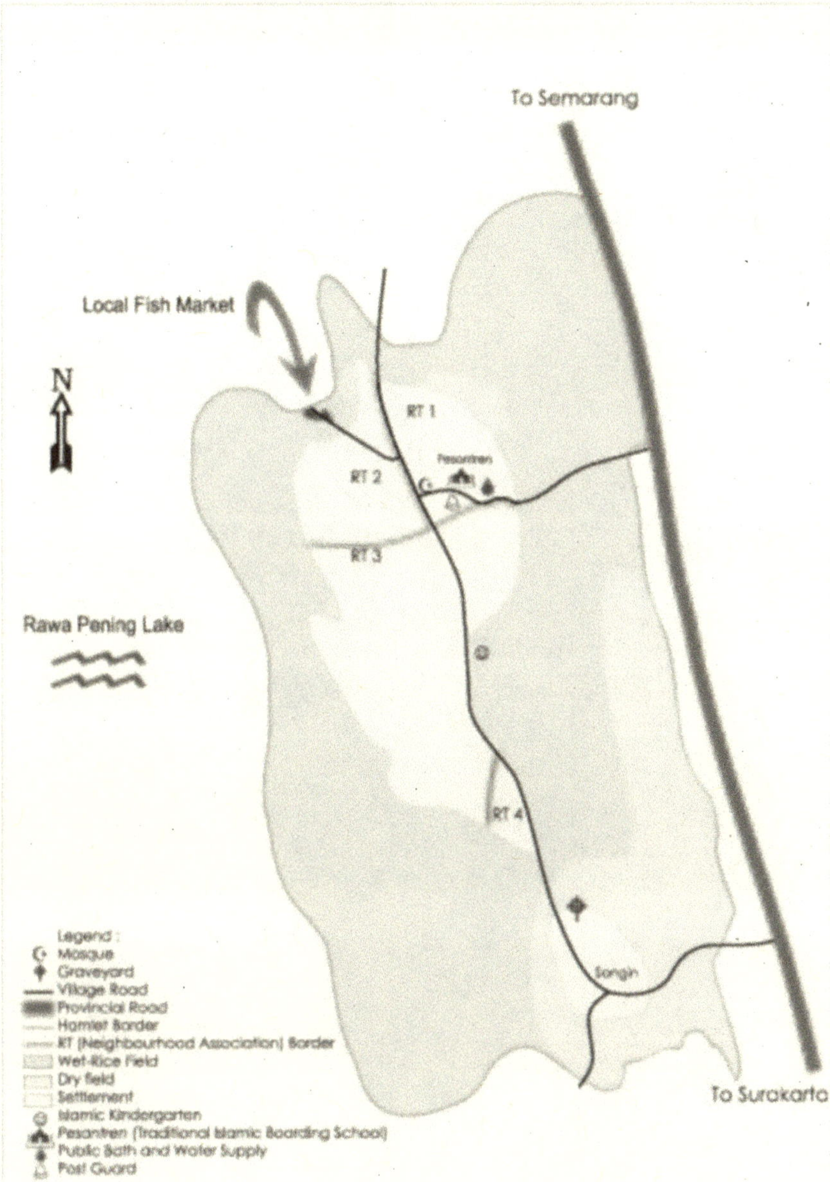

Map 6 Gudang Hamlet

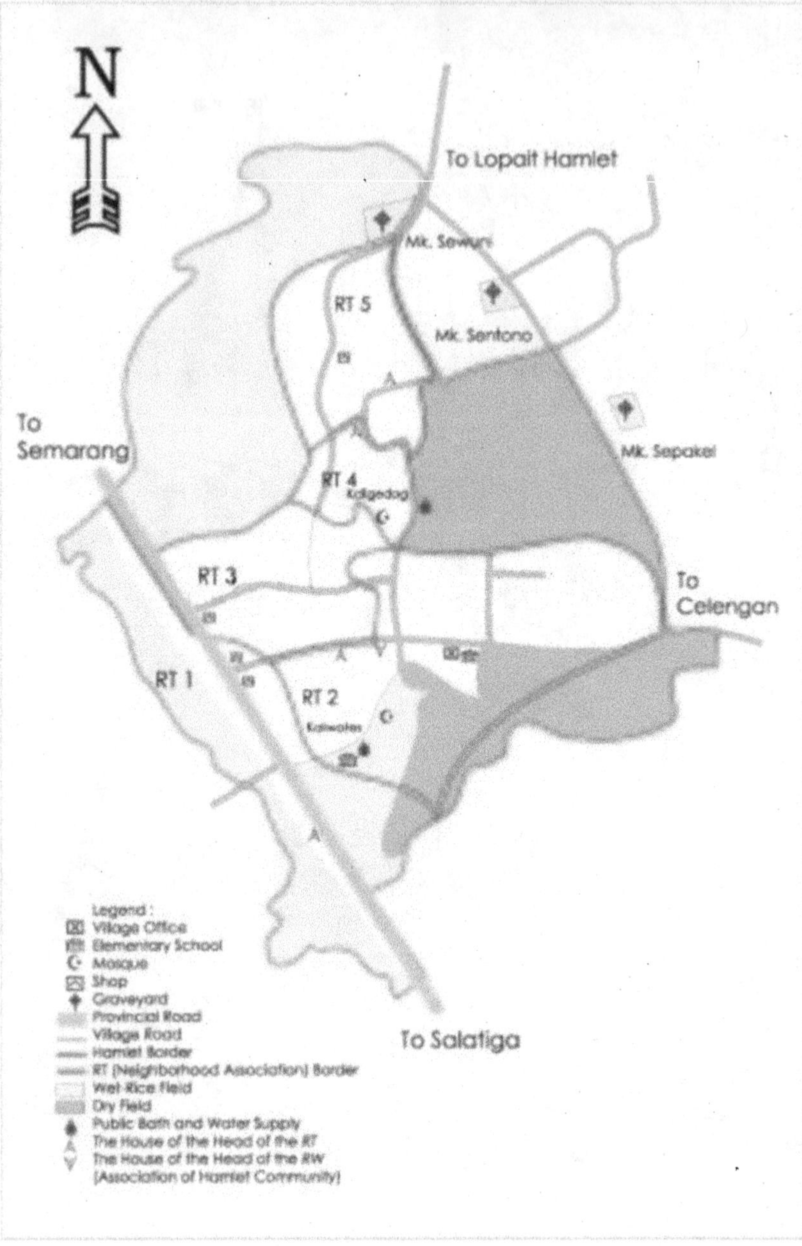

Chapter 5

The Socio-Religious Values of the Three Hamlets of Lopait and Their Relationship to People's Participation in Development

The aims of this chapter are to describe the present socio-religious values of the three hamlets of Lopait, and to examine the relationship between these socio-religious values and the people's participation in development programmes in their respective hamlets. The fact that the population of all three hamlets is ethnically Javanese and mostly professes to be Muslim, does not imply that it represents a single socio-religious value system. In fact, as has been demonstrated in Chapter Two, hamlet identity remains strong despite the government's efforts to integrate these hamlets within one official village boundary. Apart from the contribution of different historical backgrounds to the formation of the communities in these three hamlets, the constant interaction of these hamlets with the 'outside world', in terms of their adaptation and response to development programmes and policies, has contributed to further shaping of particular social structures and local values in each hamlet.

It is not sufficient, however, to describe the local values of these three hamlets as the reactions and responses of the people to external forces. The most important aspect in describing the local socio-religious values lies in understanding the belief system within each of these hamlets (Geertz, 1973: 123-5).[1] This belief system includes religious concepts, myths, moral principles and rituals (Steeman, 1973: 43).[2] In regard to rituals, there has been a marked tendency among interpretive anthropologists to look at ritual as a 'text'. The significance of this approach lies in what the ritual 'says' rather than what it does to the people. Such an approach, while useful, was ill-conceived, since people often participate in rituals with different needs,[3] perceptions and

---

[1] See also Talcott Parsons, *Structure of Social Action*, 1937: 427; and Emile Durkheim, *The Elementary Forms of the Religious Life*, 1965: 419.

[2] For an extensive discussion on the relationship between belief systems and local values, see Talcott Parsons and Edward A. Shils, eds., *Toward a General Theory of Action*, 1951: 162-183; Clifford Geertz, *The Interpretation of Cultures*, 1973: 113-127; and Robert W. Hefner, *Hindu Javanese, Tengger Tradition and Islam*, 1985: 18.

[3] For the relationship between 'needs' and 'values', see Clyde Kluckhohn, "Values and Value-Orientation in The Theory of Action: An Exploration in Definition and Classification." In T. Parsons and E. A. Shils, eds., *Toward a General Theory of Action*,

interpretations of the event (Hefner, 1985: 269). The present research has therefore, sought to explain not only what the ritual means for the people, but also what it does to the people.

The significance of the different variants within the Muslim community in Java have long been indicated;[4] however, there are a number of different ways of looking at these variants. Geertz (1960), for example, viewed the *abangan* (syncretic-animistic) religious system as the basic stratum of the Javanese culture; consequently, the *santri* (devout Muslim) tradition was regarded as the foreign culture and the 'counter-tradition' (Geertz, 1968: x). Among those who disagreed with Geertz was Nakamura (1976), who refused to see the *abangan* as an independent variant, let alone as the indigenous Javanese culture. Nakamura viewed the *abangan* tradition only as a phenomenon within the on-going process of the Islamisation of Java.[5]

A number of concerns have been expressed in regard to Geertz's concept of *santri-abangan-priyayi variants* (1960)[6] applied to Javanese Muslims as a whole. In fact, in many parts of Java, the terms *santri* and *abangan* are either unknown or have different meanings. In Besuki, East Java, for example, the landless farm labourers are called *santri* (Hefner, 1985: 242). In Lopait, the term *santri* refers exclusively to the students at *pesantren* (traditional Islamic school).[7] Mark R. Woodward's study of Islam in the Sultanate of Yogyakarta identified a further classification of *santri* into the '*white santri*' and the '*red santri*' (1989: 150). While in the north-west coast of Central Java, Bagelen and

---

1951: 425-427; and Edward C. Tolman, "A Psychological Model." In T. Parsons and E. A. Shils, eds., *Toward a General Theory of Action*, 1951: 285-290.

[4] In the late nineteenth century a Dutch missionary, C. Poensen mentioned two variants within the Muslim community in Java, which he called the *abangan* (those who did not strictly observe the Islamic faith) and the *putihan* (those who strictly followed the teaching of Islam), see C. Poensen, "Iets over Javaansche Naamgeving en Eigennamen." *Mededeelingen Vanwege het Nederlandsche Zendeling Genootschap* 14 (1870): 312. However, it was Clifford Geertz, in his book, *The Religion of Java* (1960), who gave the first comprehensive description of these variants. For a thorough review of Geertz's concept of the *santri, abangan, priyayi* variants, see H. W. Bachtiar, "The Religion of Java: A Commentary." *Majalah Ilmu-Ilmu Sastra Indonesia* 5 (1973): 85-115.

[5] This theory views the *santri* belief system as the basic layer of Javanese culture, see Matsuo Nakamura, *The Crescent Arises over the Banyan Tree*, 1976: 1-24; C. C. Berg, "The Islamization of Java." *Studia Islamica* 4 (1955): 111-192; and Zamakhsyari Dhofier, "Santri-Abangan Dalam Kehidupan Orang Jawa: Teropong dari Pesantren." *Prisma* 5 (1978): 64-72.

[6] According to Geertz, "*abangan*, representing a stress on the animistic aspects of the over-all Javanese syncretism and broadly related to the peasant element in the population; *santri*, representing a stress on the Islamic aspects of the syncretism and generally related to the trading element (and to certain elements in the peasantry as well); and *priyayi*, stressing the Hinduist aspects and related to the bureaucratic element" (1960: 6).

[7] This is believed to be the original meaning of the term *santri*, see Koentjaraningrat, *Kebudayaan Jawa*, 1984: 208.

Banyumas, the term *abangan* has the concept of despicability referring to those who do not take religion seriously (Koentjaraningrat, 1984: 208). In Kebumen, the *santri-abangan-priyayi* framework simply did not exist (Alexander, 1987: 16).

As elsewhere in the third world, 'modernity' has called for a new religious vocabulary and social identity, both at local and national levels. The dynamics of this change appear in a number of micro-studies on rural Javanese belief systems which indicated the complex reality of contemporary (New Order) Indonesia.[8] As belief systems are very much bound up with the totality and the dynamics of the social reality, both at local and national levels (Hefner, 1990: 238-9), it is even more difficult to make a generalised classification of the Muslim community in Java into strictly the *santri* and *abangan* variants (Woodward, 1989:7). For the purpose of our discussion, it is sufficient to say that these variants are not static. The dynamics of these variants could be seen as the result of either the 'adaptive' strategy of the *abangan* tradition (Geertz, 1968), or the success of and reaction against the Islamisation process (Nakamura, 1976), or the search for new social identity in response to the socio-political development and policies in the modern Indonesian nation state (Hefner, 1985: 239).

Irwan Abdullah's recent study of Jatinom (1994) can be seen as an attempt to understand the dynamic interactions between religious values and socio-economic progress (modernity) of a semi-urban community, both locally and in the wider context. He identified significant contributions of these dynamic interactions in shaping the values and identity of the trading elite of Jatinom. In a sub-district level study, Irwan Abdullah classified the Muslim community in Jatinom into three categories.[9] First, the *Islam KTP* (ID-card Muslims), described as those Muslims who were ignorant of Islamic concepts. Most of them belonged to the lower classes and maintained the traditions of the *Agami Jawi* (Javanese syncretic-animistic belief system).[10] The second category were people who followed Islamic concepts and customs, but did not stick to pure Islamic values. Most of the people in this category regularly attended Friday prayers, practised the *shalat* (prayer five times a day) and fasted during the

---

[8] See for example, Robert W. Hefner, *The Political Economy of Mountain Java*, 1990; Irwan Abdullah, *The Muslim Businessmen of Jatinom*, 1994; Gillian Hart, *Power, Labor and Livelihood*, 1986; Pradjarta Dirdjosanjoto, *Memelihara Umat*, 1994; Jennifer Alexander, *Trade, Traders and Trading in Rural Java*, 1987; and Koentjaraningrat, 1984.

[9] According to Irwan Abdullah, this classification was made by the elite-trader Muslim reformists (the followers of Muhammadiyah) of the Jatinom sub-district. Unfortunately he failed to take account of the classification made by the lower class agrarian *abangan* community in Jatinom (1994: 89-91).

[10] For an extensive reading of the *Agami Jawi*, see Koentjaraningrat, 1984: 310-427; Niels Mulder, *Mysticism and Daily life in Contemporary Java*, 1975; and Harun Hadiwijono, *Man in the Present Javanese Mysticism*, 1967.

month of *Ramadhan.* At the same time they were also involved in various kinds of *slametan* (ritual feasts), which are strictly forbidden for the followers of Muhammadiyah (modernist Islamic organisation) (cf. Hefner, 1985: 104). The third, the 'true followers of Islam' (followers of Muhammadiyah), are those who lived according to the rules and values of Islam. These 'true followers of Islam' were almost exclusively the trading elite of Jatinom. The self identification of the trading elite of Jatinom as the true followers of Islam suggests that, in spite of the massive secularisation brought by extensive government development programmes, religious orientation remained one of the major aspects in shaping the groups' values and identity in the Jatinom sub-district.[11]

In Lopait, the devout Muslim (*santri*) is called the *tiyang agami* (religious person), which distinguishes him from the rest of the community. Some features which characterise this group are regular attendance at the Friday prayers and evening *pengajian* (recitation of the *Qur'an* and study session),[12] the practice of *shalat*, and fasting during the month of *Ramadhan*. These *tiyang agami* in Lopait are exclusively the followers of the *Nahdlatul Ulama* (the orthodox Muslim organisation).[13] Even with such commonality in religious practices among the *tiyang agami,* it is still difficult to categorise them into a single value-orientation group. The historical background of each hamlet, the ecological setting, the means of livelihood, and the different responses of each hamlet to supra-village policies have also contributed to the formation of their distinct value orientations. The value orientation of devout Muslims in Celengan, for example, as we shall see later in this chapter, is closer to the values of the rest of the Celengan community than to the devout Muslims in

---

[11] Irwan Abdullah also identified other important aspects which shape group values in Jatinom, namely livelihood and social class (1994: 91-93).

[12] The *pengajian malam* (evening recitation of the *Qur'an* and study session) is held twice a week in Calombo and Celengan hamlets, and once in 35 days [*selapan*] in Gudang hamlet.

[13] NU (*Nahdlatul Ulama*) is the Arabic phrase for the council of Muslim Scholars. The organisation was founded in 1926 by K. H. Abdul Wahab Hasbullah, K. H. Asnawi, K. H. Hasjim Asj'ari and others. The formation of NU was, to some extent, motivated by or a reaction against the Muslim modernist movements of Muhammadiyah, which was founded by H. Ahmad Dahlan in 1912. Throughout its history the appeal of NU has been largely to the rural-agrarian Javanese, while its rival organisation, the Muhammadiyah, has its supports from urban-based merchants. In the Soekarno era, politically the orthodox Muslim largely affiliated to the NU, while the modernists mostly supported the Masyumi (the modernist Muslim party). For further reading see Deliar Noer, *The Modernist Muslim Movement in Indonesia 1900-1942*, 1973; B. J. Boland, *The Struggle of Islam in Modern Indonesia*, 1971; James L. Peacock, *Purifying the Faith: The Muhammadiyah Movement in Indonesian Islam*, 1978b; and Clifford Geertz, *The Social History of an Indonesian Town*, 1965.

Gudang and Calombo hamlets.[14] On the other hand, the value orientation of devout Muslims in Gudang are more closely associated with the devout Muslims in Calombo than to the rest of the Gudang community. With such complex interactions and strains within a religious cluster (i.e. the devout Muslims), it is important to look at different factors which shape the value orientation of each hamlet.

1. The Socio-Religious Values of Calombo

The local leaders of Calombo are generally proud of the way Calombo has been depicted as a Muslim hamlet. Socio-culturally, politically as well as economically, Islamic concepts and values seem to have been deeply rooted among the population. However, unlike most *santri* villages in Java, which have a long history of established Islam, the *santri* tradition of Calombo was a recent development.[15] Only some 30-40 years ago did Islam begin to effectively influence the group's values and identity in Calombo hamlet.

1.1. Rituals and Religious Concepts

In the late 1950s Fatekurohman, the son of the *kyai* (Islamic religious teacher) in Gading village who married a resident of Calombo, began his career as a *kyai* (religious teacher) in Calombo hamlet.[16] From an interview with the *kyai,* it appears that during the early days of his career, the majority of the people in Calombo were followers of the *Agami Jawi.* Therefore, he described his task as bringing the people of Calombo to the 'pure' teaching of Islam. Over the years, this process of 'religious purification' significantly affected the socio-religious as well as cultural values of the people.

1.1.1. The Concept of *Taqdir* and the Ritual of *Ruwatan*

The following are the areas where the teachings of Islam, as presented by *kyai* Fatekurohman, have changed the local concepts and values. First, the concept of *taqdir* (destined by Allah) and the ritual of *ruwatan* (religious ritual to free someone from a spell, bad luck or a state of disgrace).[17] Previously, the ritual of

---

[14] Long before the New Order development programmes were introduced, Geertz had identified significant differences between value orientations of the rural and urban *santri* of Mojokuto (1965b: 89). See also J. Alexander, 1987: 15-16.

[15] See for example, the long history of Islam establishment in Jatinom (Abdullah, 1994: 81-88) and in Tayu (Dirdjosanjoto, 1994: 54-81).

[16] The work was pioneered by his father in the late 1940 and '50s. The people of Calombo began to refer to him as *kyai* only after he had founded the *pesantren* (Islamic traditional school) and the mosque in Calombo in the mid sixties.

[17] Those who were considered under a spell, disgrace or bad luck, so as needing to be freed (*ruwat*) are the *Kendana-kendini* (a family with only two children, male and female), the *Ontang-anting* (a family with only one child), the *Julung-wangi* (a child

ruwatan was a common practice in Calombo hamlet as in many other parts of rural Central Java. In most cases, the ritual was led by an experienced *dalang* (the performer at a shadow-play performance), who would, among other things, perform an all-night shadow-play. Interestingly, so called 'unfortunate' children were not the only ones who received the magic deliverance of the *ruwatan*. Others attending were equally enthusiastic in seeking a blessing from the ritual. The *ruwatan* was, therefore, very much a public ritual, where all the audience, and in fact, the whole hamlet community was involved in seeking magic deliverance or blessing from the event.

The *kyai*'s main objection to the *ruwatan* was not so much the ritual celebration itself, but the concept which underlay it. The *ruwatan* ritual assumed the possibility of changing the *taqdir* of Allah. Since it was not possible to perform a *ruwatan* ritual with an agenda other than the magical deliverance from one's 'bad fate', the ritual was gradually abandoned. Thus, in the conflict between *ruwatan* and *taqdir*, between the concept that 'the world is evil' and the concept of the sovereign *taqdir* of Allah, and between the long life struggle to escape from afflictions and the struggle to surrender (Islam) to the *taqdir* of Allah,[18] it was the *taqdir* of Allah which prevailed.

While the concept of *taqdir* has strongly emerged in the life of the people of Calombo, one should not, however, assume that it was accepted without reserve. Calombo's concept of *taqdir* was expressed very clearly in the struggle over the electricity project in Calombo in 1993. The people of Calombo became very anxious, having to wait for three years to get access to electricity, and had received no indication that they would be successful. While all explanations from the village and sub-district officials had failed to calm the people, the *kyai*'s simple speech at the Friday prayer succeeded. In his speech, the *kyai* simply asked the people to accept the *taqdir* of Allah in this matter. That was to accept that the time had not come for the people of Calombo to have electricity. A good number of people accepted this *taqdir* without reserve, while others simply did not dare to challenge the religious authority of the *kyai*. It needs to be noted that the concept of *taqdir* as held by the people of Calombo did not lead into extreme fatalism. As was apparent in the case of the electricity project, the *kyai*'s interpretation of the event as the *taqdir* of Allah only came after all efforts had failed. Others simply adopted this interpretation on the merit of the socio-religious authority of the *kyai*.

---

born at the sun rise), *Julung-pujud* (a child born on a journey), *Margana* (twins, one dark, the other light skinned), and *Dampit* (twins, male and female). For further reading, see, Koentjaraningrat, 1984: 376-378.

[18] Islam literally means 'surrender to the will of Allah'.

1.1.2. The Process of Rationalisation,[19] Magic and *Suronan*[20]

A number of studies on Islam and entrepreneurial (economic) development in Java show that Islamic reform has stimulated the rise of local business groups (Kuntowijoyo, 1971; Nakamura, 1976; De Jonge, 1989; Abdullah, 1994). Earlier, Lance Castles (1967) was also able to establish significant links between entrepreneurial (economic) development and the process of Islamic purification and reformism in Kudus, Central Java. Unfortunately, these studies have mostly concentrated on the reform (modernist) Muslim groups of Muhammadiyah as opposed to the orthodox (traditional) Muslim groups of the NU. In fact, H. De Jonge (1989) suggested that the rise of the local business groups in Parindu, Madura had been achieved through the changes in traditional values. With this in mind, we will now look at the process of rationalisation of religious concepts in Calombo hamlet.

In Javanese traditional belief, the first day of the month of *Sura* in the Javanese calendar is considered *kramat* (sacred, associated with some supernatural power).[21] People observed this sacred day by preparing ritual offerings to the guardian spirit at sacred (*kramat*) places, such as under a big tree, at a water spring, or a particular sacred tomb. Those who owned *pusaka* (sacred heirlooms)[22] would normally perform the annual ritual bath for them.

---

[19] The term was employed by Max Weber (1930; 1947; 1948; 1964) as his central thesis, where he believed that history moves toward rationalisation. This process of rationalisation covers various aspects in life, such as individual actions, economic organisations and institutional arrangements. Further he believed that this process of rationalisation can not proceed without spiritual change in terms of "the increasing systematization of religious ideas and concepts, the growth of ethical rationalism, and the decline of ritual and magical elements in religion" (Morris, 1990: 69). See also Clifford Geertz, *Peddlers and Princes: Social Change and Economic Modernization in Two Indonesian Towns*, 1963b: 143; Talcott Parsons, 1937: 500-533; and H. H. Gerth and C. Wright Mills, eds., *From Max Weber: Essays In Sociology*, 1948: 323-359.

[20] *Suronan* is a ritual observance of the first day of the month of *Sura* in the Javanese calendar, which is also the first day of the year in the Muslim calendar.

[21] *Kramat* renders a magical or supernatural power, associated with either a particular place, a certain day or date, or a *pusaka* (sacred object/heirloom), which are considered holy or sacred. It is derived from the Arabic word *karamat*, which means, 'the miracle of the saints', see Mark R. Woodward, *Islam in Java: Normative Piety and Mysticism in the Sultanate of Yogyakarta*, 1989: 170-171.

[22] *Pusaka* are sacred objects with some magical power (*kesakten*). Most powerful *pusaka* are associated with a particular powerful person in Javanese or Islamic history. Woodward observed that some of these powerful *pusaka* have played an extremely important role in the Javanese state cult. Since the power of the sultanate of Yogyakarta is concentrated in these most powerful *pusaka*, they are stored in the innermost portion of the court. Most *pusaka* (including those owned by ordinary Javanese) are given a ritual bath once a year on the first day of the month of *Sura*, see Mark R. Woodward, 1989: 166-7, 199-213. For further reading see, B. R. Anderson, "The Idea of Power in Javanese Culture." In Claire Holt, ed., *Culture and Politics in Indonesia*, 1972: 1-69.

The rituals are conducted at midnight entering the first day of the month of *Sura*.

With regard to the *Suronan* ritual in Calombo, the *kyai* mentioned his two main objections. First, to revere the magical power of sacred objects was considered *sjirk* (associating other powers or objects with Allah).[23] Second, Islam also forbids observance of a certain date or month as *kramat* (sacred). Both to revere the magical power of a *pusaka* and to observe a certain month as *kramat* were condemned as undermining the power of Allah. It should be noted, however, that magic itself has a place in the theology of the Javanese Muslim (Woodward, 1989: 226).[24] In fact, the *pesantren* in Calombo has been known as one of the centres of the *Asmaul Husna* (In the name of Allah), a kind of *santri* mystical movement (*tarekat*),[25] which includes an art of self defence.

Like most of the mystical movements in Java, *dzikir* (repeatedly reciting certain portions of the *Qur'an* as a meditation exercise) stands in the centre of the *Asmaul Husna* ritual (cf. Koentjaraningrat, 1984: 392). The majority of the people in Calombo, including women and children, as well as people from other villages in Central Java have joined this *tarekat*. The ritual takes place every Friday afternoon and is usually led by the *kyai*'s eldest son.[26] New members are required to undergo ritual cleansing.[27] The weekly ritual begins with *dzikir*; only after reciting portions from the *Qur'an* a few hundred times can the participant be filled with inner (invisible) power. Reportedly, an eleven year old member of the *Asmaul Husna* was able to lift a huge banana tree (12 inches in diameter) without much effort.

---

[23] The word is derived from the Arabic *shirk* which means polytheism. There have been different views among the traditionalist *santri* as to the legality, morality and the ultimate consequences of the magical power and the ownership of *pusaka*. Some tried to dissociate the magical power from *sjirk* through a system of classifications between legal and illegal magic; most, however, tend to regard magical power as an ethical rather than a doctrinal issue, see Mark R. Woodward, 1989: 225-233.

[24] Classical Middle Eastern Islam does not deny the reality of magical power. Spells and amulets are mentioned in the *Qur'an*, *Hadith* and works of prominent Muslim theologians, such as Ibn Khaldun and al-Ghazzali, see D. B. MacDonald, *Development of Muslim Theory, Jurisprudence and Constitutional Theory*, 1909; F. Rosenthal, *Ibn Khaldun, The Muqaddimah, An Introduction to History*, 1980; and E. Gellner, *Muslim Society*, 1981.

[25] The word is derived from the Arabic *tariqah*, a *Sufi* (Muslim mystical leaders) order. For further reading of *Sufism*, see R. A. Nicholson, *Studies in Islamic Mysticism*, 1921; and M. Smith, *Studies in Early Mysticism in the Near and Middle East*, 1931.

[26] He received his training at the famous *pesantren* of Gontor in East Java. For further reading on how a *tarekat* leader is prepared, see Koentjaraningrat, 1984: 407-409.

[27] Most *tarekat* have a set of cleansing rituals for their new members; however, the forms and requirements of this ritual vary from one *tarekat* to another. To join the *tarekat* 'Silamba' in Karanganyar (Central Java), for example, one has to drink a glass of milk and eat a piece of bread which have been mystically prepared by the leader (teacher) of the *tarekat*. In Calombo (*Asmaul Husna*), a new member is required to eat the innards of a rooster.

Magic was not, obviously, the reason behind the *kyai's* objection for the *Suronan* ritual. It was rather the worship of sacred objects, such as a *keris* (Javanese dagger) and other charms, which according to the *kyai*, distracted the people's attention from the greatness of Allah. Even though the religious (Islam) 'purification' in Calombo did not remove magic from its rituals, it did gradually move the people's religious concept toward rationalisation. The second objection which the *kyai* raised in regard to the *Suronan* ritual, namely, the belief that certain dates and months were *kramat* (sacred), seemed to indicate this process of rationalisation.

The first day of the month of *Sura* in the Javanese calendar, which is also the new year's day (1st. *Muharam*) in the Muslim calendar continues to be celebrated in Calombo. However, the content, as well as the notion of the celebration (ritual) is different. Food or flowers are no longer offered under the big tree or at the water spring. Neither is there the ritual washing of the *pusaka*. In fact, the *Suronan* ritual has been largely abandoned by the people of Calombo. Nowadays, on the night before the first day of the month of *Sura* (*Muharam*), the people celebrate the Muslim new year. Just like the old days, the people stay awake the whole night, but now instead of praying to the spirits under the big tree or at the water spring, they recite the *Qur'an* in the Mosque. The notion of the ritual is also different. The *Suronan* ritual was performed out of fear, whose purpose was to appease the guardian spirits, while the notion of the First *Muharam* is an expression of thankfulness.

1.1.3. *Bersih Makam* (The Ritual Cleansing of the Graveyard)

The ritual of *bersih makam* in Calombo is performed prior to the month of *Ramadhan* (the Muslim fast month).[28] The ways in which this ritual is performed in the three hamlets of Lopait represent clearly the three different socio-religious values. Originally, the ritual of *bersih makam* in Calombo involves the physical cleansing of the graveyard, prayers addressed to the souls of the *leluhur* (ancestors)[29] and food offerings given to the ancestors. Nowadays, the ritual begins with a *kerja bhakti* (mutual work) to clean up the site (graveyard), which is followed by prayers being offered for the souls of the ancestors and the deceased relatives, who were buried there, to be accepted in the sight of God. Finally, the foods which they brought are distributed to those who have taken part in the *kerja bhakti*.

---

[28] This is distinct from the ritual of *Ziarah* (visits to the tombs of the saints and holy men of Islam), which is also a well established practice (as an act of piety) among the Javanese Muslims. For further reading on the practice of *Ziarah* in Java, see James J. Fox, "Ziarah visits to the Tombs of the Wali, the Founders of Islam on Java." Paper prepared for the Monash University Annual Winter Lecture Series, 10 August 1989.

[29] The *leluhur* (ancestors) include the soul of the founding fathers of the village, the guardian spirits, the deceased parents, grand-parents and other older relatives.

In Celengan hamlet, the ritual of *bersih makam* is performed twice a year, in the month of *Sapar* and *Ruwah*[30] in the Javanese calendar.[31] Apart from the act of physical cleansing of the site and the scattering of flowers, central to the ritual is a *slametan* (ritual feast).[32] The *slametan* performed in this occasion is similar to that of a 'death *slametan*' (Geertz, 1960: 78).[33] It is believed that the deceased parents or grandparents come to the *slametan* and eat the odour of the food. The ritual conveys an expression of respect for the deceased parents, grandparents and other ancestors.

The people of Gudang performed the ritual of *bersih makam* in the month of *Rejeb* of the Javanese calendar, a month earlier than the other two hamlets. The purpose of this ritual is to seek for a blessing (from the ancestors) to observe the religious exercise of the fast month. The ritual begins with a *kerja bhakti* to clean up the graveyard. It was followed by collecting all the food prepared for the ritual (*ambeng*). Next was the *tahlilan* (the *dzikir* or recitation of *Laailaaha Illallah*, by reciting "*la ilaha illallah*"), which lasted for some 15 minutes. At the final stage was the actual communal feast (*slametan*), where the foods were distributed to and eaten by all the participants.

The notions of the ritual of *bersih makam* as performed in these three hamlets were distinct one from another. In Calombo hamlet, the purpose of the ritual is to pray for the souls of the deceased parents, grandparents and other relatives, to be accepted in the sight of God. In Celengan, the ritual conveys an expression of respect to the ancestors. While in Gudang hamlet, the ritual was meant to seek blessings from the ancestors, to observe the Islamic religious exercise of fasting.

---

[30] The name of the month of *Ruwah* comes from the Arabic *arwah*, meaning 'souls of the dead'.

[31] The twelve lunar months of the Javanese calendar are *Sura* (*Muharam* in the Muslim calendar), *Sapar, Mulud, Bagdamulud, Jumadilawal, Jumadilakir, Rejeb, Ruwah, Pasa, Sawal, Sela*, and *Besar*.

[32] The root word, *slamet* denotes a state of well being, safety and security (Sullivan, 1992: 90). Geertz described *slametan* as the central institution of the *abangan* (syncretic-animistic Javanese) culture (1960: 11). Woodward, however, argued that the religious goals of the *slametan* are rooted in the local interpretation of the *Sufi* theory of mystical union (1989: 52). Further more, Jennifer Alexander also reported that *slametan* are constantly recurring features of village life in the *santri* district of Kebumen (1987: 16). In general, the reformist Muslim strongly rejected the *slametan*. The followers of *agami Jawi* (Javanese religion), on the other hand, preserved most of the rituals. The traditionalist (orthodox) Muslim tended to stand in-between; they favoured most of the *slametan* with Islamic contents, see James L. Peacock, *Muslim Puritan, Reformist Psychology in Southeast Asian Islam*, 1978: 44.

[33] Geertz identified four major types of *slametan*: First, those in connection with life crises - birth, circumcision, marriage and death; second, those associated with Muslim ceremonial calendar; third, those concerned with social integration of the village, such as the ritual of *bersih desa* (village cleansing); and fourth, the *slametan* for special occasions such as, one assigned for a new job, moving to a new house, illness, or taking a new personal name (1960: 30).

1.2. The Socio-Cultural Orientation

1.2.1. Arts and Entertainment

The process of 'religious purification' has moulded other aspects of community life in Calombo hamlet. The sophisticated traditional Javanese marriage ceremony, for example, has largely been abandoned. The Muslim marriage ceremony (*ijab kabul*) which traditionally represented a minor part in Javanese marriages (Koentjaraningrat, 1984: 136; Geertz, 1960:56), has become increasingly central to the ceremony. With the exception of a few richer households, most marriages in Calombo have been made simple, consisting of only the *ijab kabul* in the Mosque and some simple *slametan* at the bride's house.[34] Instead of a simple *slametan*, a richer household would lay on a feast together with entertainment for the public (the hamlet populations and the relatives of both sides). The entertainment performed at the wedding celebration also reflected the strong influence of the orthodox Islam tradition in Calombo. The art of entertainment is called *terbangan*, an elaborate chanting taken from portions of the *Qur'an* or from the history of the prophet Mohammed, in which some musical instruments called *terbang* (a small drum) are beaten.

During the field research in 1992-1994, it was found that no household in Calombo owned a TV. The closest cinema was in the town of Salatiga, which is some seven kilometres away. The only modern entertainment accessible for the population of Calombo was the *layar tancap*, a movie cinema set out temporarily on a sports ground, with neither roof nor chairs. Once in every three or four months a cigarette company set out this kind of entertainment in Tuntang sub-district, as a means to advertise their products. This rather infrequent encounter with modern media and entertainment (TV, movies, etc.), has to some extent preserved the central role of the *kyai* in shaping the local values.[35]

1.2.2. The Spirit of *Gotong-Royong* (Co-operative Labour)

The role of *gotong-royong* practice in the implementation of development projects in the Calombo hamlet has been analysed in Chapter Four. The analysis suggests that most of the project implementations in Calombo have been carried out through some kind of *gotong-royong* practices. Compared to the implementation of development projects in Celengan and Gudang hamlets,

---

[34] Economic considerations might also have contributed to this marriage ceremonial change, see Koentjaraningrat, 1984: 136.

[35] By the end of my field research in late 1994, electricity became available to the people of Calombo. Very soon, a number of households purchased TV sets, either through credit or cash. With this access to national and global information and cultures through the media (TV), the social development of Calombo in the next ten years will take a different course altogether and thus provide ground for further study.

the role of the *gotong-royong* practice in Calombo has been recorded as being more significant. However, a proper *gotong-royong* spirit with its basic virtues of egalitarianism, generosity, and consideration could not be assessed only through the degree of the *kerja bhakti* (voluntary work) practised in development projects. One needs to go beyond the role of *gotong-royong* in such formal occasions, and look at its role in the daily life of the people.

There are different types of *gotong-royong* practice in rural Java.[36] One is the *gotong-royong* to help a neighbour to build or renovate his house, known as *sambatan*. Traditionally, *sambatan* involved a one day co-operative construction of a house (usually made of wood), between sunrise and sunset. In the Calombo and Celengan hamlets, *sambatan* remained a very common practice. On occasions, when the owner of the house was among the poorer households in the hamlet, not infrequently, the *sambatan* was extended for several days. Reportedly, such a practice is dying out in many modernised villages, especially when people in those villages began to build permanent (*tembok* or brick) houses (Sullivan, 1992: 95). Such is the case in Gudang hamlet, where most of the house construction in recent years has been undertaken by local developers or groups of professional labourers. Only in the case of extremely poor households did the close neighbourhood help with house construction.

1.3. Summary

A change of ritual observance in Calombo hamlet has also occurred in the ritual of *bersih desa* (village cleansing). The ritual which was formerly intended to clean the hamlet from evil spirits, has been transformed to become simply a *kerja bhakti* to clean up the physical appearance of the hamlet (roads, ditch, public bath). From a number of changes which occurred in the ritual observance as well as the cultural expression of the people of Calombo, one could readily detect the ongoing process of Islamisation ('religious purification') and rationalisation of religious concepts. These processes of Islamisation and rationalisation have not been as dramatic as a reformist Muslim would expect, but they were significant in shaping the socio-religious values of the people. Most apparent was the change in their concept of life, where the people of Calombo have a more positive view on life and less fear of evil (destructive) spirits. The change in the ritual of *bersih makam* also brought

---

[36] In an extensive study in two villages in Central Java, Koentjaraningrat identified seven types of *gotong-royong* practice, namely, *tulung-layat* (in times of bereavement and calamity); *gugur-gunung* (to execute major development projects); *slametan* (ritual feast); *sambatan* (helping to build or renovate a neighbour's house); various phases of agricultural production; *nyadran* (graveyard cleansing); and other activities related to the duty of the landholders to help the poorer households, such as *bawon* (share cropping), see Koentjaraningrat, *Some Social-Anthropological Observations on Gotong-Royong Practices in Two Villages in Central Java*, 1961: 29.

realisation that the living are more powerful than the dead. The souls of the ancestors no longer have control over them; in the past they prayed to the dead, now they pray for the dead. Together with the positive concept of life and the diminishing fear of 'destructive' spiritual powers, this realisation of the potency of life has, to some extent, encouraged creativity and productivity.

Both *wayang* (shadow play) mythologies and the *slametan* ritual, which were perceived as the core of the traditional Javanese belief (Darmaputera, 1988; Geertz, 1960), have largely been abandoned. As a result, the totalistic world view (Darmaputera, 1988: 110) and the Javanese concept of tolerance (Anderson, 1965: iii) derived from the *wayang* mythologies and the *slametan* ritual have very little relevance in the daily life of the people of Calombo. Interestingly, instead of modern entertainment and secular celebrations, as in many villages, it was the orthodox Islamic concepts, ideas, entertainment and rituals, which have replaced the traditional Javanese core belief. The concept of *nrima* (passive attitude toward life)[37] has been replaced by the concept of *ikhtiar* (work, effort) and of *sedhekah* (giving of alms).[38] And the hierarchical world-view of the traditional Javanese has gradually been replaced by the egalitarian concept of *umma* (Islamic community).[39] It seems that it was this concept of *umma*, which has, to some extent, intensified the practice of *gotong-royong* in Calombo hamlet.

2. The Socio-Religious Values of Celengan

Celengan hamlet consists of a religiously mixed community, with some 18 percent Christians, 4 percent Buddhists, 15 percent *santri* (*tiyang agami* or devout Muslims) and 63 percent nominal Muslims. It needs to be noted, however, that the difference between the devout Muslims and the nominal Muslims in Celengan is not as antagonistic as between the *santri* and the *abangan* in Geertz's terms. Apart from the observance of the *shalat* (prayer five times a day) and the regular attendance at Friday prayer by the devout

---

[37] Although the concept of *nrima* conveys the idea of 'active' acceptance of one's place in the universe, which denotes the quality of one's patience, endurance and perseverance (Darmaputera, 1988: 97; Kodiran, 1971: 347), quite often, it leads to conformity and produces a passive attitude toward life. The concept of *taqdir* in Calombo, on the other hand, is not a static concept. It is closely related to time (dispensation), and could only be revealed through *ikhtiar* (work, effort).

[38] *Amal* (charity) and *sedhekah* (giving of alms) to the poor are amongst the most important aspects of the *kyai*'s religious concept. Since the *kyai* sees his role as the channel of God's grace to the world, accumulation of wealth in the world is also an important aspect in the theology and practice of the followers of orthodox Islam in Java, see, Zamakhsyari Dhofier, "Islamic Education and Traditional Ideology on Java." In J. J. Fox, ed., *Indonesia: The Making of a Culture*, 1980: 268-269.

[39] The sense of community as equal believers is very important in the theology of Islam (*Sunni*), see, Clifford Geertz, *Islam Observed*, 1968: 76-77; Mark R. Woodward, 1989: 140; and Irwan Abdullah, 1994: 155.

Muslims, there are many similarities between them. In regards to general norms, values and life-style, the devout Muslims in Celengan are closer to the nominal Muslims, and even to the Christians in Celengan than to devout Muslims in Calombo and Gudang hamlets. Accordingly, this religious heterogeneity creates no divisions or tensions within the hamlet. Compared to the Gudang and Calombo hamlets, *kerukunan* (harmonious relationship) and tolerance within Celengan hamlet appeared to be much higher. The traditional values of *Kejawen* (Javanese belief system) seem to be much stronger in socially uniting the people of Celengan, than are the religious differences in causing divisions.

2.1. Christianity in Celengan

The first conversions to Christianity occurred in the early 1960s. The early growth of the church was very slow; prior to 1965, reportedly, there were only six Christian families (households) in Celengan hamlet.[40] As in many parts of Java, following the 1965 aborted *coup d'etat* and the banning of the PKI (Indonesian Communist Party) in 1966, a large number of the population of Celengan, who were mostly members of the BTI (Indonesian Farmer Front) turned to Christianity for political protection.[41] Between 1966-1968 the number of Christians in Celengan increased significantly. By the end of 1968 the majority of the population were either members or sympathisers of the Christian faith (Purnomo and Sastrosupono, 1986: 101-103).[42] However, between 1969-1970, as Indonesia regained socio-political stability, the people

---

[40] Organisationally, the Church in Celengan belongs to the GKJ (*Gereja Kristen Jawa*, Javanese Christian Church) denomination. Both theologically and organisationally GKJ is mostly influenced by the Gereformeerd Church in the Netherlands. For an extensive reading on the history and development of the GKJ, see J. A. C. Rullman, *De Gereformeerde Zending in Midden Java*, 1970; J. D. Wolterbeek, *Babad Zending Ing Tanah Djawi*, 1938; and Hadi Purnomo and M. S. Sastrosupono, eds., *Gereja-Gereja Kristen Jawa: Benih Yang Tumbuh dan Berkembang di Tanah Jawa*, 1986.

[41] In most cases, people who had not been registered as members of one of the five official religions (Islam, Protestantism, Roman Catholicism, Hinduism and Buddhism) were accused of being PKI supporters. Since the Muslims, especially members of the Ansor (NU Youth Organisation) were behind the massacre of the PKI supporters in rural Java, the alleged communist supporters mostly turned to religions other than Islam for protection. For further readings on the growth of Christianity and Hinduism in the aftermath of the 1965-1966 bloodshed, see M. C. Ricklefs, "Six Centuries of Islamization in Java." In N. Levtzion, ed., *Conversion to Islam*, 1979: 100-128; M. L. Lyon, "The Hindu Revival in Java: Politics and Religious Identity." In James J. Fox, ed., *Indonesia: The Making of a Culture*, 1980; and Clifford Geertz, "Religious Change and Social Order in Soeharto's Indonesia", in *Asia* 27 (1972): 62-84.

[42] Reportedly, the membership of GKJ increased from 56,471 in late 1965 to 115,000 in the early 1970s. For further reading on this mass 'conversion' within the GKJ, see Susilo Darmowigoto, *Pemashuran Injil Kerajaan Allah di Wilayah Sinode GKJ*, 1969.

of Celengan reconsidered their religious allegiance. Former religio-cultural obstacles which had hindered most of the people of Celengan hamlet from becoming Christian prior to the 1965-1966 bloodshed, such as the requirement to abandon the *slametan*, the food offerings and circumcision rituals, re-surfaced. As a result, the Church in Celengan lost a large majority of its members and sympathisers. Most of the people turned to either Buddhism or Islam which allowed them to keep the *slametan*, food offerings and the circumcision rituals. It needs to be noted, however, that those who remained in the Church were not necessarily free of syncretism. A large number of those who chose to remain in the Church privately continued to observe *slametan* and other rituals of the Javanese traditional belief system (Purnomo and Sastrosupono, 1986: 138-139).

In the early 1970s, as the Church (local) leadership was gradually handed down to the local Christians (with the formation of the local Presbytery), the Church undertook a major change with regard to their policies on the ritual observance of the Javanese traditional belief system. The aim of the policy change was partly to 'contextualise' the Gospel, but more importantly to regain former Church members who had left due to conflicts with Javanese traditional rituals. The Church leaders have, therefore, adopted a rather mild stance on the issue.[43] However, this mild policy did not succeed in attracting their former members; instead, it has encouraged some of the existing Church members who had privately maintained the traditional Javanese rituals to continue the observance of the rituals openly.

2.2. Rituals and Religious Concepts

As in many other parts of rural Java, *slametan* stands at the centre of socio-religious rituals in Celengan hamlet.[44] While it is true that *slametan* can be found in most rural Javanese villages, apart from the reformed Muslim (Muhammadiyah) villages (Hefner, 1985: 104; Alexander, 1987: 16), the content as well as the notion of the ritual itself often differed from one place to another. Hefner's study of the Tengger in East Java, for example, indicated that "what Tengger regard as a *slametan* differs significantly from the lowland event of the same name." (1985: 104). In most cases, the differences in both the content and the notion of *slametan* are largely determined by the religious orthodoxy of the Muslim Javanese communities (Hefner, 1985: 105-112).

Regardless of their religious affiliations, most of the people of Celengan observe the *slametan* ritual. The orthodox Muslims prefer to call it *tahlilan*

---

[43] This policy change in regards to the Javanese traditional rituals was also reported to occur in many other parts of Java in the 1970s (Purnomo and Sastrosupono, 1986: 108).

[44] For an extensive reading on *slametan* rituals see, Clifford Geertz, *The Religion of Java*, 1960.

(recitation of the *Laailaaha Illallah*),[45] the Christians refers it as *bidstond* (prayer gathering),[46] and the nominal Muslims, who are mostly followers of the *Agami Jawi* (Javanese belief system) often call it *kenduren* (prayer meal). The most common *slametan* are rituals to commemorate or to celebrate a person's life passage- birth, circumcision, marriage and death. The *slametan* to celebrate birth, and to commemorate a deceased family member are observed in a relatively modest way, with attendance of some 20 to 30 male guests,[47] within one's own *RT* (neighbourhood association) (Dirdjosanjoto, 1994: 97). On the other hand, the *slametan* to celebrate circumcision and marriage are generally attended by a larger number of guests, depending on the socio-economic status of the host.

2.2.1. *Slametan* to Commemorate A Deceased Family Member

The *slametan* for the third day, the seventh day, 40 days, 100 days, first anniversary, second anniversary, and 1,000 days after one's death are largely preserved by the Muslims, the followers of the *Agami Jawi*, as well as by the Christians in Celengan.[48] Much of the settings, the foods and the sequence of the ritual of *slametan* in these three communities are similar. The only obvious difference appears in the way prayers are offered. Whatever the religious orientations, the *kenduren* (*bidstond* or *tahlilan*) ritual to commemorate a deceased family member in Celengan is simple and straightforward.

Since the Church in Celengan does not have a pastor or a vicar, a Christian *bidstond (kenduren)* is either led by a clergyman from the Church in Blotongan (Salatiga) or, in most cases, by one of the local Church elders. The *bidstond* is usually attended by Church members, close relatives and immediate neighbours within the *RT* (neighbourhood association). The leader initiates the ritual by

---

[45] Within the *santri* community, the *slametan* to give thanks to God is called the *tasyakuran*.

[46] Like *slametan*, the term *bidstond* serves a large variety of socio-religious purposes. One performs *bidstond* (*bistonan*), to occupy a new house, taking a new job, and most commonly, to observe rites of passage, see H. Purnomo and Sastrosupono, 1986: 138.

[47] In most cases, women help with the food preparation and remain in the kitchen throughout the ceremony. Both in Javanese traditional *slametan* and Muslim *tahlilan*, all the participants are male, see Geertz, 1960: 12-14. Although it is still uncommon, and has not been very successful, the Christian *bidstond*, has to some extent, encouraged women to join the ritual.

[48] Frank L. Cooley observed that while the Synod of the GKJTU (*Gereja Kristen Jawa Tengah Utara*, The Christian Church of the Northern Central Javanese) did not encourage the local churches to observe Javanese *rites de passage*, it was a common practice among local churches, especially in the rural area, to observe this set of rituals with a *bidstond*, see Frank L. Cooley, *Benih Yang Tumbuh III: Memperkenalkan Gereja Kristen Jawa Tengah Utara*, 1975: 53. It seemed that, while the GKJ held a rather stronger policy against these Javanese traditional rituals, most of these rituals continued largely to be practised by its members, especially those living in the rural areas, see H. Purnomo and Sastrosupono, 1986: 139.

giving an introductory speech on behalf of the host. In a traditional Javanese *slametan*, this speech is called *ujub* (Geertz, 1960: 12; Hefner, 1985: 106).[49] Following the introductory speech he leads the attendance in singing a hymn. In most cases, only a handful of people sing along with him, the rest, the non-Christians especially, simply sit with their heads bowed. Next, the leader reads a portion from the Bible, with a very brief commentary related to the context of the occasion. The prayer which follows the Bible reading is a very general one, to ask God's blessings for the host, the guests and the food. As the ritual ends, the food is served for the guests and some is sent to neighbours and friends who are not present at the ritual.

Those attending the *bidstond* are free to make their own interpretation of the ritual (Darmaputera, 1988: 113-116). The clergyman understands his task as being to comfort the family of the deceased person; on the other hand, the host sees the purpose of the *bidstond* as bringing peace to the soul of the deceased person.[50] The guests may have yet another interpretation different from that of the clergyman and the host, depending on their religious orientations. This particular type of *bidstond* was initially meant to retain the 'horizontal' or the social aspect of *slametan* ritual and, to some extent, abandon the 'vertical' (sacred) aspect of *slametan*, namely the belief of the participation of the souls of the deceased in the ritual feast, which was considered by the Church as unbiblical (Cooley, 1975: 53; Purnomo and Sastrosupono, 1986: 139). In reality, however, a large number of the Christians in Celengan retain this vertical aspect of the *slametan*. For them the idea of this *bidstond* is not primarily to worship God, but to show respect to the deceased parents or other older relatives in a Christian way. Apart from the main Christian ritual of *bidstond* which is presided over by a clergyman, most often the host also privately prepares a *bucu* (a small *tumpeng* [ceremonial dish of rice served in a cone shape]) and a cigarette, if the deceased is a male, or a betel leaf, if the deceased is a female. To avoid offending the clergyman, the *bucu* is placed in the inner part of the house or in the bed room of the deceased.[51]

It seems that the church's adoption of this set of rituals for commemorating a deceased family member, or to be more precise, the insertions of the church's

---

[49] The speech was delivered in a very formal 'high Javanese', and normally consists of an expression of gratitude for his neighbour's attendance, a statement of the purpose of the *slametan*, and a request for blessings of those present, as well as an apology for any inadequacy in the ceremony.

[50] The *bidstond* at the third and the seventh day are initially meant to comfort (*bidstond panglipuran*) the family members of the deceased. On the other hand, the *bidstond* at the 40 days, 100 days and the rest are meant to commemorate (*bidstond peringatan*) the deceased person.

[51] Among the followers of the *Agami Jawi*, the *bucu* is placed in the centre of the house or in the living room. People also prepare *bucu* for their deceased parents and grandparents on certain sacred days, such as *Senin Pon* and *Selasa Kliwon* in the Javanese Calendar.

liturgy (hymn and prayer) into this traditional *kenduren* ritual, have had a modest impact, in terms of value change. Even though the vertical aspect of the traditional *kenduren* ritual, namely the concept of maintaining one's relationship with the spirits by offering them food, has been suppressed within the formal ritual (*bidstond*), it does not mean that the people have completely abandoned it. It seems that because the Church in Celengan has no clear teaching on the (immanence of) guardian spirits, it was unable to address the issue adequately. As a result, the Church simply ignores it, leaving Church members to decide whether to deal with these spirits privately (outside the formal Church ritual/*bidstond*), as most of them have done, or to abandon their belief in the existence of guardian spirits altogether.[52] Furthermore, the other aspects of this *kenduren*, namely the socio-mystical unity with the deceased parents and grand-parents, as well as the social unity of the participant, have largely been implicitly maintained in the *bidstond*.

The Muslims, both the *tiyang agami* (devout Muslims) and the nominal Muslims of Celengan also, commemorate the third day, the seventh day, 40 days, 100 days, the first and second anniversaries and the 1,000 days after one's death by a *yasinan*[53] and a *tahlilan*. The third day and seventh day rituals are called the *yasinan*, while the 40 days, 100 days and the other following rituals are called the *tahlilan*. Both rituals are led by a local *dukun* (a specialist in Javanese traditional spiritual knowledge).[54] The only death ritual led by a *santri*, in fact by the *modin* (village religious [Muslim] official)[55] himself is the

[52] The synod's policy on circumcision and death rituals remained indecisive for quite a long period, until recent years (Purnomo and Sastrosupono, 1986: 138-139). With regard to GKJTU, up to the late 1970s it had been very busy solving its internal problems, such as organisation, finances, leadership, and especially its relationship with the GKJ. Accordingly the synod did not have sufficient time to address the socio-cultural issues between the Church and Javanese socio-religious traditions. Frank L. Cooley observed that a number of sensitive encounters between the Church and the Javanese socio-religious traditions were left for the local Church leader to decide (1975: 52-56).

[53] From *surah yasin*, the 37th. *surah* in the *Qur'an*.

[54] The term *dukun* is used for a wide variety of Javanese traditional specialists. In Tengger, East Java, the priest is called *dukun*, thus the chief priest is a *lurah dukun* (Hefner, 1985: 8, 50). In general, the term *dukun* is associated with the exercise of some supra-natural power, and sometimes he is referred to as a sorcerer (*dukun santet*) or a magical healer. There are other *dukun*, however, which have nothing to do with any super-natural power, such as *dukun bayi* (traditional mid-wife) and *dukun sunat* (traditional circumcision specialist). For further reading on the role of *dukun* in traditional Javanese communities, see Koentjaraningrat, 1984: 422-427; and R. Hefner, 1985: 108-110.

[55] A *modin* is elected for life by his fellow villagers and (then) ratified by the local government. One of the main qualifications is a good command of Islamic law. His duties include preparing a corpse for burial, conducting marriage and divorce ceremonies, giving advice on inheritance according to Islamic law, and so forth, see C. Geertz, 1960: 206-207.

burial ritual.[56] The fact that the present *modin* of Lopait is a *santri* of Gudang hamlet, who is also a member of the village elite in Gudang, explains why the role of the *santri* in the death rituals (even among the *santri* community) in Celengan hamlet is kept very low. As has been discussed in Chapters Three and Four, the people of Celengan considered the village elite at Gudang hamlet as an instrument of the supra-village structure to socio-politically suppress the people of Celengan. Thus, it appears that the hamlet identity of Celengan is somewhat stronger than their religious (*santri*) orientation.

At present, there are three prominent *dukun* in Celengan who are considered qualified to lead the *yasinan*, the *tahlilan* and the other *kenduren* rituals, namely Sukarno (70 years), Parin (60 years) and Marto (80 years). In a *yasinan*, the ritual begins by the Islamic greeting from the *dukun* in charge. Then follows the two main elements of the ritual, namely the *al-fatehah* and the reading of five to ten verses from the *surah yaṣin.* Finally, after the prayer for the meal the *dukun* will utter the *al-ichlas* (whole-heartedly accepted) prayer. The *tahlilan* ritual is somewhat similar; instead of reading the *surah yasin*, the *dukun* recites the *Laailaaha Illallah.* And the reading *al-fatehah* is replaced by the pronouncement of the *mantera* (magic spells).[57] Apart from these slight differences in the elements of the ritual as described above, the meals (*bucu*), and the other ingredients of the ritual, such as the red and white roses, the clear water in a bowl, as well as the burning of incense are all the same. Just as the Muslims are passively participating in the Christian *bidstond*, so are the Christians attending these 'Muslim' rituals without uttering the prayers, but they are free to interpret the events individually. So, during the time of prayer, the Christians pray according to their own beliefs.

The religious concept behind the *yasinan* and the *tahlilan* is to *ngirim donga* (to send prayers for the deceased ones). Both the *tiyang agami* (devout Muslim) and the followers of *Agami Jawi* (*Kejawen*), believe that the souls of the deceased remain in the village for a period of time. The *Kejawen* believe that the souls of the deceased are either wandering around the house or remain near the grave. During this period of time, they (the living) have the responsibility not only to show respect to their deceased parents and grand-parents, but also to provide food (*bucu*) for them. The *Kejawen* believes that

---

[56] Since a *modin* is both a Muslim (*santri*) leader as well as a village level government (Department of Religious Affairs) representative, Geertz's description of the problem of ritual dependency of the *Kejawen* followers to the *modin* in the burial ritual (1973: 153-158), should not be understood only in terms of religious dependency (Nakamura, 1976), but also in terms of government administrative necessity. Only the *modin* has the legal right to issue death certificates for deceased Muslims, so to bury a Muslim without his knowledge could be considered an illegal act.

[57] According to a respondent who is a devout Muslim in Celengan, the *dukun* obtained these specific *mantera* (magic spells) by undergoing *laku* (an act of *samadhi* [meditation] or fasting for a period of time).

after this period of time (1,000 days),[58] the souls of the dead will either become spirits or by the aid of *kenduren* performed by the living, they are making an upward journey to the seven heavens. The *kenduren* for commemorating the 1,000th day after death, the most elaborate ritual, is observed to celebrate the completion of their journey, when the souls finally reach their union with God (Woodward, 1989: 174; Geertz, 1960: 75). The *tiyang agami*, on the other hand, believes that the souls of the deceased remain in the grave until the end of the world (*Al-Qiyama*) (Koentjaraningrat, 1984: 383). During which time, the *tiyang agami* are to pray that the souls of the deceased may find a resting place and a state of peace in the grave, to be forgiven by God and, finally, to be accepted in the sight of *Allah* (Woodward, 1989: 174).[59]

Unlike the Church in Celengan which did not address the "issue of fear of the (guardian) spirits" (Cooley, 1975: 56), the *tiyang agami* (devout Muslims) addressed the issue in a confrontational way. While the foods, the odour of flowers, the burning of incense and the pronouncement of the magic chants (spells) are considered the main elements of a traditional Javanese *kenduren*, the main elements of a *tahlilan* is the *tahlil* (recitation of the *Laailaaha Illallah*) and the reading of the *Qur'an*, both the *al-fatihah* (the first *surah* of the *Qur'an*) and the *surah yasin*. The *tahlil* and the reading of the *Qur'an* are believed to have some magical power to drive away the evil spirits. Thus, within a Muslim *kenduren* (both *yasinan* and *tahlilan*) participants are also free to make their own interpretation. The followers of *Kejawen* would focus their attentions on the aspects of the rituals which they consider to be the most essential in terms of their responsibility to the dead, such as the burning of incense and the prayer meal. On the other hand the *tiyang agami* would concentrate on the reading of the *Qur'an* and the recitation of the *tahlil*. The Christians who also attend the ceremony would concentrate on something else.

---

[58] After 1,000 days the corpse is thought to have decayed entirely, which means the fate of the (soul of the) dead has been decided and thus the responsibility of the living (family members) has ended.

[59] Both Javanese and Islamic views on the afterlife are ambiguous. The length of time the souls of the deceased remain in or near the grave is unclear for both the *Kejawen* and *tiyang agami*. Some of the followers of *Kejawen* believe that after 1,000 days, the souls of the deceased reach the state of *sempurna* (complete or perfect), to be considered as *leluhur* (ancestors), who are worthy to receive offerings. Other believe that after 1,000 days the souls vanish (as the body has completely become dust), and so breaks the connection between the dead and the living. The *tiyang agami* are also uncertain about the time souls spend in the grave. Different from what is commonly believed, that the souls remain in the grave until the day of judgement, Al-Ghazzali stated that the souls "remain in the graves for two or three months, after which they are flown up to the garden (heaven) on birds" (Smith and Haddad, 1981: 52). For further reading on Javanese and Islamic views on death, see Mark R. Woodward, 1989: 172-176; Clifford Geertz, 1960: 72-76; James L. Peacock, 1978: 84-86; and J. Smith and Y. Haddad, *The Islamic Understanding of Death and Resurrection*, 1981.

The death rituals as observed by these different religious groups in Celengan have largely retained the notion of traditional Javanese *kenduren*, namely to maintain harmony in the existence of the living. While new aspects, such as the concern for the salvation of the dead (the devout Muslims), and the concern for the emotional state of the living (the Christians) do emerge in the observance of the death rituals in Celengan, the majority of the people remain largely concerned with the maintenance of harmony, both between the living and the dead, and among the living themselves.

2.2.2. The Ritual of *Bersih Dhusun* (Village Cleansing)

Although the Calombo and Gudang hamlets have their own *bersih dhusun* ritual (at hamlet level), the ritual in Celengan hamlet is considered as representing the whole village of Lopait. Compared to the observance of the *bersih dhusun* ritual in Calombo and Gudang hamlets, which has become little more than just a routine *kerja bhakti* (mutual work), the ritual in Celengan has been the most celebrated one.[60] While traditional Javanese rituals have been dying out in many parts of Java due to the massive inflow of and the intensive interaction with modernity, the traditional *bersih dhusun* ritual in Celengan has been more celebrated during the 1980s and early 1990s.

As has been discussed in Chapter Three, in the late 1970s and 1980s, socio-politically as well as economically, Celengan hamlet was under tremendous pressure. As most of the population of Celengan had been members of the BTI (Farmer Front, associated with the communist party), the policies of the local and regional governments toward Celengan seemed to be based on suspicion. As a result, the socio-political and the economic status of the people of Celengan was severely harmed. These external pressures have, to some extent, strengthened their hamlet identity, and have produced awareness for the need of a greater social unity within the hamlet. It is within this very context, that the resurgence of the *bersih dhusun* ritual in Celengan hamlet in the 1980s and early 1990s has occurred.[61]

The *bersih dhusun* ritual in Celengan is held in *Sapar*, the second month of the Javanese lunar calendar, at the night prior to the *Jumat* (Friday) *Kliwon*.[62] It

---

[60] Koentjaraningrat also observed that in most cases, the full notion of the *bersih dhusun* ritual is maintained in more remote villages, as compared to the villages which are close to cities (1984: 376), see also Clifford Geertz, 1960: 83. Geertz's description of a *bersih dhusun* ritual in Mojokuto is an example of a ritual which has lost its notion and became a mere routine village activity (1960: 82).

[61] Robert Hefner observed that the Hindu reform movement in Tengger in the 1970s and 1980s was a response to a national (New Order) policy, which was brought about by the integration of Tengger into the 'outside world' (1985: 264-265). See also Lyon's (1980) report on the Hindu revival in Java following the 1965 massacre.

[62] The Javanese month is 35 days; it combines the Javanese five-day market week (*Legi, Paing, Pon, Wage and Kliwon*) with the Western seven-day week (*Minggu, Senin,*

involves *slametan* at the grave of the founder or the *danyang* (guardian spirit) of the hamlet,[63] *kerja bhakti*, and an all night shadow play performance. While the purpose of the ritual includes the physical (especially the main water spring which symbolises the source of life for the whole village) and the spiritual cleansing of the village, the *bersih dhusun* is originally designed to strengthen the social bond among the members of the village (hamlet) community by putting an end to all the existing enmity (Geertz, 1960: 83; Koentjaraningrat, 1984: 375). The idea of spiritual cleansing is not to drive the spirits out of the village (hamlet), but to call for all members of the hamlet community to cleanse their minds from wickedness, sins and other inappropriate thoughts and deeds which might cause calamity. The Javanese believe that the universe, and to some extent, the village (the small universe) is maintained by a state of 'balance and harmony' (Darmaputera, 1988: 120-125).[64] As calamity and destruction are perceived to come whenever this state of balance and harmony is disturbed, *slametan bersih dhusun* is needed to correct the relationship between the living and the dead, between humanity and nature, between the spiritual and material worlds, and among the fellow members of the hamlet community (Geertz, 1973: 129-131). As far as the relationship between individuals is concerned, Ann Ruth Willner has rightly said that it requires every individual to subdue elements of potential discord and dissonance (1970: 258).

More than any other *slametan* rituals, regardless of religious differences (with their different interpretations of the event), the whole community of the hamlet is encouraged to participate in the *bersih dhusun* ritual. Thus, at the end of the *slametan*, the *tiyang agami* would pray to Allah for protection and blessings in the coming year, the Christians would pray to Jesus, and the followers of *Agami Jawi* would pray to the *danyang* (guardian spirits). The notion of *rukun* (harmonious relationship) among the members of the hamlet community and of respect to the ancestors (including and most importantly the founder of the hamlet) are repeatedly emphasised and symbolised throughout the ritual. The theme of the all night shadow play performance, which is the finale to the ritual, yet again emphasised the notion of balance, harmony and respect.

The *bersih dhusun* ritual, therefore, did not only express the socio-religious values of the people of Celengan, but more importantly, it strengthened them. The people have strategically revitalised the *bersih dhusun* rituals to meet their

---

Selasa, Rebu, Kemis, Jumaat, Sebtu). With the combination of these two systems, there are 35 possible separate days.

[63] This grave is considered sacred and believed to hold some magical power. Reportedly most of the candidates for the office of village head in Lopait, had visited this grave and prayed for blessing from the guardian spirit prior to the election.

[64] Benedict R. O'G. Anderson, in his book *Mythology and The Tolerance of the Javanese* (1965) gave an excellent exposition of the Javanese's worldview of balance and harmony.

need for stronger social unity and hamlet identity. This explains why, in spite of the large numbers of people from Celengan who have worked in the urban areas, this and other related Javanese traditional rituals have been largely preserved.

2.3. The Socio-Cultural Orientation

Apart from the shadow play performance, *ketoprak* is a very popular entertainment for the people of Celengan. They not only enjoy *ketoprak* (Javanese popular theatre) but are also proud of having a group of *ketoprak* performers. Both the shadow play and the *ketoprak* have been the most popular entertainment in the *nagaragung* area (the centre of the Mataram Kingdom as well as of the *Kejawen* tradition), since the mid-nineteenth century (Koentjaraningrat, 1984: 223).[65] Traditionally, *ketoprak* takes up Javanese popular sagas, such as Anglingdarma, Damarwulan, Arya Penangsang, and Jaka Tarub. In its development, however, it is quite common for a *ketoprak* to also perform portions of the Islamic saga of *Wali Sanga* (the nine founding fathers of Islam in Java). Nowadays, Muslims,[66] Christians, and even the government have made use of *ketoprak* to convey their message to the rural people. In mid-1991, the *ketoprak* group of Celengan made an all night performance at a Christian wedding celebration in Lopait village; interestingly, one of the stories they performed was Paul's conversion, taken from the book of Acts of the Christian Bible. On other occasions, the same *ketoprak* group performed the success story of the *Wali Sanga* in introducing Islam in Java. Sometimes the *ketoprak* was also used to convey the government's development programmes, such as family planning and transmigration (Abdullah, 1994: 13). It needs to be noted, however, that whatever the story being performed, *ketoprak* seemed to almost always use a Hindu-Javanese kingdom as the background (see, Geertz, 1960: 289).

The shadow play performance is too expensive for the people of Celengan and is largely considered as (more) sacred, than *ketoprak*. Therefore, the shadow play is generally performed only once a year at the *bersih dhusun* ritual. Unfortunately, in recent years, the *ketoprak* group has become less

---

[65] The shadow play performance seemed to be very popular both in the courts as well as among the *tiyang alit* (small, rural people). On the other hand, in its development, the *ketoprak* seemed to be considered more as a folk-entertainment, see Koentjaraningrat, 1984: 223-227, 286. Clifford Geertz suggested that *ketoprak* was invented as late as 1923 (1960: 289).

[66] Irwan Abdullah reported that the reformist Muslims (followers of Muhammadiyah) in Jatinom refused to transmit Islamic teachings with the help of *ketoprak* or any other traditional art or performance. While such policy is common among the reformist Muslims, it has put them in a difficult position, since the majority of the people in Jatinom, like their traditionalist Muslim counterparts, enjoyed both *ketoprak* and shadow play performance, see Irwan Abdullah, 1994: 99.

active and has rarely given a public performance, mostly due to the migration of a number of its key players to urban jobs. Although the performance of this traditional Javanese entertainment has become less frequent, it seems that the traditional Hindu-Javanese values of tolerance which underscore these traditional performances remain strong in the daily life of the people of Celengan.

It needs to be noted that during the field research, the only entertainment beside the traditional performances was, like in Calombo hamlet, the *layar tancap* (a temporary movie theatre set out in the sub-district sports ground, with neither chairs nor roof). Just like the Calombo hamlet, Celengan had no access to electricity, and accordingly, until 1994, no one was recorded as owning a TV set. The lack of adequate means of transportation between Celengan and the closest movie theatre (in Salatiga), especially in the evening, has made this modern entertainment (cinema) relatively unpopular among ordinary people of Celengan. It does not mean that the movie theatre was foreign or unknown to the people, but that it has not replaced the traditional Javanese values expressed in the *ketoprak* and shadow play performance. Having said that, it needs to be borne in mind that, in regard to Celengan and Calombo hamlets, major infrastructural developments have taken place between 1995-1996, and both hamlets now have access to electricity. At the same time they have good (improved) quality asphalt roads which give them easy and direct access to the main provincial road. These significant developments will undoubtedly bring changes to the values, norms and life-style of the younger generations, which are now beginning to slowly emerge. These socio-cultural changes will therefore call for further research in the years to come.

2.4. Summary

In spite of religious heterogeneity, Celengan hamlet demonstrates a socio-culturally unified community. Unlike in many other villages in Java, the traditional Javanese values of tolerance and harmony in Celengan have not faded away. In fact, they have become stronger in the 1980s and early 1990s. This reversed socio-cultural phenomenon was caused not by geographical isolation but by the 'socio-political isolation' of the 1970s and 1980s (imposed by the supra-village administration). This 'socio-political isolation', as described in Chapter Three, has produced the 'need' for a distinctive hamlet identity and a stronger social unity among the population of Celengan. There were two ways in which the people of Celengan responded to this need. First, they tried, as much as possible, to dissociate themselves (socio-economically) from the other hamlets within Lopait village. As a result, a large number of people have migrated to Jakarta for urban jobs. This step was mostly taken by younger people of working age. Second, those who remained in the hamlet have found a way to return to their common Javanese traditional values. One way in which these values have been recaptured is by the resurgence of traditional Javanese rituals and social activities. Thus reviving the Javanese traditional rituals and social activities was a strategy to meet their 'need'. It must be added, however, that this strategy would not have been very successful if both 'salvation religions' (Weber, 1948; 1964), the Christian and the Muslim, had been able to sharply transform the socio-religious values of the Javanese in Celengan.

3. The Socio-Religious Values of Gudang

In terms of religion, 122 out of 128 households in Gudang hamlet are registered as Muslim, the rest (six households) are Christian. Unlike Calombo and Celengan hamlets, the tension between the devout Muslims and the nominal Muslims is quite apparent. As the value orientation of the nominal Muslims in Gudang has moved from *Kejawen* into secularism, the tension is not so much between *Kejawen* and *santri*, but largely between the values of orthodox Islam and secularism. *Kejawen* values have not been completely abandoned, but as in many other parts of Java, the massive development (modernisation) programmes of the New Order administration, and the increasing integration of Gudang hamlet into the 'larger world' (urban and national) have gradually undermined the Javanese traditional values.

Gudang, with its several socio-cultural groupings, represents a very complex socio-religious system. Firstly, the orthodox Muslims in Gudang are oriented toward the *kyai* in Calombo hamlet. Secondly, the more dominant group of secular Muslims have their orientation toward Golkar (the government party) and toward economic development. Thirdly, there are those who have preserved the Javanese traditional values of *Kejawen*. With the exception of the orthodox Muslim group, the distinctions between the rituals and the social activities of the other two groups are not always clear. In general, however, the traditional ritual with its values is gradually fading away. Many traditional rituals have lost their full meaning and have become mere routine activities. Similarly, since the orthodox Muslim group is less dominant, and more oriented toward Calombo hamlet, the Islamic rituals are not fully celebrated in Gudang hamlet. On a number of Islamic religious occasions, such as Friday prayer[67] and the *shalat Idul Adha,*[68]some devout Muslims of Gudang prefer to observe the rituals in Calombo hamlet, where these Muslim rituals are generally more meaningfully celebrated.

---

[67] Especially so, when the *imam masjid* (the priest of the mosque) of Gudang, who is also the *modin* of Lopait village, for whatever reasons, did not preside over the ritual in the Mosque of Gudang.

[68] Muslim feast that commemorates Abraham's offering his son 'Ishmael'.

3.1. Ritual and Religious Concept: The Ritual of *Merti Desa*

The socio-religious polarity within Gudang hamlet has encouraged the hamlet leaders to make some adjustments to some ritual observances in order to accommodate the interests of these different groups. The way in which Gudang hamlet distinguishes the ritual of *merti desa* (the spiritual cleansing of the hamlet) from the physical cleansing of the hamlet, which they call *bersih desa*, is unique. It seems that this unusual division of the physical and the spiritual cleansing of the hamlet was a strategy to accommodate the different socio-religious groups within the hamlet. Both activities, however, are mainly associated with the economic prosperity of the hamlet, which is symbolised by the success of the (*paddy*-field) harvest. Therefore, the *bersih desa* and the *merti desa* are observed in *Rejeb*, the seventh month of the Javanese calendar, just after the main harvest period.[69]

The *bersih desa* is observed a week prior to the *merti desa* ritual. The *bersih desa* in Gudang is simply an annual (major) *kerja bhakti* by the whole hamlet community (regardless of their socio-religious orientations). This activity is to clean up the village public facilities such as roads, bridges, Mosque, and especially, the main public water supplies of 'Kaligedog' and 'Kaliwates'. There is no ritual or religious flavour attached to this *kerja bhakti*.

Unlike the *bersih desa*, the ritual of *merti desa* is observed only by those who have either partly or fully maintained the traditional Javanese belief system. The ritual of *merti desa* concentrates in the two main public water supplies of Gudang and at the house of the village head. Apart from the placing of *sesajen* (offering presented to spirits), there is no formal ritual in the two main public water supplies of 'Kaligedok' and 'Kaliwates'. The main ritual of *merti desa* takes place in the house of the village head. Every participant (representing his household) brings two *ambeng* (food offerings on an winnowing tray) to the ritual. The poorer households (the landless farm labourers) are required to bring only one *ambeng* each, while the landowners and the richer households are required to bring two *ambeng*. The first *ambeng* contains rice and a variety of side dishes, and the second *ambeng* contains *jajan pasar* (various little between-meal snacks from the market).[70] It appears that there are only a handful of (mostly elderly) people who really both understand

---

[69] This *merti desa* ritual in Gudang probably originated from the sort of harvest festival common to other cultures. However, it does more than just celebrate the harvest. It was initially meant to drive away any pest, plague, famine or other epidemic in the coming year.

[70] Different traditional Javanese rituals generally require different sets of food offerings, which serve their symbolic meanings. Koentjaraningrat observed a consistency of the symbolic meaning of each of the items of the food offerings, according to their names, colours and functions (1984: 365). For the (original) symbolical meanings of these food offerings, see J. van Baal, "Offering, Sacrifice and Gift". In *Numen* 23 (1975): 161-178; S. Koperberg, "Het Betreden der Aarde (Tedak Siten)". In *Djawa* 14 (1934): 213-214; and Clifford Geertz, 1960: 41-49.

the symbolic meanings of the food offerings and care about them. Most, for example, did not buy the *jajan pasar* directly from the market as it should be done traditionally (Geertz, 1960: 48-49). And some even, for the sake of efficiency, mixed the items of the *jajan pasar* with similar snacks produced by modern food companies. The symbolic meaning of these food offerings as a means to communicate with the spiritual beings (Van Baal, 1975) seems to have died out.

There have been some major changes in the observance of the *merti desa* ritual since beginning in the early 1980s. Prior to the 1980s, once the foods were collected in the middle of the room the *bekel*, as the traditional leader of the hamlet would utter an Islamic prayer. After the prayer, the foods were served, which was then followed by the climax of the ritual, the shadow play performance. In 1980 the last traditional *bekel* of Gudang died and his function was replaced by the modern institution of *kadus* (hamlet head).[71] The following year, based solely on economic reason, his son, who is the chairman of the *RW* (hamlet community association), proposed to remove the shadow play performance from the *merti desa* ritual. His proposal was unanimously supported by the modern minded elite of the hamlet and thus accepted by the hamlet community. The poorer households did not raise much objection, because financially, they contributed very little to the ritual. Moreover, the increasing economic pressures of the 1980s have sapped their capacity to survive economically.

Over the years, one could not only notice the decreasing number of people who observed the *merti desa* ritual, but also the decline of the people's enthusiasm in celebrating it. The removal of the shadow play from the ritual probably had an impact on the decline in the observance of *merti desa* ritual. However, most people referred to the ongoing infestation of mice in their paddy fields as the main cause. Some of the respondents complained that while the *merti desa* ritual was kept every year, their harvests were not satisfactory from the mid-1980s through to the early 1990s. The mice destroyed a large portion of their crops year after year. Neither the *merti desa* nor the modern technologies have been able to solve this problem completely. As a result, they have, to some extent, lost confidence in both the ritual and the technology.

3.2. The Socio-Cultural Orientation

Gudang hamlet is a typical developing Javanese agricultural village, where 'modernity' has largely eroded the traditional Javanese values of *gotong-royong* (mutual help), tolerance and harmony. The *sambatan* (mutual help to build a neighbour's house) has largely been abandoned, except for the very poor households. Even though some of the *slametan* rituals are maintained,

---

[71] See in Chapters Four and Five, for a thorough discussion on this institutional change and how this change has influenced socio-political life at the local levels.

they have not been observed with their full notions of tolerance (Anderson, 1965) and harmony (*rukun*), both among the fellow villagers and between the living and the dead (cf. Geertz, 1960). For some, *slametan* in Gudang has become a routine social activity; others maintain it out of fear of the spirits. Thus, as opposed to the *santri* hamlet of Calombo, which has abandoned the vertical (spiritual) aspect and maintained the horizontal (social) aspect of *slametan*,[72] Gudang has abandoned the social aspect, and to some extent, maintained the spiritual aspect of *slametan*.

Compared to the Calombo and Celengan hamlets, Gudang has at least two advantages in the area of communication and information to and from the outside world. First, its settlements lie on both sides of the Semarang-Surakarta provincial road, and second, because of that, many of its inhabitants, especially those who live near the road, have had access to electricity for a long time. The number would certainly be higher if we include those, as was common in many other parts of rural Java, who illegally divert electricity to the more remote houses.[73] These two advantages have enabled Gudang to interact with the outside (modern) world much sooner than the other hamlets. But more importantly, the socio-cultural background of the educated-*pegawai* (civil servants) or the '*new priyayi*' class which dominates Gudang hamlet, proves to have always been very responsive to modern culture (cf. Kartodirdjo, *et al.*, 1987: 22-23).

3.3. Summary

To a large extent, modernity, with its commercialisation and market economy as well as its individualistic nature, has largely prevailed over the traditional horizontal-social values of harmony, togetherness and sharing arrangements in Gudang hamlet. Although some aspects of the traditional 'sharing arrangements' can still be found in village life, such as the arrangement of the food offerings where the richer households have a double responsibility, they are fading away. Together with the ongoing process of *santrinisasi* (bringing nominal Muslims to become true adherents of Islam), this influx of modernity have encouraged religious as well as socio-cultural polarisation within Gudang hamlet.

Unlike the horizontal-social values, the traditional vertical-sacred value of spirit belief has not been drastically eroded. While the (guardian) spirits are still feared by much of the population, this state of fear does not strongly affect the everyday life of the people. The people only review their relationship with

---

[72] It appears to be very common among the *santri* (devout Muslim) community in Java, see E. Darmaputera, *Pancasila and the Search for Identity and Modernity in Indonesian Society*, 1988: 115.

[73] Not until late 1994 did the whole population of Gudang have access to electricity.

supernatural beings when something terrible happens to them;[74] otherwise they just take it for granted that the spirits will not harm them if they have not been upset in the first place. Accordingly, this 'modern culture' has not only changed the economic pattern of the people, it has also redefined some traditional religious rituals to fit the new values.

4. The Value Orientations of the Three Hamlets

One way in which the process of value change within these three Javanese hamlets will be assessed is by employing the cross-cultural measurement instrument developed by Florence Kluckhohn (Kluckhohn and Stordtbeck, 1961). She identified five value orientations which are common to all cultural settings and their range of variations (1961:10). The five orientations are: man's relation to man, man's relation to time, man's relation to activity, man's relation to nature and man's relation to human nature (life) (see Table 2.1). This instrument has been used in many different cultural settings (Cancian, 1975: 15), including the Javanese cultural setting of the 1960s and 1970s (Koentjaraningrat, 1971; 1993) and early 1980s (Darmaputera, 1988). The following data were gathered through a set of questionnaires (Instrument C, Appendix 1) directed to all the respondents and the key informants in the three hamlets.

4.1. Views Regarding Human Relationship within a Community

The majority of the population in both Calombo (69.7 percent) and Celengan (91.7 percent) hamlets considered maintaining *kerukunan* (harmony) among fellow villagers as the most essential aspect of living together in a community. The reason for their choice, is however, quite different. While for the traditional Javanese community of Celengan 'harmony' is essential for the maintenance of safety (*aman*), peacefulness (*tentrem*) and smoothness (*lancar*) in all the community's activities (functions), for the *santri* hamlet of Calombo a community is created (predestined) by Allah for the people who live in it to be able to complement each other. While the emphasis on community life is the same, the motives are different. On the one hand, Celengan seems to stress the importance of the functions of the whole community as a unit; on the other hand, Calombo stresses the importance of one's compliance to the *taqdir* (predestined will) of Allah.

Gudang represents different views altogether. 68.8 percent of the respondents in Gudang stated that co-operation between two individuals or more can only be justified when they pursue a common goal(s) or serve an

[74] In traditional Javanese belief system, one has to constantly maintain the balance and harmony between the living and the supernatural beings.

individual interest(s).[75] Since hierarchy is an important aspect in the '*new priyayi*' (*pegawai* or civil servant) class community, where kinship loyalty often prevails over rationality (Kartodirdjo, *et al.*, 1987: 170), the role of the leaders (elite) is very important in setting up the common goal(s). For the poorer households, however, this common goal (s) could mean exploitation, and their individual interest(s) could be as modest as the need for (social) acceptance within the hamlet community. This appeared in some of the responses from the poorer households, which indicated that their participation in *kerja bhakti* (mutual/voluntary work) and other hamlet activities was mainly motivated by fear of social isolation from the rest of the hamlet community.

4.2. Views regarding People's Attitude toward Time

There are only 24.2 percent of the respondents in Calombo, 4.4 percent in Gudang and none in Celengan, who not only wished for economic improvement but also believed that economic change was possible and, more importantly, are ready to work at it when opportunity (capital) comes. This does not mean that the other respondents are economically static or have never longed for economic improvements. Certainly most, if not all, respondents desire to improve economically. It does mean, however, that only a few of them do really want to change their future and work towards it, or work with a view to changing their future.

Most of the respondents in Calombo (75.8 percent), Gudang (66.7 percent) as well as Celengan (66.7 percent), while probably yearning for economic improvement, tend to focus their efforts on maintaining their present economic status. The group are inclined to use their resources to secure their future (not to change it), that is to maintain the present status in the future. They view the future with a passive eye. Instead of accumulating their resources for changing their future, they preserve their resources to respond to any unfortunate happening in the future.

One-third of the respondents in Celengan and 24.4 percent of the respondents in Gudang appear to be mostly concerned with their present status. There are at least two groups which belong to this category. First, there are those who are extremely poor, so that all their energies and resources are consumed to meet their very basic (daily) needs. Second, there are those who tend to spend their resources on improving their present social status. While no doubt they would also wish for economic improvement, they have not thought of either accumulating their resources to change their future or preserving them in order to maintain their present economic status.

From the comparison of this particular value orientation between these three hamlets, it appears that the *santri* (devout Muslim) values of Calombo, with the

---

[75] 12.5 percent of the respondents went even further, believing that one should co-operate with others only when the co-operation benefits oneself.

kyai's 'religious purification' programme, have enabled more people in Calombo (24.2 percent) to view their future pro-actively. The majority of the respondents in the three hamlets, however, remained largely concerned with maintaining their present economic status. They view their future with a rather passive attitude, reacting and preparing to react to what might happen in the future. While the future is both unchangeable and uncontrollable, they believe, people can and should protect themselves from the unexpected. For the third category of people, who mostly live within the traditional Javanese values of Celengan (and partly in Gudang), there is very little concern for the future. Since the future is unpredictable, it is the present (not the future) socio-economic status and needs which mostly concern them.

4.3. Views regarding People's Attitude toward Work

In regards to activities or jobs, 31.1 percent of the respondents in Gudang and 18.2 percent in Calombo have signified real concern for the quality and achievements of their work or activities. Unlike most traditional rural Javanese, this group of people describe 'success' in primarily economic terms, and as in all modern societies they value the notions of competition and achievement. From the questionnaires and interviews, it appears that most of them prefers jobs where they can set the limits of achievement themselves, and have the liberty to achieve them.

A large number of the respondents in both hamlets (57.8 percent in Gudang and 66.7 percent in Calombo), however, largely undervalue the notions of 'competition' and 'achievement'. In regard to income earning activities, this second group prefers employment with a certain income, such as the civil service, rather than a similar vocation within a private company where both the salary and the competition are higher. Although they would of course wish for a good salary, the motives for seeking civil service employment seem to be primarily based on job security and not so much on the higher salary. The increasing economic pressures in rural life seem, to some extent, to have changed the value orientation behind this choice for civil service. Earlier, Koentjaraningrat observed that in the 1970s and 1980s the large majority of the *tiyang alit* (small/poor people) of rural Java wanted to become civil servants. Reportedly, their primary motive was improvement of social status, from being a *tiyang alit* to becoming a *priyayi* (1984: 444). Nowadays, while a large number of the people in Gudang and Celengan hamlets continue to aspire to the civil service, the motive is primarily economic.[76] This change of value orientation, from one of primary concern for social status to another primarily

[76] Within this second group, there are four respondents in Gudang and four in Calombo who have chosen the civil service vocation primarily for the improvement of their social status. The rest of the respondents in the Gudang (11.1 percent) and Calombo (15.2 percent) mostly related their activities or jobs to their service to *Allah*.

concerned for economic security (income stability), has been quite modest compared to the value change which has occurred within the first group above. Within this second group, the people have not chosen the civil service primarily for the best (possible) salary. In regards to activities or jobs, they remained largely concerned with 'being' or 'being-in-becoming' a civil servant, and have very little concern for the 'doing',[77] which includes the concern for the quality of the job, for the accumulation of resources (capital) and maximisation of achievement.

The respondents of Celengan gave a different view regarding their attitudes towards activities or jobs. When they were asked about their job expectations for their children (and why), most (93.3 percent), responded to the effect, 'that's up to the children themselves'.[78] Next, when they were asked, the reasons for their answer, interestingly, 62.5 percent of them responded that, 'every person has a different ability. I only desire my children to follow an occupation which *cocok* (fits) and *sesuai* (is appropriate) with their ability and assigned place in the universe'.[79] Others have identified the significance of the notion of *cocok* as a typical expression of the *Kejawen* value of harmony (Darmaputera, 1988: 125; Anderson, 1965: 5). Geertz accurately summed up the Javanese concept of *cocok*:

> *Tjotjog*[80] means to fit, as a key does in a lock, as an efficacious medicine does to a disease, as a solution does to an arithmetic, as a man does with the woman he marries (if he does not, they will divorce). If your opinion agrees with mine we *tjotjog*; if the meaning of my name fits my character (and if it brings me luck), it is said to be *tjotjog*. Tasty food, correct theories, good manners, comfortable surroundings, gratifying outcomes are all *tjotjog*. In the broadest and most abstract sense, two items *tjotjog* when their coincidence forms a coherent pattern which gives to each a significance and a value it does not in itself have. There is implied here a contrapuntal view of the universe in which that which is important is what natural relationship the separate elements have to one another, how they must be arranged to strike a chord and to avoid dissonance. And as in harmony, the ultimately correct relationships are fixed, determinate and knowable . . .(1973: 129-130).

It is interesting to note how the traditional Javanese value of harmony in Celengan hamlet has accommodated the notion of economic progress on the one hand, and has retained the expressions of their traditional values as a socio-

[77] Florence Kluckhohn classified people's attitude toward activity (job) into three types, namely the 'being', the 'being-in-becoming', and the 'doing' (1961: 12). See also Table 2.1.

[78] It needs to be noted, there are only 3 respondents in Celengan who wished to become civil servants.

[79] 7.1 percent added that whatever the occupation of their children in the future, they hoped it would meet their daily needs.

[80] *Tjotjog* is the old Indonesian spelling (prior to 1972) for *cocok*.

political strategy to strengthen their hamlet identity on the other hand. As stated above, they believe that people's attitude toward job or activity is fixed and determinate, on the other hand, this research detected a significant number of people (23.4 percent of the respondents) who are increasingly concerned with the idea of economic progress. These respondents believe that while their children should decide for themselves the occupations which are *cocok* and *sesuai* for them, these occupations should enable them to make economic progress. As a lasting and happy marriage is considered *cocok*, so is a job which brings economic progress to the family.

Therefore, the attitude of the people of Celengan towards 'work' is neither a 'being', because the kind of the occupation itself was not very important for them, nor a 'doing', because the end achievement is not the main issue in seeking a job.[81] The main issues for them are the concepts of *cocok* and progress. An occupation is like a shirt, which can be changed when it is no longer *cocok* for the occasion. Modernity has largely left intact the traditional Javanese expression of harmony (*cocok*) in Celengan, but changed the notion from an inward subjective feeling of *tentrem* (peaceful mind), self-fulfilment and contentment, to an outward yearning for (economic) progress.

4.4. Views Regarding Human Nature

Koentjaraningrat observed that both the ordinary rural Javanese farmers and the *priyayi* (elite) viewed life in the world as series or episodes of suffering, which one should accept with endurance and total submission (1984: 437).[82] This present research, however, found that none of the three hamlets under investigation seems to fit this description. All the respondents in Calombo, for example, have a positive attitude towards life. However, they viewed life from a number of different perspectives. Twenty-four percent of the respondents felt good about their life, because their daily economic needs were sufficiently met. The majority of the respondents in Calombo (54.5 percent), however, felt good about their life on the ground that their spiritual (religious) needs were sufficiently met. The purpose of life is both an act of devotion to God and to enjoy His grace, which includes one's responsibility, as well as opportunity, to meet the economic needs of one whole family. There is one important aspect of Calombo's understanding of the purpose of life which distinguished it from the other two hamlets, that is the aspect of 'enjoying God's grace'. The understanding that the purpose of life is partly to enjoy God's grace has

[81] This 'neither-nor' approach to 'conflicts' is also a typically Javanese expression; see Eka Darmaputera, 1988: 122-123.

[82] This concept of life as episodes of suffering is often thought to lead to an attitude of *nrima* (whole heartedly accepting one's fate). And *nrima* has been mostly identified as the essence of the fatalistic nature of the Javanese, see Koentjaraningrat, 1984: 345-347; Eka Darmaputera, 1988: 130; and Niels Mulder, *Kepribadian Jawa dan Pembangunan Nasional*, 1986: 41.

consequently provided a space for the development of 'individual' dreams within the community in Calombo. In traditional Javanese community, one does not separate individuality from surroundings. Just like the universe and time, the primary surroundings (family, hamlet) are regarded as having authority over oneself (individual). Therefore, individuality, initiative and individual dreams are considered dangerous and inappropriate (Mulder, 1986: 35). Here we see an example of how the process of the *kyai*'s 'religious purification' in Calombo has enabled some people not only to view life positively, but also creatively.

93.3 percent of the respondents in Celengan hamlet viewed their life positively. However, unlike Calombo, the majority viewed life either from the perspective of inward experiences, such as *tentrem* (peaceful mind), *ayem* (contentment) and both mental and physical health (44.6 percent), or from the economic perspective (46.2 percent). In Gudang hamlet, both the 77.8 percent of respondents who viewed life positively, and the 22.2 percent who viewed life with a negative attitude, saw it mostly from the economic perspective. Those who were content with their economic status tended to view life positively,[83] while those who were not content either accepted their fate (*pasrah*), and thus viewed life with a negative attitude (13.3 percent), or have made some efforts to change their present economic status (6.7 percent). This last group represents a few more modern-minded people in Gudang who believed that people should have some control over the surroundings, the time, and to some extent, the future.

As a whole, the majority of the people in the three hamlets view life with a positive attitude. With only very few exceptions, life is no longer viewed as a series of sufferings, either to be fled from through messianic movements (*kebatinan*) or to be accepted with an attitude of *pasrah* (fatalism). This present research has also detected the emergence of a new value orientation regarding people's view on life (human nature). 36.4 percent of the respondents in Calombo, 6.7 percent of the respondents in Gudang, and five percent of the respondents in Celengan hamlet view life as neither bad nor good. For them, life is not 'is', but 'will be'. It seems that, the *kyai*'s orthodox Muslim concept of *ikhtiar* (initiative, finding a way, making an effort) in Calombo, has been largely responsible for the emergence of this new value orientation.

[83] Those who felt content with their economic state, both in Gudang and Celengan hamlets, or those who viewed life positively on the ground of contentment over their economic states, did not necessarily belong to the richer households. A large number of these people probably just barely met their daily needs. The emphasis has mostly been on inward feeling of contentment, and not so much on their actual economic achievements.

4.5. Views regarding People's Relation to Nature

The majority of the respondents in Calombo (87. 9 percent) and Celengan (61.7 percent) basically view people's relation to nature as complementary and reciprocal. Nature is regarded as God's provision for human beings; in return, man has the responsibility to maintain nature. Even though the people of Calombo and Celengan seem to view their relation to nature in the same way, they have, however, set out from different belief systems. For the devout Muslims of Calombo, nature and its resources are considered as God's provision; people's attitude in utilising them is, therefore, determinant on the perpetuity of God's blessings. The people of Celengan hamlet, on the other hand, argue that nature should not be exploited much beyond its normal (traditionally known) capacity, otherwise, it would interrupt the balance and harmony of the universe.

The people of Gudang (66.7 percent of the respondents) and also a significant number of people from Celengan (38.3 percent) view people's relation to nature in a different way. They argue that God has equipped man with intellectual capacity to maximise the utility of nature and its resources for the benefits of human beings. Therefore, nature may be and should be effectively exploited for the maximum results for human beings. It appears that this view has largely been influenced by their occupation. As a large number of people in Gudang and Celengan work as urban commuters or temporary urban migrants, their income-earning activities have much less frequent contact with the surrounding nature (environment), and therefore, they have very little concern for its preservation. The view, which the people of Calombo mostly hold (above), has also been partly influenced by the income-earning activity of the people, as fishermen in Rawa Pening lake. Hereby we discovered the interactive negotiations between Islam and income-earning pattern within Calombo hamlet. At a number of points we have seen how the 'religious purification' in Calombo made a significant contribution to the process of value change and rationalisation, while in other cases Islam in Calombo seems to choose to serve the interests of the traditional economic pattern of the people.

5. The Relation Between Socio-Religious Values and Participation in the Three Hamlets of Lopait: A Synopsis

The different value orientations of the three hamlets have, to some extent, influenced the way in which some of the development programmes have been implemented in these hamlets. While in terms of the speed of overall economic development, with a number of infrastructural advantages, Gudang has been considerably faster than Calombo and Celengan hamlets, in terms of participation Gudang was the lowest.[84] In Celengan, people's participation was

[84] Although Table 6.1 indicates that the level (scores) of participation in Celengan was the lowest, the field data also recorded that people's participation in activities which are

high when the project served the community's need of stronger social unity. On the other hand, participation appeared to be relatively low when the project was perceived to be undermining hamlet identity.[85] In Calombo, where the role of the *kyai* was very dominant in almost every stage of development programmes, both participation and the incidence of poverty reduction were the highest among the three hamlets. Unlike Celengan, however, the main motive behind people's participation in Calombo were the Islamic concepts of *amal* (charity for the sake of *Allah*), *ibadah* (acts of devotion to *Allah*) and *umma* (Islamic Community) with its egalitarian nature (Abdullah, 1994: 151).

5.1. Calombo Hamlet

5.1.1. The Decision-Making Stage

It appears that hamlet identity in Calombo, which had been largely shaped by the process of 'Islamic religious purification' and to some extent, by the socio-political isolation imposed by the supra-village administrations, has instigated the identification of most of the projects implemented in Calombo hamlet. The identification of the construction of the bridge in *RT* IV and the construction of the building for the Islamic kindergarten are two most obvious examples, where the initial motives behind the identification of the projects were based on the need to assert the 'Islamic' as well as the local identity of Calombo against the other hamlets in Lopait, as well as against the village and supra-village administrations. Although they were formally selected at the *rapat dusun* (hamlet leaders meeting), together with the construction of the road in *RT* IV, and the construction of the main road of Calombo hamlet, these projects were first identified at the evening *pengajian* (recitation of the *Qur'an* and study sessions).

The identification of the other two projects, namely the refurbishment of the Mosque and the refurbishment of the public water supply (*MCK*) by the *kyai* were obviously motivated by religious needs as well. However, since the *kyai* is regarded as the sole authority in religious matters and the 'owner' of these facilities, there was less space for the people to participate in the identification, selection and planning stages of these projects. Thus the seeming lack of participation at the identification stage of these two projects was mainly caused by the nature of the *kyai*'s leadership. As a whole, therefore, the identification

---

seen to serve in strengthening the social bond of the hamlet community was significantly high. This seemingly lower participation in the government's development projects, and evidently higher participation in the projects which either meet their needs of hamlet identity or were motivated by it, was their very strategy, not only to survive (Slamet, 1982), but to effectively respond to the external pressures (Scott, 1976).

[85] It needs to be noted, however, that this 'traditional collectivism' was not entirely cultural but also a social strategy for survival. Therefore, it would fully function mostly when their hamlet (social) identity and their collective welfare were at risk.

stage of most of the development projects implemented in Calombo hamlet between 1989 and 1994 has been considerably informed by the local (Islamic) socio-religious values.

With regard to the project selection phase, the absence of *golongan cikal-bakal* (founding fathers) and the egalitarian nature of the concept of *umma* have to some extent influenced the way in which most projects were selected in Calombo hamlet, i.e., through a voting system. Apart from the two religious projects above, all the other projects implemented in Calombo were selected through voting either in a *rembug dhusun* (traditional village meeting) or *rapat dusun* (hamlet leaders meeting) forum. Interestingly, this voting system was totally absent in the project selection phase in Gudang and Celengan hamlets. The significant role of this voting system at the project selection phase in Calombo was probably shaped by two local socio-religious factors, first, the egalitarian nature of the concept of *umma*, and second, a strategy of the Muslim leaders of Calombo to assert their new Islamic hamlet identity by a deliberate move or departure from the traditional functions of *rembug dhusun*. In many rural Javanese villages where the traditional structure with its patronage relationship between the elite (*golongan cikal-bakal*) and the poor still prevails, *rembug dhusun* often functions mainly to serve the interest of the elite (Jay, 1969; cf., Johnston and Clark, 1982; Chambers, 1983). The people attend the *rebug dhusun* mostly to affirm what has been decided by the rural elite.

5.1.2. The Planning and Implementation Stages

As has been illustrated in Chapter Four, people's participation both in the planning and implementation stages in Calombo hamlet was significantly high. The people of Calombo attributed their active involvement at these stages of development to their Islamic belief. 18 out of 33 or 55.4 percent of the respondents in Calombo viewed their involvement in the planning and implementation stages as *amal* (charity for the sake of *Allah*) and *ibadah* (acts of devotion to *Allah*). Apart from this religious conviction, the high degree of socio-religious homogeneity and the relatively small size of the population in Calombo hamlet added to the exclusiveness of the hamlet community, which in turn produced both a deeper sense of solidarity and greater social pressures, especially in the implementation stage.

While it is true that religious conviction and socio-religious pressures have made some direct contribution to the substantial participation in the planning and implementation stages of development in Calombo, it was the fact that most of these projects had been identified and selected by the people themselves, and thus met their strongest needs,[86] which probably motivated the people most. Moreover, compared to Celengan and Gudang hamlets, most of the heads of households in Calombo engaged in types of livelihood which

[86] As has been discussed earlier in Chapter Six, these strongest needs had been largely shaped by their socio-religious value.

allowed them to participate more both in the planning and implementation stages.[87]

5.1.3. The Sharing of Benefits Stage

As clearly demonstrated in Chapter Four, the sharing of development benefits was often closely related to the level of people's participation in the decision-making process. This was evidently the case with Calombo hamlet, where people's participation both in the decision-making process and the sharing of benefits stage were relatively high. It seems that as the egalitarian nature of the concept of *umma* influenced the project identification and selection in Calombo, it also apparently affected the sharing of benefits stage. 93.6 percent of the respondents in Calombo claimed to have benefited from the projects and most of them said they made use of the facilities on a daily basis, both for their economic and non-economic activities.

5.1.4. Conclusion

It appeared that throughout the stages in the project cycle, people's participation in Calombo hamlet was relatively high. Participation at the decision-making stage seems to have direct implications for the other stages in the project cycle, especially in the sharing of benefits stage. The relatively high level of participation at the planning and implementation stages was made possible by the types of livelihood engaged in by most of the population of Calombo, which allowed them to spare a considerable time, energy and attention for developing their hamlet.

As a whole, the homogeneity of political affiliation, the pattern of livelihood, the economic structure and the religious orientation in Calombo hamlet have to some extent contributed to substantial participation in development. However, the primary credit should go to the role of the *kyai* in initiating the process of what he himself considered 'religious purification', and, to some extent, also a 'religious rationalisation'. The constant interactions and negotiations between this religious rationalisation and the influx of modernity, as well as with the socio-economic needs of the people, have eventually produced the new value orientation presently emerging in Calombo hamlet. In regard to human relationships within the community, the concept of *umma* (Islamic egalitarian community) seems to dominate the people of

[87] Most of the fishermen of Calombo work only two to three hours in the afternoon to set out their nets, and between two to three hours in the early morning to gather the fish they have caught. The more educated younger working group were mostly commuting urban employees in Bawen or Salatiga, which are only six and seven kilometres from Calombo respectively. As most village meetings were conducted after the evening *pengajian*, their occupations did not hinder them from attending and participating in the planning stage. The urban employees of Celengan, on the other hand, were mostly temporary migrant employees in Jakarta.

Calombo. This concept of *umma* has not only encouraged participation in development, but has also facilitated significant poverty reduction in Calombo.

For the Muslims of Calombo, the future is solely in the hands of Allah. But since someone will recognise his *taqdir* (the predestined will of Allah) only after it has come to pass, the role of *ikhtiar* (initiative) becomes very important. This concept of *ikhtiar* has enabled an increasing number of people in Calombo to view the future proactively. One's place in the universe is not something which one should passively accept, with an attitude of *pasrah* (fatalism), but should be continually sought after through *ikhtiar*. It needs to be noted, however, that *ikhtiar* has always been understood within the context of *umma* (the whole hamlet community), and is motivated by or understood as an act of devotion to *Allah*. As the development process has been perceived by the people of Calombo within this context, they have viewed their participation in development programmes as *amal* (charity for the sake of *Allah*) and *ibadah* (acts of devotion to *Allah*).

In addition to the contribution of the local Muslim socio-religious values in motivating the people of Calombo to participate in the development process, one should also recognise the role of the *kyai* in shaping and strengthening the hamlet identity of Calombo. This hamlet identity has undoubtedly made a significant contribution to the substantial participation in Calombo.

5.2. Celengan Hamlet

5.2.1. The Decision-Making Process

Compared to Calombo, people's participation at the decision-making stage in Celengan was very low. There were at least two factors which brought about this low level of participation. First, most of the development projects implemented in Celengan between 1989-1994 had been identified and selected by the village and supra-village administrations. This excessive involvement of the supra-village structures in the development process of Celengan which was primarily meant to guard against any political activities of the ex-followers of the PKI (the Communist Party), has in many ways prevented the people from participating in the socio-economic development of their hamlet. Second, the banning of the Communist Party (PKI) in 1966 cost Celengan most of their local (hamlet) leaders. Some of them were arrested in the late 1960s, the rest chose to migrate to Jakarta and other urban sites in the early 1970s. The lack of a strong local leadership as well as the absence of any grass-roots local organisations have badly affected the people of Celengan, especially in terms of their effort to organise themselves in effectively developing their own hamlet.

It should also be noted that since many households from Celengan who earned their income from urban employment (especially in Jakarta) had been able to make significant economic progress, economic development was closely associated with urban employment. Within this context, development projects in Celengan have been viewed as less significant or less associated with economic progress. To some extent this explains why the relations between socio-religious values and participation at the decision-making stage in Celengan was weak.

5.2.2. The Planning and Implementation Stages

People's participation both at the planning and implementation stages in Celengan was also low. As with the decision-making stage, the relations between the socio-religious values and this low level of participation in the planning and implementation stages was very weak. The low level of participation at the planning stage was primarily caused by the excessive involvement of the supra-village structures, which left very little space for the people of Celengan to be involved in the planning stage. As reported earlier, none of the 60 respondents in Celengan were either taking part in or sitting on the committee of any of the development projects. Moreover, as apparent in Table 6.1, a significant proportion of the respondents in Celengan (45.9 percent) had to some extent been prevented from participating in the implementation stage by their type of livelihood.

5.2.3. The Sharing of Benefits Stage

The inaccurate identification of development projects, mostly by the village and supra-village administrations, has largely impeded the people of Celengan from benefiting from the development projects in their hamlet. Accordingly only 35.6 percent of the respondents in Celengan claimed to have benefited from the projects. Similarly to the previous stages in the project cycle, the relations between the socio-religious values of Celengan and this low level of participation in the sharing of benefits stage was not readily apparent.

5.2.4. Conclusion

As has been discussed in Chapter Four, the external political and economic pressures and the extensive involvement of the local and regional governments in the development process in Celengan have undermined people's participation. Rituals and religious concepts have not functioned as the source of motivation, instead, they have become instruments to search for hamlet identity and to strengthen social unity within the hamlet. As strengthening social unity and hamlet identity became the perceived needs of the hamlet, participation in development as well as other social activities have also been viewed as instruments for meeting these needs. Accordingly, people would participate in development projects only if the projects would either strengthen the social bond within the hamlet community or reinforce hamlet identity. Although the people of Celengan have been notably religious, religions and the traditional Javanese socio-religious value of harmony have had very little direct influence on people's participation in Celengan hamlet.

5.3. Gudang Hamlet

5.3.1. The Decision-Making Process

Most of the projects implemented in Gudang hamlet between 1989-1994 were identified and selected by the rural elite (traditional village elite who mostly belong to the richer income group of Gudang). The traditional village structure of Gudang, with its pattern of socio-economic differentiation and strong domination by a small powerful local elite, has severely undermined people's participation at the decision-making stage. As has been discussed in Chapter Four, project identification and project selection in Gudang were evidently biased toward the interest of the rural elite. In most cases the patronage relationship between the elite and the poor has left the poor with very little say at the meetings where these stages took place. Projects identified by the elite were generally accepted without argument. It appears that this traditional village structure with its patronage relationship has been one of the major determinants for people's low participation at the decision-making stage in Gudang.

5.3.2. The Planning and Implementation Stages

Just as in Calombo and Celengan hamlets, the planning stage in Gudang was very much related to the identification and selection processes of the projects. It appeared that the general pattern in Lopait was that those who identified a project were generally asked to plan its implementation, or at least were expected to play a major role in the planning stage. Accordingly, two out of the seven projects under investigation were identified and planned by the sub-district administration. Five were identified by the rural elite; of these, only one involved ordinary members of the community in the planning.

At the implementation stage the picture was quite different, as people's participation in Gudang was rather high (see Table 6.1). Four out of five construction projects were implemented through some forms of *kerja bhakti* (voluntary/mutual work), which involved a large number of people or sometimes even the whole hamlet community. It needs to be noted, however, that as shown in Table 6.1, some 60 percent of those who participated in the implementation stage indicated that to some extent their participation in the *kerja bhakti* had been under some form of socio-cultural pressure. To consider this 'qualitative' factor in measuring participation in the implementation stage in Gudang, one would come to the conclusion that while in actual project implementation participation was rather high, in terms of 'self-motivated' meaningful participation it was much lower. This 'qualitative' analysis, therefore, suggests that there were other major determinants for participation at the implementation stage, apart from the traditional village structure.

The adoption of the 'modern' values of individualism, competition and the exploitation of resources for the highest outcome has to some extent promoted both the overall economic growth and the widening of the socio-economic polarisation within Gudang hamlet. Together with the traditional village structure and the integration of Gudang into a wider world, the adoption of these 'modern' values created an increasing economic pressure among the poorer households. As economic pressure steadily increased, especially among the poorer households, the possibility of enjoying immediate economic benefits of development projects became one of the main motivating factors for participation. Since most of the project identification in Gudang was biased toward the interest of the rural elite, the quality of participation at the implementation stage was very low.

5.3.3. The Sharing of Benefits Stage

Some 60 percent of the respondents in Gudang claimed to have benefited from the development projects. However, the development benefits have not been equally distributed. As the project identifications were mostly biased toward the interest of the rural elite, they were the ones who benefited most from these projects. As a result, the development programmes in Gudang have delivered fewer benefits to poorer households. As with the decision-making stage, the traditional village structure with its patronage relationship has to some extent undermined participation at the sharing of benefits stage in Gudang hamlet.

5.3.4. Conclusion

As modernity prevailed, especially among the elite, and economic pressures steadily increased among the poor, the core value orientation of Gudang has also shifted from traditionally socio-cultural to primarily economic. However, the expression of this value change has largely been restricted by the traditional village structure which remained considerably strong in Gudang hamlet.

While the traditional village structure with the socio-cultural pressures that accompanied it was among the main causes for the low level of participation at the decision-making and planning stages, the increasing economic pressure, and thus, the 'immediate economic benefits' of the projects was a major determinant for participation at the implementation stage in Gudang hamlet. This does not mean that the other hamlets have had no concern for the economic aspect of development. It does, however, demonstrate that, as with the socio-religious (Muslim religious purification) expressions in Calombo and the socio-cultural (social unity and hamlet identity) needs in Celengan, the economic aspect (immediate benefits) of the development projects became the main incentive for a low quality type of participation in Gudang.

5.4. Comparative Analysis

One way in which the future trend of the relationship between socio-religious values and participation in rural Java can be discerned is by identifying different factors which determined the relationship between them in the development processes of the three hamlets of Lopait.

As described earlier in this chapter as well as in Chapter Three, the socio-religious values of Calombo, especially the application of the Islamic concepts of *amal* (charity for the sake of *Allah*) and *ibadah* (acts of devotion to *Allah*) to people's participation in development, have in many ways contributed to the substantial participation in development. However, it was the process of 'religious purification' which led to the adoption of Islam (*santri*) as the group (hamlet) identity of Calombo, that has primarily produced the strong link between the socio-religious values and participation in Calombo.

To some extent, the homogeneity of the political affiliation has strengthened the Islamic identity, which in turn, contributed to the substantial participation in Calombo. In addition, the pattern of livelihood in Calombo (fishermen) did not only allow the people to spare more time for participation in development, it also encouraged the formation of an independent mentality, which in turn, produced creativity and a self-reliant attitude. Together with the pressure from socio-political isolation imposed by the supra-village administrations and the charismatic socio-religious leadership of the *kyai*, these factors have influenced the way in which socio-religious values in Calombo relate to people's participation in development.

In spite of the religious plurality, Celengan in the 1980s witnessed the revival of the traditional Javanese values of *Kejawen*, which became the uniting force against the supra-village socio-political pressure. The 'ineffectiveness' of both Islam and Christian in introducing alternative social identity and values for the people to address their socio-political as well as religio-cultural problems has to some extent encouraged the substantiation of the traditional Javanese values as the hamlet identity in Celengan.

While it was true that the notion of 'balance and harmony' in Celengan's religiosity did not encourage the idea of market competition and aggressive individualism, in reality, the people of Celengan have been able to accommodate the notion of economic progress on the one hand, and the notion of balance and harmony on the other hand (see Section 4.4.3). Instead of the inward feeling of self-contentment and the notion of *tentrem* (peaceful mind), an increasing number of people in Celengan have viewed economic progress as a sign of harmony between oneself and one's livelihood.

From the experience of Celengan hamlet, it appears that the Javanese traditional values of 'balance and harmony' are not necessarily inimical to economic development, as others have suggested (Mulder, 1986; Koentjaraningrat, 1993). The effect of this accommodation of the notion of economic progress into the traditional Javanese values in Celengan has to some extent generated motivation for economic progress. However, since efforts and activities to organise the people of Celengan have been constantly under (political) suspicion and thus undermined by the supra-village administrations, the Javanese traditional values of Celengan have very little space to express themselves in motivating the people to participate in the development process in Celengan hamlet.

Since an ex-PKI stronghold was generally regarded as politically more threatening for the New Order than an NU stronghold, the socio-political pressure imposed by the supra-village administrations and the extensive involvement of the village and supra-village administrations in the development process in Celengan have been much more severe than those imposed on Calombo. As has been indicated above, this extensive external involvement, which was partly motivated by political suspicion, has largely prevented the people of Celengan from participating in the development process, especially in the decision-making stage.

While the fisherman type of livelihood in Calombo generated an independent and self-reliant mentality, the prevalence of landless farm labourers in Celengan has encouraged the formation of a more dependent mentality. Although the percentage of landless farm labourers in Celengan has declined from 70.4 percent in 1980 to 31.1 percent in 1994 (Table 5.6), the dependent mentality, a feature which often accompanies this type of occupation, remains dominant in Celengan hamlet.

Apart from the socio-political pressure, the extensive involvement of the village and supra-village administrations and the type of livelihood engaged in by the people of Celengan, another factor which prevented the people of Celengan from actively participating in the decision-making stage was the lack of local leadership. As most of the hamlet leaders had either been arrested by the New Order government or had left the hamlet for urban jobs, the only local leader in Celengan was the *dukun* (shaman; traditional healer). Unlike the *kyai* in Calombo, the *dukun* of Celengan did not establish his authority by mobilising followers around himself. While the *kyai* viewed his primary function as to perform 'religious purification' mostly through intensive teaching of the *Qur'an*, the functions of the *dukun* in Celengan were primarily dealing with traditional rituals and healing services. Furthermore, Islam does not recognise a separation between socio-political and religious matters, a concept which took the *kyai*'s influence beyond the religious sphere. On the other hand, in most cases the influence of the *dukun* in Celengan was limited to the religious sphere. These differences between a *kyai* and a *dukun* explain why the *dukun* in Celengan did not make a significant contribution to the process of development as did the *kyai*.

Gudang represents a different socio-religious setting altogether; unlike Celengan and Calombo hamlets, there was socio-religious polarisation in Gudang, mainly between the *santri* (devout Muslims) and the secular Muslims. The *santri* of Gudang have their orientation toward the *kyai* in Calombo, while the secular Muslims gathered around the *golongan cikal-bakal* (traditional elite) of Gudang who were mostly civil servants and belonged to the higher income group.[88] The *santri* represent the traditional Islamic values, while the new *priyayi* (traditional elite; civil servants) represent modern secular values. Although the process of *santrinisasi* in recent years has considerably increased the number of devout Muslims in Gudang, the traditional elite remains very dominant. Apart from these two opposing groups there was a considerable number of people in Gudang, mostly poor peasants (*wong cilik*), who did not belong to either of these groups. The majority of these people observed the Javanese traditional belief with varied intensity, and retained much of its values.

As the social context of the *santri* in Calombo and Gudang was very different, their roles and contributions to the development process in their respective hamlets were also different. Unlike Islam in Calombo which has become the hamlet identity with the *kyai* as the central figure, the *santri* in Gudang were the losers. Within this context, the primary concern for the *santri* of Gudang was to establish Islam as the dominant force. Since most projects were identified and selected by the traditional elite, whom they considered secular, irreligious and ungodly, they did not primarily view participation in development as *amal* (charity for the sake of *Allah*) and *ibadah* (acts of devotion to *Allah*), as did the *santri* of Calombo. It needs to be noted however that unlike the poor peasants of Gudang, the *santri* were not totally excluded from the decision-making process. A number of projects under investigation were identified by the Muslim leaders.

The effect of the rapid process of *santrinisasi* in Gudang in recent years has been slightly overshadowed by the massive influx of goods and modernity. In the language of Indonesian development planning, development is conceived as modernisation, with the government as the innovator and the carrier of this process and the people as the object of change (Selosoemardjan and Braezeale, 1993). This is especially true in Gudang hamlet, where a large number of those belonging to the traditional elite were civil servants. This traditional elite has thus viewed itself as the carrier of the process of modernisation in Gudang.

As discussed earlier in this chapter, although the people of Gudang still preserve a number of Javanese traditional rituals, the symbolic meaning and the spiritual significance of these rituals seems to have faded away. Together with the influx of 'modern values' and the process of *santrinisasi*, the economic pressure of the 1980s contributed to the decreasing importance of Javanese traditional rituals in the life of the people of Gudang. The diminishing of the spiritual significance of the Javanese traditional rituals in Gudang has two implications. First, it reduced the role of belief in public life in Gudang, especially among the rural elite and the poor peasants, and second, it indicated

---

[88] The division between these two socio-religious groups was not always clear-cut, for obviously there were members of the traditional elite and some civil servants who were devout Muslims and thus belonged to the *santri* group.

the level of influence traditional belief had in the individual and social life in Gudang hamlet.

Within this context, just as the traditional elite viewed themselves as the carrier of the process of modernisation, the *santri* of Gudang viewed themselves as the defender of Islamic values in the development process against prevailing secular values.

To some extent, the experience of the three hamlets of Lopait illustrates the complexity of the process of value-change in rural Java, and how they relate to participation in development. In the case of Calombo, as Islam has been substantiated to be the social identity of the hamlet community, it will most likely continue to supply the *santri* of Calombo with motivation for participation and progress. It should be noted, however, that the intensity and the weight of this motivation may vary from time to time, depending on the other factors, such as a change in the supra-village attitudes toward Calombo, or a major change in the livelihood of the people.

With regard to Gudang, it appears that the tension between the *santri* and the secular Muslims will increase in intensity. Although presently the traditional elite with its modern secular values seems to prevail in Gudang, a further political inclination toward Islam at the national level together with the ongoing process of *santrinisasi* would most likely change the balance of power in Gudang hamlet. Should this happen, Islam will certainly become the main force in the social life of Gudang; however, it is unlikely that Islam will function as the hamlet identity of Gudang in the same way it does in Calombo. It appears that whoever takes control of Gudang's socio-political life, whether the *santri* or the traditional elite, the tension and competition between the two socio-religious groups will remain.

The direction of the process of value-change in Celengan and their relation to participation is much more difficult to predict. There are many different factors which could influence the course of socio-economic change as well as value change in Celengan. Although supra-village pressure was one of the major determinants for value change in Celengan, no one could guarantee that if the pressure were lifted the revival of Javanese traditional rituals would not die out, just as in Gudang, or whether it will express itself more freely and provide motivation for participation and economic progress. Moreover, there are other potential factors such as the Church and the *tiyang agami* (devout Muslims) who could influence the course of the process of value change and its relation to participation in Celengan hamlet.

Chapter 6

Conclusion

1. Religion and Development

1.1. Muslim Religious Reform and Participation

A number of field-studies have suggested that religious values have made significant contributions to economic change in different parts of Asia (Bellah, 1957; Kuntowijoyo, 1971; Wang, 1990; Abdullah, 1994). The process of *santrinisasi* (Islamic religious 'purification') in Calombo which has stimulated people's participation in development as well as reinforcing the poverty-reduction process, further confirms the role of such religious values in accelerating sustainable economic development.[1] There are three important points which need to be made here. Firstly, there are of course other socio-cultural and political factors which have encouraged the people of Calombo to participate in development projects. Compared to the roles of the *kyai* and his 'religious purification', however, the impact of these socio-cultural and political factors on participation has been quite modest.

Secondly, participation is not the only important factor for successful rural economic development. There are other factors such as macro economic policies, market competition, infrastructure and resources which could accelerate or hinder the process of economic development. Gudang is a good example of how the infrastructure, the regional political policies and the macro development policies have accelerated overall economic development. However, the absence of any meaningful participation in the development process has denied the poorer households in Gudang the opportunity to benefit from development programmes. The development process in Gudang has generally benefited the richer households, as a result, the percentage of poorer households increased from 22.4 per cent in 1980 to 28.3 per cent in 1994 (Table 5.8). While it is true that participation alone does not produce rapid economic growth, it does, however, provide greater awareness of opportunities for delivering directly development benefits to the poorer households and thus, reduce the number of people living under absolute poverty, as in the case of Calombo.

---

[1] Huub de Jonge's (1989) study in Parindu, Madura also demonstrated similar phenomena, where Muslim religious reform stimulated the appearance of local business groups.

Thirdly, the process of 'religious purification' in Calombo should not be viewed simply as a replacement of the traditional Javanese belief system with 'pure' Islamic teaching. The nature of Islam in Calombo itself has been largely shaped by the ongoing dialogue and negotiation between Islam and the local social-structure, the supra-village policies and the influx of modernity. In other words, the socio-religious values did not result from theological content alone. One has to go further, not only to describe how Islam has been understood by the people, but more importantly, how this particular religion has actually functioned within the community.

1.2. Socio-Religious Values and 'Action'

The experience of Calombo suggests that, when religion functions as a group identity, 'action' (participation) tends to conform to socio-religious values. Celengan and Gudang hamlets on the other hand, demonstrated different sorts of relations between religion and development, or between socio-religious values and 'action'. Unlike Calombo which has discovered its group identity in Islam, the people of Celengan are still in the process of recovering their traditional Javanese values as their group identity. The hostile external political pressures upon Celengan have, to a large extent, shaped the perceived need of the people as stronger group identity.[2] This need has in turn informed 'action'. Within this context, religion (the traditional Javanese rituals) functions as an instrument to attain this perceived need. This relation between perceived need and religion should not, however, be understood as a one-way communication. To some extent, it was true that the perceived needs have taken part not only in the rediscovery but also in the reshaping of the traditional Javanese belief system in Celengan. However, the converse was also true, that the traditional Javanese belief system informed the people of Celengan of the way in which they should respond to the external pressures as such. In the case of Celengan hamlet, therefore, 'action' conforms to religious values only when in accord with the perceived need of the people to strengthen the hamlet identity. While the experience of Calombo seems to correspond to the Parsonian theory of the 'Socialised Actor', where values serve as a standard or paradigm for selection among the alternatives of 'action' or 'orientations' (Parsons, 1951: 12-14),[3] the experience of Celengan tends to correspond to the "Social Identity Approach" developed by Peter Berger and Thomas Luckmann (1966), Erving Goffman

---

[2] It has been discussed at length, both in Chapters Five and Six, that this perceived need for stronger hamlet identity was their strategy for socio-cultural, economic and political survival against external pressures.

[3] Unlike the "static internal state" of the (individual) values in the theory of Socialised Actors, the experience of Calombo suggested that the conformity of "action" to the religious values were based on the ongoing interaction" between the religious values and the other social aspects within the community.

(1967) and others.[4] This 'Social Identity Approach' suggests that values affect 'action' by specifying 'action' which will cause others to validate a particular identity (Cancian, 1975: 137).[5] This explains why the relations between the values of the minority religious groups in Celengan hamlet (Christian and orthodox Muslim) and 'action' appeared to be very weak. The people's responses and reactions toward government's development programmes were not mainly motivated by their individual religious convictions, but cognitively (strategically) chosen or developed to validate their social identity.

The government's development policy and the rapid integration of Gudang into the wider (urban) world has, to some extent, been responsible for the acceleration of class polarisation within Gudang. While the increasing class polarisation has gradually diminished their common socio-cultural values, the capitalistic nature of Indonesian urban life has, to a large extent, stimulated and intensified the commercialisation of exchange in Gudang. Therefore, 'action' (participation) has been largely determined by its economic benefits. As was described in Chapter Four, the practice of participation in Gudang has mostly benefited the elite at the expense of the poorer households. Since there was little evidence of immediate (direct) economic benefits attached to participation, people's participation in Gudang has been very low. This lack of participation has nothing to do with either the religion or the cultural identity of the people.[6] Thus, the immediate economic benefits, and not the socio-religious values, have been the main motive and consideration for 'action' in Gudang hamlet.

In regard to the theory of action, the study of the three hamlets of Lopait has thus suggested that the relationship between socio-religious values and 'action' can not be adequately explained by a single theory, either by the 'Socialised Actor' theory or by the 'Social Identity Approach'. Each theory has only been useful for explaining the relationship between socio-religious values and 'action' in a particular context. In fact, neither theory adequately explains the relationship between socio-religious values and 'action' in Gudang. In general, therefore, it appears that the relationship between socio-religious values and 'action' tends to be stronger, when a particular belief (religion) is shared by a group and has become the group identity of this particular community.

---

[4] See, Howard S. Becker, *Outsider*, 1963; Peter Berger and Thomas Luckmann, *The Social Construction of Reality*, 1966; Erving Goffman, *Interaction Ritual*, 1967; and J. Douglas., ed., *Understanding Everyday Life*, 1970. For a comprehensive summary of this approach, see Francesca Cancian, *What Are Norms?*, 1975: 135-147.

[5] See the discussion on these two theories of action in Chapter One.

[6] The increasing religious polarisation within Gudang hamlet has contributed to the gradual isolation of belief from social life; see the discussion on the ritual change in Gudang hamlet in Chapter Seven.

2. Development Policy and Participation

With regard to the development process in Lopait village as a whole, government policies at national and regional levels have evidently brought considerable socio-economic change. It needs to be noted, however, that the development benefits have not been equally distributed among the hamlets within Lopait village. Even within Gudang hamlet, to which most of the economic development policies have been directed, there was clear evidence of unequal distribution of benefit between the richer and the poorer households. To some extent, the experience of Lopait village and especially of Gudang hamlet indicates that government's commitment to deliver "equitable distribution of development and its gain" (Republic of Indonesia, 1987: 36) and to promote "active participation in development of all layers of the community" (Republic of Indonesia, 1983: 17) has been impeded primarily by the socio-cultural and socio-political factors at the local level. The patronage relationship between the (traditional) elite and the poor (cf., Prijono and Prijono, 1983), as well as the collaboration between the elite and the supra-village administrations (cf., Hart, 1986), have delivered the development benefits mostly to the elite. The failure of the supra-village administrations to anticipate this typical problem of a traditional social structure, where a small powerful elite group often exploits the poorer households (Johnston and Clark, 1982; Chambers, 1983), has excluded the poorer households from the benefits as well as meaningful participation in development.

As the 'village' has been considered as the community unit for the implementation of development programmes, the socio-cultural values and needs of Gudang hamlet were regarded as the values and needs of the whole village.[7] Consequently, the socio-religious values and needs of Calombo and Celengan hamlets which were different from those of Gudang were largely disregarded. As meaningful participation is often related to the local socio-religious values (Selosoemardjan and Breazeale, 1993) and local 'needs' (Buijs, 1979), in Celengan hamlet, therefore, participation in some of the development programmes which were identified by the supra-village administrations was recorded low. With regard to Calombo hamlet, participation was recorded very high when the projects were identified and selected by the local people, and thus reflected the local religious values and met the local needs. On the other hand, extensive involvement of the supra-village administrations in the execution of hamlet level development has considerably weakened people's participation.

Unintentionally, the hostile socio-political policy against Calombo and Celengan hamlets, as described in Chapters Three and Four, has produced considerable motivation among the people in these two hamlets to strive for

[7] For a general discussion of the structure of Indonesian local administration, see Chapter Four. For the implementation of this administrative structure in Lopait village, see Chapter Five.

socio-economic development outside the government's development programmes (cf., Buijs, 1979). The people of Calombo, who drew their strength and motivation from Islamic teachings, chose a self-reliant development, and thus accelerated participation.[8] The people of Celengan responded to hostile external pressures in three ways; first, by leaving the village for better paid urban jobs; secondly, by strengthening their hamlet's socio-cultural identity and social unity (Buijs, 1979), and thirdly, by demonstrating a passive attitude toward governmental development programmes (Scott, 1976). To some extent, therefore, the substantial participation in Calombo hamlet and the revival of the traditional Javanese ritual in Celengan hamlet were (indirect) positive outcomes of the hostile external pressures.

3. Implications for Policy on Rural Development

The study of the three hamlets of Lopait has examined the different roles of religion in the process of social change in rural Java. In certain contexts religion has stimulated participation as well as promoting equal distribution of development benefits (cf., Abdullah, 1994). The role played by religion in economic development has varied from one social context to another. Often it changed the value orientation of the people by initiating the process of rationalisation (Weber, 1947; Peacock, 1978b); elsewhere, it also created a positive working ethic (Bellah, 1957; de Jonge, 1989). In a different context, as has been clearly demonstrated in Calombo hamlet, it also functioned as a group identity, which has effectively substantiated the concern for the poor.[9] Regardless of the important roles religion (belief system) has played, the ongoing process of change in the wider social context, as well as the government's policies at national and local levels, have continued and will continue to play the most significant roles in shaping the social structure of rural Java.

While it is true that participation alone does not necessarily lead to poverty alleviation, nor does it claims to be the only important factor for effective poverty eradication process, to some extent the experience of the three hamlets of Lopait indicates some forms of correlation between people's participation in decision-making process and an equitable distribution of development benefits. With regard to Calombo hamlet, although in terms of poverty-reduction it has achieved considerable success, in terms of development policy it has left no pattern at all. Moreover, one has to wait and see whether the substantial

[8] Although a reaction to socio-political pressures often produces new socio-cultural (religious) values which are generally more self-reliant (Abdullah, 1994: 163), it is ethically difficult to find justification for such a policy out of these experiences.

[9] See the discussion on the concept of *umma* (Islamic community) in Chapter Seven, which conveys the notion of social justice (Abdullah, 1994: 174).

poverty reduction in Calombo will in turn generate substantial economic growth, or whether there will be a repetition of what happened among the reformed Muslims of Jatinom, where at a certain stage, the process of economic development became stagnant because of the lack of 'systematic business organisation' (Abdullah, 1994). It therefore, appears that the experiences of the three hamlets of Lopait do not provide a model or even a pattern for economic development in rural Java. There are, however, some useful hints and implications which could be drawn from their experiences, and used as a parameter for future development policy.

Firstly, although different (government) development programmes, such as *Kejar Paket A* (literacy programme), *Posyandu* (rural health cadre) and the Green Revolution inputs and credit have in various degrees benefited the rural people, it was the infrastructural development such as road construction which has made the major contribution to the overall increase in household income in Lopait. This infra-structural development has not only provided the rural people access to higher income urban jobs (cf. Manning, 1988), but has also reduced real transport costs of goods being traded to nearby market towns, and thus increased the competing power of rural products (cf. Booth, 1979; Hefner, 1990). Together with the infra-structural developments, the improved education standard in Lopait and the development of new industrial towns of Ungaran, Klepu and Bawen have also made significant contributions to employment change and increased household income.

Secondly, since the group identity in many parts of rural Java is found mostly at a hamlet (and not a village) level (cf., Dirdjosanjoto, 1978; Tjondronegoro, 1984; Schulte Nordholt, 1987b), one way in which participation can be stimulated is by making a necessary administrative change. Instead of 'village' (*desa*), hamlet (*dukuh*) should be considered as the lowest level administrative unit for the implementation of development programmes.[10] Another way to do it is by simply redefining the village boundaries, according to the domain of the major socio-religious values and group identity. Either way, the new structural-administrative unit must correspond to the domain of the socio-religious (cultural) values and the group identity of a particular community.

[10] This structural change at the hamlet-village levels will certainly, have consequences for the other administrative levels as well. As has been suggested in Chapter Four, the sub-district administration and not the village level administration should be considered the third level administrative unit, after the province and district administrative levels. This structure implies that the major responsibility for rural development will be in the hand of the 'more educated' *camat* (sub-district head), rather than the secondary educated *lurah* (village head). This structure will increase efficiency and effectiveness of the rural development process by firstly, trimming the unnecessary bureaucracy (the village level), secondly, putting a more educated official (*camat*) to be in charge of the execution of the rural development programmes, and thirdly, by meeting the socio-religious (cultural) values and the perceived needs of each particular community unit.

Thirdly, the generalisation approach of the development policy (and programmes) in rural Indonesia has produced less than potential benefits for the rural development process. While such common development policy made the execution of development programmes a lot easier for the government, it has largely failed to recognise the significance of local values and needs. As Niels Mulder (1986) indicated, while co-operative programmes could be quite successful among some cultural settings outside Java, their implementation in rural Java has largely been unsuccessful.[11] Earlier, Koentjaraningrat (1971) had also noticed the potential problem of cultural plurality in Indonesia for the formulation of a development policy. This thesis further confirms the failure of the universal development policy (at a national level) in adequately addressing all the specific needs of different local communities (hamlets) in Java. Further comparative research on the implementation of the *IDT* (*Inpres Desa Tertinggal*, presidential instruction for the poverty reduction programme throughout rural Indonesia), or any other national development programme recently implemented in the different parts of Indonesia would therefore be of significance for the formulation of future development policies.

Finally, from the experience of the three hamlets of Lopait, it appears that participation in the decision-making process was more directly correlated to the sharing of development benefits. On the other hand, the government's tool for assessing participation in rural development is mostly based on the actual contribution at the implementation stage (Republic of Indonesia, 1983: 17), which as has been demonstrated in the Lopait case, has much less implication for delivering development benefits to the poor. One way in which the quality of people's participation in rural development could be improved so as to promote equitable distribution of development benefits, is by redefining participation and revising the existing measurement, especially with one which gives proper weight to the decision-making process of development.

The New Order's strong commitment to broad-based economic growth since its inception, together with the massive external funding of development (foreign aid) and the increase in the international price of oil in the 1970s were among the major factors in Indonesia's spectacular economic growth (Cheetham and Peters, 1993; Booth, 1996). While in terms of macro economic growth, most economic observers have almost unanimously praised the achievement of the New Order administration (Hart, 1986; Dirkse *et al.*, 1993), in terms of poverty alleviation they were less unanimous, and in terms of equal distribution of development benefits they were generally concerned for the government's failure to deliver on its commitment. Even though a large number of micro studies in rural Java, including this present research, indicate that the government's development programmes have in varying degrees benefited the rural population of Java (Hart, 1986; Kasryno, 1986; Hefner,

[11] For a study of village level co-operatives in West Java, see H. T. Kalo, Makali and G. Wiradi, *Perkembangan Koperasi di Pedesaan Jawa*, 1980.

1990, Jatileksono, 1994), there has been an increasing concern for an unequal distribution of the development benefits. At the micro level, this present study has indicated a number of factors which have contributed to this unequal distribution of development benefits. One of these factors which appeared to be very significant in the development processes in the three hamlets of Lopait was the lack of people's participation in the decision-making stage. As participation in the decision-making stage was closely related to the participation in the sharing of benefit stage, the exclusion of the rural poor from the decision-making process implied prevention from equal access to development benefits. Accordingly, this study suggests that a number of modifications and adjustments are needed both in the government's policy design and in the programme implementation, so as to allow more meaningful people's participation in the decision-making process.

4. The Rural Javanese and Modernity

At the beginning of this thesis, a question was posed as to whether the rural Javanese social structure has undergone major transformation to become a totally commercialised, individualised and class polarised capitalist system (Collier, 1978; Husken and White, 1989) or whether it has retained much of its traditional-communal and egalitarian (shared poverty) nature (Geertz, 1984; Mulder, 1986). In response to this question, this thesis has pointed out at least two crucial points. Firstly, it has extensively demonstrated, that there are no common (single) Javanese set of socio-cultural values as such; and it is even doubtful whether such common values ever really existed. This does not mean, however, that there are no common aspects to socio-cultural values found in many different parts of rural Java, both in the past and at the present.

Secondly, the social complexity of rural Java has greatly increased in recent years as a result of the substantial development of infrastructure, the improvement of transportation, and the rapid influx of goods and information. The experience of the three hamlets of Lopait has clearly rebutted the commonly held view on the process of transformation in rural Java, which has mostly interpreted social change as simply a replacement of traditional communal life with an impersonal and commercialised type of society. There have been complex and varied factors (local politics, macro policy, religious purification, ecological setting, pattern of livelihood, historical background and so forth) which have determined the process, the speed and even the direction of social change in the three hamlets of Lopait. It needs to be noted that this constant encounter between the traditional cultural values and the other aspects of social life mentioned above, is evidently not a one-way inflow of values. The ongoing interactions and negotiations between different social aspects, and most importantly, between the local and the wider social context have added to the complexity of the present social structure of the Javanese rural community. The question which we posed at the beginning of this discussion appears to over-simplify the process of change in Javanese social structure, and can be only an initial point of departure.

Appendix

The Field Research and the Questionnaires

1. The Field Research

The field research began in July 1993, with three months of intensive observation in the three hamlets. At the end of this period, the first draft of socio-economic descriptions and the belief structure of the three hamlets was produced. The observation was done mostly by unstructured interviews with the formal (*pamong*, village administrators) and informal leaders of the hamlets, such as the *kyai* of Calombo, a retired *pamong* of Gudang and a senior member of *Kejawen* in Celengan, and other elderly people who are natives of these hamlets.

The next stage was the data collecting phase. The first step was to make a list of all development projects implemented in the three hamlets between 1989-1993. These data were collected through interviews with the *kadus* (hamlet head) of each hamlet, and from the *monografi desa* (village demographic register, continually updated). Considering the limitation of time and resources, I selected 7 projects in each hamlet (comprising physical development projects, such as road constructions and mosque reconstruction, and non-physical projects such as education and health) investigation.

The second step was to choose two key informants for each project, and follow this up by in-depth interview with each of them (Instruments B and C). The third step, was to take a random sample for each hamlet, representing different social classes (poor, middle and rich, see the Introduction for the method of classification). The total number of households who have been formally interviewed, including the key informants, was 138 (30 per cent from each hamlet). This random survey aimed first, at assessing people's participation in development projects in their respective hamlet (Instrument A), and second, to cross check the data on value orientation of each hamlet collected through field observations (Instrument C). The data collecting phase was completed by the end of June 1995. During this phase, direct observation was carried out in the area of rituals and social events, such as *slametan* (Javanese communal feasts), traditional wedding ceremonies, *kerja bhakti* (voluntary labour), and *sambatan* (voluntary helping a neighbour in constructing a house or preparing a feast).

2. Instrument A (source: respondents)

Objectives:

1. To assess people's participation in the development process
2. To examine people's motivations for participation

A.1 Questions related to the stage of identifying a particular type of project:

A.1.1 Is the interviewee participating in this stage? (if not, skip to question #5).

A.1.2 In what capacity is the interviewee involved? What kinds of things is the interviewee doing? What has the interviewee invested (money, time, manpower, materials, other)?

A.1.3 What has the decision making process been like since the interviewee first decided to Participate in the project?

A.1.4 For what reason did the interviewee decide to participate? What is the relationship between the interviewee's reasons for his participation and his beliefs?

A.1.5 If the interviewee is not participating, what are his reasons? What is the relationship between the interviewee's reasons for not participating and his beliefs?

A.2 Questions related to the planning stage for the Particular type of Project:

A.2.1 Is the interviewee participating in this stage? (If not, skip to question #5).

A.2.2 In what capacity is the interviewee involved? What kinds of things is the interviewee doing? What has the interviewee invested (money, time, manpower, other)?

A.2.3 What is the planning process like?

A.2.4 For what reasons did the interviewee decide to participate? What is the relationship between the interviewee's reasons for his participation and his beliefs?

A.2.5 If the interviewee is not participating, what are his reasons? What is the relationship between the interviewee's reasons for not participating and his beliefs?

A.3 Question related to the implementation stage of a particular project:

A.3.1 Is the interviewee participating in this stage? (If not, skip to question #5).

A.3.2 In what capacity is the interviewee involved? What kinds of things is the interviewee doing?

What has the interviewee invested (money, time, manpower, materials)?

A.3.3 What is the implementation process like?

A.3.4 For what reasons did the interviewee decide to participate? What is the relationship between the interviewee's reasons for his participation and his beliefs?

A.3.5 If the interviewee is not participating, what are his reasons? What is the relationship between the interviewee's reasons for not participating and his beliefs?

A.4 Question related to the sharing of a particular project's benefits:

A.4.1 Is the interviewee reaping any benefits from the project? (If not, skip to question #5).

A.4.2 What benefits has the interviewee enjoyed?

A.4.3 How is the sharing of benefits determined?

A.4.4 For what reasons did the interviewee choose to enjoy the benefits of this project?
What is the relationship between these reasons and an interviewee's beliefs?

A.4.5 If the interviewee has decided not to share in the project's benefits, what are his reasons?
What is the relationship between these reasons and the interviewee's beliefs?

A.5 Question related to the maintenance stage of a particular project:

A.5.1 Is the interviewee participating in this stage? (If not, skip to question #5).

A.5.2 In what capacity? What is he actually doing? What has he invested?

A.5.3 What is the process involved at this stage?

A.5.4 For what reasons did the interviewee decide to participate?
What is the relationship between the interviewee's reasons for his participation and his beliefs?

A.5.5 If the interviewee is not participating, what are his reasons? What is the relationship between the interviewee's reasons for not participating and his beliefs?

3. Instrument B (source: key informants of each project)

Objectives:

1. To describe the development process in the three hamlets of Lopait
2. To assess people's participation from the perspective of the key informants

B.1 Related to the stage of project identification:

B.1.1 In what forum were types of project first identified/discussed? Who attended?
B.1.2 Who led the discussion to identify the types of project?
B.1.3 What types of projects were identified in the discussion?
B.1.4 Which individuals proposed which projects?
B.1.5 What was your role in this stage?

B.2 Related to the stage of determining what projects would be chosen:

B.2.1 What was the primary reason for choosing this project?
B.2.2 What was your role in this stage?
B.2.3 What type of decision making process was used to choose this project; including the role of other parties in this process?
B.2.4 Did any party disagree with the decision; how was this problem solved?

B.3 Related to planning stage:

B.3.1 What was your role in this stage?
B.3.2 What was the process used for this planning stage; including the role on other parties?
B.3.3 What is including in the plan (state all of its aspects)?
B.3.4 What problems arose during the planning stage; how were they resolved?

B.4 Related to the project implementation stage:

B.4.1 What was your role in this stage?
B.4.2 What was the implementation process used; including the role of other parties?
B.4.3 What problems arose during this stage; How were they resolved?

B.5 Related to the sharing of project benefits stage:

B.5.1 Have you share in the benefits of this project?
B.5.2 What benefits have those involved enjoyed?
B.5.3 What other parties have enjoyed benefits?
B.5.4 Which benefits have been enjoyed by which parties?
B.5.5 How was the sharing of project benefits determined and applied?
B.5.6 What problems arose during this stage; How were they resolved?

B.6 Related to the maintenance stage:

B.6.1 What was your role in this stage?
B.6.2 What was the role others in this stage?
B.6.3 Methods for this maintenance?
B.6.4 What problems arose; how were they resolved?

B.7 Reasons for one's participation:

B.7.1 Why did you initiate the realization of this project?
B.7.2 What is the relationship between your reasons for this initiation and your beliefs?

4. Instrument C (source: respondents and key informants)

Objectives:

1. To describe the socio-cultural (religious) values in the three hamlets
2. To explain the role of religion in shaping the socio-cultural values
3. To comparatively examine the responses and reactions of the three hamlet communities to modernity

4.1 Instrument C.1: Comparative Value Orientations

C.1.1 Views regarding people's relation to other people: Within this sub-village how does the interviewee think that personal relationships should be carried out?

a. Maintain relational harmony within the community.
b. Maintain cooperation among members of the community for the common good.
c. Use community co-operation for personal gain.
d. Grant each person freedom based on their individual needs.
e. .....

Please give reasons for choice.

C.1.2 Views regarding people's relation to nature: How does the interviewee view the relationship between man and the surrounding natural resources?

a. They are a God-given gift, of which people may partake in moderation.
b. They are a resource which man should both put to active use and preserve for future generations.

c. They are an expendable resource which people may exploit for his immediate gain.
d. ......

Please give reasons for choice

C.1.3. Views regarding people's relation to time: If the interviewee receives money in addition to his regular income (for example: inheritance), what does he do with it ?

a. Saves it
b. Purchases land
c. Uses it as business capital
d. Renovates his house
e. Buys a vehicle
f. Buys a TV
g. Fixes up a grave-site
h. ....

Please give reasons for choice.

C.1.4 Views regarding people's attitude to activity/work: What profession does the interviewee hope to see his children in.

a. Farmer
b. Shop/small restaurant owner
c. Military personnel
d. Administrator/official
e. Civil servant
f. Trader
g. Private business person
h. ....

Please give reasons for choice

C.1.5 Views regarding people's attitude to life/human nature:
5.1 What does the interviewee believe to be the aim of human life?
5.2 What is the interviewee's opinion of the life he's lived so far?

a. Bad
b. Good
c. Bad but making an effort to improve it
d. ....
Please give reasons for choice.

C.1.6 What does the interviewee consider the most important doctrine/ teaching in his belief?

C.1.7 Why is this doctrine/teaching most important for the interviewee?

4.2 Instrument C.2: Traditional Values and Modernity

C.2.1 In choosing a school for his children, what are the interviewee's most important considerations:

a. A quality school
b. An inexpensive school
c. Not far from home
d. Knows the teachers
e. Religious affiliation
f. ....
g. ....

Please choose two considerations : ...., ...

C.2.2 If a member of the interviewee's family falls ill, where does he take them for treatment:

a. A doctor in Salatiga/Ambarawa
b. Public hospital in Salatiga/Ambarawa
c. Community health centre
d. Medical aide(paramedic)
e. Traditional healer
f. Other: ....

Please state reasons ....

C.2.3 Within this sub-village, who does the interviewee consider successful? Why does he consider them successful?

C.2.4 Within this sub-village, who does the interviewee think has achieved happiness? Why does he consider them happy?

C.2.5 Within this sub-village, who does the interviewee consider to be poor? Why does he consider them poor?

C.2.6 If the interviewee could choose, which of the following would he choose for himself?

a. Wealth
b. Position

c. Respect
d. Education
e. Power/supernatural power
f. Health/longevity
g. Happiness
h. ....

Please choose three ...., ..., ...

5. INSTRUMENT D: (source: respondents; key informants, formal and informal leaders of each hamlet)

Objectives:

1. To describe the pattern of employment in each hamlet
2. To assess household income in each hamlet
3. To examine the pattern of relationship between employment, income, education, sex, and age
4. To establish local classification of income groups within each hamlet

5.1 Instrument D-1: Personal / Household Data

1. Name of Head of Household (HH):
2. Age of HH:
   a. 15-24
   b. 25 - 49
   c. 50 - 59
   d. 60 or older
3. Place of Birth: ....
4. Hamlet in which HH currently resides: ....
5. Number of members in family:
   a. Age of wife: ....
   b. Age and sex of first child: ....
   c. Age and sex of second child: ....

   d. Age and sex of third child: ....
   e. ....
   f. ....

6. Education:
6.1 Highest level of education completed by HH:
   a. elementary/primary school
   b. junior high school

c. senior high school
d. university
e. attended but did not graduate from elementary/primary school
f. no formal education
g. ....

6.2 Highest level of education completed by spouse (wife):
6.3 Highest level of education completed by first child:
6.4 Highest level of education completed by second child:
6.5 Highest level of education completed by third child:
6.6 ....
6.7 ....

7.1 Main occupation of HH :
a. Owner farmer (Including Share-Croppers):
a1. ....hectares of *sawah* (wet-rice field)
a2. ....hectares of *tegalan* (dry field)
b. Landless farm labourers
c. Fisherman
d. Self-employed; Home industry
e. Businessman/woman
f. Rural salaried employee
g. Urban employee
h. Trader
i. Unskilled casual non-farm labourer
j. Civil servant; Armed Forces; Retired
k. ....

7.2 Average monthly Income earned from this occupation: Rp.
7.3 Other occupation(s) of HH:................................; ....
7.4 Average monthly income earned from this occupation(s): Rp.
7.5 Total average monthly income earned by the HH: Rp...........................

8.1 Occupation of other family member (wife):
a. Owner farmer (Including Share-Croppers):
a1. ....hectares of *sawah* (wet-rice field)
a2. ....hectares of *tegalan* (dry field)
b. Landless farm labourers
c. Fisherman
d. Self-employed; Home industry
e. Businessman/woman
f. Rural salaried employee
g. Urban employee
h. Trader
i. Unskilled casual non-farm labourer
j. Civil servant; Armed Forces; Retired

k. ....

8.2 Average monthly Income earned from this occupation: Rp.
8.3 Other occupation(s):...; ....
8.4 Average monthly income earned from this occupation(s): Rp.
8.5 Total average monthly income earned: Rp

9.1 Occupation of other family member; First child (M/F):
a. Owner farmer (Including Share-Croppers):
a1. ....hectares of *sawah* (wet-rice field)
a2. ....hectares of *tegalan* (dry field)
b. Landless farm labourers
c. Fisherman
d. Self-employed; Home industry
e. Businessman/woman
f. Rural salaried employee
g. Urban employee
h. Trader
i. Unskilled casual non-farm labourer
j. Civil servant; Armed Forces; Retired
k. ....
9.2 Average monthly Income earned from this occupation: Rp.
9.3 Other occupation(s):...; ....
9.4 Average monthly income earned from this occupation(s): Rp.
9.5 Total average monthly income earned: Rp..................

10.1 Occupation of other family member; Second child (M/F):
a. Owner farmer (Including Share-Croppers):
a1. ....hectares of *sawah* (wet-rice field)
a2. ....hectares of *tegalan* (dry field)
b. Landless farm labourers
c. Fisherman
d. Self-employed; Home industry
e. Businessman/woman
f. Rural salaried employee
g. Urban employee
h. Trader
i. Unskilled casual non-farm labourer
j. Civil servant; Armed Forces; Retired
k. ....
10.2 Average monthly Income earned from this occupation: Rp.
10.3 Other occupation(s):...; ....
10.4 Average monthly income earned from this occupation(s): Rp.
10.5 Total average monthly income earned: Rp

11. Other (regular) family income:
a. Renting a land/house; Rp. ....
b. Monthly interest from money deposited in the bank; Rp
c. ....; Rp. ....
d. ....; Rp. ....

12. Total average monthly household income: Rp.

14. Religious affiliation of HH:
a. Muslim
b. Buddhist
c. Christian
d. ....
e. ....

13. Other relevant information:
a. ....
b. ....
c. ....

5.2 Instrument D-2: Local Classification of Income Groups

Following Mubyarto and Soetrisno (1985), this study employed the anthropological approach to social analysis as the principal method to describe the overall socio-economic settings of Lopait, especially for the classification of income groups within each hamlet. To some extent, this method of classification is an attempt to break away from the standard approaches to development research, where the researchers calculated the total incomes of each respondent and grouped them into income categories created by the researchers or by other external (national or international) agencies. In Lopait, the respondents themselves were asked to create income categories, by defining prosperity, and by identifying whom they consider as *tiyang gadah* (rich people), *cekapan* (middle income group) and *tiyang mboten gadah* (poor people) within their respective hamlet. These three categories of income group are local classifications.

1. Within this hamlet, who does the interviewee consider as *tiyang gadah* (rich/more than sufficient) (list 5-10 households) ? Why does he consider them rich? Within the categories of *tiyang gadah, tiyang cekapan, tiyang mboten gadah*, what was each household's economic status in 1980?

2. Within this hamlet, who does the interviewee consider as *tiyang cekapan* (middle/sufficient) (list 5-10 households) ? Why does he consider them *cekapan*? Within the categories of *tiyang gadah,*

tiyang cekapan, tiyang mboten gadah, what was each household's economic status in 1980?

3. Within this hamlet, who does the interviewee consider as *tiyang mboten gadah* (poor/not sufficient) (list 5-10 households) ? Why does he consider them poor? Within the categories of *tiyang gadah, tiyang cekapan, tiyang mboten gadah*, what was each household's economic status in 1980?

These local categories of income group in the three hamlets were then quantified by placing them within the range of incomes earned by the people in each income group, which had been collected through Instrument D-1 above. Using this methodology, the study established the estimated income categories as viewed by the local people. Accordingly, the *tiyang gadah* (the rich households) are those with average income per capita more than US$ 350. The *tiyang cekapan* (middle income households) are those with an average per capita income between US$ 135 - US$ 350. And the *tiyang mboten gadah* (poor households) are those with the income per capita below US$ 135 (see Table 6.1).

It is interesting to note that this locally developed poverty line of US$ 135 in Lopait village was much closer to the average expenditure per capita in rural Indonesia in 1993 of US$ 142 (BPS, 1994a) than to the poverty line adopted by the government of US$ 100 (BPS, 1994b). This poverty line is, however, still much lower than the World Bank poverty line of US$ 275 (World Bank, 1990a).

Table 6.1. Community Determined Income Groups and Estimated Household Income Levels

	poorer household/ *tiyang mboten gadah* in US$[1]	middle income group/ *tiyang cekapan* in US$	richer household/ *tiyang gadah* in US$
Calombo, 1994	below 134	134-337	above 337
Gudang, 1994	below 140	138-381	above 381
Celengan, 1994	below 132	132-363	above 363
Estimated levels employed by this study	below 135	135-350	above 350
Average expenditure on rural Indonesia 1993	142	n/a	n/a
National poverty line, 1993	100	n/a	n/a
World Bank poverty line, 1990	275 (lower poverty line)	n/a	n/a

[1]The Exchange rate in 1994 was US$1=Rp. 2,215

5.3 The Data collection method for the 1980 Household Classification

The 1980 household classification data were not based on information gathered through instrument D-1. Instead they are estimations given by the village (hamlet) officials and counter checked by other key informants and the respondents.

With regard to this 1980 household classification, the first task was to establish the estimated household classification in the early 1980s, relying mostly on the data collected from the village and hamlet officials. Once the estimated household classification in each hamlet was established, the data were counter checked by the information gathered through the key informants, the respondents (see Instrument D-2 above) and the local informal leaders (chairmen of the *RT* and *RW*) in each hamlet. In addition the respondents were asked to compare their present income category (1994) with that of the 1980.

Glossary

abangan	nominal Muslim
agami Jawi	Javanese religion
al-fatihah	the first surah of the Qur'an
aliran	cultural-religious political alliances in Java
amal	religious charity
ambeng	winnowing tray
Ansor	Islamic youth organisation
Bandes (Bantuan desa)	central government grants for village development
bekel	traditional village leader
bengkok	village's farm lands temporarily given to village administrators as their salary
bersih desa/bersih dhusun	village cleansing
bersih makam/nyadran	ritual of graveyard cleansing
bidstond	Christian prayer gathering
Bimas (Bimbingan massal)	agricultural extension programme (Green Revolution)
bondo desa	village farm lands as a source for village incomes
BTI (Barisan Tani Indonesia)	Farmer Front, associated with the communist party
bucu	ceremonial dish of rice served in a cone shape
bupati	administrative head of a district (kabupaten)
camat	administrative head of a sub-district (kecamatan)
carik	village secretary
D. I. (Daerah Istimewa)	special region
dai (da'i)	Muslim preacher
dalang	wayang (shadow play) performer
danyang	guardian spirit
desa/dhusun	village
dukun	traditional healer-may or may not use magic means to cure
dusun/dukuh	hamlet

dzikir	portions of Qur'an or other sacred texts used in Sufi meditation exercise
Golkar (Golongan Karya)	government political party
golongan cikal-bakal	the family of founding fathers of the village
gotong-royong	mutual assistance; co-operative labour
Idul Adha	Muslim feast to commemorate Abraham's offering of Ismael
IDT (Inpres Desa Tertinggal)	government grants allocated for alleviating rural poverty
ijab kabul	Islamic marriage ceremony
ikhtiar	work; effort
Inmas (Intensifikasi Massal)	rice intensification programme
Inpres (Instruksi Presiden)	Presidential Instruction for Special Grants Programmes
Insus (Intensifikasi khusus)	rice special intensification programme
iuran wajib	obligatory donation
jajan pasar	various little between-meal snacks from the market
kadus (kepala dusun)	hamlet head
kamituwa	traditional office of vice to the village head
kecamatan	administrative sub-district
kejar (kelompok belajar) paket A	government literacy programme
Kejawen	Javanese belief system; Jevenese mysticism
kenduren	ritual feast
kerja bhakti	mutual (voluntary) work
ketoprak	Javanese popular theatre
KKN (Kuliah Kerja Nyata)	social outreach by university students
Koramil	sub-district level army commanding officer
kramat/keramat	sacred; hold some magical powers
KTI (Kawasan Timur Indonesia)	Eastern Indonesia
KUA (Kantor Urusan Agama)	religious (Islam) department at sub-district level
KUD (Koperasi Unit Desa)	village co-operative
kyai	religious teacher
layar tancap	a temporary movie theatre set out in a sport- ground
leluhur	ancestors
LKMD	

(Lembaga Ketahanan Masyarakat Desa)	village resilience institution
LSD (Lembaga Sosial Desa)	village social institution
lurah	village head
mancanegara	part of Mataramese realm outside the negarigung
mantera/mantra	magic spell
Masyumi	modernist Muslim party
MCK (mandi cuci kakus)	rural public bath
merti desa	traditional harvest feast
modin	mosque official; village religious (Islamic) official
Muhammadiyah	modernist Islamic organisation
mushola/langgar	Muslim prayer house
nagaragung	area immediately surrounding the Mataram court
nrima	passive attitude toward life; accepting one's fate
NU (Nahdlatul Ulama)	Muslim scholars' organisation
ojek	motor-cycle used as taxi
padat karya	labour intensive development programme
pamong desa	village administrators
pasisir/pesisir	part of Maratamese realm lying on the north coast
PDI (Partai Demokrasi Indonesia)	Indonesia democratic party
pegawai (negeri)	civil servant
Pelita (Pembangunan Lima Tahun)	Five year development plan
Pemilu (Pemilihan Umum)	general election
pengajian	recitation of the Qur'an; study sessions
Perda (peraturan daerah)	provincial legislation
Perumka (Perusahaan Kereta Api)	National Railway company
Perusda (Perusahaan Daerah)	provincial company
pesantren	Islamic traditional (boarding) school
PKI (Partai Komunis Indonesia)	Indonesian Communist Party
PKK (Pendidikan Kesejahteraan Keluarga)	family welfare movement
PNI (Partai Nasional Indonesia)	Indonesia nationalist party
pos kamling (pos keamanan lingkungan)	guard post
posyandu (pos pelayanan terpadu)	rural health cadre; primary health care post
PPP (Partai Persatuan Pembangunan)	United Development Party; Muslim party
priyayi	elite group; administrative (pegawai) class
pusaka	sacred heirlooms
puskesmas (Pusat Kesehatan Masyarakat)	local (rural) health centre

R. I.	Republic of Indonesia
rapat dusun	hamlet (leaders) meeting
rembug desa (dhusun)	traditional village meeting
Rhamadan	the first month of the Muslim calendar
Riyaya (Idul Fitri)	Muslim feast at the end of the month of fasting
RT (Rukun Tetangga)	neighbourhood association
rukun/kerukunan	social harmony
ruwatan	ritual to free someone from a spell or bad luck
RW (Rukun Warga)	hamlet community association
sajen/sesajen	offerings presented to the spirits
salat/shalat	Muslim liturgical prayer performed five times per day
sambatan	mutual help to build a neighbour's house
santri	devoted Muslim
sawah	wet (irrigated) rice field
sedekah/sedhekah	alms-giving
selapan	every 35 days
slametan	ritual/communal feast
Sufi/Shufi	mystical (Islam)
Suronan	traditional ritual on the first day of the month of Sura in the Javanese calendar
syahbandar/shahbandar	harbourmaster
tahlilan	recitation of Laailaaha Illallah
taqdir	determined by Allah
tarekat	a Sufi order
tegal/tegalan	dry field
terbangan	Islamic musical entertainment (terbang a small drum)
tiyang alit	socially small people; poor; commoners
tokoh masyarakat	informal leaders
ujub	opening speech in a slametan
umma	Islamic community
Wali sanga	the nine Islamic saints who believed to have brought Islam to Java
warung	prepared-food stall
wayang (kulit)	shadow play performance
wudlu/wudhu	cleansing (wash) before a Muslim prayer
yasinan	from yasin the 37th surah of Qur'an

Abbreviations of Journals and Publishers

BKI	Bijdragen to de Taal-, Land- en Volkenkunde (Contributions to the Philology, Geography and Ethnology [of the Netherlands East Indies], Published by the Royal Institute of Philology, Geography and Ethnology [of the Netherlands East Indies]).
CSIS,	Centre for Strategic and International Studies
ESCAP	Economic and Social Commission for Asia and the Pacific
FAO	Food and Agricultural Organisation
HKTI	Himpunan Kerukunan Tani Indonesia (Indonesia's Farmer's Union)
IFAD	International Fund for Agricultural Development
ILO	International Labour Organisation
IMF	International Monetary Fund
IRRI	International Rice Research Institute
KITLV	Koninklijk Instituut voor Taal-, Land- en Volkenkunde (Royal Institute for Philology, Geography and Ethnology [of the Netherlands East Indies]), Leiden
LP3ES	Lembaga Penelitian, Pengkajian dan Pengembangan Ekonomi (Institute for research and economic development studies)
TBG	Tijdschrift voor Indische Taal-, Land- en Volkenkunde uitgegeven door het (Koninklijk) Bataviaasch Genootschap van Kunsten en Wetenschappen (Journal of Indonesian Philology, Geography and Ethnology, Published by the Royal Batavian Society of Arts and Sciences)
TKII	Tijdschrift van het Koninklijk Instituut van Ingenieurs, Afdeeling Nederlandsch-Indie (Journal of the Royal Institute for Engineering, the Netherlands East Indies Section)
TNI	Tijdschrift voor Nederlandsch-Indie (Netherlands East Indies Journal)
UNRISD	United Nations Research Institute for Social Development
VKI	Verbandelingen van het Koninklijk Instituut voor Taal-, Land- en Volkenkunde (van Nederlandsh-Indie) (Publications of the Royal Institute for Philology, Geography and Ethnology [of the Netherlands east Indies])
Bappenas	Badan Perencanaan Pembangunan Nasional (National Development Planning Board)
BPS	Biro Pusat Statistik (Central Bureau of Statistic)
SUSENAS	Survey Social Ekonomi Nasional (National socio-economic survey)

Bibliography

A. Manuscripts and maps

Arsip Nasional Republik Indonesia, Jakarta:
"Algemeen Verslag der Residentie Semarang over het Jaren 1837-1878"

"Kaart van Midden Java (van 1825-1830)". Krijgsgeschiedenis van Nederl. Indie, No. 4. Batavia and Den Haag: Kolff, 1895-1897.

Kaart van Sala Tiga en Omba Rawa met Omstreken (1891). Batavia: Topographisch Bureau, 1897.

B. Articles, PAPERS and newspapers

Alexander J. and P. Alexander. "Labour Demands and the 'Involution' of Javanese Agriculture." ***Social Analysis*** 3 (1979): 22-44

-----"Shared Poverty as Ideology: Agrarian Relationship in Colonial Java." ***Man*** (N. S.) 17 (1982): 597-619.

Albert, Ethel M. "The Classification of Values." ***American Anthropologist*** 58 (1956): 221-248.

Anderson, A. G. "Rural Market in West Java." ***Economic Development and Cultural Change*** 28 (1980): 753-777.

Anderson, Benedict R. O'G. "The Languages of Indonesian Politics." ***Indonesia*** 1 (1966): 89-116.

-----"Old State, New Society: Indonesia's New Order in Historical Perspective." ***Journal of Asian Studies*** 42 (1983): 477-496.

Arief, Sritua. "Who Benefits from Economic Growth: The Indonesian Experience." ***The South East Asian Economic Review*** 1.1 (1980): 1-12.

Asad, Talal. "Anthropological Conceptions of Religion: Reflections on Geertz." ***Man*** (N. S.) 18 (1965): 237-259.

Baal, Jan van. "Offering, Sacrifice and Gift." ***Numen*** 23 (1975): 161-178.

Bachtiar, H. W. "The Religion of Java: A Commentary." ***Majalah Ilmu-Ilmu Sastra Indonesia*** 5 (1973): 85-115

Berg, C. C. "The Islamization of Java." ***Studia Islamica*** 4 (1955): 111-192.

Bernsten, R. H., B. H. Siwi and H. M. Beachell. "The Development and Diffusion of Rice Varieties in Indonesia." Paper prepared for the International Rice Research Conference, 29 April 1981.

Bleeker, P. "Fragmenten eener Reis over Java, Reis Langs de Noordkust van Midden Java." ***TNI*** 1 (1850): 1-48.

Booth, Anne. "The Agricultural Survey, 1970-75." ***Bulletin of Indonesian Economic Studies*** 15 (1979): 45-68.

-----"Counting the Poor in Indonesia." ***Bulletin of Indonesian Economic Studies*** 29.1 (1993): 53-83.

-----"Indonesia Economic Development in the Soeharto Era." Paper prepared for the SBU-CAFOD-CIIR Seminar on UK/Indonesia Economic Relations, South Bank University, 17 July 1996.

Booth, Anne and R. M. Sundrum. "The 1973 Agriculture Census." ***Bulletin of Indonesian Economic Studies***, 12.2 (1976): 90-105.

Budiardjo, Miriam. "Perkembangan." ***Gatra***, 19 August, 1995: 38-39.

Cernea, M. "Farmer Organisation and Institution Building for Sustainable Development." ***Regional Development Dialogue*** 8.2 (1987): 1-19.

Collier, William L. "Food Problems, Unemployment, and the Green Revolution in Rural Java." ***Prisma*** 9 (1978): 38-52.

-----"Improved Cropping Patterns, Labor Absorption, and Small Rice Farm Mechanization in Java." Paper prepared for the joint A/D/C-IRRI Workshop on Consequences of Small Rice Farm Mechanization. Los Banos, Philippines, 14-18 September 1981(a).

Collier, William L., *et al.* "Recent Changes in Rice Harvesting Methods; Some Serious Social Implications." ***Bulletin of Indonesian Economic Studies*** 9.2 (1973): 36-45.

-----"Choice of Technique in Rice Milling on Java." ***Bulletin of Indonesian Economic Studies*** 10.1 (1974): 106-120.

-----"Acceleration of Rural Development of Java." ***Bulletin of Indonesian Economic Studies*** 18 (1982): 84-101.

-----"A Preliminary Study of Employment Trends in Lowland Javanese Village." Research Report submitted to the United States Agency for International Development, 1988.

Daroesman, R. "Survey of Recent Developments." ***Bulletin of Indonesian Economic Studies*** 17.2 (1981): 1-41.

Dhofier, Zamakhsyari. "Santri-Abangan Dalam Kehidupan Orang Jawa: Teropong dari Pesantren." ***Prisma*** 5 (1978): 64-72.

Dick, H. "Survey of Recent Development." ***Bulletin of Indonesian Economic Studies*** 18 (1982): 1-38.

Economic Commission for Latin America. "Popular Participation in Development." ***Community Development Journal*** 8.2 (1973): 77-93.

Eisenstadt, S. N. "Some Reflections on the Significance of Max Weber's Sociology of Religion for the Analysis of Non-European Modernity." ***Archives de Sociologie des Religions*** 32 (1971): 29-52.

Finterbusch, K and W. A. van Wicklin. "The Contribution of beneficiary participation to development project effectiveness." ***Public Administration and Development*** 7 (1987): 1-23.

Forum Keadilan. "Wawancara Letjen (pur.) Sayidiman Suryohadiprojo." 6 Novermber 1995: 80-84.

-----"Bergairah Politik, Berbaju Sosial." 20 November 1995: 13-14.

Fox, James J. "Ziarah Visits to the Tombs of the Wali, The Founders of Islam on Java." A paper prepared for the Monash University Annual Winter Lecture, 10 August 1989.

Fruin-Mees, W. "Pieter Franssen's Journaal van zijn Reis naar Mataram in 1630 en Eenige Wegen naar de Hofplaats." ***TBG*** 64 (1926): 395-422.

Gatra. "Akhirnya Naro Melakukan Kudeta." 21 October 1995: 39-40.

-----"Gebrakan Para Mantan." 11 November 1995: 22-24.

Geertz, Clifford. "Religious Belief and Economic Behaviour in a Central Javanese Town." ***Economic Development and Cultural Change*** 4 (1956): 134-158.

----- "Ritual and Social Change: A Javanese Example." ***American Anthropologist*** 59 (1957): 32-54.

-----"The Javanese Kijaji: The Changing Role of a Cultural Broker." ***Comparative Studies in Society and History*** 2 (1959-1960): 200-249.

-----"Religious Change and Social Order in Soeharto's Indonesia." ***Asia***, 27 (1972): 62-84.

-----"Culture and Social Change: The Indonesian Case." ***Man*** (N. S.) 19 (1984): 511-532.

Gezelius, Helena. "Popular Participation in Development: Some Different Interpretations." Unpublished manuscript, 1989.

Graaf, H. J. de. "De Verdwenen Tjandi te Salatiga." ***BKI*** 114 (1958): 117-120.

Graaf, H. J. de and Th, G. Th. Pigeaud. "The Eerste Moslimse Vorstendommen op Java: Studien over de Staatkundige Geschiedenis van de 15de en 16de Eeuw." ***VKI,*** Vol. 69, 1974.

Hague, W., *et al.* "Towards a Theory of Rural Development." ***Development Dialogue*** 2 (1977): 7-137.

Hefner, Robert. "Islamizing Java? Religion and Politics in Rural East Java." ***Journal of Asian Studies*** 46 (1987): 533-554.

Higgins, Benjamin. "Survey of Recent Development." ***Bulletin of Indonesian Economic Studies*** 8.1 (1972): 1-31.

Hinkson, J. "Rural Development and Class Contradiction on Java." ***Journal of Contemporary Asia*** 5 (1975): 327-336.

Hugo, Graeme. "Circular Migration." ***Bulletin of Indonesian Economic Studies*** 13 (1977): 57-66.

Husken, Frans. "Landlords, Sharecroppers, and Agricultural Labourers: Changing Labour Relations in Rural Java." ***Journal of Contemporary Asia*** 9 (1979): 140-151.

-----"Capitalism and Agrarian Differentiation in a Javanese Village." ***Masyarakat Indonesia*** 11 (1984): 140-151.

Ihalauw, John. "Mengkaji Penebas." ***Cakrawala***, November-December, 1974: 225.

Jacoby, Eric H. "Effects of the 'Green Revolution' in South and Southeast Asia." ***Modern Asian Studies*** 6.1, January 1971.

Jayasuriya, S. K. and R. T. Shand. "Technical Change and Labor Absorption in Asian Agriculture: Some Emerging Trends." ***World Development*** 14.3 (1985): 415-428.

Jones, G. W. "Links between Urbanization and Sectoral Shift in Employment in Java." ***Bulletin of Indonesian Economic Studies*** 20 (1984): 120-159.

Kahin, George McT. "Soekarno tak Ingin Ada Pertumpahan Darah." ***Tiras***, 5 October 1995: 47-52.

Kano, Hiroyoshi. "The Economic History of Javanese Rural Society: A Reinterpretation." ***The Developing Economies*** 17 (1980): 3-22.

Kluckhohn, Clyde. "The Scientific Study of Values." Toronto: University of Toronto Installation Lectures, 1958.

Kluckhohn, Florence R. "A Method for Eliciting Value Orientations." ***Anthropological Linguistic*** 2 (1960): 1-23.

Koperberg, S. "Het Betreden der Aarde (Tedak Siten)." ***Djawa*** 14 (1934): 213-214.

Korten, D. C. "Community Organization and Rural Development: A Learning Process Approach." ***Public Administration Review*** 40.5 (1980): 480-511.

Kuntowijoyo. "Economic and Religious Attitudes of Entrepreneurs in a Village Industry: Notes on the Community of Batur." ***Indonesia*** 12 (1971): 47-55.

Labovitz, Sanford and Robert Hagedorn. "Measuring Social Norms." ***Pacific Sociological Review*** 16 (1973): 283-304.

Liddle, R. W. "Evolution from Above: National Leadership and Local Development in Indonesia." ***Journal of Asian Studies*** 32.2 (1973): 287-309.

Manning, Chris. "Rural Economic Change and Labour Mobility. A Case Study from West Java." ***Bulletin of Indonesian Economic Studies*** 23 (1987): 52-79.

Maurer, Jean-Luc. "Agricultural Modernization and Social Change: The Case of Java over the Last Fifteen Years." ***Masyarakat Indonesia*** 11.2 (1984): 109-119.

Mochida, O. "Brown Planthoppers Reduce Rice Production." ***Indonesian Agricultural Research and Development Journal*** 1.1 (1979): 2-8.

Mubyarto. "Ada Petunjuk Keliru Memahami IDT." ***Kompas***, 11 July 1995.

Mubyarto, Loekman Soetrisno, and Michael R. Dove. "Problems of Rural Development in Central Java: Ethnomethodological Perspectives." ***Contemporary Southeast Asian Studies*** 5.1 (1983): 41-52.

Mulder, J. A. Niels. "Aliran Kebatinan as an Expression of the Javanese Worldview." ***Journal of Southeast Asia Studies***, 1 (1970): 105-114.

Nasikun. "Redefinisi Kriteria Batas Ambang Kemiskinan Berwawasan Martabat Manusia." Paper presented at the monthly seminar of the Centre for Rural and Regional Development Studies (P3PK), Gajah Mada University, 7 June 1993.

Nasution, Abdul Haris. "Catatan 50 Tahun Indonesia." ***Gatra***, 19 August 1995: 40-41.

Ortner, Sherry B. "Theory in Anthropology since the Sixties." ***Comparative Studies in Society and History*** 26.1 (1984): 126-166.

Poensen, C. "Iets over Javaansche Naamgeving en Eigennamen." ***Mededeelingen Vanwege het Nederlandsche Zendeling Genootschap*** 14 (1870): 304-321.

"Reis van den Gouverneur-Generaal Van Imhoff over Java in het Jaar 1746." ***BKI*** 1 (1853): 291-440.

Republika. "Tiap Tahun 50,000 Hektar Sawah Dikonversi." 11 October 1995.

-----"Penelitian BPS: Bawah Maju, Lapisan Atas Maju Lebih Cepat." 13 October 1995.

-----"Rapim II Golkar; Kesenjangan, Isu Pokok Menjelang Pemilu 1997." 18 October 1995.

-----"Isu Kesenjangan akan Rugikan Parpol." 19 October 1995.

-----"Bila Program IDT Gagal, Kredibilitas Pemerintah Terpengaruh." 20 October 1995.

Rietveld, P. "Non-Agricultural Activities and Income Distribution in Rural Java." ***Bulletin of Indonesian Economic Studies*** 22.3 (1986): 106-117.

Roche, Frederick C. "Critical Lands in East Java: Development Problems and Potentials." ***Economic Problems*** 26 (1984): 1-6.

Sairin, Sjafri. "Beberapa Masalah Derep: Studi Kasus Yogyakarta." ***Prisma*** 5 (1975): 59-67.

Sajogyo. "Garis Kemiskinan dan Kebutuhan Minimum Pangan." ***Kompas***, 17 November, 1977.

-----"Lapisan Masyarakat yang Paling Lemah di Pedesaan Jawa." ***Prisma*** 7.3 (1978): 3-14.

Schulte Nordholt, N. G. "De Positie van de Lurah: Een Kritische Baschouwing naar Aanleiding van Enkele Lurah-verkiezingen in Midden-Java. ***BKI*** 138 (1982): 98-128.

Schweizer, Thomas. "A Century of Change in the Javanese Rural Economy." Paper prepared for the Panel on Contemporary Indonesia at the Annual association of Southeast Asian Studies in the UK (ASEASUK) Conference. Cambridge, 23-25 March, 1988.

Sinaga, Rudolf. "Rural Institutions Serving Small Farmers in the Village of Sukagalih, Garut Regency, West Java." Report submitted to the ESCAP Expert Group Meeting on Rural Institutions Serving Small Farmers, Bangkok 13-17 December 1976.

-----"Implications of Agricultural Mechanisation for Employment and Income Distribution." ***Bulletin of Indonesian Economic Studies*** 14.2 (1978): 102-111.

Slinkers, L. H. and J. E. de Meijer. "De Waterwerken in de Afdeeling Demak." ***TKII*** (1891-1892): i-xxi.

Soetrisno, Loekman. "Kelembagaan Desa dan Kelembagaan Masyarakat Desa: Prospek pada Program Umum HKTI dan Pencapaian Tujuan-Tujuan HKTI." Paper presented at the Workshop on the Formulation of HKTI's General Programme, 4-6 April 1989.

Stoler, Ann. "Some Socio-Economic Aspects of Rice Harvesting in a Javanese Village." ***Masyarakat Indonesia*** 2 (1975): 51-87.

-----"Rice Harvesting in Kali Loro." ***American Ethnologist*** 4 (1977a): 678-698.

-----"Class Structure and Female Autonomy in Rural Java." ***Signs*** 3 (1977b): 74-89.

Stone, Russel A. "Religious Ethic and the Spirit of Capitalism in Tunisia." ***International Journal of Middle East Studies*** 5 (1974): 260-273.

Temple, Gordon P. "Migration to Jakarta." ***Bulletin of Indonesian Economic Studies*** 11.1 (1975): 76-81.

Timmer, Peter C. "The Choice of Technique in Rice Milling in Java." ***Bulletin of Indonesian Economic Studies*** 9 (1973): 57-76.

-----"The Political Economy of Rice in Asia." ***Food Research Institute Studies*** 14.3, 1975.

Tiras. "Wawancara A. M. Fatwa: Sistem Kepartaian Sekarang Belum Kondusif." 9 November 1995: 46-52.

-----"Peran Dai dalam Pemilu." 18 April 1996: Appendix A-H.

Utami, W. and J. Ihalauw. "Some Consequences of Small Farm Size." ***Bulletin of Indonesian Economic Studies*** 9.2 (1973): 46-56.

Van Goens, Ryckloff Volckertsz. "Reijsbeschrijving van den Weg uijt Samarangh nae de Koninckliјke Hoofdplaets Mataram, mitsgaders de Zeeden, Gewoonten ende Gegeringe van den Sousouhounan, Groot Machtigste Koningk van 't eijlant Java." ***BKI*** 4 (1856): 307-350. (Reprinted in H. J. de Graaf, ed., ***De Vijf Gezantschapsreizen van Rijklof van Goens, naar het Hof van Mataram, 1648-1654***. 's-Gravenhage: Martinus Nijhoff, 1956).

Van Milaan, P. W. "Beschouwingen over het 17e Eeuwse Mataramse Wegennet." ***Sociaal Geographische Mededeelingen*** 4 (1942): 205-239.

Van Niel, Robert. "Nineteenth-Century Java: Variations on the Theme of Rural Change." Southeast Asian Social Studies Association Conference Paper, Ohio University, 1983.

Wang, Gungwu. "The Culture of Chinese Merchants." Working Paper Series No. 57, Joint Centre for Asia Pacific Studies, University of Toronto-York University, 1990.

Wardhana, Ali. "Indonesia, Asia-Pacific, and the Global Economy: New Dimensions and the Challenge of Regional Community Building." Paper presented at the CSIS seminar, Jakarta 17 October 1995.

White, Benjamin. "Population, Employment and Involution in a Javanese Village." ***Development and Change*** 7 (1976): 267-290.

-----"Political Aspect of Poverty, Income Distribution and their Measurement: Some Examples from Rural Java." ***Development and Change*** 10 (1979): 91-114.

-----"Agricultural Involution and Its Critics: Twenty Years after Clifford Geertz," Working Paper, series no. 6. The Hague: Institute of Social Studies, 1983.

C. Books and Monographs

Abdullah, Irwan. ***The Muslim Businessmen of Jatinom.*** Ph. D. Thesis, Universiteit van Amsterdam, 1994.

Ahmad, Imam. "Agama: Jawaban atau Pertanyaan?" In LP3ES, ***Agama dan Tantangan Zaman***, pp. vii-xlii. Jakarta: LP3ES, 1985.

Alatas, Syed Hussein. "Religion and Modernization in South-East Asia." In Hans-Dieter Evers, ed., ***Modernization in South-East Asia***, pp. 153-169. Singapore: Oxford University Press, 1973.

Albert, Ethel M. "Value System." In David L. Sills, ed. ***International Encyclopaedia of the Social Science***, Vol. 16. New York: The Free Press, 1968.

Alexander, Jennifer. ***Trade, Traders and Trading in Rural Java.*** Singapore: Oxford University Press, 1987.

Alexander, Paul; P. Boomgaard; B. White., eds. ***In the Shadow of Agriculture.*** Amsterdam: Royal Tropical Institute, 1991.

Amaluddin, Moh. ***Kemiskinan dan Polarisasi Sosial, Studi Kasus di Desa Bulugede, Kabupaten Kendal, Jawa Tengah***. Jakarta: University of Indonesia Press, 1987.

Anawati, George C. "Philosophy, Theology & Mysticism." In Joseph Schacht and C. Bosworth, eds., ***The Legacy of Islam***, pp. 350-392. Oxford: Clarendon Press, 2nd. ed., 1974.

Anderson, Benedict R. O'G. ***Mythology and the Tolerance of Java.*** Ithaca: Cornell University Press, 1965.

----- "The Idea of Power in Javanese Culture." In Claire Holt, ed., ***Culture and Politics in Indonesia***, pp. 1-69. Ithaca: Cornell University Press, 1972.

----- "Perspective and Method in American Research on Indonesia." In Benedict Anderson and Audrey Kahin, eds., ***Interpreting Indonesian Politics: Thirteen Contributions to the Debate***, pp. 69-83. Ithaca; Cornell University Press, 1982.

----- ***Language and Power: Exploring Political Cultures in Indonesia.*** Ithaca: Cornell University Press, 1990.

Anderson, Benedict R. O'G. and Ruth T. McVey. ***A Preliminary Analysis of the October 1, 1965 Coup in Indonesia.*** Ithaca: Monograph Series, Modern Indonesia Project Cornell University, 1971.

Anderson, Benedict R. O'G. and Audrey Kahin, eds. ***Interpreting Indonesian Politics: Thirteen Contributions to the Debate.*** Ithaca: Cornell University Press, 1982.

Antlov, Hans and Thommy Svensson. "From Rural Home Weavers to Factory Labour: The Industrialization of Textile Manufacturing in Majalaya." In P. Alexander *et al.*, eds., ***In the Shadow of Agriculture***, pp. 113-126. Amsterdam: The Royal Tropical Institute, 1991.

Arief, Sritua. ***Consumption Patterns in Indonesia: An Econometric Study***. Jakarta: Sritua Arief Associates, 1978.

Arief, Sritua and Adi Sasono. ***Indonesia: Dependency and Underdevelopment.*** Kuala Lumpur: META, 1980.

Arndt, H. W. "Banking in Hyperinflation and Stabilization." In B. Glassburner, ed., ***The Economy of Indonesia: Selected Readings***, pp. 359-395. Ithaca: Cornell University Press, 1971.

Bamberger, M., ed. ***Reading in Community Participation***. Washington, DC: Economic Development Institute of the World Bank, 1986.

Banton, Michael. ***Anthropological Approaches to the Study of Religion***. London: Tavistock Publications, 1966.

Barker, Randolph, Robert W. Herdt and Beth Rose. ***The Rice Economy of Asia***. Washington DC: Resources for the Future, 1985.

Bastin, John. ***Raffles' Ideas on the Land Rent System in Java***. The Hague: Nijhoff, 1954.

Becker, Howard S. ***Outsider***. New York: The Free Press, 1963.

Bellah, Robert N. ***Tokugawa Religion***. New York: The Free Press, 1957.

-----, ed. ***Religion and Progress in Modern Asia***. New York: The Free Press, 1965.

-----"Reflections on the Protestant Ethic Analogy in Asia." In S. N. Eisenstadt, ed., ***The Protestant Ethic and Modernization: A Comparative View***, pp. 243-251. New York: Basic Books, 1968.

Benda, Harry J. ***The Crescent and the Rising Sun***. The Hague and Bandung: W. Van Hoew Ltd., 1958.

Berger, Peter and Thomas Luckmann. ***The Social Construction of Reality***. New York: Doubleday, 1966.

Bhadwi, A and A. Rahman, eds. ***Studies in Rural Participation***. New Delhi: Oxford and IBM Publishing, 1982.

Bhasin, K. ***Towards Empowerment***. Rome: FAO, 1985.

Biersack, Aletta. "Local Knowledge, Local History: Geertz and Beyond." In Lynn Hunt, ed., ***The New Cultural History***, pp. 72-96. Berkeley and Los Angeles: University of California Press, 1989.

Birowo, Achmad T. and Gary E. Hansen. "Agricultural and Rural Development: An Overview." In Gary E. Hansen, ed., ***Agricultural and Rural Development in Indonesia***, pp. 1-27. Boulder: Westview, 1981.

Boland, B. J. ***The Struggle of Islam in Modern Indonesia***. The Hague: Martinus Nijhoff, 1971.

Boeke, J. H. ***Economics and Economic Policy of Dual Societies, as Exemplified by Indonesia***. New York: Institute of Pacific Relations, 1953.

Boggs, Carl. ***Gramsci's Marxism***. London: Pluto Press, 1976.

Booth, Anne E. and Peter McCawley, eds. ***The Indonesian Economy during the Soeharto Era***. Kuala Lumpur: Oxford University Press, 1981.

Booth, Anne E. and R. M. Sundrum. "Income Distribution in Indonesia: Trends and Determinants." In R. G. Garnaut and P. T. McCawley, eds., ***Indonesia: Dualism, Growth and Poverty***, pp. 455-485. Canberra: Research School Of Pacific Studies The Australian National University, 1980.

Bose, Swadesh R. "Has Economic Growth Immiserized the Rural Poor in Indonesia? A Review of Conflicting Evidence." In G. B. Hainsworth, ed., ***Village-Level Modernization in Southeast Asia***, pp. 53-69. Vancouver and London: University of British Columbia Press, 1982.

Bromley, Daniel W., ed. ***Making the Common Work: Theory, Practice, and Policy***. Institute for Contemporary Studies, 1992.

Bryant, Coralie and Louise G. White. ***Managing Rural Development with Small Farmer Participation.*** West Hartford: Kumarian Press, 1984.

Buijs, H. Y. ***Access and Participation***. ICA Publication No. 33. Leiden: Institute of Cultural and Social Studies Leiden University, 1979.

Burger, D. H. ***De Ontsluiting van Java's Binnenland voor het Wereldverkeer***. Wageningen: H. Veenman & Zonen, 1939.

-----***Structural Changes in Javanese Society: The Village Sphere.*** Ithaca: Cornell University Press, 1957.

Burkey, Stan. ***People First: A Guide to Self-Reliant, Participatory Rural Development***. London and New Jersey: ZED Books Ltd., 1993.

Carey, P. B. R. "Aspects of Javanese History in the Nineteenth Century." In Harry Aveling, ed., ***The Development of Indonesian Society***, pp. 45-105. Queensland: The University of Queensland Press, 1979.

Castles, Lance. ***Religion, Politics and Economic Behaviour in Java: The Kudus Cigarette Industry***. New Haven: Yale University Southeast Asia Studies, Cultural Report Series, No. 15, 1967.

Castillo, C. T. ***How Participatory is Participatory Development: A Review of the Philippine Experience***. Manila: Philippine Institute for Development Studies, 1983.

Cernea, M. ***Putting People First: Sociological Variables in Rural development***. Oxford: The Oxford University Press, 1985.

Chambers, Robert. ***Managing Rural Development: Ideas and Experience from East Africa***. Uppsala: Scandinavian Institute of African Studies, 1974.

-----***Rural Development: Putting the Last First***. London: Longmans, 1983.

Chandler, G. N. ***Periodicity, Mobility and the Distribution of Consumer Durable: A Study of Village Market Trade in D. I. Yogyakarta, Indonesia***. M. A. Thesis, Monash University, 1982.

Cheetham, Russell J. and R. Kyle Peters Jr. "Poverty Reduction during the New Order Government." In Dirkse *et al*., eds., ***Development and Social Welfare; Indonesia's Experiences under the New Order***, pp. 17-36. Leiden: KITLV Press, 1993.

Christie, Anthony. "Natural Symbols in Java." In G. B. Milner, ed., ***Natural Symbols in Southeast Asia***. London: School of Oriental and African Studies, 1978.

Cician, Francesca. ***What are Norms?, A Study of Beliefs and Action in a Maya Community***. Cambridge: Cambridge University Press, 1975.

Cohen, J. M. and N. T. Uphoff. ***Rural Development Participation: Concepts for Measuring Participation for Project Design, Implementation and Evaluation***. Working Paper, Rural Development Committee. Ithaca: Cornell University, 1976

Collier, William L. "Agricultural Evolution in Java". In Gary. E. Hansen, ed., ***Agricultural and Rural Development in Indonesia***, pp. 147-173. Boulder: Westview Press, 1981(b).

Cooley, F. L. ***Indonesia: Church and Society***. New York: Friendship Press, 1968.

-----, ed. ***Benih yang Tumbuh 3: Gereja Kristen Jawa Tengah Utara***. Jakarta: LPS (the Research Department) of the Indonesian Council of Churches, 1975.

Cribb, R., ed. ***The Indonesian Killings of 1965-1966; Studies from Java and Bali***. Clayton: Centre for Southeast Asian Studies, Monash University, 1990.

Crouch, Harold. ***The Army and Politics in Indonesia***. Ithaca: Cornell University Press, 1978.

-----"The Trend to Authoritarianism: The Post-1945 Period." In Harry Aveling, ed., ***The Development of Indonesian Society***, pp. 166-204. Quensland: The University of Queensland Press, 1979.

Darmaputera, Eka. ***Pancasila and the Search for Identity and Modernity in Indonesian Society***. Leiden: E. J. Brill, 1988.

Darmowigoto, Susilo. ***Pemashuran Injil Kerajaan Allah di Wilayah Sinode GKJ***. Salatiga: GKJ, 1969.

Day, Clive. ***The Policy and Administration of the Dutch in Java***. Kuala Lumpur: Oxford University Press, 1972.

De Jonge, Huub. "Perkembangan Ekonomi dan Islamisasi di Madura." In Huub de Jonge, ed. ***Agama, Kebudayaan dan Ekonomi***, pp. 83-110. Jakarta: Rajawali Press, 1989.

De Jonge, J. K. J. and M. L. van Deventer, eds. ***De Opkomst van het Nederlandsch Gezag in Oost-Indie Verzameling van onuitgegeven Stukken uit het Oud-Koloniaal Archief.*** 16 vols. 's-Gravenhage: Martinus Nijhoff, 1862-1909.

Development Alternatives Inc. ***Strategies for Small Farmer Development: An Empirical Study of Rural Development Projects.*** Boulder: Westview Press, 1975.

Dewey, Alice G. ***Peasant Marketing in Java.*** New York: The Free Press of Glencoe, Inc., 1962.

Dhofier, Zamakhsyari. "Islamic Education and Traditional Ideology on Java." In James J. Fox, ed., ***Indonesia: The Making of a Culture***, pp. 263-272. Canberra: Research School of Pacific Studies, The Australian National University, 1980.

-----***Tradisi Pesantren: Studi tentang Pandangan Hidup Kyai.*** Jakarta: LP3S, 1982.

Dirdjosanjoto, Pradjarta. ***Memelihara Umat: Kyai di antara Usaha Pembangunan dan Mempertahankan Identitas Lokal di Daerah Muria.*** Ph. D. Thesis, Vrije Universiteit, 1994.

Dirdjosanjoto, Pradjarta., *et al.* "Socio-Economic Aspects of the Population around the Rawa Pening Lake, Pilot Study in the Village of Candirejo." In Friedhelm Goeltenboth, ed., ***Rawa Pening Profect Report*** Vol. 1, No. 2, pp. 102-250. Salatiga: Satya Wacana University, 1978.

Dirkse, Jan-Paul, Frans Husken and Mario Rutten, eds. ***Development and Social Welfare; Indonesia's Experiences under the New Order.*** Leiden: KITLV Press, 1993.

Djojohadikusumo, Sumitro. ***Trilogi Pembangunan dan Ekonomi Pancasila.*** Jakarta: Induk Koperasi Pegawai Negeri R. I., 1986.

Dohrenwend, B. S. ***Some Factors Related to Autonomy and Dependence in Twelve Javanese Villages.*** Ithaca: Cornell University Press, 1957.

Dove, Michael R., ed. ***The Real and Imagined Role of Culture in Development; Case Studies from Indonesia.*** Honolulu: University of Hawaii Press, 1988.

Douglas, J., ed. ***Understanding Everyday Life.*** Chicago: Aldine, 1970

Durkheim, Emile. ***The Elementary Forms of the Religious Life.*** Translated by Joseph Ward Swain. New York: The Free Press, 1965.

Eisenstadt, S. N., ed. ***The Protestant Ethic and Modernization: A Comparative View.*** New York: Basic Books, 1968.

Elson, R. E. ***The Cultivation System and 'Agricultural Involution'.*** Melbourne: Monash University, Centre of Southeast Asian Studies, 1978.

-----***Sugar and Peasants; The Social Impact of the Western Sugar Industry on the Peasantry of the Pasuruan Area, East Java, from the Cultivation System to the Great Depression.*** Ph. D. Thesis, Monash University, 1980.

Evers, Hans Dieter, ed. ***Modernization in South-East Asia.*** Singapore: Oxford University Press, 1973.

Fagg, Donald R. "Authority and Social Structure: A Study of Javanese Bereaucracy." Unpublished Doctoral Thesis (Harvard University), 1958.

Falcon, W. P., W. O. Jones, and S. R. Pearson., eds. ***The Cassava Economy of Java.*** Stanford: Stanford University Press, 1984.

Fasseur, C. ***Kultuurstelsel en Koloniale Baten; De Nederlandse Exploitatie van Java 1840-1860.*** Leiden: Universitarie Pers, 1974.

Feith, Herbert. ***The Decline of Constitutional Democracy in Indonesia.*** Ithaca: Cornell University Press, 1962.

Fernandez, W., ed. ***People's Participation in Development.*** New Delhi: The Institute of Social Studies, 1981.

Fernandez, W. and R. Tandon ***Participatory Research and Evaluation***. New Delhi: Indian Social Institute, 1986.

Fernando, M. R. ***Peasants and Plantation Economy; The Social Impact of the European Plantation Economy in Cirebon Residency from the Cultivation System to the End of the First Decade of the Twentieth Century***. Ph. D. Thesis, Monash University, 1982.

Fox, James J., ed. ***Indonesia: The Making of a Culture***. Canberra: Research School of Pacific Studies, 1980.

Furnivall, J. S. ***Netherlands India: A Study of Plural Economy***. Cambridge: Cambridge University Press, 1939.

Galjart, B. F. ***Peasant Mobilization and Solidarity***. Assen: Van Gorcum, 1976.

Geertz, Clifford. "The Javanese Village." In G. William Skinner, ed., ***Local, Ethnic and National Loyalties in Village Indonesia***, pp. 34-41. Cultural Report Series No. 8. New Haven: Yale University Southeast Asia Studies, 1959.

-----***The Religion of Java***. Chicago: The University of Chicago Press, 1960.

-----***Agricultural Involution: The Process of Ecological Change in Indonesia***. Berkeley and Los Angeles: University of California Press, 1963(a).

-----***Peddlers and Princes: Social Development and Economic Change in Two Indonesian Towns***. Chicago: University of Chicago Press, 1963(b).

-----***The Social History of an Indonesian Town***. Cambridge, Mass.: MIT Press, 1965(a).

-----"Modernization in a Muslim Society: The Indonesian Case." In Robert N. Bellah, ed., ***Religion and Progress in Modern Asia***, pp. 93-108. New York: The Free Press, 1965(b).

-----"Religion as a Cultural System." In M. Banton, ed., ***Anthropological Approaches to the Study of Religion***, pp. 1-46. New York: I. A. Praeger, 1966.

-----***Islam Observed, Religious Development in Morocco and Indonesia***. New Haven: Yale University Press, 1968.

-----***The Interpretation of Cultures***. New York: Basic Books, 1973.

Geertz, Hillary. ***The Javanese Family: A Study of Kinship and Socialization***. Glencoe, The Free Press, 1961.

Gellner, E. ***Muslim Society***. Cambridge: Cambridge University Press, 1981.

Ghai, D. ***Participation in Development: Some Perspectives from Grass-roots Experiences***. Geneva: UNRISD, 1988.

Gibbs. A. "Agricultural Modernization, Non-Farm Employment and Low-Level Urbanization: A Case Study of a Central Luzon Sub-Region." Ph. D. Thesis, University of Michigan, 1974.

Godoy, Ricardo and Christopher Bennett. ***Diversification among Coffee Smallholders in the Highlands of South Sumatra, Indonesia***. Working Paper. Cambridge, Mass.: Harvard Institute for International Development, 1987.

Goeltenboth, Friedhelm. "The Rawa Pening Lake; Background Information, Facts and Problems." In F. Goeltenboth, ed., ***Proceedings of the First Seminar in Aquatic Biology and Aquatic Management of the Rawa Pening Lake***. Salatiga: The Rawa Pening Project, Satya Wacana University, 1978.

Griffin, K. ***The Political Economy of Agrarian Change***. London: Macmillan, 1974.

Goffman, Erving. ***Interaction Ritual***. Chicago: Aldine, 1967.

Guinness, Patrick. ***Harmony and Hierarchy in a Javanese Kampung***. Singapore: Oxford University Press, 1986.

Hadiwijono, Harun. ***Man in the Present Javanese Mysticism***. Baarn: Bosch & Keuning NV, 1967.

Hainsworth, Geoffrey B., ed. ***Village-Level Modernization in Southeast Asia***. Vancouver: The University of British Columbia, 1982.

Handboek voor Cultuur en Handelsonderneming in Nederlandsch-Indie. Amsterdam: J. H. Bussy, 1888.

Hansen, Gary E. ***The Politics and Administration of Rural Development in Indonesia***. Berkeley and Los Angeles: University of California Press, 1973.

-----, ed. ***Agricultural and Rural Development in Indonesia*** Boulder: Westview Press, 1981.

Hardjono, Joan. "Rural Development in Indonesia: the 'Top-Down' Approach." In David A. M. Lea and D. P. Chaudhri, eds., ***Rural Development and the State***, pp. 38-65. London and New York: Methuen, 1983.

Hart, Gillian. ***Power, Labor, and Livelihood: Processes of Change in Rural Java***. Berkeley: University of California Press, 1986.

Hart, G.; A. Turton; B. White, eds. ***Agrarian Transformations: Local Processes and the State in South East Asia***. Berkeley: University of California Press, 1989.

Hatley, Ron., ed. ***Other Java Away from Kraton***. Clayton, Australia: Monash University Press, 1984.

Hayami, Yujiro and Masao Kikuchi. ***Asian Village Economy at the Cross-Roads: An Economic Approach to Institutional Change***. Baltimore: Johns Hopkins University Press, 1982.

Hazell, P. B. and A. Roell. "Rural Growth Linkage: Household Expenditure Patterns in Malaysia and Nigeria." IFPRI Research Report No. 41. Washington DC: International Food Policy Research Institute, 1983.

Hazell, P. B. and C. Ramasamy. ***Green Revolution Reconsidered: The Impact of High Yielding Rice Varieties in South India***. Baltimore and London: Johns Hopkins University Press, 1991.

Hefner, Robert. ***Hindu Javanese: Tengger Tradition and Islam***. Princeton: Princeton University Press, 1985.

----- ***The Political Economy of Mountain Java***. Berkeley: University of California Press, 1990.

Henket, N. H. ***De Aanleg van Spoorwegen op Midden-Java***. Amsterdam: J. C. Schlomann, 1886.

Heytens, P. "Technical Change in Wetland Rice Agriculture." In S. Pearson *et al.*, eds., ***Rice Policy in Indonesia***. Ithaca: Cornell University Press, 1991.

Hofsteede, W. M. F. ***Decision-Making Process in Four West Javanese Villages***. Nijmegen: Katholieke Universiteit Nijmegen, 1971.

Hopkins, N. S. "Participatory Decision Making and Modern Cooperatives in Mali." In J. Nash, J. Dandler and N. S. Hopkins, eds., ***Popular Participation in Social Change***. Paris: Mouton, 1976.

Horikoshi, Hiroko. ***Kyai dan Perubahan Sosial***. Jakarta: P3M, 1987.

Hugo, Graeme. ***Polulation Mobility in West Java***. Yogyakarta: Gajah Mada University Press, 1978.

Huisman, Henk. ***Planning for Rural Development: Experiences and Alternatives, Cases from Indonesia and Lesotho***. Ph. D. Thesis, Universiteit Utrecht, 1994.

Huizer, G. ***Boerenverzet in Latijns-Amerika***. Nijmegen: SUN, 1976.

----- ***Guiding Principles for People's Participation Projects***, Rome: FAO

Hunter, G. ***Modernizing Peasant Societies: A Comparative Study in Asia and Africa***. London and New York: Oxford University Press, 1969.

-----"Research on Cooperatives in East Africa: Review/Note." Mimeographed. London: Overseas Development Institute, 1971.

Husken, Frans and Benjamin White. "Java: Social Differentiation, Food Production, and Agrarian Control." In Hart, Gillian, Andrew Turton and Benjamin White, eds., ***Agrarian Transformation: Local Processes and the State in Southeast Asia***, pp. 235-265. Berkeley and Los Angeles: University of California Press, 1989.

Ibrahim A., S. Siddique, and Y. Hussain, eds. ***Reading on Islam in Southeast Asia.*** Singapore: Institute of Southeast Asian Studies, 1985.

Inayatullah. ***Cooperatives and Planned Change in Asia***. Geneva: UNRISD, 1970.

Jatileksono, Tumari. "Varietal Improvements, Productivity Change, and Income Distribution: The Case of Lampung, Indonesia." In Cristina C. David and Keijiro Otsuka, eds., ***Modern Rice Technology and Income Distribution in Asia***, pp. 129-171. Boulder and London: Lynne Rienner Publishers, 1994.

Jay, Robert R. ***Religion and Politics in Rural Central Java.*** New Haven: Yale University Press, 1963.

-----***Javanese Villagers: Social Relations in Rural Modjokuto***. Cambridge, Mass.: MIT Press, 1969.

Johnston, Bruce F. and William C. Clark. ***Redesigning Rural Development, A Strategic Perspective.*** Baltimore and London: The Johns Hopkins University Press, 1982.

Jratunseluna and NEDECO. "Report of Prefeasibility of Rawa Pening." Internal Report, 1972.

-----"A Proposal for Cleaning the Lake of the Floating Aquatic Weeds Including Recommendations for Maintenance and Scientific Research." Internal Report, 1974.

Kahin, George McT. ***Nationalism and Revolution in Indonesia***. Ithaca: Cornell University Press, 1952.

Kahn, Joel. "Ideology and Social Structure in Indonesia." In Benedict Anderson and Audrey Kahin, eds., ***Interpreting Indonesian Politics: Thirteen Contributions to the Debate***, pp. 92-103. Ithaca: Cornell University Press, 1982.

Kalo, H. Thamrin, Makali and Gunawan Wiradi. ***Perkembangan Koperasi di Pedesaan Jawa.*** Rural Dynamics Series No. 15. Bogor: Center for Agro Economic Research, 1980.

Kartodirdjo, Sartono. "Agrarian Radicalism in Java: Its Setting and Development." In Claire Holt, ed., ***Culture and Politics in Indonesia***, pp. 75-125. Ithaca: Cornell University Press, 1972.

-----***Protest Movements in Rural Java: A Study of Agrarian Unrest in the Nineteenth and Early Twentieth Centuries***. Singapore: Oxford University Press, 1973.

Kartodirdjo, S., A. Sudewo, and S. Hatmosaprobo. ***Perkembangan Peradaban Priyayi.*** Yogyakarta: Gajah Mada University Press, 1987.

Kartohadikoesoemo, Soetardjo. ***Desa***. Bandung: Sumur Bandung, 1965.

Kasryno, Faisal. "Structural Changes in Rural Employment and Agricultural Wage in Indonesia." In Yang Boo Choe and Fu Chen Lo, eds., ***Rural Industrialization and Non-Farm Activities of Asian Farmers***, pp. 183-208. Seoul: Korean Rural Economic Institute/ Asian and Pacific Development Centre, 1986.

-----"Labor absorption in Rural Indonesia." In F. Kasryno *et al.*, eds., ***Toward a Balanced Structure of Rural Economic Development***. Bogor: Center for Agro Economic Research, 1988.

Keeler, Ward. ***Javanese Shaddow Plays, Javanese Selves.*** Princeton: Princeton University Press, 1987.

Kleyn, R. H. ***Het Gewestelijk Bestuur op Java.*** Ph. D. Thesis, P. Sommerwill, Leiden, 1889.

Kluckhohn, Clyde. "Values and Value Orientations in the Theory of Action: An Exploration in Definition and Classification." In T. Parsons and E. Shils, eds., ***Toward a General Theory of Action***, pp. 388-433. Cambridge, Mass.: Harvard University Press, 1951.

Kluckhohn, Florence R. and Fred Strodtbeck. ***Variations in Value Orientations***. New York: Row, Paterson, 1961.

Kodiran. "Kebudayaan Jawa." In Koentjaraningrat, ed., ***Manusia dan Kebudajaan di Indonesia***, pp. 327-350. Jakarta: Penerbit Djambatan, 1971.

Koentjaraningrat. ***Some Social-Anthropological Observations on Gotong Royong Practices in Two Villages of Central Java***. Ithaca: Cornell University Press, 1961.

-----"Changing Cultural Value Orientation of Javanese Peasants." In Geoffrey B. Hainsworth, ed., ***Village-Level Modernization in South-East Asia***, pp. 43-52. Vancouver and London: The University of British Columbia, 1982.

-----***Kebudayaan Jawa***. Jakarta: Balai Pustaka, 1984.

-----, ed. ***Villages in Indonesia***. Ithaca: Cornell University Press, 1967.

-----"Aneka Warna Manusia dan Kebudayaan Indonesia dalam Pembangunan." In Koentjaraningrat, ed., ***Manusia dan Kebudayaan di Indonesia***, pp. 371-391. Jakarta: Penerbit Djambatan, 1971.

-----***Kebudayaan, Mentalitas dan Pembangunan***. Jakarta: Gramedia, 16th. ed. 1993.

"Kota Madya Salatiga, Suatu Laporan Survey Tentang Keadaan Sosial Ekonomi dan Pembangunan Daerah." Report. Salatiga: Satya Wacana University, 1975.

Kumar, Ann. "Developments in Four Societies over the Sixteenth to Eighteenth Centuries." In Harry Aveling, ed., ***The Development of Indonesian Society***, pp. 1-44. Quensland: Queensland University Press, 1979.

Kusnaedi. ***Membangun Desa; Pedoman untuk Penggerak Program IDT, Mahasiswa KKN, Kader Pembangunan Desa***. Jakarta: Penebar Swadaya, 1995.

Laceulle, F. A. E. ***Eindverslag over het Desa Autonomie Onderzoek op Java en Madura***, 1929.

Landau, Y. H., *et al.*, eds. ***Rural Communities, Intercooperation and Development***. New York: Praeger, 1976.

Lay, Cornelis. ***Ketimpangan dan Keterbelakangan di Indonesia***. Monograph No. 5/1993. Yogyakarta: Gajah Mada University, 1993.

Leys, C. "Political Perspectives." In D. Seers and L. Joy, eds., ***Development in a Divided World***. Middlesex: Penguin Books, 1971.

Liem, Thian Joe. ***Riwajat Semarang; Dari Djamannja Sam Poo Sampe Terhapoesnja Kongkoan***. Semarang-Batavia: Boekhandel Ho Kim Yoe, 1931.

LPU-UKSW "Proyek Rawa Pening II." Report. Salatiga: Satya Wacana University, 1977.

Long, Norman. ***An Introduction to the Sociology of Rural Development***. Boulder: Westview Press, 1977.

Lovely, d'Eden. ***Itoe Bidadari dari Rawa Pening***. Semarang: Boelan Poernama, 1929.

Lyon, M. L. "The Hindu Revival in Java: Politics and Religious Identity." In James J. Fox, ed., ***Indonesia: The Making of a Culture***, pp. 205-220. Canberra: Research School of Pacific Studies, The Australian National University, 1980.

MacAndrew, Colin., *et al.* "Regional Development Planning and Implementation in Indonesia: The Evolution of a National Policy." In R. P. Misra, ed., ***Regional Development, Essays in Honour of Masahiko Honjo***. Singapore: Maruzen, 1982.

MacDonald, D. B. ***Development of Muslim Theory, Jurisprudence and Constitutional Theory***. New York: Charles Scribner's Sons, 1909.

Mackie, J. A. C. "The Golkar Victory and Party-Aliran Alignments." In Oey Hong Lee, ed., ***Indonesia after the 1971 Elections***, pp. 60-75. London: Oxford University Press, 1974.

Mandoyokusumo, K. P. H. ***Serat Raja Putra Ngayogyakarta Hadiningrat***. Yogyakarta: Bebadan Museum Karaton Ngayogyakarta Hadiningrat, 1988.

Manning, Chris. ***The Green Revolution, Employment, and Economic Change in Rural Java: A Reassessment of Trends under the New Order***. Singapore: Institute of Southeast Asian Studies, 1988.

Marcus, George and Michael Fischer. ***Anthropology as Cultural Critique: An Experimental Moment in the Human Sciences***. Chicago: University of Chicago Press, 1986.

Marsono. ***Peranan Pamong Pradja dalam Administrasi Pemerintahan Daerah di Indonesia***. Jakarta: U. P. Pradja, 1968.

Maskun, Sumitro. ***Pembangunan Masyarakat Desa: Asas, Kebijaksanaan, dan Manajemen***. Yogyakarta: Media Widya Mandala, 1993

Maurer, Jean-Luc. "Some Consequences of Land Shortage in Four Kelurahan of the Kabupaten Bantul." Mimeograph. Yogyakarta, 1973.

May, Brian. ***The Indonesian Tragedy***. London: Routledge and Kegan Paul, 1978.

McVey, Ruth. "Nationalism, Islam and Marxism: The Management of Ideological Conflict in Indonesia." Introduction to Sukarno, ***Nationalism, Islam and Marxism***. Ithaca: Cornell University Press, 1970.

Mears, Leon A. and Sidik Moeljono. "Food Policy." In Anne Booth and Peter McCawley, eds., ***The Indonesian Economy during the Soeharto Era***, pp. 23-61. Kuala Lumpur: Oxford University Press, 1981.

Meesook, Oey. "Comments on Professor Sayogyo's Calculations of the Extent of Poverty in Rural Java, 1970 to 1976." Mimeographed. Washington: World Bank, 1978.

Moertopo, Ali. ***Some Basic Thoughts on the Acceleration and Modernization of 25 Years' Development***. Jakarta: Centre for Strategic and International Studies, 1973.

Morris, Brian. ***Anthropological Studies of Religion, An Introduction Text***. Cambridge: Cambridge University Press, 1990.

Mortimer, Rex. "Indonesia: Growth or Development?" In R. Mortimer, ed., ***Showcase State: The Illusion of Indonesia's 'Accelerated Modernisation'***, pp. 51-66. Sydney: Angus and Robertson, 1973

-----***Indonesian Communism under Soekarno: Ideology and Politics, 1959-1965***. Ithaca: Cornell University Press, 1974.

Mubyarto. "The Fixation of Agricultural Policy in Indonesia: An Historical Perspective." In N. Hainsworth, ed., ***Village-Level Modernization in Southeast Asia: The Political Economy of Rice and Water***, pp. 27-41. Vancouver and London: University of British Columbia Press, 1982.

-----"Strategi Pembangunan Pedesaan." In Mubyarto and Sartono Kartodirdjo. ***Pembangunan Pedesaan di Indonesia***, pp. 3-83. Yogyakarta: Gajah Mada University Press, 1988.

Mubyarto and Loekman Soetrisno. "Rural Development in Indonesia, Past Experience and Future Policies." In R. P. Misra, ed., ***Rural Development, Capitalist and Socialist Paths***, pp. 3-262. New Delhi: Naurang Rai Concept Publishing Company, 1985.

-----***Integrated Rural Development:Indonesia***. Dhaka, Bangladesh: Centre on Integrated Rural Development for Asia and the Pacific (CIRDAP), 1989.

Mulder, J. A. Niels. "Mysticism and Daily Life in Contemporary Java." Ph. D. Thesis, Universiteit van Amsterdam, 1975.

-----***Kepribadian Jawa dan Pembangunan Nasional***. Yogyakarta: Gajah Mada University Press, 6th. ed. 1986.

-----***Individual and Society in Java, A Cultural Analysis***. Yogyakarta: Gajah Mada University Press, 2nd. ed. 1992.

Mulder, M. "Moeilijkheden van de Minder Machtigen bij het Leren van Participatie." In P. J. D. Drenth, ed., ***Arbeids-en Organisatie-Psychologie***. Deventer, 1973

Myrdal, Gunnar. ***Asian Drama: An Inquiry into the Poverty of Nations***. New York: Pantheon, 1968

Nakamura, Matsuo. ***The Crescent Arises over the Banyan Tree: A Study of the Muhammadijah Movement in a Central Javanese Town***. Ph. D Thesis, Cornell University, 1976.

Nagazumi, Akira. ***The Dawn of Indonesian Nationalism: The Early Years of the Budi Utomo, 1908-1918***. Tokyo: Institute of Developing Economies, 1972.

Naylor, R. "The Rural Labor Market in Indonesia." In S. Pearson *et al.*, eds., ***Rice Policy in Indonesia***. Ithaca: Cornell University Press, 1991.

Ndraha, Taliziduhu. "Beberapa Catatan tentang Kemungkinan Pembinaan Struktur Organisasi Pemerintahan Desa." Mimeograph. Malang: Biro Research dan Publikasi IIP, No. 63, 1973.

Nicholson, R. A. ***Studies in Islamic Mysticism***. Cambridge: Cambridge University Press, 1921.

Noer, Deliar. ***The Modernist Muslim Movement in Indonesia, 1900-1942***. Singapore: Oxford University Press, 1973.

Nuningsih, Retno and Budi Sukardjo. "Socio-Economic Aspects of the Village Communities Surrounding the Rawa Pening Lake." In F. Goeltenboth, ed., ***Proceedings of the Second Seminar in Aquatic Biology and Aquatic Management of the Rawa Pening Lake***, pp. 366-405. Salatiga: The Rawa Pening Project, Satya Wacana University, 1979.

Oakley, Peter. ***The Monitoring and Evaluation of Participation in Rural Development***. Rome: FAO, 1988.

Oakley, Peter and D. Marsden. ***Approaches to Participation in Rural Development***. Geneva: International Labour Office, 1984.

Oakley, Peter., *et al.* ***Projects with People: The Practice of Participation in Rural Development***. Geneva: International Labour Office, 1991.

Ong Hok Ham. ***The Residency of Madiun; Priyayi and Peasant in the Nineteenth Century***. Ph. D. Thesis, Yale University, 1975.

Palmer, Ingrid. "Rural Poverty in Indonesia, with Special Reference to Java." In ***Poverty and Landlessness in Rural Asia***. Geneva: International Labour Organization, 1977.

Palte, Jan G. L. ***The Development of Java's Rural Uplands in Response to Population Growth: An Introductory Essay in Historical Perspective***. Yogyakarta: Gajah Mada University Press, 1984.

Parsons, Talcott. ***Structure of Social Action***. New York: McGraw-Hill, 1937.

-----***The Social System***. Glencoe: Free Press, 1951

Parsons, Talcott and Edward A Shils, eds. ***Toward a General Theory of Action***. Cambridge, Mass.: Harvard University Press, 1951

Paul, Samuel. ***Community Participation in Development Projects***. Discussion Paper No. 6. Washington DC: World Bank, 1987.

Payer, Cheryl. ***The Debt Trap. The IMF and The Third World***. Harmondsworth: Penguin, 1974.

Peacock, James L. ***Muslim Puritans: Reformist Psychology in Southeast Asian Islam***. Berkeley, Los Angeles: The University of California Press, 1978(a).

-----***Purifying the Faith: The Muhammadiyah Movement in Indonesian Islam***. Menlo Park, California: The Benjamin/Cummings Publishing Co., 1978(b).

Pearse, Andrew. ***Seeds of Plenty, Seeds of Hope***. Oxford: Clarendon Press, 1980.

Pearse, Andrew and M. Stiefel. ***Inquiry into Participation: A Research Approach***. Geneva: UNRISD, 1979.

Penny, David and Masri Singarimbun. ***Population and Poverty in Rural Java: Some Economic Arithmetic from Srihardjo***. Ithaca: Cornell University Press, 1973.

Pigeaud, Th. G. Th. ***Javaansche Volksvertoningen. Bijdrage tot de Beschrijving van Land en Volk***. Batavia: Volkslectuur, 1938.

Polak, B. "Construction and Origin of Floating Islands in the Rawa Pening." Bogor: Contr. Gen. Agricultural Statistic, No. 121, 1951.

Prabowo, Dibyo and Sajogyo. "Sidoarjo, East Java, and Subang, West Java." In Gary E. Hansen, ed., ***Agricultural and Rural Development in Indonesia***, pp. 68-78. Boulder: Westview Press, 1981.

Prijono, Yumiko Mizuno and Prijono Tjiptoherijanto. ***Demokrasi di Pedesaan Jawa***. Jakarta: Penerbit Sinar Harapan, 1983.

Purnomo, H. and Sastrosupono, eds. ***Gereja-Gereja Kristen Jawa; Benih yang Tumbuh dan Berkembang di Tanah Jawa***. Yogyakarta: Taman Pustaka Kristen, 1986.

Raffles, Thomas Stamford. ***The History of Java***, 2 vols. London, 1817

Rahman, Md. A. ***Some Dimensions of People's Participation in the Bhoomi Sena Movement***. Geneva: UNRISD, 1981

-----***Grass-roots Participation and Self-Reliance***. New Delhi: Oxford and IBH Publishing Co., 1984.

-----"Participation of the Rural Poor in Development." Mimeographed. Geneva: ILO, 1985.

Ricklefs, M. C. ***Jogjakarta Under Sultan Mangkubumi 1749-1792: A History of The Division of Java***. London: Oxford University Press, 1974.

-----"Six Centuries of Islamization in Java." In N. Levtzion, ed., ***Conversion to Islam***, pp. 100-128. New York: Holmes and Meier, 1979.

-----***A History of Modern Indonesia***. London and Basingstoke: The Macmillan Press, 1981.

Rosenthal, F. ***Ibn Khaldun, The Muqaddimah, An Introduction to History***. Princeton: Princeton University Press, 1980.

Rouffaer, G. P. "Vorstenlanden." In ***Adatrechtbundels,*** Vol. 34, 1931: 233-378.

Rullman J. A. C. ***De Gereformeerde Zending in Midden Java***. Baarn: Uit Zendingcentrum, 1970.

Ruthenberg, Hans. ***Farming Systems in the Tropics***. 3d ed. Oxford: Clarendon Press, 1980.

Sairin, Sjafri. ***Javanese Trah, Kin-Based Social Organization***. Yogyakarta: Gajah Mada University Press, 1992.

Sajogyo. ***Modernization without Development in Rural Java***. Bogor: Research Centre for Rural Sociology, 1972.

Salam, Solichin. ***Sejarah Partai Muslimin Indonesia***. Jakarta: Lembaga Penjelidikan Islam, 1970.

Saptari, Ratna. The Differentiation of a Rural Industrial Labour Force: Gender Segregation in East Java's Kretek Cigarette Industry, 1920-1990." In Alexander,

P., P. Boomgaard, and B. White, eds., ***In the Shadow of Agriculture***, pp. 127-150. Amsterdam: Royal Tropical Institute, 1991.

Schrieke, B. O. J. ***Ruler and Realm in Early Java***. Vol. 2 of ***Indonesian Sociological Studies: Selected Writings of B. Schrieke***. 2 vols. The Hague: Van Hoeve, 1957.

Schrieke, J. J. ***De Lagere Inlandsche Rechtsgemeenschappen in Indonesie***, 1921.

Schulte Nordholt, N. G. "From LSD to LKMD: Participation at the Village Level", in Philip Quarles van Ufford, ed., ***Local Leadership and Programme Implementation in Indonesia***, pp. 31-53. Amsterdam: Free University Press, 1987(a).

-----***Ojo Dumeh, Kepemimpinan Lokal dalam Pembangunan***. Jakarta: Pustaka Sinar Harapan, 1987(b).

Schumacher, E. F. "Pandangan Ekonomi Budha." In LP3ES, ***Agama dan Tantangan Zaman***, pp. 80-90. Jakarta: LP3ES, 1985.

Schwarz, Adam, ***A Nation in Waiting: Indonesia in the 1990s.*** Sydney: Allen & Unwin, 1994.

Scott, James C. ***The Moral Economy of The Peasant***. New haven: Yale University Press, 1976.

Selosoemardjan. ***Social Changes in Jogjakarta***. Ithaca: Cornell University Press, 1962.

Selosoemardjan and Kennon Breazeale. ***Cultural Change in Rural Indonesia: Impact of Village Development***. Surakarta: Sebelas Maret University Press, 1993.

Shari, Ishak and Jomo Kwame Sundaram. "Malaysia's Green Revolution in Rice Farming: Capital Accumulation and Technological Change in a Peasant Society." In G. B. Hainsworth, ed., ***Village-Level Modernization in Southeast Asia***, pp. 225-254. Vancouver and London: University of British Columbia Press, 1982.

Shrimpton, R. ***Community Participation in Food and Nutrition Programs: An Analysis of Recent Government Experiences***. Ithaca: Cornell University Press, 1989

Sider, Ronald, ed. ***Evangelicals and Development: Towards a Theology of Social Change***. Exeter: The Paternoster Press, 1981.

Simanjuntak, P. J. "Government Programmes Aimed at Improving Rural Development." In J. B. Kristiadi *et al.*, ***Report of a Workshop in Indonesia on Employment Creation Strategy for Rural Development***, pp. 55-73. Jakarta: Goethe Institut, 1987.

Singarimbun, Masri. "Perubahan-Perubahan Sosial-Ekonomi di Miri Sriharjo (1989)." In David H. Penny, ed., ***Kemiskinan: Peranan Sistem Pasar***, pp. 169-179. Jakarta: University of Indonesia Press, 1990.

Singer, Milton. "Max Weber and the Modernization of India." In Andreas E. Buss, ed., ***Max Weber in Asian Studies***, pp. 28-45. Leiden: E. J. Brill, 1985.

Sjahrir. ***Basic Needs in Indonesia; Economics, Politics and Public Policy***. Singapore: Institute of Southeast Asian Studies, 1986.

Skinner, G. William, ed. ***Local, Ethnic and National Loyalties in Village Indonesia***. New Haven: Yale University Southeast Asia Studies, 1959.

Slamet, Ina E. ***Pokok-Pokok Pembangunan Masyarakat Desa***. Jakarta: Bhratara, 1965.

-----***Cultural Strategies for Survival: The Plight of the Javanese***. Rotterdam: The Comparative Asian Studies Programme, 1982.

Slamet, Y. ***Pembangunan Masyarakat Berwawasan Partisipasi***. Surakarta: Sebelas Maret University Press, 1993.

Smith, J. and Y. Haddad. ***The Islamic Understanding of Death and Resurrection***. Albany: State University of New York Press, 1981.

Smith, M. ***Studies in Early Mysticism in the Near and Middle East***. London: Routledge & Kegan Paul Ltd., 1931.

Smyth, Ines. "A Critical Look at the Indonesian Government's Policies for Women." In Dirkse *et al*., eds., ***Development and Social Welfare; Indonesia's Experiences under the New Order***, pp. 117-129. Leiden: KITLV Press, 1993.

Soedjatmoko. "Cultural Motivation to Progress: The 'Exterior' and The 'Interior' Views." In Robert N. Bellah, ed., ***Religion and Progress in Modern Asia***, pp. 1-14. New York: The Free Press, 1965.

----- "Iman, Amal dan Pembangunan." In LP3ES, ***Agama dan Tantangan Zaman***, pp. 3-12. Jakarta: LP3ES, 1985.

Soemarsaid, Moertono. ***State and State-Craft in Old Java: A Study of the Later Mataram Period, 16th to 19th Century***. Ithaca: Cornell University Press, 1968.

Soentoro., *et al.* ***Land Tenure and Labor Markets in East Java, Indonesia***. Bogor: Agro Economic Survey, 1981.

Soewardi, H. ***Respons Masyarakat Desa terhadap Modernisasi Produksi Pertanian Terutama Padi***. Yogyakarta: Gajah Mada University Press, 1976.

Stapel, F. W. ***Geschiedenis van Nederlandsch-Indie***. Nederlandsche Historische Bibliotheek 16. Amsterdam: Menlenhoff, 1930.

Steeman, Theodore M. "Religious Pluralism and National Integration." Ph. D. Thesis, Harvard University, 1973.

Stinson, W. ***Creating Sustainable Community Health Projects: The PRICON Experience***. Maryland: Centre for Human Services, 1987.

Sudaryanto, Tahlim and Faisal Kasryno. "Modern Rice Variety Adoption and Factor-Market Adjustments in Indonesia." In Cristina C. David and Keijiro Otsuka, eds., ***Modern Rice Technology and Income Distribution in Asia***, pp. 107-127. Boulder and London: Lynne Rienner Publishers, 1994.

Sullivan, John. ***Local Government and Community in Java, An Urban Case-Study***. Singapore: Oxford University Press, 1992.

Suparlan. "Foreword." In C. Geertz, ***Abangan, Santri, Priyayi dalam Masyarakat Jawa***. Jakarta: Pustaka Jaya, 1981.

Suparmoko., *et al.* ***Penyerapan Tenaga Kerja pada Intensifikasi Penanaman Padi dan Pengolahan Padi di Jawa dan Bali***. Yogyakarta: Gajah Mada University, 1972.

Surianingrat, B. ***Wewenang, Tugas dan Kewajiban Camat***. Bandung, 1976.

Suryo, Djoko. "Social and Economic Life in Rural Semarang under Colonial Rule in the Later 19th. Century." Ph. D. Thesis, Monash University, 1982.

Sutherland, H. A. ***Pangreh Pradja; Java's Indigenous Administrative Corps and Its Role in the Last Decades of Dutch Colonial Rule***. Yale University Press, 1973.

-----***The Making of a Bureaucratic Elite, The Colonial Transformation of Javanese Priyayi***. Singapore: Singapore University Press , 1979.

Suwondo, Kutut. "Changes in the Means of Obtaining Income of the Inhabitants Around the Rawa Pening." In F. Goeltenboth, ed., ***Proceedings of the First Seminar in Aquatic Biology and Aquatic Management of the Rawa Pening Lake***, pp. 167-195. Salatiga: The Rawa Pening Project, Satya Wacana University, 1978.

Tichelman, F. ***The Social Evolution of Indonesia: The Asiatic Mode of Production and Its Legacy***. The Hague: Martinus Nijhoff, 1980.

Timmer, C. Peter. "The Formation of Indonesian Rice Policy: A Historical Perspective." In Gary E. Hansen, ed., ***Agricultural and Rural Development in Indonesia***, pp. 33-43. Boulder: Westview Press, 1981.

Tjondronegoro, Sediono M. P. "Elite and Masses: Trends in Recognition and Alienation." In H. Soebadio and C. A. due Marchie Sarvars, eds., ***Dynamics of Indonesian History***, pp. 377-395. Amsterdam: North-Holland, 1978.

-----***Social Organization and Planned Development in Rural Java***. Singapore: Institute of Southeast Asian Studies, 1984.

-----"Administrative and Institutional Problems." In Dirkse, Jan-Paul ***et al.***, eds., ***Development and Social Welfare; Indonesia's Experiences under the New Order***, pp. 159-183. Leiden: KITLV Press, 1993.

Tolman, Edward C. "A Psychological Model." In Talcott Parsons and Edward A. Shils, eds., ***Toward a General Theory of Action***, pp. 279-361. Cambridge, Mass.: Harvard University Press, 1951.

Triyono, Lambang and Nasikun. ***Proses Perubahan Sosial di Desa Jawa***. Monograph No. 3/1992. Yogyakarta: Gajah Mada University, 1992.

United Nations "Report of the Economic and Social Council," 58th. Session, Supplement no.3, New York, 1975.

UNRISD. ***Rural Cooperatives as Agents of Change: A Research Report on a Debate***. Geneva: UNRISD, 1975.

Uphoff, N. T.; J. M. Cohen, and A. A. Goldsmith. ***Feasibility and Application of Rural Development Participation: A State-of-the-Art Paper***. Rural Development Committee Monograph Series, No. 3. Ithaca: Cornell University, 1979.

Uphoff, Norman and Milton Esman. ***Local Organization for Rural Development; Analysis of Asian Experience***. Ithaca: Rural Development Committee, Cornell University, 1974.

Utrecht, Ernst. "The Military and the Elections." In Oey Hong Lee, ed., ***Indonesia after the 1971 Elections***, pp. 76-87. London: Oxford University Press, 1974.

Van Deventer, JSZ, S. ***Bijdragen tot de Kennis van het Landelijk Stelsel op Java***. 3 vols. Zalt-Bommel: Joh. Norman en Zoon, 1865-1866.

Van Niel, Robert. ***Java Under Cultivation System: Collected Writings***. Leiden: KITLV Press, 1992.

Van Ossenbruggen, F. D. E. "Java's Monca-pat: Origins of a Primitive Classification System." In P. E. de Josselin de Jong, ed., ***Structural Anthropology in the Netherlands, A Reader***, pp. 30-60. The Hague: Martinus Nijhoff, 1977.

Van Vollenhoven, C. ***De Indonesier en Zijn Grond***. Leiden: E. J. Brill, 1919.

-----***De Ontdekking van het Adatrecht***. Leiden: E. J. Brill, 1928.

Vogt, Evon Z., and Ethel Albert, eds. ***People of Rimrock***. Cambridge Mass.: Harvard University Press, 1966.

Vries, E. de. ***Landbouw en Welvaart in het Regentschap Pasoeroean; Bijdrage tot de Kennis van de Sociale Economie van Java***. Ph. D. Thesis, Landbouwhoogeschool Wageningen, 1931.

-----***Masalah-Masalah Petani Jawa*** (The Indonesian translation of de Vries' Inaugural speech entitled, "Problemen van de Javaanse Landbouwer", 13 June 1947). Jakarta: Bhratara, 1972.

Waal, E. ***Aantekeningen over Koloniale Onderwerpen***, Vols. 1-10. 's-Gravenhage: Martinus Nijhoff, 1865-1867.

Ward, Ken. ***The 1971 Election in Indonesia, An East Java Case Study.*** Monash Papers on Southeast Asia, No. 2, 1974.

Warsito, Rukmadi. "Pergulatan Hidup Kaum Nelayan di Tengah-Tengah Pemanfaatan Rawa Pening." In F. Goeltenboth, ed., ***Proceedings of the Second Seminar in Aquatic Biology and Aquatic Management of the Rawa Pening Lake***, pp. 234-283. Salatiga: The Rawa Pening Project, Satya Wacana University, 1979.

Weber, Max. ***The Protestant Ethic and the Spirit of Capitalism***. Translated by Talcott Parsons. London: Allen & Unwin, 1930.

-----***The Theory of Social and Economic Organization***. Translated by Talcott Parsons and A. M. Henderson. New York: Oxford University Press, 1947.

-----***From Max Weber: Essays in Sociology***. Translated and Edited by H. H. Gerth and C. Wright Mills. London: Routledge & Kegan Paul Ltd., 1948.

-----***The Sociology of Religion***. Translated by E. Fischer. Boston: Beacon Press, 1964.

-----***Economy and Society***. Edited by Guenther Roth and Claus Wittich. Berkeley: University of California Press, 1978.

Wertheim, W. F. "Islam Before and After the Elections." In Oey Hong Lee, ed., ***Indonesia after the 1971 Elections***, pp. 88-96. London: Oxford University Press, 1974.

White, Benjamin. "The Economic Importance of Children in a Javanese Village." In Moni Nag, ed., ***Population and Social Organization***, pp. 127-146. The Hague: Mouton, 1973.

Willner, Ann Ruth. "The Neotraditional Accommodation to Political Independence: The Case of Indonesia." In Lucian W. Pye, ed., ***Cases in Comparative Politics: Asia***, pp. 242-306. Boston: Little, Brown and Company, 1970.

Wiradi, Gunawan and Chris Manning. ***Landownership, Tenancy and Sources of Household Income; Community Pattern from a Partial Recensus of Eight Villages in Rural Java***. Bogor: Centre for Agro Economic Research, 1984.

Wolterbeek, J. D. ***Babad Zending ing Tanah Djawi***. Yogyakarta: Rebens, 1938.

Woodward, Mark R. ***Islam in Java: Normative Piety and Mysticism in the Sultanate of Yogyakarta***. Tucson: The University of Arizona Press, 1989.

World Bank. ***Indonesia; Policies for Growth and Employment***, Washington DC: IBRD, 1985.

-----***World Development Report: Poverty***. New York: Oxford University Press, 1990(a).

-----***Indonesia; Poverty Assessment and Strategy Report***. Washington DC: World Bank, 1990(b).

-----***Indonesia; Strategy for a Sustained Reduction in Poverty***. Washington DC: World Bank, 1990(c).

-----***World Development Report***. New York: Oxford University Press, 1995.

D. Legal and official sources

Bijblad No. 9308. "Regelen Omtrent de Vereniging en Splitsing van Desa's op Java en Madura met unitzondering van de Vorstenlanden." Gouvernementsbesluit No. 13, 28 October 1919.

Central Bureau of Statistics (BPS), Jakarta. ***Kemiskinan dan Pemerataan Pendapatan di Indonesia 1976-1990.*** (1992).

-----***Statistical Pocketbook of Indonesia 1992.***

-----***Statistical Year Book of Indonesia***, 1993(a).

-----***Welfare Indicators***, 1993(b).

-----"Laporan Kepada Bapak Presiden Mengenai Penetapan Desa Miskin 1993." Jakarta 5 August 1993(c).

-----"Hasil Perhitungan Jumlah dan Persentase Penduduk Miskin Tahun 1993." (1994a).

-----"Penduduk dan Desa Miskin Indonesia 1993." (1994b).

Direktorat Pembangunan Desa Propinsi Jawa Tengah. "Laporan Hasil Survey Mikro Kecamatan Tuntang, Kabupaten Dati II Semarang, Propinsi Dati I Jawa tengah, 1984-1985."

Dutch Colonial Government's Decrees on the Election of Village Head in Java: Staatsblad No. 13, 1819; Regeeringslement 1855, Chapter 71: 3; Staatsblad No. 47, 1878; Staatsblad No. 212, 1907.

Government's Acts on Village Administration: Perda (Regional Decree), Central Java No. 1, 1973; UU (Legislation) No. 5, 1974; UU No. 5, 1979.

Lopait Village. "Laporan Monografi Data Dinamis Desa Lopait." (Monthly Village-Level Statistical Reports), From June 1988 to April 1994.

Perumka (Perusahaan Umum Kereta Api). "Data-Data Lokomotif Tua." Museum Kereta Api Ambarawa, nd.

Perusda (Perusahaan Daerah) Perkebunan Tlogo Tuntang Salatiga, 1992.

Republic of Indonesia. ***Decree of The People's Consultative Assembly of the Republic of Indonesia No. II/MPR/1983 on the Guidelines of State Policy***.

-----***Indonesia's Fundamental Efforts in Building Abiding Peace and Social Justice***, 1987.

-----***Indonesia Develops: Repelita V, Five Year Development Plan 1989/1990 - 1993/1994***.

Semarang District. "Kabupaten Semarang Dalam Angka." (Annual Statistics of Semarang District), 1982; 1983; 1993; 1994.

Tuntang Sub-District. "Statistik Kecamatan Tuntang, Kabupaten Semarang." (Annual Statistics of Tuntang sub-district), 1982; 1988; 1989.

-----"Formulir Isian Monografi Kecamatan." (Statistics of Tuntang Sub-District, updated every six months), 1993-1995.

Index

This GLOBAL THEOLOGICAL VOICES Series Listing

David Emmanuuel Singh (ed.)
Jesus and the Cross
Reflections of Christians from Islamic Contexts
2008 / 978-1-870345-65-1 / x + 226pp

The Cross reminds us that the sins of the world are not borne through the exercise of power but through Jesus Christ's submission to the will of the Father. The papers in this volume are organised in three parts: scriptural, contextual and theological. The central question being addressed is: how do Christians living in contexts, where Islam is a majority or minority religion, experience, express or think of the Cross? This is, therefore, an exercise in listening. As the contexts from where these engagements arise are varied, the papers in drawing scriptural, contextual and theological reflections offer a cross-section of Christian thinking about Jesus and the Cross.

Sung-wook Hong*
Naming God in Korea
The Case of Protestant Christianity
2008 / 978-1-870345-66-8

Since Christianity was introduced to Korea more than a century ago, one of the most controversial issue has been the Korean term for the Christian 'God'. This issue is not merely about naming the Christian God in Korean language, but it relates to the question of theological contextualization—the relationship between the gospel and culture—and the question of Korean Christian identity. This book examines the theological contextualization of the concept of 'God' in the contemporary Korean context and applies the translatability of Christianity to that context. It also demonstrates the nature of the gospel in relation to cultures, i.e., the universality of the gospel expressed in all human cultures.

August 2008

REGNUM STUDIES IN MISSION
Series Listing

Kwame Bediako
Theology and Identity
The Impact of Culture upon Christian Thought in the Second Century and in Modern Africa
1992 / 1-870345-10-X / xviii + 508pp

The author examines the question of Christian identity in the context of the Graeco–Roman culture of the early Roman Empire. He then addresses the modern African predicament of quests for identity and integration.

Everett A Wilson
Strategy of the Spirit
J.Philip Hogan and the Growth of the Assemblies of God Worldwide, 1960 - 1990
1997/1870345231/214

Everett Wilson, a long-time Pentecostal missionary among the Hispanic people, wrote a well-researched contribution on the life and role of J. Philip Hogan, as the primary architect of the missionary work of the U.S. Assemblies of God (AG). The main strength of this work is the vast amount of material and information the author was able to collect, and the enjoyable descriptive way he presents the data as well as an evaluation that readers can easily comprehend.

Christopher Sugden
Seeking the Asian Face of Jesus
The Practice and Theology of Christian Social Witness in Indonesia and India 1974–1996
1997 / 1-870345-26-6 / xx + 496pp

This study focuses on contemporary wholistic mission with the poor in India and Indonesia combined with the call to transformation of all life in Christ with micro-credit enterprise schemes. 'The literature on contextual theology now has a new standard to rise to' – Lamin Sanneh (Yale University, USA).

Hwa Yung
Mangoes or Bananas?
The Quest for an Authentic Asian Christian Theology
1997 / 1-870345-25-8 / xii + 274pp

Asian Christian thought remains largely captive to Greek dualism and Enlightenment rationalism because of the overwhelming dominance of Western culture. Authentic contextual Christian theologies will emerge within Asian Christianity with a dual recovery of confidence in culture and the gospel.

August 2008

Keith E. Eitel
Paradigm Wars
1999 / 1-870345-12-6 / x + 140pp
The Southern Baptist International Mission Board Faces the Third Millennium

The International Mission Board of the Southern Baptist Convention is the largest denominational mission agency in North America. This volume chronicles the historic and contemporary forces that led to the IMB's recent extensive reorganization, providing the most comprehensive case study to date of a historic mission agency restructuring to continue its mission purpose into the twenty-first century more effectively.

Samuel Jayakumar
Dalit Consciousness and Christian Conversion
Historical Resources for a Contemporary Debate
1999 / 81-7214-497-0 / xxiv + 434pp
(Published jointly with ISPCK)

The main focus of this historical study is social change and transformation among the Dalit Christian communities in India. Historiography tests the evidence in the light of the conclusions of the modern Dalit liberation theologians.

Vinay Samuel and Christopher Sugden
Mission as Transformation
A Theology of the Whole Gospel
Regnum Books (1999), 522pp, ISBN: 0870345133

This book brings together in one volume twenty five years of biblical reflection on mission practice with the poor from around the world. The approach of holistic mission, which integrates proclamation, evangelism, church planting and social transformation seamlessly as a whole, has been adopted since 1983 by most evangelical development agencies, most indigenous mission agencies and many Pentecostal churches. This volume helps anyone understand how evangelicals, struggling to unite evangelism and social action, found their way in the last twenty five years to the biblical view of mission in which God calls all human beings to love God and their neighbour; never creating a separation between the two.

Christopher Sugden
Gospel, Culture and Transformation
2000 / 1-870345-32-0 / viii + 152pp
A Reprint, with a New Introduction, of Part Two of Seeking the Asian Face of Jesus

Gospel, Culture and Transformation explores the practice of mission especially in relation to transforming cultures and communities. - 'Transformation is to enable God's vision of society to be actualised in all relationships: social, economic and spiritual, so that God's will may be reflected in human society and his love experienced by all communities, especially the poor.'

August 2008

Bernhard Ott

Beyond Fragmentation: Integrating Mission and Theological Education

A Critical Assessment of some Recent Developments in Evangelical Theological Education

2001 / 1-870345-14-2 / xxviii + 382pp

Beyond Fragmentation is an enquiry into the development of Mission Studies in evangelical theological education in Germany and German-speaking Switzerland between 1960 and 1995. This is carried out by a detailed examination of the paradigm shifts which have taken place in recent years in both the theology of mission and the understanding of theological education.

Gideon Githiga

The Church as the Bulwark against Authoritarianism

Development of Church and State Relations in Kenya, with Particular Reference to the Years after Political Independence 1963-1992

2002 / 1-870345-38-X / xviii + 218pp

'All who care for love, peace and unity in Kenyan society will want to read this careful history by Bishop Githiga of how Kenyan Christians, drawing on the Bible, have sought to share the love of God, bring his peace and build up the unity of the nation, often in the face of great difficulties and opposition.' Canon Dr Chris Sugden, Oxford Centre for Mission Studies.

Myung Sung-Hoon, Hong Young-Gi (eds.)

Charis and Charisma

David Yonggi Cho and the Growth of Yoido Full Gospel Church

2003 / 1-870345-45-2 / xxii + 218pp

This book discusses the factors responsible for the growth of the world's largest church. It expounds the role of the Holy Spirit, the leadership, prayer, preaching, cell groups and creativity in promoting church growth. It focuses on God's grace (charis) and inspiring leadership (charisma) as the two essential factors and the book's purpose is to present a model for church growth worldwide.

Samuel Jayakumar

Mission Reader

Historical Models for Wholistic Mission in the Indian Context

2003 / 1-870345-42-8 / x + 250pp

(Published jointly with ISPCK)

This book is written from an evangelical point of view revalidating and reaffirming the Christian commitment to wholistic mission. The roots of the 'wholistic mission' combining 'evangelism and social concerns' are to be located in the history and tradition of Christian evangelism in the past; and the civilizing purpose of evangelism is compatible with modernity as an instrument in nation building.

Bob Robinson

Christians Meeting Hindus

An Analysis and Theological Critique of the Hindu-Christian Encounter in India

2004 / 1-870345-39-8 / xviii + 392pp

This book focuses on the Hindu-Christian encounter, especially the intentional meeting called dialogue, mainly during the last four decades of the twentieth century, and mainly in India itself.

Gene Early

Leadership Expectations

How Executive Expectations are Created and Used in a Non-Profit Setting

2005 / 1-870345-30-4 / xxiv + 276pp

The author creates an Expectation Enactment Analysis to study the role of the Chancellor of the University of the Nations-Kona, Hawaii, and is grounded in the field of managerial work, jobs, and behaviour, drawing on symbolic interactionism, role theory, role identity theory and enactment theory. The result is a conceptual framework for further developing an understanding of managerial roles.

Tharcisse Gatwa

The Churches and Ethnic Ideology in the Rwandan Crises 1900-1994

2005 / 1-870345-24-X / approx 300pp

Since the early years of the twentieth century Christianity has become a new factor in Rwandan society. This book investigates the role Christian churches played in the formulation and development of the racial ideology that culminated in the 1994 genocide.

Julie Ma

Mission Possible

Biblical Strategies for Reaching the Lost

2005 / 1-870345-37-1 / xvi + 142pp

This is a missiology book for the church which liberates missiology from the specialists for every believer. It also serves as a textbook that is simple and friendly, and yet solid in biblical interpretation. This book links the biblical teaching to the actual and contemporary missiological settings with examples, thus making the Bible come alive to the reader.

Allan Anderson, Edmond Tang (eds.)

Asian and Pentecostal

The Charismatic Face of Christianity in Asia

2005 / 1-870345-43-6 / approx. 600pp

(Published jointly with APTS Press)

This book provides a thematic discussion and pioneering case studies on the history and development of Pentecostal and Charismatic churches in the countries of South Asia, South East Asia and East Asia.

August 2008

I. Mark Beaumont

Christology in Dialogue with Muslims

A Critical Analysis of Christian Presentations of Christ for Muslims from the Ninth and Twentieth Centuries

2005 / 1-870345-46-0 / xxvi + 228pp

This book analyses Christian presentations of Christ for Muslims in the most creative periods of Christian-Muslim dialogue, the first half of the ninth century and the second half of the twentieth century. In these two periods, Christians made serious attempts to present their faith in Christ in terms that take into account Muslim perceptions of him, with a view to bridging the gap between Muslim and Christian convictions.

Thomas Czövek,

Three Seasons of Charismatic Leadership

A Literary-Critical and Theological Interpretation of the Narrative of Saul, David and Solomon

2006 / 978-1-870345484 / 272pp

This book investigates the charismatic leadership of Saul, David and Solomon. It suggests that charismatic leaders emerge in crisis situations in order to resolve the crisis by the charisma granted by God. Regarding Saul, the book argues that he proved himself as a charismatic leader as long as he acted resolutely and independently from Samuel his mentor. He failed, however, because in Samuel's shadow he could not establish himself as a charismatic leader.

Jemima Atieno Oluoch

The Christian Political Theology of Dr. John Henry Okullu

2006 / 1-870345-51-7 / xx + 137pp

This book reconstructs the Christian political theology of Bishop John Henry Okullu, DD, through establishing what motivated him and the biblical basis for his socio-political activities. It also attempts to reconstruct the socio-political environment that nurtured Dr Okullu's prophetic ministry.

Richard Burgess

Nigeria's Christian Revolution

The Civil War Revival and Its Pentecostal Progeny (1967-2006)

2008 / 978-1-870345-63-7 / xxii + 347pp

This book describes the revival that occurred among the Igbo people of Eastern Nigeria and the new Pentecostal churches it generated, and documents the changes that have occurred as the movement has responded to global flows and local demands. As such, it explores the nature of revivalist and Pentecostal experience, but does so against the backdrop of local socio-political and economic developments, such as decolonisation and civil war, as well as broader processes, such as modernisation and globalisation.

August 2008

David Emmanuel Singh & Bernard C Farr (eds.)

Christianity and Cultures

Shaping Christian Thinking in Context

2008 / 978-1-870345-69-9 / x + 260pp

This volume is a way of marking an important milestone, 25th anniversary, of the Oxford Centre for Mission Studies (OCMS). The papers here have been exclusively sourced from Transformation, a quarterly journal of OCMS, and seek to provide a tripartite view of Christianity's engagement with cultures by focusing on the question: how is Christian thinking being formed or reformed through its interaction with the varied contexts it encounters? The subject matters include different strands of theological-missiological thinking, socio-political engagements and forms of family relationships in interaction with the host cultures.

Tormod Engelsviken, Ernst Harbakk, Rolv Olsen, Thor Strandenæs (eds.)

Mission to the World

Communicating the Gospel in the 21st Century:
Essays in Honour of Knud Jørgensen

2008 / 978-1-870345-64-4 / 472pp

Knud Jørgensen is Director of Areopagos and Associate Professor of Missiology at MF Norwegian School of Theology. This book reflects the various main areas of Jørgensen's commitment to mission. At the same time it focuses on the main frontier of mission, the world, the content of mission, the Gospel, the fact that the Gospel has to be communicated, and the context of contemporary mission - the 21st century.

Al Tizon

Transformation after Lausanne

Radical Evangelical Mission in Global-Local Perspective

2008 / 978-1-870345-68-2 / xx + 281pp

After Lausanne '74, a worldwide network of radical evangelical mission theologians and practitioners use the notion of "Mission as Transformation" to integrate evangelism and social concern together, thus lifting theological voices from the Two Thirds World to places of prominence. This book documents the definitive gatherings, theological tensions, and social forces within and without evangelicalism that led up to Mission as Transformation. And it does so through a global-local grid that points the way toward greater holistic mission in the 21st century.

Bambang Budijanto

Values and Participation

Development in Rural Indonesian.

2009 / 978-1-870345-70-5

Socio-religious values and socio-economic development are inter-dependant, inter-related and are constantly changing in the context of macro political structures, economic policy, religious organizations and globalization; and micro influences such as local affinities, identity, politics, leadership and beliefs. The three Lopait communities in Central Java, Indonesia provide an excellent model of a rich and complex negotiations and interactions among all the above factors. The book argues that the comprehensive approach in understanding the socio-religious values of each local community is essential to accurately describing their respective identity which will help institutions and agencies, both governmental and non-governmental, to relate to these communities with dignity and respect.

Young-hoon Lee*

The Holy Spirit Movement in Korea

Its Historical and Theological Development

2009 / 978-1-870345-67-5

This book traces the historical and theological development of the Holy Spirit Movement in Korea through six successive periods (from 1900 to the present time). These periods are characterized by repentance and revival (1900-20), persecution and suffering under Japanese occupation (1920-40), confusion and division (1940-60), explosive revival in which the Pentecostal movement played a major role in the rapid growth of Korean churches (1960-80), the movement reaching out to all denominations (1980-2000), and the new context demanding the Holy Spirit movement to open new horizons in its mission engagement (2000-). The volume also discusses the relationship between this movement and other religions such as shamanism, and looks forward to further engagement with issues of concern in the larger society.

David A. Kerr, Kenneth R. Ross (eds.)

Edinburgh 2010: Mission Then and Now

2009 / 978-1-870345-73-6

No one can hope to fully understand the modern Christian missionary movement without engaging substantially with the World Missionary Conference, held at Edinburgh in 1910. As the centenary of the Conference approaches, the time is ripe to examine its meaning in light of the past century and the questions facing Christian witness today. This book is the first to systematically examine the eight Commissions which reported to Edinburgh 1910 and gave the conference much of its substance and enduring value. It will deepen and extend the reflection being stimulated by the upcoming centenary and will kindle the missionary imagination for 2010 and beyond.

August 2008

Ande Titre

Leadership and Authority

Bula Matari and Life - Community Ecclesiology in Congo

2009 / 978-1-870345-72-9

This book proposes that Christian theology in Africa can make a significant development if a critical understanding of the socio-political context in contemporary Africa is taken seriously. The Christian leadership in post-colonial Africa has cloned its understanding and use of authority on the Bula Matari model, issued from the brutality of colonialism and political absolutism in post-colonial Africa. This model has caused many problems in churches, including dysfunctions, conflicts, divisions and lack of prophetic ministry. The book proposes a Life-Community ecclesiology for liberating authority, where leadership is a function, not a status, and 'apostolic succession' belongs to all the people of God.

Alan R. Johnson

Leadership in a Slum

A Bangkok Case Study

2009 / 978-1-870345-71-2

This book looks at leadership in the social context of a slum in Bangkok from an angle different from traditional studies which measure well educated Thais on leadership scales derived in the West. Using both systematic data collection and participant observation, it develops a culturally preferred model as well as a set of models based in Thai concepts that reflect on-the-ground realities. This work challenges the dominance of the patron-client rubric for understanding all forms of Thai leadership and offers a view for understanding leadership rooted in local social systems, contrary to approaches that assume the universal applicability of leadership research findings across all cultural settings. It concludes by looking at the implications of the anthropological approach for those who are involved in leadership training in Thai settings and beyond.

August 2008

OTHER REGNUM TITLES

Vinay Samuel, Chris Sugden (eds.)
The Church in Response to Human Need
1987 / 1870345045 / xii+268pp

Philip Sampson, Vinay Samuel, Chris Sugden (eds.)
Faith and Modernity
Essays in modernity and post-modernity
1994 / 1870345177 / 352pp

Klaus Fiedler
The Story of Faith Missions
1994 / 0745926878 / 428pp

Douglas Peterson
Not by Might nor by Power
A Pentecostal Theology of Social Concern in Latin America
1996 / 1870345207 / xvi+260pp

David Gitari
In Season and Out of Season
Sermons to a Nation
1996 / 1870345118 / 155pp

David. W. Virtue
A Vision of Hope
The Story of Samuel Habib
1996 / 1870345169 / xiv+137pp

Murray Dempster, Byron Klaus, Douglas Petersen (eds.)
The Globalization of Pentecostalism
A Religion Made to Travel
1999 / 1870345290 / xvii+406pp

Peter Johnson, Chris Sugden (eds.)
Markets, Fair Trade and the Kingdom of God
Essays to Celebrate Traidcraft's 21st Birthday
2001 / 1870345193 / xii+155pp

Deryke Belshaw, Robert Calderisi, Chris Sugden (eds.)
Faith in Development
Partnership Between the World Bank and the Churches of Africa
2001 / 978-0821348482 / *246pp*

August 2008

Robert Hillman, Coral Chamberlain, Linda Harding
Healing & Wholeness
Reflections on the Healing Ministry
2002 / 978-1- 870345-35- 4 / xvii+283pp

David Bussau, Russell Mask
Christian Microenterprise Development
An Introduction
2003 / 1870345282 / xiii+142pp

David Singh
Sainthood and Revelatory Discourse
An Examination of the Basis for the Authority of Bayan in Mahdawi Islam
2003 / 8172147285 / xxiv+485pp

For the up-to-date listing of the Regnum books, see:
http://www.ocms.ac.uk/docs/Regnum_Studies_In_Mission_Listing.pdf.
http://www.ocms.ac.uk/docs/Global_Theological_Voices_Listing.pdf.

regnum

Regnum Books International

Regnum is an Imprint of The Oxford Centre for Mission Studies
P.O. Box 70, Oxford, OX2 6HB
Web: www.ocms.ac.uk/regnum

In partnership with Paternoster (except *-marked titles)
Web: www.authenticmedia.co.uk/paternoster

August 2008